Successful Sport Management

Successful Sport Management

Second Edition

Edited by

Herb Appenzeller

Guy Lewis

Carolina Academic Press / Durham, North Carolina

Learning Resources
Centre

12165298

ISBN 0-89089-661-5
LCCN 00-106586

Carolina Academic Press
700 Kent Street
Durham, North Carolina 27701
Telephone 919/489-7486
Fax 919/493-5668
E-mail: cap@cap-press.com
www.cap-press.com

Printed in the United States of America.

Contents

Acknowledgments

The editors wish to express their gratitude to all who contributed to making *Successful Sport Management* available to the many professionals who work in the field. The contributing authors not only accepted and met deadlines but re-ordered personal schedules to give each chapter continuing attention as it was prepared for publication.

We appreciate the Lexis Company for giving us the rights to *Successful Sport Management*. We particularly want to thank Edwin Jackson for his assistance in our acquiring the rights to update and enhance the book with nine new chapters.

We thank Carolina Academic Press for permission to include two chapters from *Risk Management In Sport: Issues and Strategies* in this text. The chapters are Gil B. Fried's "The Americans with Disabilities Act and Sport Facilities" and David Maraghy's "Event Management: A Practical Approach."

Appreciation is due Dr. Keith Sipe, publisher of Carolina Academic Press for his vision and support in developing a series of sport management and sport law publications. We also want to express our gratitude to Kathy Kay who uses her expertise to make good books even better.

Finally, we thank Ann Terrill Appenzeller for her tireless work and counsel in every phase of the book. Her suggestions and advice and knowledge of sport management enhanced the editing of the book.

Introduction

Guy Lewis

Sport management has existed as an activity from at least the time of the ancient Greeks, reflecting the importance of sport in the lives of men. Sport management in modern times, however, has not developed professionally as rapidly as management in other industries, perhaps reflecting a continuing association in the public mind of sport with play and management with work. Effective operation of sport-related activities is, nevertheless, essential for the pleasure of players and spectators alike and for maintaining the cash flow that makes this pleasure possible. *Successful Sport Management* draws on the experience of twenty-five professionals to provide, in a single volume, a reference manual for all those whose responsibilities include management of sport and associated business. The key element in the development of a professional field is a body of knowledge, a literature rich both in volume and substance. While this volume is not a work in which the subject matters that make up the field of sport management are exhaustively described or perfectly integrated, it does highlight the substance of an increasingly important literature and hopefully, by so doing, contributes to the definition of the discipline of sport management.

Successful management is essential to all segments of the sport industry, professional or amateur, school or club, private or government at any level, community or individual. Whatever the location of the management function, the same basic requirements are present: namely, effective and efficient management of personnel, program, marketing, information, facilities and legal responsibilities. The six parts of this work are devoted to these topics. Selected general documents are included in the individual chapters to enable a manager to draw new elements from his or her operating philosophy.

With each part the chapters follow a logical order dictated by the management function. Part 1, Human Resource Management, begins with a consideration of the contribution of recruitment and training to the development of an effective staff, continues with a discussion of time management, and concludes with techniques for dealing with stressful situations. Part 2, Program Management, covers development of program philosophy and objectives, the mechanics of scheduling, budgeting and financial management, equipment control and provision of medical services for teams and/or spectators. Part 3, Marketing Management, begins with a description of the characteristics of sport marketing and then suggests ways of marketing events, marketing services, raising funds, and increasing ticket sales through promotions, and focuses attention on internal marketing. In Part 4, Media and Information Management, the discussion of public relations is extended, the benefits of computer applications to sport management tasks are assessed and the impact of options in the use of technology is measured. Running throughout this section is attention to the question of media relations. Part 5, Facility and Event Management, poses and answers questions concerning contractual arrangements among sponsoring agencies and host facilities, the philosophy of operating a public access facility, the management of individual events, and the internal ongoing management of activity centers. Part 6, Legal Management, provides an introduction to risk assessment and reduction, specific terms of contracting with participants, suppliers and staff, an individual chapter on team sport contracts and an overview of the law pertaining to public assembly facilities.

Those who choose to read Successful Sport Management as a single work rather than as a series of topical chapters will find that there is some material common to several of the chapters. This is inevitable, both because the chapters are intended as stand-alone units and because some principles of management are a constant from setting to setting. This measure of overlap also suggests, however, that professionals independent of each other in their day-to-day operations increasingly find common ground in defining the essential problems and strategies of sport management. The editors and authors hope that, as the body of information on sport management increases, the arrangement of that information can become increasingly precise through conferences and additional publications. When this happens, sport management will take its place as an appropriately recognized branch of the management field.

Successful Sport Management

Part 1

Human Resource Management

The long-term successful performance of any organization is ultimately the responsibility of leadership.

David K. Scott

Chapter 1

Staff Recruitment, Selection, Retention, and Termination

John Billing

Introduction

Personnel constitute the primary resource of most sport organizations. The goal of human resource management is to obtain competent employees and provide the means for them to function optimally. Sport organizations are people-oriented operations, consisting of persons as producers, as products and as consumers. This contrasts to many other businesses that deal with raw materials, automated machinery and indirect public sales. The fact that sport organizations are so people-oriented elevates personnel management to a primary function in organizational management. In addition, the human problems of management are often the most complex due to the variability of human nature and behavior. Therefore, the management of the personnel resources of any sport organization is paramount to the success of the organization.

Human Resource Management Defined

Human resource management involves all the ways in which employees interact in both the formal and informal context of the organization. Typical aspects of employee management include:

1. Obtaining competent employees;
2. Assigning employees effectively;
3. Motivating employees to perform optimally;
4. Stimulating the professional growth and development of employees;
5. Evaluating and compensating employees fairly; and
6. Retaining or dismissing employees.

The decision to employ a person is an extremely important undertaking. Making a poor hiring selection costs the organization in many ways. Employees represent a substantial financial commitment when viewed over their entire career. The cost in time and effort to recruit and train the new employee is substantial. In addition, the unpleasant consequences of having to dismiss an employee and the resultant bad feelings and potential loss of productivity until a replacement is found are all negative results of poor employee selection.

Human Resource Handbook

Each organization should develop a human resource handbook which is distributed to all employees upon joining the organization. This handbook should clearly state the major policies, practices , and responsibilities of the employer and the employees. It is a guidebook to proper behavior in the organization. Human resources handbooks often contain such items as: mission statement, organizational chart, application process, hiring procedures, holiday, sick and vacation policies, salary and reward policies, appraisal procedures, grievance procedures, termination policies, fringe benefits, harassment and grievance issues, dealing with disabilities, injury compensation, and retirement procedures.

Most government and state agencies will have well developed human resource procedures which apply to all employees. Private and charitable organizations need to develop specific guidelines to meet the needs of their particular organization. In all cases legal counsel should be consulted in the development of these procedures statements and administrative or governing boards should review and approve them. These publications represent important protection for both the employee and the employer.

Professional and Hourly Employees Defined

Since sport organizations are people-intensive operations, every staff selection is of primary importance. Normally, organizational personnel are classified as either professionals or hourly employees. Professional employees are those occupying higher-level positions in the organization and who do not have fixed work schedules, do not punch time clocks or have standard benefit packages. They are expected to perform specific duties for the organization that are not directly linked to a fixed day/hour work schedule. Hourly employees, by contrast, usually have very specific day/hour schedules, often are required to keep records of their work time, may have specified lunch and break times, receive specified vacation time and sick leave and are not expected to work "after hours" without additional compensation. In general, administrators, managers, coaches, public relation officers and similar appointees are considered professional employees. Secretaries, ticket office employees, equipment managers, janitors and security officers are considered hourly employees. The hourly employees may be considered support personnel to the professional segment of the organization.

Place of the Organizational Chart in Staffing

All staffing selections must begin with the administrative organizational chart. This chart should clearly depict the lines of authority and responsibility of the various members of the unit. The chart identifies the basic structure of the organization and where each employee fits into the scheme of operation. All employees should be familiar with this chart and understand how their positions and duties contribute to the composite structure.

Job Description

Each position within the organization should be explained in a job description which details the major responsibilities, who the individual is responsible to and who they supervise. The job description should be in sufficient detail to succinctly portray the essence of the duties. The composite of all the position descriptions for the organization details the total assignment of responsibilities and serves as a means of communicating the formal operation of the unit. (Example is located in Appendix 1 at the end of this chapter.) Job descriptions should be reviewed and updated annually as conditions change.

Position Announcements

Position announcements are public advertisements of positions to be filled. They should be carefully constructed to depict the primary duties as identified in the organizational position description and should also include information on appropriate qualifications, salary, benefits, starting date and how to apply. Many organizations now require extensive advertising of openings including direct mail announcements to educational institutions and to similar organizations, newspaper advertisements, listings in appropriate placement services and at professional meetings. In many sport organizations word of mouth remains a primary mode for communicating position openings. Administrators from one sport team or athletic department ask their friends in similar organizations if they can suggest appropriate candidates. The recommendation from a highly respected colleague is often the most important credential a candidate can possess.

A reasonable time period should be provided after the opening is announced before closing the search for a professional position. This allows sufficient time for candidates to learn of the opening and submit their applications. An exception to this practice is often employed when selecting new head coaches. Many times a very short period is all that is provided and only a few preselected candidates are considered. This is considered necessary to prevent the disruption which would occur with a lengthy search process.

Usually a selection committee reviews applicants and selects several as the most promising candidates. These finalists are often invited for a visit which allows the candidate to see the new situation in person and for numerous interviews with officers of the organization. The qualifications of each finalist should be thoroughly checked for accuracy and their references contacted. Often the materials submitted by the applicant will be vague as to the actual duties which the applicant performed. A check with former employers and references can confirm the exact nature of a candidate's former duties and how effectively the duties were performed. Many positions are formally filled with the signing of an employment contract. Others involve only a letter of appointment or a standard employment form. In all instances, some official employment document should be signed by both the employer and employee. The employee should also receive written notification of all benefits which are provided as part of the employment.

Recruitment — Cautions and Strategies

An important question to be answered when filling positions is whether it is desirable to fill the positions from within the existing staff via promotion or transfer or to seek outside applicants. It is the philosophy of many organizations always to look within to promote loyal and competent employees as a preference to bringing in new outside personnel. This practice has the advantage of building staff morale and a conscious effort by employees to achieve and thus earn their way to more desirable positions. It rewards loyalty and provides a strong base for tradition and standardization of operation. However, many outsiders may have qualifications superior to any current members of the organization. They will be more likely to provide new ideas and approaches to their assigned duties. In most instances, it is best to solicit applicants from both within and without the organization. Careful judgment will then produce the best selection from the potential candidates.

Staff Training

The training of personnel consists of the entire spectrum of job development beginning with familiarization of new employees to the organization and to their duties, specialized on-the-job training, career development and retooling. The employee should see this process as career development designed to make the employee a more effective member of the organization.

It is essential that new employees be assimilated into the organization with minimal stress to the employee and the ongoing operation. This is best accomplished by some means of formal or informal training. Specific mechanisms should be in place for introducing the new employee to the job duties and the important items of "how it's done here." Often a specific supervisor is charged with providing this introductory information. This process also happens informally with interaction among co-workers. Established employees should be encouraged to help "educate" the new employee and all other employees should be tolerant and understanding of the minor errors a new employee is likely to make. New employees should be specifically encouraged to ask questions about anything which is unclear and should also feel they have someone to turn to during this introductory period of employment.

Many positions in sport organizations require some on-the-job training to familiarize the new employee with specific equipment, machinery, or facility operation. Specific plans to provide this knowledge and experience must be a part of the orientation of new employees on the staff of most support units including: janitorial, maintenance, grounds crew, lighting and media crews, and security.

Career development is the long-term commitment of the organization to the improvement and advancement of its employees. Opportunities are often provided or encouraged which allow employees to upgrade their skills, increase their education and acquire new abilities which might contribute to their current job performance or qualify them for advancement. Some organizations will make these opportunities available free of charge or grant released time for career development. Others may pay a portion of the cost or merely encourage persons seeking advancement to acquire the additional skills. A current example is the need for employees at many levels to become familiar with computer capabilities. Many records are now being computerized. Ticket sales and distribution, maintenance schedules, inventories, as well as financial accounts and personnel records, all benefit from computerization. This is but one example of the need for staff development which will continue to increase in our rapidly changing society. Employees in management positions may be encouraged or required to take courses in time management, communication skills, risk assessment or whatever new techniques may be beneficial to sports organizations in the future.

Performance Appraisals

Performance appraisals are the essence of personnel management. They are the means for evaluating employee effectiveness and a basis for producing change in the work behavior of each employee. The task of assessing performance is a difficult and extremely complex undertaking when all of the organizational and interpersonal ramifications are considered. For these reasons, significant planning and managerial attention should be devoted to the appraisal process.

Performance appraisals are a systematic means for making decisions concerning salary levels, promotions, raises and training needs as well as evaluating ongoing effectiveness of employees. Some organizations require performance appraisals at regular intervals while others allow managers to utilize them at the administrator's discretion. Most often, organizational policies will require a formal performance appraisal prior to any promotion, awarding of merit raises, or dismissal of an employee. In every case, appraisals provide the opportunity for employee and supervisor to discuss the employee's job performance and to identify any desired redirection of efforts.

Typically, performance ratings have been developed based on personality traits, work habits, job behaviors, and job results. Regardless of the essential focus, current law requires that performance appraisals be based on job relevant criteria, and not on unrelated personal characteristics or vague items not related to job performance. For example, if appearance and dress are to be used as a rating item, the organization should be able to defend the reason for this in relation to the job. This might be easily done for a secretary or receptionist, but would be more difficult in the case of a grounds-worker or equipment manager.

Performance Traits

Often rating systems have used a generalized trait approach. Typically, traits such as: initiative, dependability, leadership, creativity, judgment and cooperation are rated on some scale using either verbal descriptions (excellent, good, average, poor) or a numerical scale (1-high, 3-moderate, 5-low). This trait format has the advantage of being almost universally useful within a large group of employees performing diverse functions. The results of these appraisals provide some general and often useful information concerning employee performance but, in many cases, the information is a vague generalization, subjectively determined by the supervisor. A rating of "average" on initiative or "low" on cooperation may not provide the employees with much useful information to improve their performance.

The trait format does offer a reference point to begin a discussion with an employee in which more specific strengths and weaknesses are specified under each general category. The benefit of this form of appraisal is its universal applicability to all employees and its ease of design and administration. Large organizations such as state universities and those utilizing union workers often use this format for all hourly employees. They are often required in the process for retention, promotions, raises and dismissals.

Management by Objectives

One currently popular technique devised to assess the accomplishments of employees in a variety of business and educational settings is termed management by objectives. This system incorporates the setting of specific goals or objectives to be accomplished, specifies an appropriate time frame and evaluates staff effectiveness based on the degree of goal attainment. The management-by-objectives format serves to focus the employee's efforts on what management considers to be the most important functions (objectives) and emphasizes measurable results as the basis for success. (Example is located in Appendix 2 at the end of this chapter.) This focus on objectives is a valuable planning tool and serves to control extraneous efforts in which employees might otherwise engage. It allows for the supervisor and employee to jointly agree on the desired accomplishments. Management by objectives does not deal directly with the employee's specific behaviors or the means that accomplish the objectives. Rather, desirable goals are may be used to a identified and the employee is allowed the freedom of various means of achieving these goals. Often an employee, such as an assistant coach or fundraiser, may appear busy all the time with piles of work, but in reality, little is actually accomplished. Management by objectives forces the employee to focus on the end results, the accomplishments.

Management by objectives entails three essential steps:

1. *Setting of objectives:* A meeting of the employee and the manager is conducted to discuss specific objectives to be accomplished. The employee is an important part of the planning process and should be actively involved in setting reasonable objectives. The end result of the meeting is specification of a number of objectives to be accomplished and a rank or priority for each. In addition, a specific time frame is identified for accomplishment and measurable indicators of success are specified.

2. *Provision of time and resources:* A reasonable period of time is allowed with the freedom to pursue the goals as the employee deems most suitable. This has the advantage of often producing substantial creativity and commitment from many workers. Reasonable resources are made available to enable accomplishment of the objectives.

3. *Performance review*: Quantitative and qualitative accomplishment of the objectives are reviewed at specified intervals. Areas of success and failure are noted and new objectives are developed or redefined to provide continued progress toward the larger goal.

Management by objectives may be most applicable to professional -level employees where greater freedom exists in time schedules and resources and where employees have the freedom to initiate new techniques and approaches. This technique provides a clear agreement between the employee and the manager as to the relative importance of the various job tasks and how success in each will be measured.

By focusing exclusively on outcomes, the management-by-objectives approach provides little guidance as to how to accomplish the desired outcomes. New employees may lack sufficient knowledge of how these might be accomplished, what resources are available and what behaviors are ethically or legally acceptable in the organization. Workers may adopt a "results at any cost" approach, where significant damage is done in the process of accomplishing the goal. In most sport organizations, the way the organization treats the public is often at least as important as an ultimate goal of winning or increasing profits. In these situations where alumni or fan identification with the team is of great importance, care must be exercised not to produce some short-term gain at the expense of a long-term loss in support. One method to reduce this undesirable consequence is to review the planned techniques for goal attainment with the supervisor. The employee still has the freedom and exercises the creativity of suggesting means for goal attainment, but approval for using these means must be obtained from supervisors.

Behaviorally Anchored Rating Systems

Another technique used to appraise employee performance which focuses on the actual job behaviors has been termed "behaviorally anchored rating systems." These systems assess the employee's performance as a series of on-the-job behaviors. This is in contrast to the management-by-objectives approach of looking at outcomes of job behavior. In the behaviorally anchored system, a set of specific statements describing desirable job behaviors is prepared. These statements describe different levels of job performance in rather specific terms which identify indicators of outstanding performance, good performance, average performance, below average performance and very poor performance. (Example is located in Appendix 3 at the end of this chapter.)

Qualitative statements describing differing levels of job performance are created for each major function or dimension of the employee's assigned tasks. An employee having seven major job functions would have a set of descriptive statements ranging from outstanding through very poor for each of these functions. These sets of behavioral indicators must be developed for each different job classification since obviously, a secretary is not expected to exhibit the same job behaviors that are appropriate to a concessions manager.

This approach to appraising job performance is similar to the current United States Tennis Association (USTA) method of ranking tennis-playing ability. For each of the USTA ranks from 1.0 through 7.0, a set of descriptive statements detailing the player's ability to consistently make various strokes and implement specific strategies is provided. Any player, coach or professional can then attempt to match these statements with the observed level of play to determine which rank best describes the current level of the player.

Similarly, supervisors using a behaviorally anchored rating system observe their employees and determine which set of descriptive statements best depicts each employee's typical performance. This rating is conducted for each of the major dimensions of the employee's job. Thus, a ticket office employee might receive a high rating on personal contact with customers, a low rating on financial record keeping and an average rating for speed of customer service. Each of these dimensions would have a set of statements describing what behaviors are typical of high, average and low performance.

The construction of behaviorally anchored rating systems can be quite time-consuming depending upon the degree of detail desired and the number of different job categories existing within the organization. They do provide an excellent means of feedback to the employee on areas of job performance needing attention and provide descriptive examples of what constitutes the desired behaviors.

It is often advantageous to have employees complete a self rating or self appraisal. Either using an identical form of the official appraisal or a written narrative of their performance. Review of the employees self rating prior to the official appraisal may provide significant insight to the supervisor as to what the employees' consider their most important accomplishments and their major short comings. Employees often self identify the very shortcomings which have been observed by the supervisor. This process often results in less resentment since it allows the employee a chance to note weaknesses in advance of the supervisor's ratings.

Each of the previously described performance appraisal techniques offers specific advantages and entails limitations. The performance-traits approach identifies broad categories of desired traits of all workers and is useful as a general evaluation technique. The management-by-objectives approach focuses on identifying goals and directly assessing progress toward those goals. The clearly described, desirable behavior of workers is the essence of the behaviorally anchored rating system. Competent managers should be familiar with each of these personnel-appraisal techniques and should select appropriate methods which will best serve their specific employees and organization.

All formal performance appraisals should become a part of the personnel file of each employee. This record documents progress or lack of progress and should be reviewed prior to each new appraisal.

The concluding portion of each performance appraisal should include a conference during which the employee and supervisor discuss the contents of the ratings assigned and either reaffirm or redirect specific employee behavior. In some organizations the employee must sign indicating his/her knowledge of the contents of the appraisal. This process offers protection for both the employee and employer should questions of retention, salary adjustment, and other factors be raised at a later date.

The conference should be viewed as a means for staff development. It is essential in providing directions for improved employee performance. Without this feedback the employees may remain essentially unaware of weaknesses in their job performance. The conclusion of the appraisal conference should always communicate confidence in the employee's ability and a helpful attitude on the part of the supervisor.

Motivating Employees

Position descriptions and performance appraisals detail the essence of each employee's expected behavior and position in the hierarchy of the organization. Fulfillment of these expectations requires employees to be motivated toward their successful accomplishment. Thus, understanding factors which affect employee motivation is essential in personnel management.

Managers often adopt one of two opposing views of the basic nature of employees. The first holds that employees are: interested in their work, take pride in accomplishments, expend a high degree of effort, are committed to the organization, are ready to accept responsibility and generally exercise good self-control and self-direction. The opposing position describes employees as: basically lazy, lacking in self-direction, working only for money, resistant to change, self-centered and uncooperative.

Obviously, neither depicts an accurate picture of all employees. However, there is some validity in each set of descriptions. There are employees who are quite positive in their approach to their assigned duties and others who are far more negative. Managers would obviously like to have an entire staff consisting of employees possessing the positive qualities. This possibility is enhanced by managers who adopt a positive expectation of each employee. These managers communicate in all their actions that they believe in and expect competent and reliable job performance. Employees sense this positive expectation and, in most cases, aspire to fulfill this role.

Positive managers also understand that an organization works most effectively when employees can satisfy their individual needs while at the same time fulfilling the organizational goals. People work to satisfy a variety of personal needs. Paramount among these are the existence needs: those related to sufficient salary to provide for housing, clothing, food and other essential materials. Once these needs are satisfied on at least an acceptable level, needs for social affiliation and personal accomplishment become of primary concern. Opportunities to fulfill these needs are the motivating factors which are available in the work environment.

Motivating factors can be classified into organizational factors and individual factors. Organizational factors are those which are provided through affiliation with the larger work unit. The most obvious of these are salary and fringe benefits. Additional organizational factors affecting motivation include the desirability of the work environment, the amount of job security, affiliation with the organization and acceptance by co-workers. Individual factors motivating job performance include the opportunity to achieve, to receive recognition, to feel pride, to work autonomously, to obtain intrinsic pleasure from the job and to provide a challenge. In situations where the work is redundant and offers little challenge and few opportunities for self-expression, the major motivation must come from organizational motivational factors. Attractive salary and benefit packages, pleasant office furnishings, up-to-date equipment, positive social climate and reasonable job security make these jobs more desirable and thus motivate employees to attempt to hold their jobs. The individual motivating factors, all related to self-esteem and accomplishment, however, are the more powerful factors for affecting most employee performance. Many employees actively seek new opportunities which provide challenges and the means to achieve promotions, status, acclaim and power, even if these are not directly associated with salary increases. Recent research has demonstrated that "transformational leadership," designed to improve or transform employees into more competent professionals, produces higher satisfaction levels that "transactional leadership," which views job performance as an exchange of duties for money.

The individual nature of human behavior necessitates that supervisors understand that each employee is a unique person motivated by a different array of organizational and individual factors. The more familiar managers are with each employee, the better able managers are to provide the incentives which will be important to that employee.

Employee motivation is directly influenced by the respect they hold for their supervisors. An ineffectual, unrespected manager produces a work climate fostering uninspired employees. Several suggestions for positive supervision leading to motivated employees include:

1. *Accept the responsibility of the administrator.* Make the decisions which are necessary and take the credit and blame for those decisions. Employees are frustrated when decisions which directly affect them are avoided or unnecessarily delayed. Never allow an employee to shoulder the blame for a decision which was made by the administrator.
2. *Delegate both responsibility and the authority to accomplish assigned tasks.* Allow employees some freedom and creativity in their means of accomplishing their assigned duties.
3. *Give credit for staff accomplishments.* Never allow the misconception to remain that an employee's achievements or ideas were those of the administrator.
4. *Be an understanding supervisor.* Attempt to see situations from the employee's perspective. Be sensitive to what is happening in the employee's total job and life at that moment in time.

All managers must remember that they are responsible for a job far too big for them to accomplish alone. They can only achieve success through effectively motivating others to perform the necessary job tasks.

Occasionally it is necessary to reprimand an employee. This can be thought of as negative motivation. Typically threats, corrections, and expressions of displeasure are necessary either to ensure acceptable employee behavior or to communicate expressions of inadequate performance. Reprimands should be factually based and directed at the act or behavior, not at the individual's personality. Statements such as "you are a poor worker," "you have no commitment to the organization," "you just don't measure up" or "you are a poor reflection of our team" attack the person rather than the undesirable behavior. Attempts to describe the specific behavior as undesirable usually prove more productive. Some examples might be: "we expect all our staff to be at their work site by 8:00 a.m."; "office staff shall refer all questions from the media to the sport information office; never comment on player-coach conflicts." These statements focus the criticism on the behavior rather than the personality of the employee. The tone and emotionality of the reprimand should be sincere, controlled and factual. Often reference to policy, procedures or job specifications is all that is necessary to remind employees of their expected performance. It is unnecessary and often unproductive to "blow-up" or show excessive emotionality.

Reprimands should generally be given in private. They should be rather short in duration but should allow the employees an opportunity to express their side of the issue. Often it is a desirable practice to begin by asking the employee to explain the situation from his viewpoint. Once the reprimand has been given, the supervisor should not hold the incident against the employee on future occasions unless the same mistake is repeated. The manager might wish to monitor the recently reprimanded behavior with the goal of reinforcing the new, desired behavior, when it is exhibited. This will help solidify this behavior and provide the employee with the feeling that the supervisor does notice when the job is done correctly.

Termination of Employment

Termination of employment may be initiated by either the employee or by the employer. Persons often choose to leave the organization for another job, personal life changes, or unhappiness with the employer. Policies and procedures should be in place for giving notice of termination, severance pay, and return of all organizational property, records, and keys. At times it is necessary to terminate employees, either due to unacceptable job performance or to changing organizational needs. If the employee has performed satisfactorily and the decision to discontinue his/her position is due to changing needs, restructuring, or new management, every effort should be made to assist the employee in the transition to a new job. Provision of a buy out, extended benefits, and assistance with new employment or relocation should be offered. When an employee is terminated "for cause" careful documentation should be retained to substantiate the reasons for dismissal and notification of any appeals or grievance provisions should be provided to the employee. This is a difficult situation and often should include an exit interview where the employees are informed of all salary, benefits, and insurance consequences and are given the opportunity to identify factors which lead to their voluntary or forced leaving of the organization.

Personnel Records

A personnel file should be established as a depository for all pertinent information concerning the employment status and productivity of each employee. These files serve the purpose of recording all aspects of employment status including: position title, contract provisions, an accounting of benefits, accumulated sick leave and vacation time. The files often also include sufficient personal information to enable the organization to contact the employee at home, to notify his physician, spouse, or next of kin in an emergency and to complete required social security, income tax and other salary-oriented financial matters.

The personnel file may also serve as a record of the employee's significant accomplishments, and as a documentation of any disciplinary actions which may have been taken. This latter use is especially important when justification may be required in a case of dismissal. Normally all official performance appraisals should become a part of the employee's personnel file.

Personnel files are considered confidential. Care should be exercised to protect the confidentiality of the employees. It is general practice that only an employee's supervisors have access to personnel files. Employees are usually permitted access to their own files, upon request. In some specific instances, evaluation materials which are a part of the employee's personnel file or personal notes made by a supervisor may not be made available to the employee. Most organizations establish guidelines for the handling and accessibility of personnel files.

Resolving Conflict

Whenever a group of people work together toward a goal there exists considerable possibility for differences of opinion as to means for goal achievement and the definition of roles. This is especially true when one employee's work relies heavily on the previous performance of other employees. The personnel of sports organizations are typically achievement oriented, strong-willed leaders who are required to interact on many matters. These organizations will produce multiple opportunities for conflict situations.

Many potential sources of conflict exist in any organization. The most common conflicts exhibited in sport organizations are conflicts which occur between athletes and coaches, between coach and administrators and between two coaches or two athletes. Clearly defined job descriptions and lines of authority will eliminate many potential conflicts; however, disagreement will still result from unclear expectations, reliance on others and interpretation of goals, policies, practices and assignments. Many other conflicts result from behavioral or personality factors which one employee finds offensive in another employee. Techniques utilized when conflict exists among two persons of equal status in the organization (i.e., two assistant coaches or two athletes) may be different from those used in situations involving different status levels. In all instances, attempts should be made to reach a solution at the lowest appropriate administrative level. If satisfactory resolution is not achieved, then higher administrative levels may be involved.

One technique for resolving conflict is nonaction; that is, simply ignoring the problem and allowing employees to work out their differences. This is sometimes appropriate in minor conflicts which are simply the result of someone having a bad day. The administrator cannot become involved in every minor conflict which may surface. In many instances, all that is needed is a little cooling-off time or space for the employees to resolve their own conflict. This does not imply that all conflicts should first be ignored, but rather, that many minor problems work themselves out if given a little time. However, it is often unlikely or impossible for the involved employees to solve major or long-standing conflicts without assistance from a supervisor or another uninvolved employee.

The most obvious method for quick resolution of a conflict is administrative decree. The administrator simply uses the formal power of position and dictates how the problem will be resolved. This option has the benefit of a rapid response and may be most appropriate when direct violations of policies and procedures are involved. Since this process does not directly involve the conflicting parties in the resolution process, it may create resentment, feelings of unfair treatment and arbitrariness which could contribute to future conflicts or reduction in job performance.

A more people-oriented approach to conflict resolution involves bringing the parties together, hearing both sides of the issue and attempting to come to a rational solution. Various alternative solutions might be discussed and the consequences of each noted. The process often results in a compromise in which both parties give in and also gain something. One advantage of this process is the heightened awareness of the position and role of each of the conflicting parties.

Often, as they become aware of the other person's situation, a compromise solution is apparent. Always attempt to find a "win-win" solution, where both parties' major concerns are satisfied. This process can also have long-term positive benefits due to greater understanding and empathy among the employees. If the administrator is not directly involved in the conflict, he can act as the negotiator or arbitrator in the resolution of these disputes. If the conflict is an administrator-employee conflict (or coach-player) the basic process of talking through the situation and seeking alternative solutions acceptable to both parties remains a possibility. In these instances, it may be helpful to involve a third party who is not directly affected by the situation as an additional source of input and to provide an unbiased viewpoint.

There remain situations in which compromise is either not possible or is clearly inappropriate. In these instances, the conflict must still be resolved and the administrator must take the initiative to implement decisive action to correct the situation. It is likely that one or both parties will be unhappy with the resolution, but for the good of the organization, some resolution is necessary. Unpleasant feelings will be lessened if the parties feel that the administrator has been open and fair in reaching a decision.

In even the most harmonious organizations, conflict situations are to be expected as employees interact to achieve their individual roles. The administrator should help foster a climate in which conflict resolution is viewed as a positive process resulting in more satisfied employees and enhanced organizational effectiveness. Staff members should be encouraged, in fact, expected, to suggest potential solutions to the problems and conflicts which arise. This is an obvious technique for requiring people to think through the problem and how a potential solution will affect others. In addition to identifying alternative solutions, this demonstrates to employees that they do have input into the decision-making process.

It is important for employees to identify areas of conflict and for administrators to attend to the prompt resolution of conflict situations. Ignoring conflict and allowing it to fester will cripple an organization and result in an eventual eruption of negative feelings and behaviors.

Grievance and Harassment Procedures

Clearly stated policies and procedures for dealing with employee grievances and harassment should be communicated to all employees of the organization. The specific rights and obligations of employees must be protected. The goal of these procedures should be to resolve the differences at the lowest possible level of the organization. Specific steps in the resolution of grievance/harassment issues should include: an initial attempt by the grieving employee to reconcile the situation, notification to the supervisor of the grievance, willingness on the part of both parties to resolve the issue, discussion with legal counsel, resolution to the issue, commitment to implement the resolution.

Summary/Conclusion

Personnel management is a challenging area of supervisory responsibility. It represents the heart of the organization since productivity relies primarily upon the individual achievements of the staff of the organization.

Efficient organizations are characterized by:

1. Clearly articulated goals, lines of authority and well-defined job descriptions.
2. Carefully selected and trained employees.
3. The regular use of performance appraisals which provide both feedback as to accomplishments and a focus for future actions.
4. Employees who are motivated and challenged to complete their assigned tasks.
5. The ability to resolve personnel conflicts in a manner which fosters individual and organizational growth.
6. The development and distribution of clear human resource policy statements.

Appendix 1

Job Description

Job Title: Equipment Manager
Primary Duties:

1. Devise and administer a procedure for distribution, collection and control of all athletic equipment and supplies.

2. Conduct an annual inventory of equipment and supplies.

3. Order all regular inventory items in a timely manner to prevent depletion of stock.

4. Assist coaches in orders of special equipment needs.

5. Supervise the maintenance of and records of all vehicles.

6. Accommodate special equipment and supply needs of visiting teams and for special events.

7. Supervise locker room and equipment room staff.

8. Supervise laundry and laundry room staff.

9. Work directly with the business manager in preparation of all equipment purchases.

10. Other duties as assigned by the Assistant Director for Operations.

Appendix 2

Management by Objectives (MBO)

DATE:

Job Title: Business Manager
Priority Objectives

Supervisor: Athletic Director
Evaluated 3–6–9–12 Months

1. Keep all accounts posted to enable up-to-date budget
   reports on the 19th of each month.   3–6–9–12

2. Prepare monthly reports showing current receipts and
   projected receipts for the remainder of the year. Identify
   the source of any projected receipts which were unrealized.   3–6–9–12

3. Prepare a budget for the upcoming year showing total
   expenditures no greater than 5% above the current year.   9

4. Make all disbursements within 30 days of billing.   3–6–9–12

5. Monitor all major categories of the budget monthly
   and anticipate if fund transfer will be necessary. Clear
   all transfers with the Director.   6–12

6. Supply monthly budget summaries to each head coach.   6–12

Appendix 3

Behaviorally Anchored Rating System (BARS)

Job Title: Ticket Clerk
Job Dimension*: ticket sales to public
Rating: Typical Behaviors

1. Customer is greeted with pleasant "hello, may I help you" or similar greeting. Clerk recognizes many customers. Clerk smiles at customer. Tickets are prepackaged and arranged for quick service. Offer is extended to show location of seats. Each customer thanked. Obvious effort is made to move line fast if people waiting. Special requests are handled in a responsive manner which does not significantly slow service to others.

2. Opens window on time, has tickets arranged and cash box prepared. Is generally helpful. Makes change correctly and quickly. Moves line rapidly.

3. Clerk performs all assigned duties but does not go out of way to be helpful. Is occasionally rude or curt with customer. Does not generally greet customers or thank them. Makes no special effort when lines are long.

4. Does not help other clerks when they are busy. Takes extended breaks. Has trouble balancing cash box. Fails to exhibit helpfulness or efficiency.

5. Customer must request service. Clerk chats with friend or on phone while customer waits. Clerk is disorganized and often late in opening. Unfamiliar with stadium seating.

---

*Ticket sales to the public is only one dimension of the total job. Others might include: record keeping, telephone orders, office security, etc. A separate BARS would be developed for each of the job dimensions.

Chapter 2

Time Management

William T. Brooks

Introduction

Effective time management is the single, most critical skill that a successful sport manager can develop. The surprising thing is that very few professional preparation programs for any field of endeavor deal with the topic of time management to any great depth or length. Success in a well-managed sports program or well-administered business need not be measured by the finite number of hours that one invests on a daily basis. What really counts is how the minutes, hours and days are maximized for peak output. The effective use of time is the key to administratively competent, professional, technically proficient and educationally meaningful programs.

Pareto Principle (The 80/20 Rule)

The Pareto Principle implies that 80% of one's results comes from 20% of one's activities. The famous 80/20 rule that "those critical elements in any set usually constitute a minority of elements" is absolutely critical to any meaningful discussion of time management. If one could consciously devote 80% of one's time to the accomplishment of activities that have a value of 80% (those activities required to accomplish clearly defined objectives), one could achieve peak effectiveness at least 80% of the time.

If the day is filled with too many items having a value of 20%, there will not be enough time to work on those activities with a "payoff" of 80%. It makes sense, therefore, to concentrate on those few activities that will yield 80% of the results. An incredible amount of the time every day can be spent on trivia unless the following single, straightforward statement is asked: "What is the payoff of this activity, 80 or 20%?"

Developing Positive Habits

Planning and managing time in a daily, weekly, monthly and yearly basis is nothing more than applying self-discipline to develop positive work habits. It is essential to determine the status of current work habits and resolve every day that time will be used wisely. With practice and self-discipline, effective time management can become a positive habit enabling the sport manager to become the master of his/her destiny.

Guidelines for Time Management

A. Setting Objectives

In time management it is essential to set objectives to know what is to be accomplished. Objectives must be specific and measured on a quantitative basis. John Billing describes goal setting as a popular management technique in "Management By Objectives" (MBO). The principles of MBO, Billing notes, can be utilized in the process of time management. "This system incorporates the setting of specific goals or objectives to be accomplished, specifies an appropriate time frame and evaluates staff effectiveness based on the degree of goal attainment." He continues by saying that: "The management by objectives format serves to focus the employee's efforts on what management considers to be the most important functions (objectives) and emphasizes measurable results as the basis for success."

Billing concludes:

Management by objectives does not deal directly with the employee's specific behaviors or the means that may be used to accomplish the objectives. Rather, desirable goals are identified and the employee is allowed the freedom of various means of achieving these goals. Often an employee, such as an assistant coach or fund-raiser may appear busy all the time with piles of work, but in reality, little is actually accomplished. Management by objectives forces the employee to focus on the end results, the accomplishments.

For example, a sport manager may establish an objective to involve no less than 70% of all students in the intramural program by March 30 of a specific year. It is critical that these objectives are realistic, placed in a time frame (the March 30 deadline for intramural involvement fits nicely here), and attainable.

It is important that objectives are compatible with one another and, perhaps most importantly, are recorded. Written objectives tend to be attained on a more regular basis than those committed to memory. There is a tendency to forget things entrusted to memory and remember those that are recorded, written and placed in front of one on a daily basis. In short, there is difficulty in remembering things not known.

It is helpful to identify those specific activities that must be undertaken, on a step-by-step basis, so that each objective can be reached. Related items should be grouped together and ranked in priority order. For example, group together academic concerns, facility matters, staffing and staff developments, personal development, long-range planning and public relations in order of importance.

B. Planning

Once the goals and objectives are set, it is necessary to develop a plan to implement them. The difference between success and failure is often the use of time through planning. Planning is nothing more than looking ahead in a systematic way. The paradox is that most people simply do not plan. There is a significant difference between planning and scheduling since a plan tells what is to be done while a schedule tells when it will be done. Sound advice, therefore, suggests that nothing is planned unless the time in which it is to occur is scheduled. Most positive things, as a rule, do not happen by accident. They are generally planned and the more carefully they are planned the better the results.

Plan, think, organize, direct, control and manage time. Remember to review the day at its end and set objectives and priorities for the next day. Write out a daily to-do list and at the end of the week write out a weekly plan. Within that plan build in specific periods with a personal priority system. The plan should then be placed where it can be seen.

C. Eliminating Major Time-Wasters

Interruptions that steal time are led by meetings, telephone calls and drop-in visitors. No single profession is exempt from poor use of time. Sales groups, service organizations, educational administrators, the legal profession, manufacturers and hundreds of other groups all join the sport manager in facing this staggering group of time-wasters.

D. Meetings

It seems that administrators at all levels spend an inordinate amount of time in meetings although many meetings are a complete and total waste of time. Several practical suggestions may prove helpful in reducing the ineffectiveness of meetings.

1. All meetings should begin and end on time.
2. There should be a prearranged agenda distributed prior to the meeting with each agenda item given a specific time for discussion.
3. Certain questions should be asked before any meeting is held, such as: "What is the purpose of this meeting?" "What will it solve?" or "Can it be solved with a memo or telephone call?" Individuals should ask "What can I contribute to the meeting?" "Why have I been invited?"
4. If there is little reason to attend, ask to be excused.

E. Telephone Calls

Most telephone calls have very little to do with anything except asking trivial questions, socializing and stealing valuable time. Unfortunately, many managers presume that persons are calling for legitimate reasons, when, in fact, they are calling for exactly the opposite reasons. Needless to say, many of the reasons for the telephone calls are things that are not related to high priority items.

It is important to set certain hours to take incoming telephone calls. Train a secretary, work-study student, graduate assistant or even fellow administrators to screen incoming calls. Watch a clock during calls to hold "on the phone" time to an absolute minimum. Return all calls at a specified time, plan calls in writing, and try standing while on the telephone.

F. Drop-In Visitors

Most drop-in visitors, like telephone calls, have little to do with high priority matters. Too often the visitors talk about the latest staff gossip, job openings, or other unimportant items. To keep those interruptions to a minimum, try some of these tips:

1. Meet visitors outside the office, stand up if they should enter the office and simply escort them out the door;
2. Don't be afraid to close doors occasionally;
3. Remove extra chairs from the office; and,
4. Go to the other person's office for meetings.

G. Allow for Unscheduled Time

Activities should be scheduled around key events by limiting or completely avoiding spending time on those activities that are not related to the attainment of predetermined objectives. Allow sufficient time to think, plan, reflect and organize. Ideally, it is good practice to allow between 25 and 40% of every day to unscheduled time to handle crises and emergencies that inevitably arise despite one's best intentions.

H. Record Every Activity

A time log or time record is the best way to objectively determine how one *really* spends time. This exercise is admittedly time-consuming and can appear to be burdensome and painstaking. At times it may even take one longer to record actual time use than it takes to carry out the function one is recording. It is absolutely imperative, however, that one conducts a time log for a one-week period several times a year to determine if work habits need changing. The time log records every activity, no matter how trivial, and is the only way to develop an accurate awareness of the use of time. One cannot wait until noon to record what one did all morning or wait until evening to remember what was done in the afternoon. For many people, a day-to-day log of actual time use is quite revealing and, in many instances, shocking. Rank each activity by importance, identifying each interruption and its specific source and content. Many sport managers conduct a time log during peak periods and again in off season. This gives an accurate evaluation of time utilization at varying periods under different conditions and pressures.

At the end of each day, when the log is kept, review the log and ask several questions. "What time was the task completed?" "How many times, and for what reasons, was it interrupted?" "What was the most productive and least productive period of the day?" "Why?" "Who or what activities can be ignored, delegated or eliminated?"

The real key is to stop a dozen times a day and ask if what is being done at the moment is the most productive and the thing that needs attention. "Is the activity a high-priority activity?" "Is it related to a high-priority objective?" Do not confuse activity with productivity by getting caught up with the trivia that can engulf and limit potential results and professional growth.

I. Provide a "Quiet Hour"

There is an old adage in time management that says, quite simply, "As the first hour goes, so goes the rest of the day." Unfortunately, many people tend to use the important first hour on very low-priority items such as drinking coffee, reading newspapers, shuffling papers and other unimportant matters. The more one accomplishes by noon, the greater the opportunity to have a productive day. Many successful sport managers develop a daily habit of setting aside a large block of uninterrupted time. This is often referred to as the "Quiet Hour" when there are no telephone calls, drop-in visitors, meetings or other distractions. It is amazing how the "Quiet Hour" can lead to the achievement of the really important things (primary objectives). Research reveals that the average manager is interrupted every six to nine minutes of the working day. It is estimated that it takes three times as long as the actual interruption to get back in track if one gets back at all. The use of the "Quiet Hour" can maximize time needed for important tasks.

J. Evaluating Work Habits

Make a concerted effort to evaluate the job's functions very critically. Identify those activities, both productive and nonproductive, that need attention on a daily basis and analyze the amount of time that is spent on each function. Many administrators find, when they evaluate their job-related habits, that they are devoting much of their time to relatively unimportant tasks by attempting to do more than it is possible to get done.

Summary/Conclusion

It is essential that the sport manager remember that all of us have time allotted in equal amounts. Time cannot be purchased, marketed or saved; it can only be spent. The secret, then, is to make the use of time a positive expenditure by disciplining oneself to develop positive time-use habits. A professional cannot afford to give it away cheaply or frivolously. By a system of evaluation, the sport manager can attempt to determine positive habits and incorporate them into a plan for a set of objectives for which one is accountable. In many ways successful sport managers do the things that the rest of us never got around to doing. Time management can become a positive habit that will build confidence and lead toward professional and capable leadership.

Chapter 3

Stress Costs and Benefits

Lynne Gaskin

Introduction

The event in our arena wasn't over until almost midnight last night and an elderly woman fell down the stairs as she was leaving. It was almost two o'clock before I got home. The alarm didn't go off this morning, and then my dog ran off when I let her out. By the time I had captured her and had finished dressing, I was late leaving the house. The fuel indicator on the car was below "E", so I had to stop for gas and got in line behind three people who were slow as snails pumping their gas and paying the attendant. When I finally got back on the interstate, I was confronted by bumper to bumper traffic and a number of drivers who confounded the already impossible situation by yelling at other drivers, blowing their horns, and making obscene gestures.

Walking into the office 45 minutes late, I'm confronted with a memo to return a call from the lawyer representing the woman who fell last night, the maintenance engineer who tells me our cooling system is malfunctioning, an audit showing our profits are down, and a reporter who wants to interview me about our security during the fight that broke out at the end of the regional basketball game yesterday afternoon. Just as I am ready to begin confronting these situations, my secretary rushes in to let me know that the tickets for next week's game have been printed incorrectly and hundreds of people are downstairs waiting to purchase these tickets that go on sale in two hours.

As I pace the office trying to decide what to do first, I can feel my heart thumping, the dryness in my mouth, the general weakness in my body, and the nervous twitch in my left eye. I feel sick to my stomach, and my head is pounding. I have an overpowering urge to run out the door and start looking for another job.

The previous account is a vivid description of stress—too much stress—built up to the point of becoming harmful (distress). Such reaction to acute or chronic stressful situations is predictable and results in the "fight or flight syndrome" so appropriately labeled by the Harvard physiologist Dr. Walter B. Cannon. When we are confronted with situations that require adjustment in our behavior, we undergo this involuntary, but predictable response. We experience an increase in our blood pressure, heart rate, rate of breathing, metabolism, and blood flow to the muscles preparing us to fight or run.

In the days of our primitive ancestors, it was appropriate to deal with enemies by fighting or running away in order to survive. Today's rational person, experiencing the same fight-or-flight response, has no such alternative. However, we must learn to use the response to our benefit or ultimately experience chronic health problems and job inefficiency.

Understanding Stress

We all have experienced stress and know something about its origins and effects. Some stress is necessary to function at one's best, but there is an optimal level of stress for each person. Stress becomes a problem when it becomes too severe and we feel a loss of control over our lives.

Individuals react differently to stress and need different techniques to relieve distress. Each person should determine his or her optimal level of stress and develop techniques for relieving distress. There is no universal formula available. Each of us has to know what stressors cause adverse effects and how to deal with them effectively to function at an optimal level.

Stress cannot be viewed solely as a negative factor, for different people react differently to similar situations. A flat tire on a vehicle may be perceived as an unfortunate occurrence and as an inconvenience to the bus driver, but to the coach whose team is on the way to an important game it is a stressful situation. The key aspects are perception and mental appraisal. What may be viewed as stress by one person may be viewed even as vitalizing for another. A snowstorm may be perceived as a harrowing experience by the sport manager with 200 boys and girls in attendance in his gymnasium for a youth soccer clinic, but it may bring a sense of euphoria to the downhill skier. Regardless of the stressor, when stress becomes excessive or builds up over a period of time, reduction in a feeling of well-being or diminished job effectiveness may result.

Stress should not be viewed solely as a personal problem, but rather as a managerial challenge for each person. Half the problem in managing stress is identifying the causes. In today's society of accelerated pace and change, technological advancement, and fluctuation in the economy, the more fully we can understand the meaning, causes, and symptoms of stress, the better prepared we will be to use it to our advantage—both in our personal and work environments (as a manager and as an employee). The goal, then, is not to avoid stress but to understand it, consider how it affects us adversely, and determine how to control potentially stressful situations.

There are several key areas to consider. One's personality and lifestyle habits are highly related to how one perceives stress and is affected by it. Assessing the stressors in one's life, recognizing the high costs of stress, and formulating a plan for reducing the harmful effects of stress are paramount in successful stress management.

Assessing Personality

An important consideration in managing stress is to acknowledge that personality may be the key to how we react to stress and that some of us may actually create too much stress for ourselves. A person with a Type A personality is described as relentlessly driven, intense, restless, impatient, irritable, aggressive, overly competitive, overly ambitious, and even hostile (Friedman and Rosenman, 1974; Gmelch and Miskin, 1993; Krohe, 1999; Sapolsky, 1998; Schaubroeck, Ganster, and Kemmerer, 1994). This individual has a compulsion to overwork, is always confronting time deadlines, and often neglects other aspects of life such as family, social occasions, and recreational activities. In contrast, Type B personality types are easygoing, relaxed, and patient. They are less competitive, less achievement-oriented, less hurried, and more likely to engage in leisure pursuits.

What type personality best describes you is an important question to consider. You may have a good indication from the previously mentioned characteristics, but stop now and respond to the checklist below. You might as well start right now to learn more about yourself and your ability to handle stress.

ASSESSING PERSONALITY TYPE
(Giammatteo and Giammatteo, 1980)

Yes	No	Don't Know		
___	___	___	1.	I'm frequently in a hurry.
___	___	___	2.	I'm typically doing several projects at the same time.
___	___	___	3.	I'm always pushed by deadlines.
___	___	___	4.	I usually take on as many (or a few more) projects as I can handle.
___	___	___	5.	I really seek recognition from my boss and/or peers.
___	___	___	6.	I believe it's important for a person to push herself or himself for success, and I seek opportunities for promotions and advancements.
___	___	___	7.	I enjoy competition in all areas.
___	___	___	8.	I really enjoy winning and hate to lose.
___	___	___	9.	My job is the most important thing in my life.
___	___	___	10.	1 sometimes feel I neglect my family by putting my job first.
___	___	___	11.	I'm usually too busy with my job to have time for many hobbies or outside activities.
___	___	___	12.	When I'm given a job, I really feel personally responsible for its success—i.e., even though others may be involved, I feel that it just won't come out as well unless I'm personally involved from start to finish.
___	___	___	13.	I have trouble trusting people easily.
___	___	___	14.	I tend to talk fast.
___	___	___	15.	When speaking, I believe in giving special emphasis to my meaning with strong vocal inflection and gestures.
___	___	___	16.	I feel some impatience in most meetings and conversations—I just wish they would speed up and get on with it.
___	___	___	17.	I tend to get irritable and lose my cool easily when obviously simple things don't go right.
___	___	___	18.	I make a list of things I must get done each day.
___	___	___	19.	I generally have strong opinions on most things.
___	___	___	20.	I don't seem to get much time to keep up with my reading.

If you answered yes to at least 15 of these statements, you probably are falling into the Type A behavior pattern.

It is important to recognize that a person's work environment often encourages and rewards the Type A behavior. Even more important, however, is the point that employees with Type A traits are approximately five times more likely to have heart attacks than employees with Type B traits (Buhler, 1993). Type A individuals, of necessity, must gain control over their own lives in order to reduce their stress level and find the optimal stress level where they function best. Otherwise, they are prime candidates for heart attacks and other serious health problems (Andrew, 1999; Krohe, 1999; Schaubroeck, Ganster, and Kemmerer, 1994). Of utmost importance is the fact that behavior is learned and can be modified. The first step, however, is to identify those aspects of one's behavior to change and then begin focusing on those areas with specific plans for accomplishing change.

Lifestyles

In addition to considering basic personality type, one must consider stress and the ability to manage stress in regard to lifestyle habits. Smoking, drinking, and eating in excess, irregular exercise, improper nutrition, inadequate relaxation, and inability to talk with others openly about problems or concerns are just a few of the health behavior problems that can contribute to poor health and chronic stress. Obviously, these behaviors must be addressed honestly and a decision made to regulate those perceived to be most hazardous to one's well-being. Each person must face these individually, for no one can improve another's health. One may seek the help of others, both personal support and professional assistance, to help effect change in any of the areas mentioned or in others; but, ultimately, each individual will decide whether to attack these concerns and what techniques are most beneficial.

Specific steps are necessary in managing stress related to lifestyle. Identify those lifestyle habits that need change. Share concerns with a member of the family, a close friend, or a colleague at work. Determine the best approach to attack the problem, and solicit another person's support to help break the habit or at least get it within the realm of reasonable control. As is the case with personality and behavior, lifestyle habits are learned and can be modified.

Assessing Stress

There are many assessment scales that have been developed to determine degrees of stress. Managers and employees who are interested in further information should consult some of the better known instruments. Probably the best known and most frequently cited assessment is the Holmes and Rahe Social Readjustment Rating Scale (1967) developed to measure the impact of life change events.

A shorter and more easily scored way of assessing one's vulnerability to stress has been developed by psychologists Lyle H. Miller and Alma Dell Smith. Consider each item and score it from one to five according to how much of the time each statement applies to you.

ASSESSING YOUR VULNERABILITY TO STRESS
(Miller and Smith, 1983)

1 = Almost always
2 = Usually
3 = Sometimes
4 = Rarely
5 = Almost Never

___	1.	I eat at least one hot, balanced meal a day.
___	2.	I get seven to eight hours sleep at least four nights a week.
___	3.	I give and receive affection regularly.
___	4.	I have at least one relative within 50 miles on whom I can rely.
___	5.	I exercise to the point of perspiration at least twice a week
___	6.	I smoke less than a pack of cigarettes a day.
___	7.	I take fewer than five alcoholic drinks a week.
___	8.	I am the appropriate weight for my height.
___	9.	I have an income adequate to meet basic expenses.
___	10.	I get strength from my religious beliefs.
___	11.	I regularly attend club or social activities.
___	12.	I have a network of friends and acquaintances.
___	13.	I have one or more friends to confide in about personal experiences.
___	14.	I am in good health (including eyesight, hearing, teeth).
___	15.	I am able to speak openly about my feelings when angry or worried.
___	16.	I have regular conversations with the people I live with about domestic problems, e.g., chores, money and daily living issues.
___	17.	I do something for fun at least once a week.
___	18.	I am able to organize my time effectively.
___	19.	I drink fewer than three cups of coffee (or tea or cola drinks) a day.
___	20.	I take quiet time for myself during the day.

___ TOTAL

To get your score, add up the numbers and subtract 20. Any number over 30 indicates a vulnerability to stress. You are seriously vulnerable if your score is between 50 and 75 and extremely vulnerable if it is over 75.

Costs of Stress and Techniques to Manage Stress

Lost productivity due to job stress costs American employers over $200 billion annually (Kedjidjian, 1995; Seaward, 1995; Solomon, 1999). Costs associated with stress-related absenteeism alone are staggering and, according to health care professionals, up to 90% of patients complain of stress-related symptoms and disorders (Cooper and Cartwright, 1994; Gibson, 1993; Kedjidjian, 1995). According to the Director of the National Institute for Occupational Safety and Health (NIOSH), American workers put in an average of 47 hours of work per week, and 75% of them believe that there is greater stress on the job than there was a generation ago (Minter, 1999; Solomon, 1999). Moreover, NIOSH also rates stress as one of the 10 leading work-related diseases (Minter, 1991), and 40% of employee turnover has been attributed to job stress (http://www.stress.org/problem.htm).

Regardless of the sector of the sport industry (e.g., amateur or professional, school or club, public or private), the costs of stress are real threats to the effectiveness of any organization. Costs related to job stress are assessed by absenteeism, employee turnover, physical and emotional health problems, workplace accidents, medical and insurance costs, job dissatisfaction, worker's compensation awards, lowered job productivity, theft, and sabotage (Gibson, 1993; Grazian, 1994; Kedjidjian, 1995; Seaward, 1995; "Study pinpoints," 1993). Stress has been related to many diseases and physical ailments, and experts have proposed that approximately 80% of all diseases and illnesses are stress-related (Seaward, 1995).

Among the most commonly mentioned diseases and physical ailments related to stress are coronary heart disease, asthma, arthritis, neck aches, backaches, tension headaches, migraine headaches, allergies, kidney problems, indigestion, diabetes mellitus, ulcers, high blood pressure, constipation, muscle spasms, diarrhea, muscular tension, and even cancer. Psychological responses to stress include anxiety disorders, depression, sexual difficulties, insomnia, family problems, and burnout. Behavioral responses may be exhibited through alcohol, drug, and tobacco abuse, accident proneness, violence, and eating disorders (Kedjidjian, 1995; Quick, Quick, Nelson, and Hurrell, 1997). Managing stress effectively can help prevent many of these job-related ailments.

There is no evidence that sports managers and others working in sports programs are any more susceptible to chronic stress than others in similar non-sport positions. There is also no evidence to indicate that sport personnel are any less susceptible. It is acknowledged, however, that the higher number of interpersonal relationships a person encounters in his or her work, the more likely stressors will present themselves. For example, people who input data into a computer system and who constantly stare at a digital display screen will not experience the same kind of stress nor the number of stress-related situations as those whose work involves consistent interaction with people—participants, coaches, spectators, officials, media representatives, salespersons, parents, and other members of the public who are consumers of sports programs. Sport managers, beware!

Business has taken two primary approaches in dealing with job stress—by (a) providing stress management programs and (b) focusing on organizational change (Brott, 1994; Kedjidjian, 1995; Minter, 1999; Sauter et al., 1999; Seaward, 1995). In the first approach, businesses frequently offer stress management, time management, and work and family training sessions; exercise programs; wellness programs; conflict management courses; and employee assistance programs (EAPs) to improve employees' ability to manage their own stress or to cope better. The second and more recent approach involves businesses identifying the causes of workplace stress and trying to eliminate or minimize them. According to authorities on stress in the workplace, the best method is a combination of the two approaches (Minter, 1999; Sauter et al., 1999).

In regard to stress management, no one way to manage stress is best. Assessing one's personality and lifestyle is mandatory. Equally important is learning about and engaging in interventions to help take control of one's own situation. Based on personal interest and preference, one should at least consider regular physical activity, eating properly, progressive muscle relaxation, meditation, rhythmic breathing, mental imagery, music therapy, yoga, and massage. The employee who takes advantage of employer-offered stress management sessions not only will be able to ingrain those positive activities in which the individual already is involved, but will be able to learn about other interventions that may be helpful. The references at the end of this chapter (books, articles, and on-line citations) provide good resources for more extensive coverage of these techniques and others that one might choose to practice. All these techniques are self-regulated and will not be effective unless the individual is motivated and chooses to practice them consistently.

In addition to profiting from participating in stress management strategies, employees also should welcome and benefit from organizational change. Collaborating with managers to identify stressful components of the workplace and taking part in strategies to minimize or eliminate these stressors will improve communication, empower employees, and enable them to exercise greater control in the workplace. According to noted researchers in job stress, lack of control, uncertainty about the work environment, and poor communication are major sources of job stress (Quick, Quick, Nelson, and Hurrell, 1997).

Regardless of the position a sport manager occupies in the sport industry, a sport manager must work with others to get the job done. Every sport manager will encounter some stress and can use it to advantage to become a more effective and efficient manager of both sports and stress. The key to stress management within the organization (regardless of the type of work situation) lies in clearly defining the workload, accepting responsibility for those things which can be controlled, and striving to enhance interpersonal relationships.

The implications are clear for the sport manager and employee. The effectiveness of the organization is undermined drastically when those who plan, organize, conduct, and assess sports programs are subjected to excessive stress in the work environment. Conscientious attention must be given to help all workers meet such situations head on.

Sport managers who are directly responsible for others working within the organization should consider specific, practical tactics to help employees function under less stressful situations.

1. Identify a specific job description for each employee. Delineate exactly what the job is and what is expected of the employee. Match the workload with the employee's capabilities and resources.
2. Set up conferences with employees to discuss stressors that they encounter, their goals for the year, job satisfaction and dissatisfaction, and suggestions for constructive change.
3. Involve employees in decision-making and change affecting their jobs.
4. Emphasize open communication, encourage employees to express their opinions freely, and give them the rationale for your proposals.
5. Involve and assist each employee in career development and future employment based on the individual's needs, interests, and abilities and the needs of the organization.
6. Give employees who are changing their job adequate time to retool or retrain so they can move into the new job with confidence.
7. Give employees consistent feedback for successful job performance and constructive feedback for unsatisfactory performance. Let employees know that they are important to the organization, valued, and appreciated. Recognize and reward meritorious service financially and through other appropriate avenues.

8. Provide employees family-friendly options to address stressors that are related to work and family—e.g., flexible work schedules, work at home, and parental leave.

9. Encourage employees to develop strong on-the-job support systems. Provide strong mentors and models for new employees or those changing jobs, and provide opportunities for social interaction among all employees.

The sport manager who incorporates these concerns will help employees function more effectively and perceive their job as a constructive and satisfying part of their lives. Each sport manager should develop managing techniques to fit the specific job related stressors of the organization.

Although the sport manager must be concerned with helping employees manage their stress, his or her first responsibility is to self. No manager can work effectively with others without first learning to function at his or her own optimal stress level. The goal of the sport manager is to gain control and convert potentially stressful situations or conditions to advantage and to the advantage of employees. There is no doubt that a wise sport manager can gain a definite advantage by learning how to handle stress effectively. Many stress-laden areas can be avoided by anticipating and planning for them.

1. Establish realistic personal goals and reorganize your life. Prioritize!
2. Identify the job-related situations that cause you the most stress.
3. Pace yourself and manage your time wisely.
4. Determine the stress reduction programs or stress management techniques that work best for you and use them consistently.
5. Recognize the limitations of management. Hire competent employees and delegate responsibility.
6. Be assertive and learn to stand up for yourself. Act in your own best interests as you continue to be concerned with others. Learn to say "no," or at least "not now."
7. Take time for yourself and maintain a support network.
8. Accept the uniqueness of your situation and make things work for you and your employees.
9. Be concerned about the well-being of employees and encourage open communication.
10. Use stress positively by working together with employees to meet deadlines.
11. Seek your own stress level and live accordingly.

One can and should anticipate stressful situations in the work environment. How can one "work smarter" and counteract the effects of too much on-the-job stress? Burke (as cited in Adams, 19890) surveyed a large number of managers, and identified the ten most frequently mentioned responses to job stress. These responses were later ranked by managers according to frequency of use to protect their health when under stress. The five most effective coping strategies with the fewest symptoms of chronic ill health associated with them were related to "working smarter"—building resistance through healthful lifestyle habits, compartmentalizing work life and home life, engaging in regular physical exercise, talking it through on the job with peers, and withdrawing physically from the situation. Five other strategies were identified as effective in coping with job stress but were less effective in regard to the number of chronic symptoms of ill health associated with them—changing to engrossing non-work activity, talking it through with spouse, working harder, analyzing the situation and changing strategy, and changing to a different work task.

Regardless of one's personality, lifestyle habits, and assessment of stressors, each person must take responsibility for managing personal stress and cannot let others manage his or her stress level. A sense of control over one's own life is the central purpose in managing stress effectively.

Summary/Conclusion

The single, most-important factor in producing harmful stressful situations is the individual's perceived loss of control of one's own destiny. Managers and employees not only can tolerate stressful situations, but can actually function effectively in potentially stressful environments. To function effectively, however, they must know that the situations and conditions are under their control.

There are several points that sport managers must consider. Become aware of what causes stress in your life and take the initiative to control your own stress. Stress reduction involves observable action. Practice stress reduction techniques and take more responsibility in managing your own stress. Recognize your needs and be realistic about your abilities. Be alert to ways in which your body reacts to stress, be aware of situations that produce these reactions, and take appropriate steps to protect your health and life. In working with employees, encourage them to participate in stress management strategies, involve them in decision making, make sure they understand their role and responsibilities in the organization, assist them in career advancement, and let them know that they are valued, contributing members of the organization.

The initial scenario described in this chapter depicts a vivid picture of harmful stress and a situation in which the sport manager had lost control in regulating stressful situations. How would the description have been different for the sport manager in control of his life?

The event at our arena wasn't over until almost midnight last night and an elderly woman fell down the stairs as she was leaving the facility. By the time our emergency medical team had completed their report and we had made sure the woman wasn't seriously injured, it was almost two o'clock before I left the building. Knowing I would be working late last night, I had arranged to go in later this morning so I didn't set my alarm. Since the dog scampered over to the neighbor's yard again when I let her out, I had to stop for gas on my way in to the office, and I got hung up in heavy traffic, I called my secretary to say I would be later than I had expected. Also, I wanted to know what had happened thus far at the office.

My secretary is quite good at his job and always follows the procedures we have established to help us function more effectively. He related several occurrences to me over the telephone.

1. The lawyer representing the woman who fell last night has already called to inquire about our medical procedures and to ask when it will be convenient for him to come over to check lighting and exit routes.
2. Our cooling system is malfunctioning. The maintenance engineer has ordered the necessary equipment and will have it installed by noon.
3. 1 have an appointment at 11:00 with a newspaper reporter, who wants to discuss the fight that broke out yesterday afternoon. Fortunately, we have an alert security force, but we do need to be more attentive to groups once they leave the building and are out in the parking lot.

On the way in to the office while I am filling up with gas and sitting in heavy traffic, I am glad to have the extra time to gather my thoughts about how I will respond to the reporter. Also, I want to be sure to commend our medical team, our maintenance engineer, and our security force for their effectiveness and efficiency. I do have to make sure, however, that the security force is aware that they should have been able to prevent the disturbance in the parking lot before it occurred. I will ask them to come up with recommendations for avoiding such situations in the future.

Walking into the office, I am greeted by my secretary who informs me that the tickets for next week's game have been printed incorrectly and hundreds of people are downstairs waiting to purchase these tickets that go on sale in two hours.

I can feel my heart rate speed up, the dryness creep into my mouth, and the twitch start in my left eye. Asking not to be disturbed for ten minutes, I go into the office, close the door, sit down in the chair by the window and begin my deep breathing exercises. It's amazing how much better I can think after I have regained control.

References

Adams, J.C., ed. (1980). *Understanding and managing stress*. San Diego, CA: University Associates.

Andrew, R. (1999). Years of living dangerously. *CA Magazine, 132*(2), 26-30.

Brott, A.A. (1994). New approaches to job stress. *Nation's Business, 82*(5), 81.

Buhler, P. (1993). Stress management. *Supervision, 54*(5), 17-19.

Cooper, C.L., and S. Cartwright (1994). Healthy mind; healthy organization—a proactive approach to occupational stress. *Human Relations, 47*(4), 455-472.

Friedman, M., and R.H. Rosenman (1974). *Type A behavior and your heart*. New York: Alfred A. Knopf.

Giammatteo, M.C., and D.M. Giammatteo (1980). *Executive well-being: Stress and administrators*. Reston, VA: National Association of Secondary School Principals. Used by permission of the authors and the publisher.

Gibson, V.M. (1993). Stress in the workplace: A hidden cost factor. *HR Focus, 70*(1), 15.

Gmelch, W.H., and V.D. Miskin (1993). *Leadership skills for department chairs*. Bolton, MA: Anker.

Grazian, F. (1994). Are you coping with stress? *Communication Briefings, 12*(5), 3.

Kedjidjian, C. (1995). How to combat workplace stress. *Safety and Health, 151*(4), 36-41.

Krohe, J., Jr. (1999). Workplace stress. *Across the Board, 36*(2), 36-42.

Miller, L.H. and A.D. Smith (1983). *Stress Audit.* Boston, MA: Biobehavioral Associates. Used by permission of the authors and the publishers.

Minter, S.G. (1991). Relieving workplace stress. *Occupational Hazards, 53,* 39-42.

———— (1999). Too much stress. *Occupational Hazards, 61*(5), 49-52.

Quick, J.C., J.D. Quick, D.L. Nelson, and J.J. Hurrell, Jr. (1997). *Preventive stress management in organizations.* Washington, DC: American Psychological Association.

Sapolsky, R.M. (1998). *Why zebras don't get ulcers: An updated guide to stress, stress-related diseases, and coping.* New York: W.H. Freeman.

Sauter, S., L. Murphy, M. Colligan, N. Swanson, J. Hurrell, Jr., F. Scharf, Jr., R. Sinclair, P. Grubb, L. Goldenhar, T. Alterman, J. Johnston, A. Hamilton, and J. Tisdale (1999). *Stress...at work.* Cincinnati, OH: National Institute for Occupational Safety and Health.

Schaubroeck, J., D. Ganster, and B. Kemmerer (1994). Job complexity, "Type A" behavior, and cardiovascular disorder. *Academy of Management Journal, 37*(2), 426-429.

Seaward, B.L. (1995). Job stress takes a global toll. *Safety and health, 151*(1) 64-65.

Solomon, C.M. (1999). Stressed to the limit. *Workforce, 78*(9), 48-54.

"Study pinpoints the causes of stress for working women" (1993). *HR Focus, 70*(9), 24.

www.jobstresshelp.com

www.stress.org

www.stress.org/problem.htm

www.stress-institute.com

www.stress-stop.com

Chapter 4

Sport Organization Leadership

David K. Scott

Introduction

The long-term, successful performance of any organization is ultimately the responsibility of leadership. However, as has been suggested in recent years by a number of management scholars and practitioners, there appears to be a dearth of truly effective leadership in many of our business and service organizations as well as in our governmental systems. Can the same be said about sport organizations? Although the answer probably depends on who is being asked, there are several other questions that might need to be considered. For example, what is meant by "effective" leadership in sport? Are organizational outcomes such as winning, maximum attendance, and profits the sole indicator of good leadership? How important is employee or athlete satisfaction as an outcome of leadership? To what extent do external groups have to be satisfied with leadership? What are the core values of sport organizations relative to their products and/or participants, and to entertainment in general? These are just a few examples of questions that must be addressed by current and future sport leaders as they assume roles of leadership for sport organizations in the new millenium.

The goal of this chapter is to provide the reader with insight for answering questions such as the ones stated above. The chapter will address elements of leadership that can be applied to both (a) individual organization leadership in sport, and (b) the broad leadership challenges within the sport industry. These two components of leadership will be referred to subsequently as "micro-leadership" (personal, small group/team, and departmental leadership) and "macro-leadership" (sport industry leadership) respectively. The sections to follow will broadly define leadership, and identify what are considered to be leadership "essentials." In addition, subsequent sections will address leadership and organizational effectiveness, problem solving through a multi-frame frame perspective, managing sport organization culture, and leadership development. The chapter will conclude with future considerations for leadership in a rapidly changing sport industry.

Leadership Challenges in Sport

From a "micro" leadership perspective, sport administrators, team owners, general managers, coaches, and others in decision-making roles of authority face a number of challenges. Financial issues, personnel problems, crisis management, public relations, and pressure from external constituents create a plethora of daily leadership problems. These are issues that often consume the business, and sometimes personal, lives of sport leaders and require tremendous leadership commitment.

From a "macro" perspective, there are a number of issues that also represent significant challenges for the sport industry in general. Some of the recent concerns that call for effective leadership intervention include gender equity, decline in sportsmanship, athlete crime, over-commercialization of sport, and professional ethics. These all represent broad leadership challenges that will likely require collaboration of leaders in sport, business, education, and possibly the government.

Defining Leadership for Sport Organizations

As one might suspect, leadership has a multitude of definitions. What most of these definitions have in common is that leadership involves vision and the ability to influence or motivate people toward goal attainment. In modern organizations, the goals attained are considered acceptable if they are both positive and mutually beneficial for the leader, the group members, and the overall organization.

In addition, there are several other descriptors of leadership that are helpful in framing the leadership phenomenon. Leadership implies that there are one or more followers. Leadership provides direction and support. Leadership creates change. Leadership is rooted in principles, morality, and ethics.

From a sport perspective, it appears that all of the above characteristics of leadership are useful in defining what sport leadership is, or what it should be. In addition, leadership in sport organizations can come from many levels. For example, in competitive sports, one can see the leadership impact that owners, general managers, athletic directors, coaches, and even athletes can have on their organizations. While ultimate leadership accountability in a sport organization rests with upper management, it should be recognized that leadership could come from "within" and not always from "above" in the organizational hierarchy.

There are also other factors involved in defining or describing leadership that should be considered. Rightly or wrongly, leadership is often proposed as a "process" and evaluated as an "outcome." In sport organizations, this is quite evident in the leadership turnover associated with losing seasons, declining attendance, and loss of financial support for a team or sport entity. Also, leadership is commonly associated with personal and/or organizational change and is often most visible in times of organizational crisis. From this perspective, sport leadership may also be thought of as an integral part of internal and external public relations.

With the above in mind, what does it take to be an effective sport leader? In order to be effective at developing vision, influencing people, achieving goals, managing change, and leading an organization through crisis situations, there are several traits, behaviors, and outcomes that are critical to effective leadership. These essential elements, identified in the next section, are the foundation for further development of both "micro" and "macro" leadership in sport.

Leadership Essentials for Sport Managers

The leadership phenomenon has been studied for decades and has evolved from purely trait theory to more modern situational, transformational, and values-based leadership. These theories have collectively produced a number of characteristics that, whether naturally occurring or developed, are generally recognized as important for a leader to possess. For example, a leader must be internally motivated, demonstrate self-confidence, and have cognitive ability. Moreover, from a standpoint of credibility, it is also important for a leader to be honest and to have knowledge and/or experience related to the enterprise being led. In addition, there are several "abilities" that leaders demonstrate which are essential to overall effectiveness. These will be discussed in some detail below. However, before proceeding it is also interesting to know what things have been identified as reducers of leadership effectiveness. The Hagberg Consulting Group (1998), in studies of U.S. corporations, recognized a number of behaviors that reduce the effectiveness of company presidents. Included are (a) poor communication of the vision, (b) excessive dominance and intolerance of disagreement, (c) self-centeredness, (d) failure to build alignment with goals, (e) lack of emphasis on teamwork, (e) arrogance and egotism, and (f) ignoring conflict. Individuals in sport leadership positions that are demonstrating one or more of these characteristics are undermining their influence on others and ultimately losing their credibility and effectiveness.

As previously mentioned, however, there are a number of leadership essentials that continually resurface in the literature regarding what *is* necessary for a leader to be truly effective. Each of these is addressed in the following discussion.

1. *Ability to obtain the trust and respect of individuals and groups.* Trust may likely be the most critical component of leadership. While trust and respect may be the result of an individual's personal charisma, previous performance, and physical or career longevity, there are a number of other traits and behaviors that are essential for the development of individual and group trust. These behaviors can generally be associated with values-based or principle-centered leadership. Bennis and Goldsmith (1997) recognized that vision, empathy, consistency, and integrity were the essential components of building and maintaining the trust of followers. Within these components, a leader who can create inspiring visions, "walk in the shoes" of followers, demonstrate consistency of purpose and action, and demonstrate integrity through ethical decision making is doing what is necessary to develop long-term trust and respect.

2. *Ability to adapt to various situations or contingencies.* Leaders of sport organizations have to make difficult decisions regarding policy, personnel, resource distribution, strategy, and a multitude of other short-term and long-term challenges. Contingency leadership theory suggests that the "situation" within which a decision must be made will dictate how a leader should approach a problem. This means that a leader may have to adapt or change from what is his or her personal leadership preference in order to produce the desired results. In competitive sport organizations, situations may change on a daily basis and one's ability to adapt to these situations is critical to effective leadership.

An issue that has to be addressed with regard to situational leadership, however, is that it is sometimes in conflict with the trust building component of consistency. A leadership oxymoron is for a leader to be adaptable to various situations while also demonstrating consistency of behavior. For example, in situations where eligibility rules or team policy have been violated, leaders in charge must take situational factors into consideration while also being concerned about how inconsistent decisions may affect the trust of group members. Although there is not an easy answer for this dilemma, it may be that the best approach is to demonstrate consistency in the process of reaching a decision that is in the best interest of the individual or groups most affected. However, at the macro-leadership level in sport, the ability to demonstrate situational adaptability requires concern for a broader constituency. Decisions that often have to be made by league commissioners and executive directors of state, national, and international governing bodies must take into account the impact of the decision on the entire association and/or industry as a whole.

3. *Ability to develop vision and clarify a path.* The ability to move beyond what "is" and visualize "what could be" is essential to leadership. Additionally, the ability to clear a path and remove obstacles for those who follow is the "action leadership" necessary to truly be an architect of change. A number of sport leaders, both present and past, have demonstrated these essentials. However, it should be noted that their decisions and what they stand for are, or were not always universally popular. While certainly not an all inclusive list, individuals such as Branch Rickey, credited with racial integration in sport, Donna Lopiano, executive director of the Women's Sport Foundation, David Stern, currently at the helm of the NBA, Mark McCormack, president and founder of IMG (International Management Group), and Billie Jean King, former tennis star and advocate of women's rights in sport have demonstrated what vision can do for the industry.

4. *Motivation and Inspiration of Followers.* Leaders are able to motivate and inspire followers to achieve and often surpass the goals of the organization. This is frequently accomplished through the personal charisma of the leader. However, the effective use of a combination of transactional and transformational leadership appears to be the right formula for success. Transactional leaders are able to motivate through the appropriate use of tangible rewards. Transformational leaders demonstrate the ability to move people beyond self-interest toward a higher level of group or organizational commitment. In many cases, transformational leaders may even move followers to a higher level of moral reasoning. In addition to personal charisma, transformational leaders are effective because of their ability to intellectually stimulate followers while providing proper individual consideration (Bass, 1990).

5. *Ability to Achieve Results.* We live in a results oriented world. No where is this more evident than in the sport industry. Although many great things happen during the process of leadership, ultimately people want to see results. Thus, effective leaders are able to produce desired outcomes in a timeframe appropriate to organizational expectations and realities. This will be discussed in more detail in the next section. However, too often, people in leadership positions become so focused on outcomes that they are willing to compromise the fundamental principles of honesty, integrity, and trust that form the foundation of true leadership. This dilemma might be referred to as "bottom-line morality." In other words, both strategic organizational constituents and society in general are often willing to overlook how something was achieved if the end result provides the notoriety and/or revenue expected. As a result, we see such things as unethical business practices, occasional athletic programs on probation, compromise of athlete

safety and health, and acceptance of what many would consider to be intolerable behavior from administrators, coaches, athletes and fans.

IDEAS AND SUGGESTIONS

- Good leaders give people the tools they need to be successful.
- Leaders need the authority to get things done but leadership is *not* synonymous with authority.
- Effective leaders are willing to share power with those who help implement the plan.

Leadership and Organizational Effectiveness in Sport

Five primary components of determining organizational effectiveness have been identified in the organizational studies literature (Cameron, 1980; Connolly, Conlon, and Deutsch, 1980; and Quinn and Rohrbaugh, 1981). These areas, relative to sport organizations, were also discussed in detail by Slack (1997). For in-depth information regarding these measures of effectiveness, the reader is referred to the above sources. The purpose here, however, is to briefly recognize these areas of organizational effectiveness and provide an overview of how they pertain to sport organization leadership. The areas of effectiveness are as follows:

1. *Goal Attainment*—based on how well an organization achieves specific outcomes that are agreed upon by its members.
2. *Use of Systems Resources*—based on an organization's ability to acquire scarce resources or "inputs" from its environment.
3. *Internal Process*—based on the internal function, flow of information, and human interaction factors such as trust, loyalty, and teamwork in the organization.
4. *Satisfaction of Strategic Constituents*—based on an organization's ability to satisfy its numerous stakeholders as well as satisfy other affiliated organizations (i.e. media, sponsors, etc.) which can help it achieve its outcomes.
5. *Competing Values*—based on the idea that no single approach to determining organizational effectiveness is wholly appropriate. Also, effectiveness is subjective and often paradoxical. For example, in competitive sport organizations winning a championship may be seen as effective, however, there may have been compromises in the "means" through which the championship was obtained.

In sport organizations, all of these measurements of effectiveness should be of concern to a leader. Additionally, it should be noted that there is often overlap and even conflict in some of the areas. For example, goal attainment can be viewed both internally and externally. In competitive sport organizations, achievement of internal organizational goals may or may not be what is expected from strategic constituents. As a result, leadership performance is often evaluated by entities whose expectations may not be realistic. From this perspective, a sport leader must have "tough skin" and perhaps be willing to evaluate personal performance based on internal organizational expectations and self-evaluation. Also, goal attainment often depends on an organization's ability to acquire the necessary resources. For example, it is unrealistic to expect a championship season from a sport team when personnel, funding, and/or media support is inadequate.

Relative to goal attainment, competitive sport organizations strive for championships, optimal attendance, satisfied customers, and ultimately increased revenue. These are all outcome-based measures that give some degree of objectivity to how well an organization is performing with regard to both internal and external expectations. As discussed in the previous section above, effective leaders achieve results. Consequently, sub-par performance relative to outcome-based measures is often attributed to poor leadership. While a number of factors other than leadership may contribute to organizational outcomes, leaders are ultimately held accountable and must be willing to accept the responsibility. In order to fulfill this responsibility and be more effective in the area of goal attainment, sport leaders need to do a good job of identifying what is truly realistic, provide the necessary structure (including policies and procedures), and develop strategies that provide goal clarity and reduce or remove obstacles along the way.

Concomitantly, it is important for a sport organization leader to demonstrate the ability to obtain resources and motivate and manage people within the organization. In a recent study of Canadian intercollegiate athletic departments (Danylchuk and Chelladurai, 1999), financial management, leadership (including supervision, motivation, inspiration, and counseling of coaches/staff), and revenue generation were among the activities perceived to be both most important and most time consuming as indicated by athletic directors.

For sport organizations, resources can include finances, personnel, facilities, equipment, and even time. Obtaining these resources is often a considerable obstacle to overcome in a highly competitive sport industry. Each level of sport is faced with its own challenge in this regard. Competition for entertainment dollars, financing of product development, balancing payroll, securing adequate media attention, and acquiring quality personnel are examples of resource oriented challenges that must be addressed by sport leaders.

Managing internal process is also a critical leadership function for sport leaders in achieving organizational effectiveness. Internal process includes components of human resource management, motivation, effective communications, group dynamics, and team building. These are areas that seem natural for "people" oriented leaders but may be quite unnatural for authority and power oriented leaders. While perhaps somewhat idealistic, it is suggested here that truly effective leadership exists only when people within a sport organization are motivated, empowered, trust one another, and are committed to each other and their leaders. This is when sport organization employees or athletes find true satisfaction, personal growth, and perhaps the most meaningful long-term impact of leadership.

Effective sport leaders must also be fully aware of the strategic constituents that will determine, and sometimes define, the organization's effectiveness. Depending on the level of competitive sport or the segment of the sport industry involved, all sport organizations must satisfy both internal and external constituents to some degree. This may present a values-based or ethical dilemma for the sport leader. For example, are athletes the primary constituents who must be satisfied in school sports? If so, should those athletes ultimately determine whether or not their leader or leaders are considered effective? With the billions of dollars in television revenue provided to professional leagues, who has the most influence on determining whether or not a league organization is effective? Does the same question exist regarding a $1,000,000 donor to a collegiate athletic department? These are valid questions that challenge leaders to "do the right thing." Certainly, sport leaders must recognize and be able to effectively manage the political issues associated with the satisfaction of constituents. This may be accomplished through strategic public relations, improved personal communication, and the demonstration of "strong will" when it comes to protecting the integrity of the organization. In this regard, effective sport leaders must also identify their role expectations and be able to maintain a principle-centered approach to managing the satisfaction of constituents. Otherwise, the outside individual or group having the most influence on an organization at any given time will ultimately determine whether or not its leader is effective.

Finally, effective sport leaders must recognize and deal with the "competing values" approach to measuring effectiveness. Although more complicated than presented here, the competing values model (Quinn, 1988), generally suggests that organizational effectiveness depends on the focus of the organization and whether outcomes to measure effectiveness are based on means or ends. In this sense, organizations that want to be successful in a highly competitive sport industry will likely have a predominant external focus that involves adaptability, productivity, goal setting, and maximum output. On the other hand, an organization with an internal focus will concentrate on such things as human commitment, internal communication, training, and group morale. However, these values often "compete" with one another. For example, this is especially true in intercollegiate sport organizations where a dilemma often exists between a sport's entertainment value, its value relative to visibility and image enhancement for the university, and its educational or developmental value for athletes. In these cases, what is considered effective by the head coach may be different than what is considered effective by the college president, the athletic director, the marketing director, or the alumni.

In modern sport organizations, leaders should be aware of all of these areas of organizational effectiveness. In addition, they should consider the many ways in which their leadership can influence positive outcomes relative to each of the areas. Over or under-emphasis on any one or more of the categories can result in catastrophe! Thus, achieving a balance is critical. While a daunting leadership challenge, it appears to be what may likely determine long-term leadership and organizational success.

Multi-frame Leadership and Problem Solving

All of the leadership challenges and measures of organizational effectiveness discussed in the previous section require that modern sport leaders be versatile. Problems are often complex and are not easily solved with simple solutions. For example, what are the solutions to the problem of increased criminal behavior by some athletes in collegiate and professional sports? Certainly, while not the norm for most athletes, the resulting negative image that is reflected upon competitive sport programs creates both a micro and macro leadership dilemma.

In addressing a problem such as the one describe above, leaders must often look beyond what appears on the surface to be the problem. Often, because of personality, background, or experience, a leader will tend to look at a problem through only one lens. This may result in a uni-dimensional approach that ultimately causes the leader to overlook more effective solutions. In addition, various situations or contexts within which problems occur often require a leader to initially "frame" a problem before immediately proceeding to a solution.

Bolman and Deal (1991) presented a multi-dimensional "framing" approach to organizational leadership that allows a leader to determine appropriate tactics for solving various organizational and perhaps even industry problems. Although Bolman and Deal's work was not written in the sport context, the fundamental principles involved are easily applied to leadership issues in sport organizations. The frames identified by Bolman and Deal were (a) structural, (b) human resource, (c) political, and (d) symbolic. The following description of these frames should help readers recognize not only their own predisposition toward one or more frames, but also how the frames relate to most if not all of the areas of organizational effectiveness.

Frames of Reference
(Bolman and Deal, 1991)

1. The *structural frame* emphasizes the traditional bureaucracy with a well-defined chain of command, clear division of labor, and specific role responsibilities. Attainment of goals is of utmost priority and leaders ensure that policies and procedures are clearly understood and followed. Structural leaders are sometimes considered taskmasters.
2. The *human resource frame* focuses primarily on meeting human needs in organizations. In this frame, leaders are sensitive to relationships and feelings and seek to lead through facilitation and empowerment. Seeking an optimal fit between the organization and each individual member is a fundamental concern.
3. The *political frame* recognizes that conflict is inevitable and that competition for scarce resources is a central feature of organizations. Political leaders need to be skillful negotiators who create coalitions, build power bases, and negotiate compromises. In the political frame, interests of powerful constituents may displace organizational goals.
4. The *symbolic frame* is rooted in the values and culture of the organization. This frame attempts to give "meaning" to organizational events. Symbolic leaders recognize and promote myth, ritual, ceremonies, and other symbolic expressions of the organization. Symbolism often defines what is acceptable and assists in establishing the organizational norms.

A brief summary of each of the frames and how they appear to relate to the categories of organizational effectiveness are presented in Figure 1.

Bolman and Deal suggested that individuals usually have a predisposition and demonstrate personal characteristics in one or two of the above frames. However, Bolman and Deal also suggested that leaders who have the capacity to be multi-dimensional have the potential to be more effective.

Going back to the problem of athlete crime that was identified in the first paragraph of this section, one can see how "framing" the problem results in a variety

	FIGURE 1	
Leadership Frame	Frame Descriptions	Related Measure of Organizational Effectiveness
Structural	Coordination and control are essential to effectiveness. Emphasis on goal attainment and policies/procedures. Leaders stress accountability and are outcome oriented.	Goal Attainment
Human Resource	Organizations exist to serve human needs. Facilitation and empowerment are important to success. Leaders are supportive and concerned for group members.	Internal Process
Political	Conflict is inevitable due to competition for scarce resources. Solutions emerge from negotiation and bargaining. Leaders develop coalitions and gain support from people with influence.	Strategic Constituents & System Resources
Symbolic	Shared values create an optimal culture. Symbols, rites, and rituals convey organizational norms and expectations. Leaders inspire through charisma.	Internal Process & Competing Values

Leadership frame information based on information contained in Bolman, L.G., & Deal, T.E. (1991). *Reframing organizations: Artistry, choice, and leadership.* San Francisco: Jossey-Bass. Organizational effectiveness information based on Cameron, K.S. (1980). Critical questions in assessing organizational effectiveness. *Organizational Dynamics, 9,* 66-80.

of potential solutions. For example, structural framing would identify the problem as one that stands in the way of overall goal attainment. A structurally oriented sport leader would likely address the problem through strict policies and procedures that are unambiguous and provide just punishments for involvement in criminal behavior.

However, framing the problem from a human resource perspective, it would be common to want to know why an athlete was involved in a crime. What was the situation and were there extenuating circumstances that may have contributed to the criminal behavior? In this frame, the leader might recognize that the individual or individuals involved need counseling and, if at all possible, an opportunity to learn from their mistakes and be reconnected to the group.

From a political frame perspective, it might be that pressures brought on by external constituents to produce a winning team resulted in compromises in the athlete selection process. In addition, how the problem is dealt with once it has happened may be influenced by the "power position" of the interested constituents. In this frame, the leader is tested with making a value decision and must ultimately do what he or she thinks is right based on principles and what is in the best interest of the organization.

Finally, the symbolic frame might suggest that a decline in overall organizational or societal values contributed to the problem. In this sense, what is needed is new "meaning" of what it takes to be a "successful" athlete, role model, and productive citizen. Leaders must then identify the symbols, rituals, and rewards necessary to establish more desirable behavioral norms.

Hopefully the above examples, although addressing one specific problem, have indicated how the multiple frame approach to leadership and problem solving could be beneficial for sport leaders in all aspects of the sport industry. All organizations eventually encounter problems that are rooted in one or more of the frames discussed in this section. As indicated previously, the leadership challenge is to successfully "frame" the problem and develop an appropriate solution strategy. Leader must remember, however, that this often requires them to think from a different perspective and be more versatile in their leadership approach.

Managing Sport Organizational Culture

Organizational culture is generally defined as the widely shared beliefs, values, and assumptions that exist at the core of an organization (Schein, 1996). Culture is not always easy to identify from external observation, but it pervades an organization and ultimately defines the norms and expectations of organizational members. In addition, several researchers from business and education have suggested that a strong positive culture is what separates the most effective organizations from those that are less effective and that leadership has a stout impact on the culture within an organization. In fact, it has also been argued (Schein, 1985) that there may be no single more important leadership responsibility than the management of culture. Certainly, in sport organizations, having everyone share a common belief system and work together toward achieving a unified goal is critical to long-term success.

Although a variety of leadership styles can be effective, one that appears to have a strong impact on the development of a positive organizational culture is transformational leadership. Transformational leaders are inspirational and empowering. According to Robbins (1996, p. 151), "Transformational leaders inspire followers to transcend their own self-interests for the good of the organization." Weese (1995) suggested that transformational leaders in recreational organizations influence a culture of "excellence and continual improvement."

The prevailing culture in an organization can often be traced to its founder or someone with strong influence on the organization. Several major league franchises, for example, have individuals in their past that established cultures which have perpetuated to some degree in their absence.

In sport organizations, one can look at the various symbols and rituals associated with a sport enterprise and get some hints of what it purports to be its values. If indeed these values are widely shared and consistently reinforced within the organization, then there is evidence of a strong culture centered around the values. For example, the innovative, controversial, and sometimes brash nature of

Nike and its leader Phil Knight provide insight into the culture that likely exists in the company. The fact that Penn State Nittany Lions football players do not have names on their jerseys symbolizes "team" oriented values. Mission statements, slogans, signs on the wall, etc., in sport related manufacturing and retail organizations tell employees and customers something about the existing or desired culture of the business.

However, observable signs of a culture do not mean that it actually exists or that is both strong and positive. The leadership challenge related to organizational culture that needs to be addressed by sport administrators, sport business owners, managers, and coaches, deals with how culture can be managed. To address this issue, a sport leader must first understand that there are three cultural situations to consider: (a) creation of a culture, (b) changing a culture, and (c) managing a culture. In new organizations without any history, culture is something that must be created. In established organizations, the leader must recognize when the current culture is inadequate for effective performance and go about the arduous process of cultural change. Finally, leaders must also recognize when things are going very well relative to an organization's performance (both internal process and outcomes) and do what is necessary to effectively manage the existing culture.

In order to be an effective culture manager in a sport organization, a leader must first define the culture as it currently exists. This may be quite evident from a surface evaluation, especially in cases where culture is weak and performance is inadequate. Franchises in disarray, athletic programs that have experienced excessive turnover, and newly formed businesses struggling to get off the ground are examples of situations where the lack of culture may be contributing to poor organizational performance.

In newly formed organizations, desired values for the infant culture should be developed through collaboration and empowerment of organizational members. In most cases, this is also true when attempting to change a culture. In cases where the existing culture is somewhat unclear, it may involve close examination of internal processes and use of individual interviews or questionnaires that help the leader determine if the desired values are indeed widely shared. If it is determined that a culture change is necessary, the leader must develop a vision for the new culture and identify essential steps necessary to proceed. Most importantly, the leader must put a system into place that supports the desired culture by consistently rewarding individuals for behaviors congruent with the ideal organizational values.

Generally, the most challenging culture management situation exists when attempting to change a culture where things are going well and organizational members have been in their positions for a long time. For example, a sport organization may have a number of managers who have been running their respective departments for years and are somewhat resistant to change. However, in a rapidly changing marketplace, it may be necessary to establish new values and ways of doing things in order to remain competitive. In this situation, it is critical for the leader to provide opportunities for organizational members to express their concerns and then provide the security necessary for them to test new ideas.

Overall, as previously mentioned, culture management may be the most challenging, yet critical component of sport organization leadership. In addition, although not discussed in detail here, one must be aware of the many "subcultures" that often exist under the umbrella of a larger culture. For example, athletic departments are divided into numerous program areas that all have their own cultures. Sporting goods manufacturers have various departments which all may have certain unique subcultures operating within them. The leadership challenge in these situations is to have central values that are crucial to overall organizational performance while allowing some degree of uniqueness in each program area.

In conclusion, there are a number of components of culture management that a sport leader should consider when guiding an organization. Establishing a distinct vision, collaborating with group members, setting and communicating clear objectives, allowing participation in decision making, providing principled leadership, and establishing proper and timely reward systems are keys to successful culture development (Scott, 1997).

IDEAS AND SUGGESTIONS

Strong culture organizations have *core values* that are readily identified by group members and that provide the rationale for decision making. Sport leaders should consider the following relative to core values:

- Establish your core values through a participative process. Get your employees or athletes involved.

- Develop no more than three to five core values

- Rank order the values so that everyone knows what comes 1st, 2nd, etc.

- *Teach* the core values to all new members of the organization. Don't just hand them a policy book.

- Make decisions (even the tough ones) consistent with the core values.

- Reinforce the core values when rewarding individuals for exceptional performance.

Adapted from K. Blanchard, "Gung Ho" Leadership Seminar (1999).

Leadership Development

Now that several of the facets of effective leadership have been discussed, what about the development and training of current and future sport leaders? Who should be responsible and what factors should be considered?

Ultimately, the responsibility for leadership training is within the individual or individuals currently in, or preparing for, leadership positions. Becoming a more effective leader generally requires a commitment to improving one's knowledge and awareness of personal leadership styles and behaviors and how they can be enhanced.

It is quite likely that numerous leaders in the sport industry acquired their leadership skills through modeling or trial and error. While many have well developed, and possibly "natural" leadership abilities, it has been determined that leadership skill can be improved through training. For students of sport management, leadership courses that examine current issues, theories, and applications relative to sport organizations and the sport industry should be required. For current leaders in the field, individuals should be willing to take the initiative to improve their knowledge and skills relative to leadership. This might be done through self-evaluation, consultation with professional leadership consultants, and/or in house workshops conducted by other sport or community leaders. In addition, current leaders should not be afraid to obtain objective feedback from organizational members regarding their own leadership performance.

The factors that need to be considered in leadership development for sport managers of course will include time available, financial considerations, and other responsibilities. However, regardless of the development methods chosen, sport managers must first acknowledge the need for personal leadership development and then continually improve their leadership skills in order to be effective in today's complex and rapidly changing sport organizations.

Sport Leadership in a New Century

Many challenges face the sport leaders of the new century. As mentioned previously, these challenges are both micro and macro in nature. Each individual sport organization has its unique problems that require careful planning, intervention, and as discussed previously, culture management by its leaders. At the macro leadership level, individuals and groups with influence on the overall sport industry face issues that may ultimately affect the delivery and impact of sport in the United States and worldwide.

Furthermore, some of what we see happening in our sport organizations and in society in general can be disturbing for current and future leaders. It is quite possible that the challenges appear so intimidating they may actually prevent people with exceptional leadership ability from pursuing positions where they feel pressure to compromise their principles, health, and/or life balance. If this occurs, true leadership will be noticeably absent and problems will worsen.

With these things in mind, what will it take to be successful as a sport leader in the 2000s? In addition to the traits, behaviors, and leadership concerns addressed in previous sections of this chapter, sport leaders should be aware of some of the current thought regarding leadership in a new millenium.

Organizational leadership in previous decades has often been characterized as authoritarian and outcome based. In this frame of reference, leaders were sometimes considered power mongers that had the political clout and/or positional authority to influence, or perhaps coerce, people to work toward goals not always understood. In some organizations this same approach to leadership exists today. Although productive but generally short-term results can be achieved through this type of leadership, important outcomes of internal process such as job satisfaction and employee morale suffer. Ultimately, the organization's performance is less than desirable and a significant change in culture is required to keep the business afloat.

Secretan (1999) suggested that "the new-story leaders who will guide the greatest organizations on Earth during the next thousand years are those who will achieve exceptional goals while honoring people at the same time - every step of the way. New-story leaders understand that the process of leadership—how you get there, how you treat people—is equally, if not more important." However, it should be recognized that these leadership values and the extent to which they are accepted are not the same in all cultures. From an international perspective, the relationship of leaders and followers is not always the same as in the United States. As indicated by Champoux (2000), "people in countries with values that specify strongly hierarchical relationships in organizations react more positively to directive approaches than to participative approaches."

Sport managers should also consider that leadership is a dynamic phenomenon that may be moving, changing positions, and ultimately serving the individuals that make up their organizations. Phrases such as "leading from behind," "turning the pyramid upside down," "leading through service," and "principle-centered or value-based leadership" have been used in recent years. These statements recognize that leaders are not always up-front issuing directives but rather that leadership is also a value based, people serving process that ultimately produces results through vision, empowerment, and support.

What is apparent is that leadership for sport, as well as for other organizations in the new century, requires (a) courage, (b) commitment, and (c) accountability. These three traits unfortunately appear to be somewhat problematic in our society. Sport leaders will not only need to discover and develop these traits within themselves, they will need to be effective models of the traits for their followers. Sport leaders will also need to realize that extraordinary organizational and industry achievements do not happen without the dedication and work of many people. The leaders of the future will not only need to provide insightful direction, they will need to be actively engaged as facilitators and supporters. Ultimately, sport leaders for the new millenium must radiate optimism and facilitate solutions that enhance the role of sport in society and satisfactorily address the diverse needs of employees, participants, and customers within this great industry.

References

Bass, B.M. (1990). "From transactional to transformational leadership: Learning to share the vision." *Organizational Dynamic, 18,* 19-31.

Bennis, W., and J. Goldsmith (1998). *Learning to lead.* Reading, MA: Perseus Books.

Blanchard, K. (1999, October). Gung-Ho Leadership Seminar, Lessons in Leadership Series. Public presentation, Albuquerque, New Mexico.

Bolman L.G. and T.E. Deal (1991). *Reframing Organizations: Artistry, choice, and leadership.* San Francisco, CA: Jossey-Bass.

Cameron, K.S. (1980). "Critical questions in assessing organizational effectiveness." *Organizational Dynamics, 9,* 66-80.

Champoux, J.E. (2000). *Organizational behavior: Essential tenets for a new millenium.* New York: South-Western College Publishing.

Connolly, T., E.M. Conlon, and S.J. Deutsch (1980). "Organizational effectiveness: A multiple constituency approach." *Academy of Management Review, 5,* 211-218.

Danylchuk K.E. and P. Chelladurai (1999). "The nature of managerial work in Canadian intercollegiate athletics." *Journal of Sport Management, 13*(2), 148-165.

Hagberg Consulting Group (1998). "How leadership effectiveness is reduced." <http://www.leadership-development.com> (6 Aug. 1999).

Robbins, S.P. (1997). *Essentials of organizational behavior.* Upper Saddle River, NJ: Prentice Hall.

Quinn, R.E. (1988). *Beyond rational management.* San Francisco, CA: Jossey-Bass.

———— and J. Rohrbaugh (1981). "A competing values approach to organizational effectiveness." *Public Productivity Review, 5,* 122-140.

Schein, E.H. (1985). *Organizational culture and leadership.* San Francisco, CA: Jossey-Bass.

———— (1996). "Culture: The missing concept in organization studies." *Administrative Science Quarterly, 41,* 229-240.

Scott, D.K. (1997). "Managing organizational culture in intercollegiate athletic organizations." *Quest, 49*(4), 403-415.

Secretan, L. (1999). "Spirit at work: Changing the world with growing companies." *IW Growing Companies* (December).

Slack, T. (1997). *Understanding Sport Organizations.* Champaign, IL: Human Kinetics.

Weese, W.J. (1995). "Leadership and organizational culture: An investigation of Big Ten and Mid-American conference campus recreation administrators." *Journal of Sport Management, 9,* 119-134.

Part 2

Program Management

Policies provide guidelines that address the specifics of actions.

John Swofford and Patricia M. Henry

Chapter 5

Scheduling for Intercollegiate Sports

John Swofford and Patricia M. Henry

Introduction

Effective scheduling is a distinguishing characteristic of every successful athletic program. This is the case because scheduling impacts upon every aspect of the athletic operation. Unless high agreement between the mission of the various teams and schedules generated is obtained, the athletic department will suffer the consequences of less than adequate performance. The success level of each team rests, in part, on the construction of a well planned schedule.

At the Division I level of intercollegiate athletics scheduling of major spectator sports is vital to the welfare of all programs conducted by the athletic department. One reason for its importance is that football, and in some instances basketball, in most institutions must not only be financially self-sustaining but must also generate funds needed for other sports. Without successful football and basketball financial stability will be virtually impossible to achieve. Scheduling also impacts upon recruiting, post-season competition, championship possibilities, season ticket sales, contributions from the private sector, student interest, faculty support and institution and department images. Consequently, it is imperative that administrators be adept at handling the requirements of scheduling for the athletic program.

Returns to be realized from scheduling are neither limited by sport nor level of play. However, returns are not likely to materialize for any sport, department or institution unless the athletic director has planned carefully and practiced skillful implementation of the plans. The principles to be applied to scheduling are basic and universal, and are thus applicable to programs of varying magnitude, including programs that have profit-making sports, revenue generating sports, nonrevenue-producing sports, and women only, men only, women and men, varsity, junior varsity and club teams. This chapter is devoted to a discussion of those things that are necessary to the development of an organized and effective approach to scheduling for intercollegiate athletics.

Philosophy and Policies

Philosophy and policy provide the beginning place for any and all matters related to scheduling. Both may be set by the board of trustees, an athletic board, the president, or left to the discretion of the athletic director. It is essential that statements are established and that they are available in writing. The authority for the statements must be documented.

The philosophy makes clear the place of the athletic program within the institution. What is to be accomplished through athletics and why the thing being sought are important to the welfare of the institution are question: that, when answered, create a framework for addressing scheduling and other matters. The philosophy will also bring institutional expectations into agreement with conference and National Collegiate Athletic Association (NCAA) or National Association of Intercollegiate Athletics (NAIA) regulations.

Policies provide guidelines that address the specifics of actions. They exist within the framework established by the philosophy. Policies act to further define the approach to scheduling and set standards to work with while making the schedule. Policies should include specific guidelines as to finance (e.g., a minimum guarantee requirement for away games, or the maximum guarantee for home games); home and away balance (e.g., always play at least six home football games, but not more than seven); types of opponents (e.g., a Division I basketball school may have a policy of scheduling only Division I opponents); geography (e.g., an East Coast team may have a policy of not traveling beyond the Mississippi River for an away contest); academics (e.g., not playing during an exam period); and time (e.g., some institutions will not play a night football game at home).

Institutions that are similar in approach to athletics will often have similar policies. However, each institution is unique and will therefore have policies particular to its needs. Policies cannot cover every circumstance and a mechanism needs to exist for the athletic director to deal with situations that are not addressed in the formal statement. This mechanism could range from simply exercising the use of judgment to gaining the approval of the president or athletic board. This, of course, is an institutional matter and should be known to the involved individuals.

Following are samples of institutional policy questions that might be addressed by the athletic director:

1. What is the standard of competition for each program? What is the expectation level of success at the conference, regional and/or national levels?
2. What is the participation level? What combination of intercollegiate varsity and junior varsity as well as club teams is the institution willing to support?
3. What are the financial parameters governing the construction of the schedule?
4. What geographic/travel limitations exist? Are there conference affiliations to be considered? If an institution supports junior varsity or club teams, are their geographical and travel limitations different than those for varsity teams?
5. What is the policy governing the mode of transportation utilized for trips? Does this policy vary from sport to sport?
6. Is it necessary or desirable to arrange schedules to enable two different teams from the same institution to travel together to a common opponent?
7. Relative to some sports, is there a limit on how man contests per week are academically permissible? Is there a difference or a preference for weekday versus weekend day contests?

8. Are contests permitted or prohibited during final examination periods?
9. Are contests permitted to be scheduled during vacation periods which fall within the athletic season?
10. Are teams who qualify permitted to participate in post-season championship competition? What are the ramifications if post-season participation falls during exams or after the academic year is concluded?

If an institution is a member of a conference, there will most certainly be guidelines and agreements relative to scheduling that should be understood by those making the schedules. Likewise it is quite important for the athletic director to be aware of scheduling parameters set forth by the national athletic governing body to which the institution belongs.

Roles of Athletic Director, Scheduler, and Coach

The director of athletics is the institutional officer responsible for enforcing all policy relative to athletics. Where scheduling is concerned the task is to generate instruments (schedules for the various sports) that will aid the department in fulfilling its mission, while following practices that are in complete agreement with policies.

The athletic director is also the chief administrative officer of the athletic department. As such, he heads a staff that has vested interests in the schedule. In the case of coaches, the schedule impacts upon the status one enjoys as a professional. While all coaches recognize the importance of the schedule to their welfare, concepts of how best to use the schedule to advantage differ greatly. Another difficulty is that on occasion coaches will insist upon scheduling practices that serve self-interest at the expense of departmental welfare.

The vast majority of athletic directors actually arrange the schedules. At some institutions scheduling responsibilities are handled by an assistant athletic director or by a scheduling officer. No matter the title of the scheduling officer, functions performed are the same. The basic arrangements are as follows:

1. Schedules for revenue-generating sports are handled independently of scheduling for other teams. This method requires much communication and coordination between coaches of revenue-generating or profit-making sports and the athletic director.

2. Depending on the structure and the needs of the department, the assignments for scheduling men's sports may be handled by one department administrator while the scheduling of women's sports is handled by another department administrator. Again, coordination and communication are necessary.

3. Some athletic departments schedule by utilizing a single scheduler. From a coordination and consistency standpoint this system works well and is dependent upon the administrative structure.

Whatever the mode of scheduling used, it is critical that final approval rest with the athletic director.

Communication between coaches and the athletic director or scheduler is a very important aspect of the scheduling process. Working within the established policy guidelines the athletic director/scheduler and coach should discuss several questions prior to the construction of the schedule. Notes of the conversations should be made part of the scheduling file.

Information gathering sessions should resolve the following matters:

1. What facility considerations exist? Is the facility shared by men's and women's teams, varsity and junior varsity teams? What other programs utilize the facility; e.g., recreational or physical education? If the facility is shared, what priorities for usage have the department or institution established so that equity exists and conflicts can be avoided?

2. What are the goals of the program? These should be incorporated in department policy and reflected in the schedule. A large majority of contests should be scheduled within the division declaration of the institution. How many contests, if any, should be scheduled in a different division? If scheduling against a lower-division opponent, how strong is the opponent? What effect would a defeat to a lower or higher-division opponent have on the team ranking, and on morale?

3. What days of the week are preferred for scheduling of contests? Is spectator attendance an important factor and how is it affected by day or time of contest?

4. Should contest days and times be consistent from week to week? Do the athletes on the team tend to have one day per week when it is better not to schedule contests because of academic reasons; e.g., labs or classes?

5. Does the institution have a policy about scheduling a contest on the Sabbath?

6. Is Monday a good day to schedule a contest, particularly if it follows a weekend of no competition or practice?

7. Should longer trips be scheduled on weekends in order to cut down on missed class time?

8. What are the vacation periods and holidays that fall during this season? How should the schedule relate to these?

9. When is the first permissible contest date of the season?

10. What opportunities and possibilities exist for post-season competition at the conference, regional and national levels? Some schedulers prefer to plan from the end of the season and work forward from that point.

11. Which opponents should be scheduled early in the season?

12. How should the strong opponents be spread throughout the season?

13. What kind of home and away balance is desired?

14. How does a long trip affect the next competition? What are the considerations of a long trip and how should long trips be balanced from year to year?

15. What considerations exist for contest starting times?

There are three occasions when basic schedule considerations might be discussed between the athletic director and coach. Prior to the schedule making process, which is during the early fall of the preceding year, scheduling strategies should be planned. Once the schedule has been developed, prior to the budget process, which is usually before the close of the first semester, a second meeting to discuss any divergence from the original schedule plan should take place. If possible, an evaluation at the end of the season of schedule considerations by the coach with the scheduler can assist in an improved schedule for the future. It is extremely important that coaches understand, appreciate, and accept the fact that final decisions rest with the athletic director. Encouragement of involvement in planning should never be handled in ways that would suggest the transfer of responsibility for the entire schedule or any part of it to a coach or to coaches. However, without meaningful involvement of coaches in the planning the idea of schedules that are acceptable to both athletic director and coach cannot be attained.

Characteristics of a "Good" Schedule

A good schedule is the end result of meeting the stated philosophy and policies of the institution. Thus, a good schedule for one institution may differ from that of another institution. Even at the same institution, good schedules vary according to sport.

At an ACC school, a good (ideal) football schedule may accomplish the following:

1. Includes all members of the Atlantic Coast Conference (ACC), five games;
2. Includes three non-conference games that encompass:
   a. one probable win,
   b. one top-twenty-type opponent,
   c. one respectable opponent that has name identification and is toss-up competitive situations;
3. Includes six home games;
4. Generates maximum financial rewards;
5. Includes games that are potential television possibilities;
6. Includes no more than two games at home or two games on the road consecutively;
7. Creates fan interest;
8. Gives a fair chance to:
   a. have a winning season,
   b. win the ACC championship,
   c. receive a bowl invitation;
9. Includes opponents that have reasonably similar academic standards;
10. Is reasonable in terms of travel;
11. Maximizes geographical exposure, institution and individual players; and
12. Contains no more than one open date after the initial game and concludes before Thanksgiving.

The basketball scheduling philosophy for a school involves a similar approach, with emphasis on travel for recruiting purposes (basketball travel is much less expensive than football on a per-trip basis because of sheer numbers) and a national flavor because of the unusual national basketball tradition that the University of North Carolina enjoys. Academics and class time missed become greater factors in basketball scheduling because 28 games are played, many of them during the week. Agreement with the policies of minimizing class time missed can be accomplished while emphasizing appealing and educational travel by working this travel into vacation periods and by chartering return flights when necessary rather than waiting for commercial flights. These strategies keep players on campus during academic sessions and return them quickly to campus if classes are meeting.

By playing two "home games" per year in two different cities in North Carolina two objectives are satisfied. Gate receipts are increased and those parts of the state have an opportunity to see the team play. This arrangement has become even more necessary because of continued sellouts on campus.

Time-Frame for the Completion of Tasks

If meetings between the athletic director and coach take place in the early fall, construction of the schedule should occur through the fall and be ready for the budget process in December. Good knowledge of the budget is necessary so that the athletic director can work within its parameters and avoid difficult schedule changes after commitments have been made.

An aid to planning is a time-frame for the completion of tasks. Items to be included will vary according to requirements that are specific to the institution and department but the following notations are likely to appear.

1. September   With basic knowledge of the budget, athletic director meets with the coach to discuss the schedule for the following year.

2. Oct.–Dec.   Athletic director contacts opponents to negotiate and firm-up the schedule.

3. December   Second athletic director-coach meeting to review the schedule. For budget purposes the schedule for the following year is basically intact.

4. Jan.–Feb.   January is generally a difficult time to contact other athletic directors. During the end of January and the month of February, the athletic director negotiates any minor changes agreed upon when meeting with the coach.

5. Feb.–April   Finalization of the budget.

6. Feb.–April   Firm-up and completion of junior varsity and club team schedules.

7. April–May   Mail out contracts for entire year.

Mechanics of a Sound Schedule

Organization is the key to success in almost any administrative function. Scheduling is no exception. Scheduling is a complex task and to complete the task successfully it is important to keep sound records of ideas, thoughts, phone calls, correspondence, future schedules, agreements to play and contracts. The first step is to develop a list of possible institutions which would help meet the objectives of your scheduling philosophy and policies. Then, put together sample "ideal" schedules which fit objectives using the institutions listed. It will take time to generate "ideal" schedules but identifying teams that satisfy selection requirements will greatly ease and facilitate planning. Once the possibilities have been examined and preferences determined, the next step is to establish contact with administrators at other institutions. If time permits, initial correspondence by mail is one approach. The telephone is a more effective tool plus it saves time. It has the added benefit of permitting discussions with other athletic directors about various "what-if 'situations, objections and complications which are everyday problems in the scheduling process. Notes should be made on each telephone call. An administration principle to adhere to when scheduling is to follow all verbal agreements in writing. Standard scheduling procedure is that once an agreement is met, a contest contract is issued by the host institution to the opponent, which is in turn signed by the administrator of the opponent and a copy returned to the host. It is also important to remember that time and date changes made verbally after the initial contract is signed should be followed up in writing.

An important skill for a good scheduler to develop is negotiating ability. A spirit of cooperation and compromise is essential. It is often not possible to construct the perfect schedule, but the closer to the ideal one comes, the higher the return to the program.

A record of contracts sent, received and returned should be maintained. It is important that before a contest takes place, both institutions possess a copy of the contract. Some institutions prefer to send a form to the opposing institutions stating that a contract has either not been received or returned for X contest, approximately one month before the start of the season.

Because there are many people and various operations within the athletic department and the institution who deal with the athletic schedule, many athletic departments develop a day-by-day schedule after the schedule has been completed and distribute this to all who work with athletic teams. Day-by-day schedules should be sent to coaches, other athletic administrators, equipment managers, travel personnel, sports information, operations and maintenance directors, the ticket office, university or college information office and anyone else who should receive such information.

If a schedule is well-planned and well-negotiated, schedule changes will be a rarity. There are times for various reasons that a change in date or time is requested and the scheduler is responsible for negotiating these changes. If such a change occurs after the schedule has been published, it is necessary to alert those involved of the exact change. It is probably appropriate to notify all those who received a day-by-day schedule in addition to the officials.

As correspondence, notes from telephone conversations, agreements to play and eventually contracts develop, it is critical to have an organized system for detailing this information. A dual-file system provides a particularly useful solution. One system would have a file for each institution contacted with regard to football and basketball—an institutional football scheduling file as well as an institutional basketball file. For example, the "Florida State Football" file would include a complete history of correspondence, phone calls, notes, agreements to play and contracts—past, present and future between the University of North Carolina and Florida State University in football. The "Kentucky-Basketball" scheduling file would contain the same for basketball. This type of information is invaluable. One file drawer is maintained for each sport and as new institutions are added to the schedules, new files are created. In addition, a contract-file system is established for each sport for the current year plus one year in advance. Example: the 1984 football contract file would contain all 11 contracts for the 1984 football season. Copies of these 11 contracts would also be in the 11 institutional files referred to above. This system provides both a history of scheduling discussions as well as a cross check of contracts by institution and by season. Therefore, it is easy to check the scheduling processes for a particular institution or summarize the contracts for an entire season.

As automated systems develop, some of which are specifically designed for intercollegiate athletic programs, some of the above information could be kept in a computer rather than in a file cabinet, although filing of certain written documents may remain necessary.

Establishing a system to organize your schedule for current and future years is a must. Long-range scheduling forms developed by Ernie Casale, former Athletic Director at Temple University, assist greatly in the accomplishment of this task. These forms are designed so that you can get a complete long-range view of your schedules over a period of years. Corresponding dates are also easy to spot from one year to the next. It is helpful to have your own code to insert into the forms beside each institution that is listed in a particular date. This code would include home (H), away (A), or a neutral site (N), plus the status of the agreement: Agreement to Play (A), Contract Sent (CS), Contract Complete (CC)—meaning the contract has been completed and signed by both institutions.

Completed forms are important records, making them a source of valuable information. Four copies should be maintained. One is kept in the athletic director's master schedule notebook in the office; another is on file with the athletic director's secretary; the third copy is passed to the director. Because of the ongoing nature of the scheduling process, the fact that athletic directors, travel extensively and the fact that scheduling opportunities often come up while at NCAA conference or committee meetings, a fourth copy of the long-range schedules should be kept in the briefcase. Its availability makes it possible to take advantage of unexpected opportunities.

The final "closing the sale" aspect of scheduling is the contract itself It should be signed and dated by the appropriate representatives of each institution, then filed in the dual-filing system and properly coded on the long-range scheduling forms. A checklist for what needs to be included in a basic football agreement includes:

1. dates the agreement is entered into;
2. site of game;
3. date of game;
4. time of game;
5. eligibility regulations of participants;
6. financial agreements, including date visiting team will be paid;
7. auditing requirement;
8. complimentary ticket arrangements for both teams;
9. number of sideline passes for both teams;
10. number and location of visiting teams;
11. how home students and faculty will be included in the game financial audit;
12. admission of band and cheerleaders;
13. control of ticket prices;
14. admission of game workers;
15. radio broadcast agreements;
16. programming concession rights;
17. game officials;
18. special event rights (e.g., Band Day, if any);
19. additional games to be played as part of the original contract agreement;
20. conditions of failure to comply with the contract; and

21. additional miscellaneous agreements.

Financial terms of the contract are, of course, very important. This may be a flat guarantee, a percentage of the gross (usually after a 15-20% operating expense has been deducted for stadium operations), or a minimum guarantee against a percentage of the gross. Whatever the agreement, it should be spelled out specifically and precisely so that problems or misunderstandings do not occur later. People change positions, and particularly with football where scheduling is often done as many as ten years in advance, it is important that all aspects of the contract be established so that it will be clear to all parties whether or not administrative changes take place.

The long-range scheduling of football games requires that tentative arrangements be completed. It is impossible to know what economic and other conditions will be five or ten years in the future. Therefore, for games scheduled that far in advance, an "Agreement to Play" is used instead of a contract. This is done in letter form and simply states the dates that the two institutions are to play and indicates that a contract specifying the financial and other terms will be negotiated within two years of the event. This agreement is then filed accordingly, and the event listed and coded on the long-range schedule.

Basketball contracts are usually shorter, but should be just as precise. A checklist for what needs to be included on a basic basketball agreement includes:

1. dates agreement is entered into;
2. site of game;
3. date of game;
4. time of game;
5. eligibility regulations of participants;
6. financial agreement and date visiting teams will be paid;
7. complimentary ticket arrangements;
8. number of seats for team parties;
9. officials' agency to make the assignment;
10. radio broadcast agreements;
11. television broadcast agreements;
12. conditions for failure to comply with contract; and
13. any miscellaneous additional agreements.

Although basketball games are generally not scheduled as far in advance as football games, agreements to play may also be used here. Guarantees are normally considerably less in basketball on a per-game basis, but the same options exist in basketball as in football—for a flat guarantee, a minimum guarantee against a percentage of the gross, or a pure percentage of the gross.

In the Atlantic Coast Conference (ACC), for example, there is no exchange of money for conference basketball games; the home team keeps all receipts. In football, it is a minimum guarantee against a percentage of the gross in the ACC.

Schedules for the entire department are maintained in a schedule book. The layout styles of schedule books vary from institution to institution. Some athletic directors prefer the entire season of one sport on one page, others would rather see all sports for a one-month period on one page. The style and organization are decisions for the athletic director to make based on what works best for him or her.

Usually, one task of the scheduler is to provide for assignment of officials Some sports are assigned officials through the conference, if the institution Is a member of a conference. Some officials are assigned via a regional bureau. if neither conference office nor regional bureau exist, the host institution is responsible for securing the game officials.

As in all other aspects of scheduling, it is imperative to follow up all communication to officials' office or bureau with written confirmation of contest date, time, place and any change in plans. The fee-structure should be established and other required plans in place for expediting payment for service and reimbursement for expenses.

The development of a good schedule requires good planning, good communication and attention to detail. The greater the number of sports to be place on the calendar, the more important these elements become. It is possible for a scheduler to accomplish this task well, especially if he or she works diligently within a planned, reasonable timetable.

Importance of Sound Scheduling

Revenue from football and men's basketball generates a large percentage of the total revenues of most intercollegiate athletic programs. Therefore, successful scheduling should maximize those revenues. However, maintaining balance in scheduling will best benefit a program over the long term. Far too often certain programs, particularly football, have scheduled strictly for dollars with little regard given to overall opportunity for success on the field over the course of a season or several seasons. Maintaining a balance of financial rewards and giving the coach and team a reasonable opportunity to enjoy a successful year will benefit a program more over time than "over scheduling" from a competitive standpoint simply to balance the budget. This is not to minimize the importance of revenues but is offered to propose that a program will be better off over the long haul by playing balanced schedules. The risk in "over-scheduling" for tremendous financial reward is that the number of victories will be reduced. Consequently, over a period of time the recruiting effort will probably suffer—thus leading to weaker teams. Attendance will probably suffer, eventually reducing revenues. Opportunities for post-season competition will suffer, thus reducing revenues, exposure and recruiting benefits. Contributions may fall and fan interest may diminish. In short, "over-scheduling" for immediate financial reward may be necessary at times, but if continued it can send a program into a negative spiral that can have devastating effects.

Scheduling can also affect recruiting. Success begets success and if the schedule doesn't afford an opportunity to be successful and consistently losing seasons are experienced it will be difficult to attract top recruits. On the other hand, if the schedule is not attractive enough—and other schools have an advantage over you in terms of travel to attractive sites and/or competing against name opponents—recruiting can also suffer.

Summary/Conclusion: Why Some Administrators Are Better Than Others at Scheduling

All administrators are not equal in terms of scheduling. Some are better than others and there are reasons for this. What do administrators that are good at the scheduling process do that others do not do? Characteristics that set apart successful schedulers from other administrators are as follows:

1. They and their institutions have a known and specific philosophy and set of policies. These serve as guidelines in the scheduling process. It is not a hodgepodge, but a systematic approach.
2. After the philosophy is established they make it a workable and active philosophy in following the policies consistently.
3. They work at the scheduling process on an ongoing basis. It is a never-ending puzzle.
4. They give it high priority and much time realizing the ramifications are extremely important.
5. They work with their coaches. It is important for a coach to have input into the scheduling process. In today's high pressure world of major college athletics, his job may well depend on scheduling decisions. It is important for the coach and athletic director to understand each other's concerns and thinking when developing a schedule.

Chapter 6

Financial Management of Sport

Nancy L. Lough

Introduction

Sport at every level appears to be financially healthy. Indications of fiscal viability are evident in the escalation of broadcast rights fees for sport properties, professional player contract increases and reports that more young people are participating in interscholastic sport than ever before. However, as each of these indicators increase, the need for a deep understanding and skillful approach to managing the money needed to produce quality sport offerings also increases. The growing number of sport properties being developed along with the amount of resources available through sponsorship and media rights suggests that securing funding for sport should be easier than ever before. Yet, with higher stakes available, the competition for athletic talent, spectators and financial support grows more and more fierce. Therefore, sport managers who will be successful in the emerging sport industry are those with an understanding of fiscal responsibility and solid preparation in financial management.

Current Economic Reality

While professional sport continues to grow and expand, the economic reality is that most major league teams are losing money. According to Howard (1999), net income has declined steadily for all leagues with the average net earning just 3% in 1996-97. The National Football League's profitability fell 30% in 1996-97, while 78% of Major League Baseball teams and 75% of National Hockey League teams finished in the red that same year. By far, Major League Baseball has experienced the most severe decline with average losses between $200 and $300 million annually since 1993. For the Cleveland Indians, the answer to securing a more stable financial position was filing with the Securities Exchange Commission offering $73.6 million in public stock for sale. This was an unprecedented move in Major League Baseball, yet a true indicator of the current economic reality of big-time professional sport.

On the college level, the recent trend has been the move by smaller colleges and universities to the National Collegiate Athletic Association's Division I classification, once thought to be reserved for large universities. With potential revenue sharing returns from conference representation in national tournaments and the potential for media attention, universities such as Portland State University have taken on the challenge of rising to Division I status. The move required increasing the number of scholarships offered, boosting coaches salaries and improving facilities. Still, university officials say they have begun to experience the benefits of media attention, typically reserved for Division I programs. Evidence of increases were seen in the donations to athletics that went from $120,000 in 1994-95 to $1.1 million in 1998-99. Football ticket sales increased by $120,000 from the previous year and corporate sponsorships jumped from 190 to 490 (DiMartino and Cohen, 1999). Figures such as these cause most intercollegiate athletic administrators to agree that the move up may well be the best strategy for financial viability.

On the interscholastic level, athletics experienced continued growth in the number of participants. On both the intercollegiate and interscholastic levels, the most significant increases in participation numbers have been evident among girls and women in sport. With one of every three girls in high school participating in sport, the need for increased funding has led coaches and administrators to become more aware of potential revenue generating opportunities. Corporate sponsorship of state high school championships has influenced school districts, leagues and even individual teams to seek sponsorships for support of athletic competitions and facilities. From the standpoint of interest, high school sport remains healthy and vital. However, when the amount of money needed to fund athletic programs is considered in accordance with decreasing budget allocations for public schools, the financial viability of high school sport becomes a concern.

Establishing the present financial climate for these three levels of sport may be the best approach to generating the interest and concern a future sport manager will need to understand the importance of finance to administration of sport programs. While the managers in the examples given above undoubtedly have an awareness of financial principles, the escalating debt and failure to secure a strong position suggests that future sport managers may need to be better prepared. Therefore, the objective of this chapter is to initiate an awareness of the financial principles that need to be understood by every sport manager. To initiate an understanding of the financial management of sport, we should begin with consideration of costs.

Cost of Operations

Interscholastic. In the public school realm, athletic teams and coaches have found the financial resources to be diminishing each year. The lack of financial support has most often resulted in special athletic fees for students who want to compete. For students who are multi-sport athletes, the fee structure may require them to pay substantial amounts of money for each sport season. Unfortunately, some high schools that require athletic fees have effectively eliminated potential talent, simply because they do not have the resources necessary to play. To address this problem, many innovative programs have secured funding through community businesses investing in sponsorship and through significant fund raising endeavors. Situations in which a coach simply manages the team and competition without needing to find some means of securing funding are growing increasingly rare.

TABLE 1

Sport	Uniforms	Equipment	Supplies	Transportation	Officials
Athletic Trainers		$400	$38,400		
Baseball	$7,700	$1,100	$19,200	$15,500	$14,900
Basketball	$23,100	$2,200	$24,500	$36,300	$35,400
Football	$40,000	$17,000	$47,800	$35,100	$24,700
Golf			$8,800	$2,800	
Track	$16,600	$4,500	$26,100	$18,200	
Soccer	$19,900	$550	$26,300	$31,700	$17,600
Softball	$3,000	$475	$22,600	$15,600	$13,200
Swimming	$4,000	$1,800	$700	$5,700	
Tennis	$5,500		$7,200	$2,100	$600
Volleyball	$7,900	$1,600	$9,000	$15,400	$13,400
Wrestling	$8,700	$300	$11,600	$11,600	$12.100
Cross Country	$8,200	$500	$5,600	12,100	
Sub-total	$144,600	$30,425	$247,800	$202,100	$131,900

The typical categories of costs that an interscholastic athletic director will need to consider are contained in Table 1. While actual costs will vary based on the number of sports offered, number of competitions, distances traveled and state regulated considerations such as officials, each of these categories represents a significant allocation of the overall budget: uniforms, equipment, equipment maintenance, supplies, transportation, meals/motel, laundry, coaching clinics, officials.

Intercollegiate sport. In 1989, the average NCAA Division I institution allocated $1.68 million for athletic scholarships. By 1995, the average was up to $2.68 million for the typical allotment of 210 scholarships (Howard and Crompton, 1995). Yet scholarships are a relatively small portion of the overall budget. Salaries for coaches, administrators and support personnel require a significant portion of the budget, in addition to travel expenses, equipment costs, marketing, academic support services, facility maintenance, athletic training, and additional complementary services. As these categories demonstrate, the cost considerations for intercollegiate athletics are considerably more complex than the typical interscholastic athletic program.

To gain a perspective of the typical revenue a NCAA Division I institution could generate to pay for the growing costs associated with competing at the Division I level, review Table 2.

In the example provided, the Division I athletic program counts on traditional revenue sources to generate just over $11 million. Non-traditional revenue sources generated 19.5% of the total revenues with approximately $2.7 million from licensing royalties, sponsorships, sky boxes, team fundraisers and special events. Yet, gate receipts, concessions, state funding, booster club, student fees, media rights, conference returns and NCAA allotments comprised over 80% of the total revenue.

Professional sport. The magnitude of the sport industry has been estimated to be around $350 billion (*The Nation*, 1998), with half of that amount considered

TABLE 2

Traditional Revenue Sources		Non-traditional Revenue Sources	
Gate receipts	$4,200,000	Licensing	$50,000
Concessions	$1,300,000	Sponsorships	$1,800,000
State funding	$2,500,000	Sky boxes	$180,000
Booster club	$1,300,000	Team fundraising	$290,000
Student fees	$705,000	Special events	$290,000
Media rights	$495,000	Sub-total	$2,900,000
Conference returns	$370,000		
NCAA allotments	$730,000		
Sub-total	$11,600,000	Total Revenues	$14,500,000

to be direct spending on spectator and participatory sport. With reports predicting continued growth well into the next century, it may be difficult to accept that many traditional revenue sources have stagnated, while the costs for operating sport programs have increased. In professional sport, the escalating salaries of players have continued to drive an emphasis on development of new and innovative revenue streams. Naming rights attributed to new sport shrines are now a standard in the professional sport industry to eliminate a portion of the debt service created when a new sport facility is built. Even fans have been required to go beyond accepting increasing ticket prices, and now find that personal seat licenses (PSLs) are required. This fee merely establishes the fan's right to purchase season tickets.

Ironically, more money is being spent on sport than ever before. Yet, with new sport properties being developed, competition for the existing resources has also become more fierce than ever before. Still, the amount of resources invested in revenue generation or fund acquisition is based primarily on the type and structure of the organization. Each of the three organizational types discussed previously have unique structures that involve differing levels of complexity. As a reflection of the relatively simple structure of a typical interscholastic athletic program, there may only be one primary athletic director with no specialized assistants in the areas of marketing, promotion or fund raising. Coaches often find their responsibilities may extend beyond the field of competition, into the community for promotion and fund raising for their program(s). Without question, coaches of high profile sports at major universities have added responsibilities that are intimately linked to promotion and fund raising. However, there are full time administrators in charge of marketing, media relations, and fund raising that simply utilize the coach's influence to enhance the efforts for the entire athletic program. As intercollegiate athletics have grown in sophistication and complexity, the personnel needed have increasingly reflected the composition of a professional sport organization. With media rights fees increasing to levels that rival those in professional sport, the difference between the two types of organizations may seem to be diminishing. However, the overall goals of these two entities vary significantly, with professional sport being run as a business designed to be profitable. Intercollegiate athletics, on the other hand, is still part of an educational structure that often is considered successful as long as they are able to generate enough revenue to operate in the black and avoid falling into debt.

Generation of Funding

Sources of income Public school budgets are based on income received from state and local taxes. Private schools utilize student tuition and other resources to fund athletic programs. In each case, booster clubs or athletic support groups can provide substantial subsidization for specific teams or programs. In one example, the $2500 budget allotted to a local high school baseball program was only a small portion, 25%, compared to the $10,000 in funding generated by the booster club. While not all sport teams can rely on significant contributions from athletic support groups, athletic directors can be instrumental in developing external resources that can be split among all athletic teams. As an example, profits generated from the sale of popcorn during lunch at a local high school have annually added up to $15,000 for the athletic program. In situations where tax support is no longer sufficient to sustain the athletic programs, innovative approaches to revenue generation, such as these, can be the key.

In intercollegiate athletics, the institutional budget determines the amount of money the athletic department will receive. The state legislature allocates the funding for most public institutions. In certain circumstances, the legislature may even consider funding special projects that require major capital outlay, such as building additions to the university's football stadium or basketball arena. However, the determination of the funding most athletic departments receive is based on the overall institutional budget. Additionally, the amount allocated by the student government to support athletics through student fees can vary widely. Even what seems to be a small portion of the overall tuition and fees cost to students may add up to significant contributions for athletic departments that maintain healthy relationships with the student government. In the intercollegiate example above, approximately $700,000 in student fees go directly to the athletic department and contributes close to 20% of the overall revenue. While this is a relatively small percentage, finding another revenue stream to account for this percentage would be challenging.

Revenue streams

To begin to understand this phenomenon, some specific concepts and terms need to be established. Revenue and profit are often discussed as if they are interchangeable terms. While the goal of generating revenue is typically to generate a profit, each term has a unique definition. Revenue is the gross income returned by an investment. Which points to the reality that it takes money to make money, even in sport. Profit is a valuable return on an investment realized as a gain. While revenue may appear to be profit, the situation often facing organizations in sport, is that the money invested may not be fully returned. Revenues are reported separately, as money comes in over time which often gives the appearance that the large amounts of revenue must in fact be profitable. But only when all of the expenses have been balanced with all of the revenue generated, can a true profit be determined.

Typically media reports the revenue generated by a sport team and therefore, establishes an image that sport has more than enough financial support. For example, Bowl game revenues can amount to millions of dollars causing spectators and fans to believe that athletic departments are providing sufficient support for all teams and programs. Yet, few understand the expense of operating the non-revenue generating sports or the revenue sharing mandated by many athletic conferences and by the NCAA. Athletic administrators understand the likelihood that a program in the same conference as a winning team will stand to gain a share of the Bowl game or championship revenue. The fact that many programs expect and often figure into their budgets this shared revenue, points to the artificial cushion that can easily disappear and create a glaring debt.

Traditional revenue streams. Sport organizations must create revenue streams and produce cash for operations. In the case of intercollegiate athletics and professional sport, large amounts of money need to be generated each year just to sustain operations at the current level. Two categories often utilized when considering revenue streams are traditional and non-traditional. Traditional revenue streams are the sources most often counted on year after year to provide significant contributions to the overall allocation of funds. Examples included in the traditional category are ticket sale/gate receipts, concessions, licensing royalties, parking, and broadcasting or media rights. In the non-traditional category, examples may include corporate sponsorships, PSLs, naming rights, endowments and other fund raising activities, and marketing innovations.

In the area of traditional revenue, ticket sales generate a significant amount of income for most sport programs. Increasingly, the value associated with the opportunity to experience women's sporting events and competitions previously offered for free has gained recognition. While spectators and fans are not yet willing to pay the same ticket price required by intercollegiate football or men's basketball, they are willing to pay and in many cases are willing to buy season tickets to women's basketball, volleyball or soccer. However, setting the price for a ticket is no simple task. A sport manager should not become too ambitious. When setting the price for a ticket there are several considerations to make. In addition to price printed on the ticket, spectators have time, travel and additional costs such as concessions, parking and merchandise. The actual price of the ticket is typically one-third of the actual cost paid to experience an event. Factors such as time spent waiting to park, waiting in concessions lines and waiting for restroom access can cause some fans to reconsider their willingness to pay. For these reasons, the sport manager and facility manager need to work together to insure a valuable and worthwhile experience for the spectators.

When increasing the price of a ticket there is a certain threshold that should be considered relative to the fan's willingness to pay. For example, increasing a ticket from $1 to $2 may not seem like a big increase. Yet, the reality is that the price was increased by 100%. In a situation where the price is extremely low, the backlash from fans is likely to be minimal. However, if a $5 ticket is increased to $10 (the exact same percentage) from one season to the next, you can expect the fans to complain. For this reason, many sport managers believe it is better to increase the ticket price a small percentage each season, rather than make a big increase in one season and risk spectator dissatisfaction. Yet, increasing a ticket price every year, may eventually result in frustration with long time fans. Thus, the decision to maintain a price for several seasons may be necessary. The most important consideration needs to lie with the faithful fans and insuring that they are not being turned away by high-ticket prices or other peripheral costs.

Season ticket sales are beneficial to the financial management process because the money is paid up front and can be figured into the budget. To accommodate those fans that want to be season ticket holders, but can not afford the price of an entire season or don't have the time available, mini-plans have been developed. A wide variety of these unique "season" ticket plans exist, all with the idea that securing money for upcoming games prior to the season benefits the overall financial status of the organization.

Concessions, merchandising, and parking were traditionally thought of as minimal contributors to overall revenue generation. However, recent innovations at new sport facilities have included the addition of restaurants and micro-breweries on the stadium or ball park concourse, and premium parking associated with specific ticket packages. Concessions can add such a large contribution to revenue generation that many organizations are reconsidering the decision to contract out the concession services. Yet, with more products desired by spectators and service considered a premium, the contracting of a professional concessionaire can prove vital to revenue generation while alleviating additional concerns during events.

Non-traditional revenue streams. In many sport examples, broadcast and media rights are traditional sources of revenue. However, with the unprecedented deals made lately in both collegiate and professional sport, the evolution of this revenue stream is far from complete. For example, broadcast rights for the NCAA men's basketball tournament known as March Madness were recently purchased by CBS for $6 billion over 11 years. Major League Baseball was only able to squeeze $815 million out of ESPN in a deal that will last from 2000 through 2005 (Lombardo, 2000). Yet, these media rights deals involve far more than the traditional broadcasting of competitions. With Internet rights added to the mix, innovations in the utilization of the sport property can be expected to unfold in new and creative ways.

Corporate sponsorship has been a growing revenue stream for many sport properties and programs. Many believe that sport could not exist today without the revenue generated from corporate support through sponsorships and advertising. Additionally, developing a licensing program has become a requirement for any sport property that has a need to protect, promote and profit from their name and image. These three P's of licensing have become increasingly important as sponsors and advertisers have found value in associating their name and image with that of a sport property. For intercollegiate athletic programs, the royalties received from the sale of licensed merchandise and memorabilia can provide a significant revenue stream. Although there is no comparing college sport with professional sport, when it comes to licensing revenue. For the NBA, the 1998-99 season was a low point with only $1 billion in worldwide retail sales. The $3 billion mark reported in 1996 was their most profitable year to date in terms of retail sales.

Additional innovations in revenue generation have included the evolution of private seat licenses (PSLs), sky boxes/loges, facility naming rights and Internet rights. In the area of fund raising, more universities are looking toward the establishment of major endowments that will provide interest on a yearly basis that can be utilized by the athletic department without depleting the source of income. Stanford University has been a leader in the securing of endowments, with the long term goal of providing full scholarship allotments for all sports through interest generated by endowments.

While these large dollar figures are far from the reach of the typical interscholastic athletic program, the trickle down effect of revenue generation strategies should be acknowledged. Sponsorship acquisition has become increasingly common in high school sport. Media rights are rare, yet radio and television coverage of high school sport has increased. Still the biggest revenue generation tool for interscholastic programs is implementation of sound fund raising strategies. Before embarking on any fund raising effort some key components should be considered. The time involvement necessary is a big key that's often overlooked. Some activities that appear to be quite simple, may in fact require a large time commitment by a number of people.

Questions that should be asked before beginning a fund raising effort

- What are the goals of the fund raiser?
- Who benefits?
- Who's involved and how?
- How much organization is required and by whom?
- How many people are needed to be effective?
- Is this an activity that can be repeated as an annual event or is it a one-time effort?
- What's the level of difficulty for those involved?
- How much money will need to be invested?
- What is the likelihood of return on that investment?

Understanding the current economic climate for sport and becoming aware of the methods utilized to generate funding are two extremely important aspects of financial management. Yet, much more knowledge is needed to understand the operation of a sport program or property. The next section will address the tools a sport manager needs to understand in order to successfully meet the challenges that lie ahead.

Accounting Applications to Sport Management

Two critical aspects of financial management that sport managers need to understand are accounting procedures and the budgeting process. Accounting records provide most of the information needed to develop the budget. When these methods are understood and utilized appropriately, accounting methods can protect an administrator or coach from misuse of funds or carelessness.

The six objectives of accounting

1. Provide data specific to each program for future planning
2. Determine the method for authorization of expenditures
3. Develop standardized contracts, purchase orders, and other forms as needed
4. Develop a standard system for authorizing payments and monitoring received goods or services
5. Provide a method for handling special funds not managed by central administrative office

6. Provide the necessary information for an audit

There are three financial statements utilized in the accounting process that need to be understood by sport managers. They include the *balance sheet, income statement*, and the *cash flow analysis*. Each of these tools assists the sport manager with financial aspects of the sport business and are crucial to planning for success.

The **balance sheet** shows the financial condition of the business and has four primary uses.

1. Illustrates change in business over time
2. Shows growth or decline in various phases of business
3. Demonstrates the ability to pay debts
4. Shows financial position through ratios

Four important terms to know in order to understand the balance sheet include **assets, liabilities, equity** and **depreciation**. Assets are simply what the business owns. The three primary assets listed on a balance sheet are (1) current assets, (2) long-term investments, and (3) fixed assets. Cash on hand, or any asset that could be converted to cash within 12 months would be considered a current asset. Any investment, such as a CD with a maturity date beyond 12 months, would be considered long-term. Fixed assets include items such as real estate (land or buildings), furniture, equipment, automobiles or other items a business own. Assets can depreciate or diminish in value over time. This concept is of importance to sport managers because depreciation can be calculated over time and become tax-deductible.

The balance sheet shows the balance of assets held compared to liabilities and owner's equity. Assets are listed on the left side, while liabilities are listed on the right. Liabilities are considered the amount of money a business owes to other parties. Current liabilities are debts that must be paid within 1 year while long-term liabilities include larger loans that do not need to be paid immediately. Both current and long term liabilities are added together to determine the total owed as liabilities. In addition to liabilities, the right side of the balance sheet lists owner's equity. The amount of money invested by owners, whether partner's or individuals, is defined as equity. Earned income is then added to the investment and withdrawals made by the owner are subtracted to determine the total owner's equity. In the case of the Cleveland Indians, and other publicly held properties, equity includes the stockholder's purchased shares of stock. Total equity is then added to total liabilities. The balance sheet should then show that the combined values equal or balance with the total assets calculated in the left column (see Table 3).

A balance sheet posting expenditures regularly should be updated and maintained by the sport manager so that those affected by the budget know the current balance.

The **income statement** shows profit or loss in the business operations. The income statement is a crucial analysis tool for determining success of a business. By comparing the cost of running a business with the sales generated, the income statement provides indication of profit or loss. The items included will depend on the type of business. To read an income statement, start at the top with gross proceeds, and follow down to the last line where net income is found (see table). Key components listed on the income statement include revenue, operating expenses, net income and a percentage column. **Gross sales** are listed under the revenue

TABLE 3

Assets			Liabilities	
Cash on hand		$10,000	Accounts Payable	$14,000
Cash in bank		$100,000	Notes Payable	$45,000
Accounts receivable		$35,000	Mortgage payments	$72,000
Inventories		$15,000	Accrued salaries	$35,000
Prepaid insurance		$36,000	Accrued taxes	$18,000
Prepaid advertising		$12,000	Shareholder equity	$1,319,000
Fixed assets—facility	$1,350,000			
Less: Reserve for facility depreciation	$125,000	$1,225,000		
Fixed assets—equipment	$90,000			
Less: Reserve for equipment depreciation	$20,000	$70,000		
Total assets		$1,503,000	Total Liabilities	$1,503,000

heading and can be defined as the total amount of revenue (excluding sales tax) that is generated. Revenue sources discussed previously, such as traditional and non-traditional, would be listed here. Progressing down the income statement, the **operating expenses** will include all other expenses a business accrues during day-to-day operations. Examples may include salaries, insurance, advertising or marketing, utilities, and rent or loan payments. **Net income** is listed at the bottom of the income statement and can be defined as the amount of money remaining after all expenses have been paid. When a net loss has occurred over the year, the amount of loss will be shown in parenthesis. Lastly, the **percentage column** on the right shows what percentage of net sales has been spent in each area of the business. This is a very useful management tool because it allows a manager to quickly assess which percentage(s) may be too high, compared to previous statements. Changes in the percentage column may assist a manager in making decisions that could lead to better utilization of resources.

The **cash flow analysis** serves a separate purpose from the previous two records discussed. The balance sheet shows the manager the business's financial condition, and the income statement shows the profit or loss, while the cash flow analysis documents the "cash in" and "cash out" typically on a monthly basis. By showing the cash sales and disbursement (expense) records, the cash flow analysis gives the manager the ability to assess the financial situation over time.

Sport is seasonal and thus effects inflows and outflows differently. Cash flow can be defined as reported net income plus amounts charged off for depreciation, depletion, amortization, and extraordinary charges to reserves that are bookkeeping deductions and not paid out in actual dollars (Regan, p. 369).

Comparing periodic records may provide patterns of cash flow that indicate a need to make adjustments at specific points in time or provide some time for strategic planning. These accounting practices vary based on the form of business ownership. However, the three financial statements discussed serve three important purposes and should be utilized together. While a much more in depth knowledge is needed to be successful in financial management, the awareness of these primary accounting procedures will allow sport managers to be prepared for the challenges ahead.

The Budgeting Process

A budget is a management plan for revenue and expenses of an organization for a period of time, usually one year. The two most important skills a sport manager will have to have relative to budgets is (1) the ability to prepare and justify the annual budget and (2) the ability to control the expenses and disbursements once the budget has been approved.

There are several advantages provided by budgeting according to Barber (1996). Seven specific advantages include:

1. Substitution of a plan for "chance" in fiscal operations. Preparation for additional staff or maintenance work that needs to be done can be accomplished with resources available.
2. Prevents over-budgeting or padding because it requires review of the entire operation in terms of funds available and revenue needs.
3. Promotes standardization and simplification of operation. Priorities and objectives are established while inefficient operations can be eliminated.
4. Provides guidelines for all staff to follow, insuring more consistency.
5. Provides factual data for evaluation by governing bodies regarding the operations efficiency.
6. Allows contributors such as the taxpaying public to see where revenues come from and where expenditures are spent.
7. Acts as an instrument for fiscal control.

There are fundamental principles that should be followed when constructing a budget. Budgets are made out annually and have individual characteristics based on the type of organization or business. Preparation of a new budget begins when the previous budget has been accepted. While top administrators at educational institutions are responsible for the overall budget, an athletic director or department head should be involved in the budget preparation process for her/his program. Just as coaches or physical educators need to be involved in the preparation of the budget for their specific program(s). This bottom-up approach provides more quality information for making budget decisions and also serves to increase staff satisfaction because their thinking was incorporated into the decision(s) that will directly affect their work. Budgets should be planned well in advance of the fiscal period for which they will be used. The fiscal year for most educational institutions is July 1 to June 30, but any 12 month period may be used depending on government regulation and local policy.

The 10 primary steps in constructing a budget

1. examining the organization's present mission, objectives and goals in relationship to the previous year's budget
2. collecting the necessary information relative to the needs, strengths, and resources of the organization
3. soliciting input from others with expertise in the collection and evaluation of information needed

4. reviewing the data collected and analyzing it in terms of what was done previously, what is required presently, and what the future may hold immediately

5. preparing the budget document in accordance with the stipulations and requirements established by the organization, or governing body

6. checking to insure the document is accurate, feasible and realistic

7. submitting a "rough draft" for critical analysis by an expert or colleague, prior to making the formal presentation to the board or administration

8. preparing prior to the presentation for anticipated questions

9. implementing the approved budget (once changes have been made as needed) with the knowledge that flexibility may be necessary as time progresses and events transpire

10. auditing the budget following the conclusion of the budget year to assist the sport manager in gaining proficiency and competence as a fiscal manager

The decision on the type of budget to use is usually based on the sophistication of the program that will be utilizing the information. However, in educational settings, the type of budget is often mandated by the educational institution or organization. For this reason a sport manager or administrator should be familiar with different budgeting procedures and be prepared to use the strengths of each when involved in the budgeting process.

Types of Budgets

Line item budget. The term *line* refers to the listing of each item as a line in the budget. This approach is one of the most simple budgeting approaches to use and understand. It can be constructed in a reasonable amount of time because the specific expenditure items that form this budget are based on information from previous years' budgets together with anticipated changes such as escalating costs, new programs or enrollment shifts. For these reasons, this approach is one of the most commonly used for physical education or athletic programs.

Program budget. The program budget separates an organization by units. For this reason it would be easily adapted to fit an athletic department or sport organization. The three components of a program budget include (1) overall organizational goals, (2) program specific goals, and (3) unique features of the program. This process is then followed by a line item budget for support. With each sport preparing a separate budget along with a narrative description of the sport's goals and the features of its program deemed most important, the athletic director can compare various budget requests and make decisions based on a more in depth understanding.

Planning-Programming-Budgeting-Evaluation System (PPBES). The purpose of the PPBES is to focus on the end product of the service provided rather than the actual cost. Additionally, providing a rationale for each of the competing units within a department can be accomplished as the PPBES provides a narrative picture of expenditures rather than simply listing the amount of money spent.

- Planning requires careful consideration of goals and objectives.

- Programming means that programs are developed to reach the established goals.
- Budgeting refers to the allocation of resources to accomplish the goals of the programs.
- Evaluation is the final step that requires assessment of the results.

Following evaluation, further planning generates the start of the next budgetary cycle. This system provides the administrator with a means of objectively evaluating programs and determining where resources should be allocated.

Zero-based budgeting. The basic premise behind this approach is that the organization begins each year with no money. A budget is then prepared by justifying each expenditure as if it is a new expense. The purpose of a zero-based budget is to control over-budgeting and waste. Each budget request is carefully considered in relationship to the overall organization. This approach has been considered a radical departure from the traditional methods described previously.

Capital budget. Long range budget items and capital expenses are covered in a capital budget. Typically, major purchases such as new facilities and equipment that are not found in operating budgets (reflecting only one year) are found in a capital budget. Capital expenditures are those which involve a significant amount of money. A narrative explanation and/or justification should be provided for each expense.

Summary/Conclusion

In the present economic environment, an understanding of basic financial principles is paramount. Sport managers and administrators will have a greater degree of success in the emerging sport industry if they understand how to manage costs, generate revenue and account for money spent.

Terms to review

- Assets: what a business owns
- Liabilities: business's debts; how much business owes to other parties
- Equity: amount of money invested by owners
- Depreciation: a decrease in value of an asset as it gets older, value diminishes
- Percentage column: a useful management tool that shows what percentage of the net sales is being spent in specific areas of the business.
- Revenue: the gross income returned by an investment
- Profit: a valuable return on an investment realized as gain

---

References

Barber, E. (1996). "Accounting and Budgeting" in B. Parkhouse (ed.), *The Management of Sport,* pp. 343-362. St. Louis, MO: Mosby.

DiMartino, Christina and Andrew Cohen (1999). "Movin' on Up," *Athletic Business* (November), 43-52.

Howard, Dennis R. (1999). "The Changing Fanscape for Big-League Sports: Implications for Sport Managers," *Journal of Sport Management* (13), 78-91.

Howard, Dennis R. and John L. Crompton (1995). *Financing Sport.* Morgantown, VA: Fitness Information Technology Inc.

Lombardo, John. (2000). Houston Goes on PSL spree. *Sports Business Journal* 37(2), 6.

Regan, Tom H., "Financing Sport" in B. Parkhouse (ed.), *The Management of Sport,* pp. 363-373. St. Louis, MO: Mosby.

Stier, William F., *Managing Sport, Fitness, and Recreation Programs*, pp. 169-192. Boston, MA: Allyn and Bacon.

"Why Sports?" (1998, August 10-17). *The Nation*, 267, pp. 3, 21.

Chapter 7

Equipment Control

Dominic Morelli

Introduction

It is important that all sport managers understand the basic elements of equipment management. An understanding of the basics will enable the sport manager to make informed decisions. This can be achieved by looking through the eyes of the person who deals directly with equipment control. The person(s) assigned this responsibility often views the task as a perpetual cycle that encompasses storing equipment, assessing needs, inventorying, maintaining inventory, issuing equipment to athletes and staff, and retrieving said equipment to return to inventory. The cycle may be altered to meet particular needs, but if the basics of it are understood, the equipment management process should be more efficient, require less manpower, and be easier for the person(s) directly controlling equipment.

Selecting and Organizing the Equipment Storage Area

The first step in controlling equipment is the selection of a proper storage area. Certain criteria must be considered when choosing or designing the equipment storage area. The location of the room should be as close to the athletes' dressing area and playing facilities as possible. If a laundry operation is included in your facility plan it should also be included in the equipment room or very near by. This area should be located on the building's ground floor with accessibility for delivery vehicles. For example, if there is a loading dock or an area where tractor-trailer vehicles can enter and exit easily it should be immediately accessible to the equipment area. This type of location makes the process of receiving, issuing and maintaining equipment more efficient.

To increase efficiency, the external design of the equipment room should be modeled after a mini-warehouse, with areas designed for receiving as well as issuing equipment. Doors in the receiving area should be large enough to accommodate substantial quantities and large pieces of equipment. This area should have ramps in place of, or in conjunction with, steps to facilitate the use of hand trucks, equipment trunks and laundry carts.

The area utilized for issuing equipment should have one main window or counter top, close to the players' locker room. The ideal design is a window with roll up closure and a counter top with storage below. Adjacent to the issue window, small individual issue-lockers should be installed. The backs of these lockers should be open to the interior of the equipment room with individually locking fronts accessible to the athlete. This "post-office box" effect saves time because it eliminates the need for "ever-present" and on-demand service throughout the day. An equipment assistant can accomplish a day's worth of issuing in a "single service" task. To ensure this process is completely efficient we must devise a method to return this equipment without human assistance. To accomplish this we install a small laundry or used equipment door approximately four feet off the floor so a bin can be placed below it, inside the equipment room to catch the used equipment. The door should be just big enough to serve its purpose but not so big that it endangers equipment room security.

Our design process now requires consideration for the interior design. In the issue area there should be an individual storage locker for each athlete that corresponds to the issue locker on the exterior of the equipment room. This individual "holding" locker should be numbered to correspond with the number assigned each athlete when he or she is issued equipment. It should be used to store equipment which does not automatically go into the issue lockers but is used frequently. The size of these lockers will depend upon the particular athlete's needs (for instance a football or field hockey locker would be much larger than one for basketball).

We must now plan for storage of the remainder of our inventory in an organized manner. In a storage area there must be ample shelving/cabinetry to store the necessary inventory. The size of the shelves and total space required depends upon the needs of a particular organization. This can be predicted by determining what you will store, how you plan to arrange it and the necessary inventory quantities. This will allow us to devise a plan for storage that we can proceed with once our storage area construction is complete.

Taking the time to organize the equipment in a neat, orderly fashion will enable us to carry out the equipment control process smoothly and easily. Basically, when the equipment is arranged in this fashion with the needs of the controller factored in, the result will be an efficient equipment operation. Arrangement of inventory is dictated by available shelf space, frequency of use, size of equipment, and purpose. Equipment similar in type or kind should be stored together in the same general area. If our plan was well thought out the location of the equipment on the shelves is already determined. All of this facilitates finding items quickly and improves the inventory process.

Security Considerations

While considering the equipment room's design, plan for the security of the storage area. The area must be a sturdy dwelling with secure locks on all doors and windows. The keys to the equipment room should be distributed only to persons who have a direct need for them. If your building has a "master key" for all doors, the equipment room should not be included on the master. Admittance to the equipment room should be restricted to persons who have business there, and athletes should never be allowed to enter in groups greater than two. Since this room often contains the largest, most valuable inventory in the athletic complex, burglar alarms and/or security cameras should be a serious consideration. The aforementioned issue lockers should be either deep enough to prevent reaching into a neighboring locker, or have removable backing. This will prevent athletes from retrieving equipment that does not belong to them. No matter what type of athletic equipment is stored, its controllers must remember the commodity being dealt with is appealing to thieves and souvenir hunters. Often there are expensive personal belongings of athletes or patrons being held in this area too. Spending extra money for security will save money and headaches caused by equipment loss.

If heavy laundry equipment is used, proper fire prevention measures, such as heat or smoke activated sprinklers and alarms, if not a part of the legal building code, should be installed. To further insure prevention of accidents a chemical storage room for volatile cleaning solutions and an eye wash station should be a part of the laundry room plan.

Using cabinets with locks instead of open shelves increases security in this area. If possible, there should be a special room where the most valuable equipment is stored. This area should be a small, locked room of shelves within the equipment room. (This is a good area to keep game uniforms, expensive items held for resale or any item that is difficult or expensive to replace.) It is often helpful to visit facilities run by organizations with similar needs to your own to gain further ideas.

Inventorying Equipment

Once equipment has been placed on the shelf in an organized manner, it is ready to be counted and considered inventory. When counting equipment, records of the item counted, its price, and its quantity by size and brand should be retained each time the inventory is conducted. These records are valuable to the equipment manager for long range planning, budgeting, predicting purchasing needs, and day to day operations. When conducting inventory, do not overlook equipment that is held outside the equipment room but is still the manager's responsibility. Such equipment may include items held in a player's locker room locker, field equipment or court accessories. Forms such as the ones shown in Appendix 1 at the end of this chapter, can be helpful when inspecting an athlete's locker and when obtaining a player's current equipment sizes. Conduct an overall manual equipment inventory count annually and check players' lockers (locker room and holding lockers) at least twice a year.

After completing an initial inventory the prudent thing to do is purchase a computer inventory program and store the inventory information in it. Different models from the very simple to the very elaborate are available and can be customized to meet your needs. If funds are not available to purchase this type of program inventory can always be kept on a spreadsheet program, which is a standard program with most computer software packages. The advantage to a custom inventory program is it can be used to input inventory information and individual player issue information, thus creating a perpetual inventory system. This allows the manager to check inventory levels at any time and creates a situation where your annual count is a check instead of a blind count. This speeds up the inventory account and makes the manager more accountable to balance out what has been purchased against what is issued and what is inventoried.

After completing the initial overall inventory, equipment needs must be determined. This process begins by assessing the equipment needs of individuals the equipment manager is responsible for outfitting. These participants must be properly fitted for equipment they will use on the playing field. Sizes may be obtained by maintaining an up to date file of locker inventory sheets and by supplying sizing questionnaires that require information pertinent to the controller's needs (see Appendix 2). With both of these methods, it will always be necessary for the controller to visually confirm these sizes are correct. This size check is most important when dealing with protective equipment.

Equipment managers must take time to learn and understand the mechanics of the equipment so that they can effectively fit and size it for the athlete. This information can be obtained by consulting authorities such as equipment manufacturers or representatives, other equipment managers, equipment catalogs and magazines, information provided with the product, clinics and seminars, professional tailors and from listening to the athletes. With proper information and guidance athletes can be sized correctly and these sizes can be filed for future use. A computer spreadsheet program is an excellent way to retain these sizes. With the proper planning and file maintenance, your spreadsheet program (see Appendix 3) can be sorted in ways (by player, by locker number, by size, etc.) that will make assessing needs much easier and more efficient.

When determining complete equipment needs, all possibilities must be explored. Investigating applicable rules and regulations will help assess equipment needs for athletic fields and playing facilities. Coaches' evaluations are the primary consideration in decisions about equipment and facility needs. Administrators, physicians, and athletic trainers who are involved in the sports program should also be consulted for equipment suggestions. It is important to plan for quantities beyond basic needs as well as replacement parts for equipment that requires frequent repair. This facilitates replacement or repair of inventory items damaged by normal or abnormal wear and tear. As a general rule, the more physical contact involved in a sport, the greater the need for periodic replacement or repair.

Budgeting

Equipment management personnel are now becoming aware of the items that will be necessary to ensure a successful operation. When managers match the ideal quantity of required items with the cost of the items, it is possible to accurately formulate a budget. Since most sports organizations operate within budget constraints, equipment managers must be prepared to formulate and submit a proposed dollar amount necessary to meet the needs of the program.

The budget process begins with the gathering of cost information for the predetermined items essential to the inventory. This information can be obtained by sending a list of items and quantities required to several sporting goods suppliers for price quotations. The lowest price should be used for budget purposes and the price bids retained for future use. Other resources for gathering dollar values include old equipment records, athletic or university business office files of old invoices or equipment catalogs.

Examine budget priorities before continuing in the budget process. Based on funds made available in the previous year the equipment manager must be smart and reasonable when requesting a budget amount. Equipment deemed "necessary" must be prioritized based on funds the manager feels are a "reasonable" request. No matter whether the equipment manager trims the budget prior to submittal or an administrator decides for him/her, priority should always be given to protective and safety equipment. The cost area devoted to an athlete's safety should never be sacrificed for ethical as well as legal liability reasons. The remaining budget categories' requests must be based on the equipment manager's observations of operational needs.

Purchasing

Once equipment appropriations are approved, equipment orders should be placed. The price bids gathered from sporting goods dealers that were used in formulating the budget can now be used in your purchasing decisions. (These bids are often only guaranteed for 30 days and time is a factor.) When selecting sporting goods suppliers, prices are not the only consideration; service is also an important factor. If an equipment supplier with lower prices is unreliable when delivering goods or servicing your account, the more expensive alternative may be the best buy when one considers the cost of phone calls, overtime and gray hair involved in prodding an undependable dealer.

Consider questions of when and how to order equipment. Target dates for ordering depend on the time of year the equipment is needed and how much lead-time is necessary to produce the equipment. As a general rule, begin the purchasing process for a particular sport as soon as the season has ended. However, this will depend upon factors such as scheduling of the sport, the manufacturers' production schedules, and the fiscal year your budget is based on. The "how to's" of purchasing are often dictated by the athletic organization's requisitioning policies and the seller's requirements in extending credit. Many organizations require equipment managers to complete purchasing requisitions which must be approved by business office personnel, who turn those requisitions into purchase orders that are then sent to equipment vendors. These purchase orders contractually bind the dealer to the equipment descriptions, quantities and prices agreed upon between the dealer and equipment manager. This prevents any arguments between vendors and purchasers over mistakenly priced equipment, incorrect quantities or unwanted items shipped to the buyer. Descriptions shown on purchase orders must be complete and precise to prevent misunderstandings that can lead to receiving incorrect items.

After placing the equipment order, the equipment controller should make periodic checks with the manufacturer/supplier to see that new equipment is scheduled to be produced and delivered on agreed upon dates. Maintain a file of phone numbers and addresses of suppliers to facilitate this process. Also, keep a running tally of monies spent out of the equipment budget in order to stay within the established budget guidelines. This is another area where the computer spreadsheet program or a special budget program can be helpful (this can also be incorporated into the aforementioned inventory program). (See basic example in Appendix 4.)

Receiving Equipment

After inventorying and inspecting deliveries, create records showing the item received, its' quantity, and the date it was received. This file is helpful in determining orders that are outstanding, verifying lead times for future ordering, evaluating the suppliers' service responsibilities and gathering information for business office receiving reports. (The receiving report is the final aspect of the business end of purchasing—this tells the business office that the purchase order has been satisfactorily completed by the vendor and you are authorizing payment for the items requisitioned for and received.) Arrange new equipment in the orderly manner for which the equipment room was designed. If equipment areas need further rearranging, the time to do it is while you are shelving new equipment (putting an item in a different spot in the equipment room may make your operation more efficient). Sometimes before the initial equipment issue, lack of space necessitates that the equipment manager store portions of the new equipment in another storage facility. In this case, do not store the equipment on shelves, just count, inspect and return the items to their shipping containers until they reach their final destination.

Issuing Equipment

With new equipment stored, the playing season is approaching and it is time to prepare to issue equipment. The first task in this process is the creation of an enumeration system for issuing equipment to the athletes. A number should be assigned to each athlete and the number should correspond to his/her dressing locker, issue locker and holding locker. All items issued to the athlete must be recognized by the identifying numeral that is etched on the equipment with a permanent marker, or screen-printed or embroidered. This system of enumeration will facilitate the equipment controller's needs for separating the athletes' equipment when it is retrieved to be laundered or inventoried. Above all we must establish a system with order that is logical and understandable.

Before the athletes' needs for equipment arise, certain items can be prepared for the anticipated future issues. Since sizes were determined earlier in the equipment process, we can now use those records to enumerate and store these items in the individual holding lockers. Cloth goods and any item with standardized sizing can be prepared for immediate issue before the athlete is present. The use of numbered mesh laundry bags or shelves with wire baskets can be used as an efficient means for controlling these everyday cloth wares.

The aforementioned computerized inventory program can be utilized as we begin issuing equipment. These inventory systems can be set up to store equipment dispersal records as the issue takes place and this will automatically reduce the amounts shown as inventory. These systems can be customized with bar codes so that you can assign equipment items as well as athletes to a bar code. A notebook identifying these codes can be kept by the issue window so that day-to-day issues can be recorded on the system quickly and efficiently. This helps the equipment manager track the location of equipment at all times, automatically creates size records, and helps alert him/her to inventory deficiencies.

The fitting of protective devices and items, which vary greatly in design and sizing (such as helmets, shoulder pads, or shoes), must be checked while the athlete is present for proper sizing. The importance of this process is even greater with young athletes because natural body growth will cause a significant change in the youngsters sizing. While fitting protective equipment and special devices, the equipment controller must offer instruction for proper wearing techniques so the athlete uses the equipment *correctly*. In addition, players' special protective needs should be explored while they are available for questions in this area (feedback from examining doctors and trainers is vital to this process).

After issuing equipment, the athletes should be made aware of equipment rules and regulations as well as the cooperation expected from them by the equipment manager. These policies should be in writing with important areas highlighted verbally in team meetings. Equipment procedures and policies should include type of equipment available to the athlete and when it is available; the system the equipment manager uses to issue and retrieve equipment and the daily procedures the player must adhere to in order to make the operations smooth and successful for both parties. Procedures for laundering equipment should be carefully explained because laundering items is a part of those daily procedures and if a participant is uncertain about what to return, when to turn it in, or how and where it is to be returned, confusion will result.

Once the equipment is issued and explained, equipment controllers must consider how the equipment is to be maintained. Primary maintenance considerations involve keeping the equipment clean, sanitary and in good repair. If the athletes' equipment is to be laundered daily, there are several ways this can be accomplished. If the equipment storage area does not have laundry facilities, a reliable outside laundry company must be contracted. The company chosen should be large enough for the organization's needs, located close to the equipment facility and above all dependable and trustworthy. Price bids and references should be obtained from competing local laundries before a final decision is made. Equipment managers with laundry facilities in-house have a much more desirable situation since time is saved and security is tighter because laundry is not transported to a different facility and is not handled by persons outside the organization. Also, having laundry equipment within the equipment room is much more cost efficient. If the initial cost of installing washers and dryers is affordable, the operation pays for itself by reducing the daily laundry costs (the bigger your operation and greater your daily laundry needs—the faster the savings will be realized). Lack of laundry facilities may also create additional equipment needs because lead-time required by outside laundries necessitates the need for additional sets of everyday apparel for each athlete. Two sets of practice gear are necessary for situations where there are internal laundry facilities (one set is being cleaned while the other one is being used), three sets may be necessary when external facilities are used.

Methods of laundering equipment must be decided upon when equipment personnel are responsible for this task. These methods can be formulated by reading labels on potential laundry items and consulting equipment manufacturers for suggestions. Also, professional laundry personnel and reputable laundry detergent dealers are helpful when considering special stain removal needs. Further ideas may be solicited from equipment controllers in similar situations.

Equipment maintenance doesn't end with laundering items. All items under the care of the equipment manager must be checked periodically for maintenance needs. The frequency of inspections depends upon the durability of the equipment, the recurrence of use and the contact involved in the sport. During a seasonal sports program, inspect protective and special equipment as often as possible. In the polices and procedures given to players, which were mentioned earlier, the player should be given the responsibility of checking his/her protective equipment daily. After the season is complete, all items should be carefully inspected for repair needs and, if necessary, sent to qualified equipment reconditioning companies. When equipment personnel become well acquainted with equipment construction, some of the repairs can be made in-house, lessening the need and expense of outside help. However, care should be taken to not alter protective equipment in a manner unsuitable for the manufacturer's safety design. If this were to happen the result is unsafe equipment and a libelous situation for the equipment manager. For example cleaning football helmets with a solvent that is not approved by the manufacturer can weaken the shell causing the football helmet to shatter on impact. The equipment manager should become proficient in equipment maintenance by learning as much as possible about the equipment.

Retrieving Equipment

When it comes time to retrieve equipment from the athlete, equipment managers must depend on records created while issuing equipment as well as their ability to judge character. No matter what the program's issue policies, or what records exist, the cooperation of the athlete is necessary to facilitate the retrieval process.

In the absence of athlete cooperation retrieval of equipment can be facilitated by requiring a mandatory payment of a deposit prior to issuing equipment, holding awards until equipment is returned, or simply by holding laundered equipment until the item in question is recovered. Other options include denying the athlete training table privileges, disciplinary action (early morning runs, stadium step runs, etc.) or denying the right to register for classes. Policies must be formulated regarding "excuses" for lost equipment, how to deal with realized losses and what the consequences of that loss will be. Working with the athletic business office the equipment manager must come up with a way to hold athletes financially responsible for lost equipment. This is the point in the equipment cycle when the computerized inventory program is the most helpful. Everything that you have issued is recorded in the program and reports of those issues can be recalled for each athlete at a moment's notice. Other methods of recording issues, which will assist in gathering equipment, are to have the athlete sign a form attesting to equipment check-out, keeping unattested issue records, or issuing the same items to each athlete. Whatever technique the equipment manager uses, equipment retrieval is the essential aspect of the equipment program.

Once equipment has been retrieved, the equipment cycle begins once again starting with the inventory stage. By retaining good records throughout different phases of the cycle, this process will become more familiar and easier to reproduce. Note areas that cause problems for the organization throughout the equipment process and work on the trouble spots before they arise again. In short, when dealing with equipment areas, be organized with the facilities, inventories and records, follow the flow of your own natural equipment cycle, be informed on all aspects of your equipment responsibilities and protect the athlete like he/she was a member of your family.

Summary/Conclusion

The sport manager should give attention and understand the basic process of equipment management no matter what his/her position in the athletic organization. This will enable the better-informed administrator to make knowledgeable decisions concerning facilities, personnel and budgeting. The areas of importance regarding equipment control begin with the location and design of the equipment room. The room must be organized sensibly and securely to achieve efficient operation. Retention of inventory and all associated records is essential to the equipment operation.

It is wise to utilize the services of coaches, administrators, physicians and athletic trainers for consultation regarding equipment needs. While budget constraints dictate the purchase of equipment, the emphasis should always be on protective and safety factors. Ethical as well as legal guidelines are influential in the purchase of sports equipment.

A system of requisitions, size records, delivery inspection, and maintaining equipment all can help ensure successful equipment management. Correct fitting of equipment must be provided and periodic sizing inspections are required. Special plans should be made for policies regarding equipment retrieval or costs for missing equipment will escalate causing budget overruns.

The sports administrator often overlooks the management of equipment when in reality it may be one of the more important duties in the sports program.

Appendix 1

Equipment Check

Date:_____

Name	Locker #	Bag	Sweat Suit	P. Pants	G. Pants	Chest	Jersey	Helmet	Facemask	Sh. Pad	Shoes

Appendix 2

Individual Sizing Sheet

HEAD

CHEST

WAIST

INSEAM

Height: _____

Weight: _____

Waist: _____

Inseam: _____

Head Size: _____

Chest: _____

Shoe Size: _____

Shoe Type: High Top or Low Top

Shoe Bottom Style: Molded or Cleated

Knee Braces: Yes or No

How to Measure

Chest: Measure around the fullest part of the chest, keeping tape up under arm and around shoulder blades: Number of inches equals size.

Waist: Measure around waist, over shirt not over slacks, at the height you would normally wear your slacks, keep one between tape and body. Number of inches equals size.

Head: Measure one inch above eyebrows the full circmference of the head.

Inseam: Take a pair of pants that fit you well. Measure from the crotch seam to the bottom of pants. Number of inches (to the nearest half) equals inseam length.

Clothing Sizes

Jacket: _____   Sports Coat: _____   T-Shirt: _____   Shorts: _____   Sweater: _____

Appendix 3

Equipment Record

Player	Jersey #	Locker #	Position	Shoe sz.	Pr. Shoe	Gm. Shoe	Wo Shoe	Pr. Turf	Shorts	Jock	Nike T
Curry	1	1	OQB	14.0	M	T	L	L	XXL	XL	XXL
Williams, D.	2	2	ORB	12.5	BHT	MS	L(13)	HT(13)	XXL	XL	XXL
Allen	3	3	OWR	11.0	B	MS	L	L(11.5)	XL	L	XL
Roberson	4	4	DLB	15.0	BHT	BHT	HT	HT	XL	L	XL

T-Shirt	Girdle	Beefy T	Helmet	F-Mask	Sh. Pads	Neck	Waist	Knee Pad	Hip Pad	Thigh	Sw. Top
XXL	XL	XXL	BM 1"	ODW	DG/QB-XL	B/RP	32	A/K	A/.75	A/K	XXL
XXL	L	XXL	V4 L	EGOP	P/34S-XL	BP	34	A/K	A/.75	B/AL-92	XXL
XXL	L	XXL	V4 L	EGOP	P/34S-L		30	A/K	A/.75	A/K	XXL
XXL	XL	XXL	V4 L	RJDW-UB	DG/56Z-XL	D-BR	36	A/K	A	DG/M	XXL

Sw. Pant	Tights	Prac. Jer.	Chest Sz.	Jersey Tp.	Inseam	Ring	Initials	Shirt	Nike Sweat	N. Jacket	1st Name
XXL	XL	48	48	QB	33	10.5	RAC	XXL	XXL	XXL	Ronald
XXL	XL	52	52	L	34	13.0	DOM	XXL	XXL	XXL	Domonique
XL	L	48	50	L	34	10.0	BLA	XL	XXL	XXL	Bosley
XXL	XL	52	52	L	34		JCR	XXL	XXL	XXL	Clay

Appendix 4

Budget Sheet

Date	Object Code	Sub	Description	Ref #1	Ref #2	R	Amount
				Beginning Balance			
				Present Balance			$0.00

Chapter 8

Sports Medicine Services

Jerald Hawkins

Introduction

Of the various services provided by a sports organization to its clientele, none is more important than medical care. Whether such care takes the form of first aid, as in the case of an injured or ill spectator, or complete injury-care and rehabilitation, as with the competitive athlete, it is the responsibility of every organization to provide quality medical care for spectators and participants. The purpose of this chapter is to identify the methods which may be utilized in providing such medical care. Because of the diversity of medical care needs of nonparticipants (spectators, employees, etc.) and active participants, it is necessary to consider two distinct aspects of medical care services: first aid and emergency care, and sports injury management.

First Aid and Emergency Care

The primary component of an organization's medical care system is that of first-aid care in the event of sudden illness or injury to one of its clients or employees. First aid is generally described as that process by which nonmedical personnel perform simple care procedures designed to alleviate the immediate threat of further injury. In the case of life-threatening injury or illness, this description may be extended to include life-saving procedures such as rescue breathing or cardiopulmonary resuscitation.

To adequately provide such services, careful planning and the development and utilization of available resources must be accomplished in the specific areas of training existing personnel to render first-aid services, providing first-aid supplies which are easily accessible and establishing a system of emergency medical care.

Every employee in the sport-related organization should be certified in both first aid and cardiopulmonary resuscitation (CPR). This is especially true for those whose daily responsibilities include direct contact with spectators and/or participants. First-aid and/or CPR instruction is available in most Communities through the American Red Cross, the American Heart Association and other voluntary health agencies. It is often possible to schedule group instruction for an entire staff, thus making it possible for certification to be obtained with minimal inconvenience to the employees. With the skills acquired through first-aid and CPR instruction, all staff members will be prepared to render first aid and emergency care whenever and wherever the need arises.

Most first-aid and emergency medical-care procedures require some form of specialized supplies. The nature of such supplies may range from cotton-tipped applicators for cleaning superficial wounds to inflatable air-splints for use in immobilizing suspected fractures and dislocations. In order for first-aid supplies to be used effectively, they must be stored in a location which allows easy access. The most efficient method of providing first-aid supplies in a sport-related facility is to assemble several "first-aid kits" and place them in a variety of locations throughout the facility. The number and specific locations of such kits will depend upon the size of the facility and the types of programs it supports. A list of the recommended contents of a first-aid kit for recreational-sports facilities may be found below.

Contents of a First Aid Kit for a Recreational Sports Facility

Adhesive compresses (Band-Aids) — Assorted sizes
Adhesive tape — Assorted widths
Alcohol (70%) — one bottle per kit
Antiseptic solution (merthiolate, betadine, etc.) — one bottle per kit
Burn ointment — one or more tubes per kit
Cotton-tipped applicators
Elastic wraps (Ace bandages) — Assorted widths
Emergency contact card — one per kit
Eye pads (sterile) — Several per kit
Gauze pads (sterile) — Assorted sizes
Gauze rolls — Assorted widths
Insect sting kit — one per kit
Manual detailing current first aid procedures
Petroleum jelly — one tube per kit
Scissors (bandage or tape style) — one pair per kit
Soap (liquid or aerosol)

Other supplies which should be stored in a central location which is easily accessible to all employees:

Blankets (preferably wool) — two or more
Litters (military type) — two or more
Splints (inflatable air style or padded wood) — Assorted lengths
Triangular bandages — one dozen or more

The third basic aspect of an effective first-aid and emergency care program is that of developing and implementing a formal, policy-based approach to first aid and emergency medical care. When a participant or spectator is injured or becomes ill, it is important that he receives care that is promptly and correctly administered. To accomplish this, it is necessary that each employee not only be trained in first-aid procedures, but also be assigned a specific role to be carried out in the event of an injury or illness in his work area. For example, ushers or pages in a spectator sport facility should be trained in basic first aid prior to being placed on the job. With this training complete, each usher or page should be assigned a specific duty within the emergency care program. Among these role assignments should be: someone to administer primary first-aid care (usually two people); someone to maintain order and decorum among the other spectators or participants who are in the immediate area; and someone to summon assistance from either on-site medical personnel or from a nearby medical facility or ambulance service. While this approach may appear somewhat simplistic and even unnecessary, the delivery of first aid to an injured spectator is too often hampered by the confusion of the moment.

To adequately prepare for effective emergency medical care, the manager of a sport-related facility must establish a positive working relationship with those agencies which will be expected to provide support services in the event of a medical emergency. In most communities, this will include the local law enforcement agency, emergency medical services, area hospital(s) and one or more physicians who may be contacted in time of need. The manager should meet with representatives of each of these support agencies to exchange information with respect to the specific role that each will play in the event of a medical emergency. At this time, the agency representative should be given the opportunity to identify the "normal procedures" of the agency while the facility manager should provide information regarding the program's first-aid and emergency-care protocol. Based on this exchange of information, an agreement should be established which will govern the relationship between the facility and support agency with respect to the specific role of each during a medical emergency. Although the specific nature of this agreement will vary according to the needs and capabilities of both parties, one basic policy should be established. During any spectator event (game, concert, etc.), emergency medical personnel should be on-site to facilitate the immediate handling of any medical emergency. It is also recommended that a physician be present at all events although this may not always be possible.

A simple, yet very important step in providing effective emergency care involves placing "emergency-contact cards" in all first-aid kits and beside all business telephones. An "emergency-contact card" is simply a small index card which contains telephone numbers which are needed in a time of medical emergency.

EMERGENCY CONTACT CARD

Ambulance: Triad Ambulance Service 555-1234
      Metro EMS Service 555-5678

Physician: Dr. John Smith (O) 555-1357
          (H) 555-2468

       or

     Dr. Mary Brown (O) 555-1470
          (H) 555-0369

Hospital: County General 555-1111

In communities where a single emergency code number has been established (e.g., 911), the "emergency contact card" may be simplified to contain only the emergency number and the names and numbers of physicians who may be contacted.

It is virtually impossible to eliminate the risk of sudden illness or injury to spectators and participants. However, it is possible to maximize the quality of emergency care provided through careful planning and the development of a systematic emergency-care plan based on the following recommendations:

1. Require all employees, especially those who work directly with program clientele, to be trained and certified in first aid and cardiopulmonary resuscitation (CPR).

2. Assemble and maintain a complete inventory of first-aid and emergency medical supplies and make these supplies easily accessible to all employees.

3. Establish an "in-house" system for providing first-aid and emergency medical care to program clientele and employees and thoroughly orient all employees with respect to this system and the specific role that each is expected to play.

4. Schedule and conduct emergency-care drills during which all employees are provided the opportunity to practice specific emergency care procedures.

5. Develop, in cooperation with local medical-support agencies and personnel, a systematic plan for emergency care which meets the specific needs of the facility and its programs.

In addition to a standard system of first-aid and emergency medical care, an organization must develop a plan for providing emergency medical care during events at which large crowds will be present. Because of the unique and complex nature of such emergency medical preparedness, this concept will be discussed in detail in a separate chapter.

Sport Injury Management

Organizations such as schools, colleges, and professional and amateur sports teams are expected to provide comprehensive medical and health care services for their athletes. The American Medical Association (AMA) stated in its "Bill of Rights for the School and College Athlete" that, while participation in sports is a privilege, it also involves some basic rights on the part of the athlete. According to the AMA, these fundamental rights include the "right to good health," supervision, a thorough preseason history and medical examination, a physician present at all contests and readily available at all practice sessions and medical control of the health aspects of athletics ("Preface" in Don H. O'Donoghue, *Treatment of Injuries to Athletes,* 4th ed. W.B. Saunders Co., 1984).

Until recently, the responsibility of a school or college to provide adequate medical and health care for its athletes was essentially viewed as a moral or ethical issue. However, the issue of medical and health care for the school or college athlete is now finding its way into the American court room as evidenced by the case of *Gillespie v. Southern Utah State College,* 669 P.2d 861 (Utah, 1983). In this case a college basketball player brought suit against a college, its basketball coach and trainer as the result of an injury he received while playing college basketball and subsequent complications resulting in the loss of a foot. The athlete claimed that the severe-injury complications were a direct result of inadequate sports-medicine care but the jury found that the athlete "was 100% negligent and such negligence was the proximate cause of his injuries." This is merely one example of the increasing frequency of sports medicine litigation and, though no definitive legal precedent has yet been established, it is apparent that schools and colleges do have some legal obligation to their athletes with respect to the availability of quality medical and health care.

Regardless of an organization's legal responsibility to its athletes, there also exists a moral and ethical obligation to provide for the health and well-being of those who represent a school, college or organization on the athletic field. This obligation not only involves the availability of qualified, on-site medical and health care personnel, but also the provision of adequate health care facilities, quality supervision and instruction, and playing conditions which promote safe participation. In short, every sports participant should be afforded the opportunity to take part in the activity of his choice with the knowledge that everything possible has been done to assure that his participation will be safe as well as enjoyable and that, in the event of an injury, he will receive immediate and effective care.

Recognition of the responsibility to provide adequate medical and health care is only the first step toward making such services available. Too often, this aspect of the total program is viewed as a "frill" or luxury. Therefore, there may be little or no planning with respect to such critical issues as the identification and utilization of qualified personnel, formal program organization and the design and utilization of adequate medical and health care facilities.

Personnel — "The Team Approach"

It has often been said that "everybody's business is nobody's business." Unfortunately, this statement accurately describes the manner in which many organizations approach the issue of providing qualified medical and health-care personnel within the total sport program. The high school or college coach may be required to not only perform his coaching duties, but also to care for the injuries sustained by his (and frequently other) athletes. Quite often, the responsibility for injury care is shared by the entire coaching staff and the issue suddenly becomes "everybody's business." In situations where personnel organization is allowed to develop according to the dictates of day-to-day needs, there is likely to be a serious lack of quality medical and health care for the participants. Even in those programs in which there is a "team physician" or "school physician" available, the absence of qualified on-site personnel (e.g., a certified athletic trainer) and the lack of a formal organizational plan for the delivery of medical and health care services will usually result in less than optimal medical and health care.

Medical and health care for sport participants may be most effectively rendered when there is a "team" of qualified professionals functioning cooperatively with the health and well-being of the participants as their common goal. While the specific composition of the "sports medicine team "may vary according to the unique needs of the organization and its Programs, three specific persons are considered essential if effective sports medicine services are to be delivered: an administrative coordinator (athletic director, sports medicine coordinator, etc.), a qualified on-site athletic trainer, and a program physician.

The administrative coordinator of a sports-injury management program is basically responsible for such administrative functions as program planning and supervision, budget development and implementation and personnel management. This role may be assumed by any one of a variety of people, depending upon the size and functional nature of the organization. In the small school or college setting, the administrative duties may be effectively handled by either the chief athletic administrator (usually the athletic director) or the head trainer. In the larger, more diverse program, it may be desirable to place administrative responsibilities in the hands of a "sports medicine coordinator," thus relieving the chief athletic administrator and head trainer of these duties. It is recommended that such a coordinator function within the purview of the chief athletic administrator and possess expertise in the areas of program administration and athletic training.

Every sports injury management program should have at least one qualified athletic trainer. This person is generally assigned the title of "Head Trainer" and assumes the primary responsibility for on-site program direction including primary injury care and rehabilitation, day-to-day administrative details and the training and supervision of student assistants. Although not essential, it is strongly recommended (and in some states required) that the head trainer be certified by the National Athletic Trainers Association (NAT) since such certification is considered the standard of professional recognition in the field of athletic training. Criteria for certification may be obtained by contacting the National Athletic Trainers Association, Greenville, North Carolina.

The third member of the "sports medicine team" is the program physician. The "team doctor," as this person is often called, functions cooperatively with the administrative coordinator and head trainer to provide such primary medical services as performing preseason medical examinations, providing consultation and recommendations relative to extended injury care and rehabilitation, providing primary medical treatment for injured athletes, and attending home athletic contests for the purpose of offering on-site injury care and supervision. Needless to say, the program physician must possess an interest in sports medicine and the desire to work, often without compensation, with injured athletes. It would obviously be desirable for the program physician to be a specialist in an area which is related to sports (e.g., orthopedics). However, the most essential qualification for a program physician is a sincere interest and desire to be a member of the "sports medicine team."

The program physician is the only member of the "sports medicine team" who is not generally an employee of the school or organization. Therefore, locating and recruiting an appropriate program physician often proves difficult. The most common method of locating a potential program physician is by identifying those physicians who already have some form of relationship with the organization. The relationship may be geographic (i.e., a physician who lives and practices in the local community), professional (i.e., a physician who is a school or organization board member), or personal (i.e., a physician with friend or family ties to the school or organization).

Once appropriate candidates have been identified, securing the services of a physician for the sports-medicine program will often depend upon the compensatory nature of the position and the duties which the physician will be expected to perform. The issue of compensation for the services of a program physician may be resolved in one of three basic ways. If the organization's budget will allow, the physician may receive monetary compensation for services rendered, usually in the form of a retainer in an amount agreed upon by all parties and specified in a contract. If financial remuneration is not possible, many states will allow institutions to provide a physician with a "gift-in-kind" statement which may be used by the physician as verification of charitable contribution in the form of donated services to the institution. If neither of these forms of compensation are appropriate, the program physician will simply serve as a "volunteer" member of the sports medicine team.

The duties or expectations of a program physician will vary, depending upon the unique needs of each program. However, the program physician is generally expected to provide the following services:

1. Compile and maintain a medical history of each program participant.
2. Conduct preparticipation physician examinations.
3. Attend all games or contests and as many practices as feasible.
4. Supervise and provide instruction to sports medicine personnel.
5. Be available to see injured program participants during regular office hours and provide treatment or referral as deemed appropriate.
6. Be "on call" for the emergency care of injured program participants at times other than during office hours.
7. Make decisions relative to the return to action of injured program participants.
8. Work closely with the other members of the "sports medicine team" in establishing policy and coordinating program activities.

When a program physician has been secured, it is imperative that his relationship with the program be spelled out in an agreement which specifically describes his duties and the form of compensation (if any) which he will receive. A sample agreement appears as Appendix 1 at the end of this chapter.

As programs and needs expand, it may prove desirable to add additional members to the basic "sports medicine team." With the recommendation of the program physician, medical specialists (e.g., orthopedist, dentist, ophthalmologist, etc.) may be included in the "sports medicine team," thus enhancing the specific services which may be provided.

Organization

All successful sports medicine programs share one common characteristic — they are well organized. Unfortunately, effective organization is not something that "just happens," but rather is the result of diligent planning and a commitment to excellence.

Several factors influence organizational success. Three factors which are critical, yet often overlooked are: the development and utilization of a formal organizational model; the establishment of policies within which the program will function; and the implementation of a system of record-keeping which will facilitate and document communication among the members of the "sports medicine team," players, coaches, and others with whom formal communication is carried on.

A formal organizational model or chart delineates the relative relationship among the various persons within the sports medicine program. The specific pattern or organization will depend upon the precise needs of the organization itself. A "Sample Organizational Model" for a small college is presented as Appendix 2 at the end of this chapter.

Without a formal organizational plan, the sports medicine program will not function as effectively as desired. At best, it will become a group of individuals, each performing the duties that he deems appropriate, inevitably resulting in a duplication in some services and a complete absence of others.

As with any organization, the sports medicine program should function according to preestablished policies. Such policies should be developed as the result of cooperative planning by the "sports medicine team," and should reflect the specific functional needs of the program. Policies should be written and implemented with respect to standard injury care and physician referral procedures, the transportation of injured athletes to and from hospitals and other medical facilities, the operation of the training room, the processing of insurance claims and other records and the specific responsibilities of staff members. These policies should be compiled and placed in a policy manual or handbook, and made available to every person involved in the program.

Record-keeping

One of the most vital concepts in program organization is that of record keeping and its influence on organizational communication. Communication is often classified as "formal," the exchange of important information or ideas that require written documentation and "informal," the exchange of less important information which requires no written documentation. Most of the communication within the sports medicine program is sufficiently important to be considered "formal" in nature, yet too often is carried out verbally. For example, an athlete or student trainer carries verbal messages from the head trainer to a physician or coach, often resulting in misunderstanding. If left unresolved, such misunderstanding may jeopardize the relationship which is essential among administrators, trainers, physicians, players and coaches. Effective record-keeping will help to alleviate many of the problems which may result from poor organizational communication.

Record forms are highly personalized communication vehicles. Therefore, it is necessary to design forms which reflect the unique needs of each program. Some typical forms are described below but it should be noted that these are presented merely for the purpose of illustration.

An essential instrument is the injury-report form (see Appendix 3 at the end of this chapter). The purpose of the injury-report form is to maximize the exchange of information among all of the parties involved in the injury management process. While a form of this type may be printed as a single sheet of paper, it is highly recommended that it be a multicopy (carbon or carbonless) instrument so that each person in the injury management process may retain a copy of the form for future reference. For example, if the form is prepared in four parts, it may be used in the following manner. After completing and signing the top portion of the form, the athlete would be given the top three copies to take with him to the attending physician. The back copy would be retained in the training room as verification that the form had been sent with the athlete to the physician. The physician would then be asked to complete the lower portion of the form based upon his evaluation of the injury and to retain the back copy for his records. The athlete would then return the two remaining copies of the form to the training room where one would be filed and the other included with any insurance claim which might be submitted.

Some of the features of this specific form which enhance its effectiveness are the multiple-copy nature of the form which provides written verification for all principal parties, the athlete's signature verifying the circumstances under which the injury occurred and the immediate care provided, and the physician's written evaluation and recommendation relative to the severity of the injury, appropriate rehabilitation and post-injury return to activity. This information may then be shared with the appropriate coach.

Since communication between the sports medicine program and the members of the coaching staff is critical to the success of both programs, the final form presented here is one designed specifically to facilitate trainer-coach communication. The injury-care recommendation form may be used to provide a written record for the coach, the sports medicine staff, and the athlete's injury file concerning any injury which will require the athlete to discontinue or alter his normal practice or same routine. Constructed as a three-part form approximately the size of a small index card, this form contains information relative to the precise nature of the injury in question, recommended procedures for caring for that injury, and the athlete's status relative to return to activity. (See Appendix 4 at the end of this chapter.) When the form has been completed and signed by the head trainer, the back copy would be given directly to the appropriate coach, providing him with a concise, written statement which answers three important questions; "What is the injury?", "How will it be cared for?" and "When and under what conditions can the athlete return to play?" The second copy of the form may be posted in the training room as a written guide for staff members in caring for the injury. The original copy of the form may be placed in the athlete's injury file for future reference. A form of this nature not only enhances communication between members of the sports medicine staff and members of the coaching staff, but also provides written documentation of staff and/or physician recommendation should future questions arise.

Although effective record-keeping requires a significant amount of time and effort, the benefits of improved program communication are well worth the time and effort invested. However, to reap these benefits, the "sports medicine team" must analyze the needs of the program and design and utilize record keeping systems which will best meet those needs.

Facilities

To a great extent, the quality of medical and health care that an organization may provide its athletes is determined by the quality of facilities utilized for this purpose. As with previous factors which have been discussed, the specific size and type of injury care facilities will depend upon the nature and scope of the programs it is expected to serve. It is not the purpose of this chapter to present a detailed discussion of facility and equipment specifications since such information is readily available in several sports medicine texts. However, it should be emphasized that all facility planning should include the direct input of all members of the "sports medicine team."

Summary/Conclusion

The manager in a sport-related organization, whether it be a spectator entertainment facility, a community recreation center, or a high school or college athletic department, assumes the direct responsibility for the health and well-being of his clientele. Therefore, every effort should be made to develop and maintain a program of medical services which will ensure the health and well-being of those he serves.

Appendix 1

Physician's Agreement

STATE OF ...)
)   PHYSICIAN'S AGREEMENT
CITY/COUNTY)
OF ....)

THIS AGREEMENT made and entered into the..day of ... 1982, by and between ....., a college having its principal place of business in ....., (hereinafter referred to as "College"), and Dr ...., a citizen and resident of .... (hereinafter referred to as "Physician").

WITNESSETH:

WHEREAS, College is desirous obtaining the services of Physician in connection with its......program, and

WHEREAS, Physician is skilled in the practice of orthopedic medicine (or other specialty) and is willing to assist College with its orthopedic (or other medical) problems in its .... program,

NOW, THEREFORE, in consideration of the covenants and promises contained herein, the parties hereto agree as follows:

1. College hereby retains and Physician agrees to be retained by College as College's orthopedic (or general medical) consultant in College's .... program for the school year 19. .-. .

2. Physician will act as a consultant with the College's coaches, trainers, athletes and other personnel with regard to orthopedic (or other) medical problems incurred by athletes in the College's .... program. Physician's consulting services shall include the attendance of all of College's games, a schedule of which is attached hereto and incorporated herein by reference, and shall also attend all scrimmages as scheduled from time to time by College, notice of which shall be given to Physician not less than 48 hours prior to such scrimmage. Physician shall also attendall/none of College's other practice sessions, excluding scrimmages, during the term of this agreement.

3. Physician shall make recommendations to the coaching staff, trainers, and other personnel as to the handling of all orthopedic (or other medical) matters with regard to the athletes in College's ..... program. Such recommendations shall include prescribing treatment for injuries and other orthopedic (or medical) problems, and recommendations for surgical and other hospital procedures when necessary. All physician charges for such surgery and other hospital procedures are not covered under the terms of this agreement.

4. As compensation for all consulting services rendered hereunder, College agrees to pay to Physician the sum of $ .... to be paid upon the execution of this agreement.

5. It is understood and agreed that Physician is an independent contractor with regard to all consulting services to be rendered hereunder, and is not acting as College's agent, employee or servant. [Optional: It is also understood that Physician is not an insurer of results in any medical treatment rendered under the terms of this agreement.]

6. This agreement is to be construed under and governed by the laws of the State of.......

IN WITNESS WHEREOF, the parties hereto have executed this agreement in duplicate originals on the day and year first above written.

      ...... College

      By:_____

      Dr...

      By:_____

Appendix 2

Sample Organizational Model

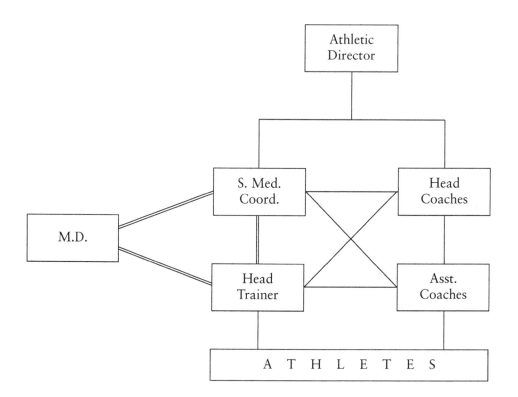

Appendix 3

Injury Report

INJURY REPORT FROM ATHLETIC TRAINER TO PHYSICIAN

Name: Sport: School:

Date of Report: Date of Injury:

Person Completing Report:

          (Athletic Trainer)   (Title)   (Phone)

Body Part Injured:

Mechanism of Injury (How? What Happened?):

Physical Findings:
Tentative Diagnosis:
Immediate Care:
Comments:

Follow Up: ☐ Physician Visit And/Or X-Rays Recommended

                ☐ Physician Visit Not Recommended

_____   _____
(Athlete's Signature)   (Trainer's Signature)

INJURY REPORT FROM PHYSICIAN TO ATHLETIC TRAINER

Name: Sport: School:

Diagnosis:
Treatment/Rehabilitation Program:

Copy of Specific Program Enclosed: Yes   No

Estimated Time Loss:

Follow Up: ☐ Must see me/another physician prior to return to practice and/or competition.

            ☐ May be checked by athletic trainer in lieu of visit to a physician.

            ☐ May return to practice and/or competition upon successful *completion* of the treatment/rehabilitation program specified above.

            ☐ May return to practice and/or competition immediately with the following modifications:

Comments:

_____   _____   _____
(Physician's Signature)   (Date)   (Phone)

Note: Keep pink copy for your records and return all other copies with the athlete.

Appendix 4

Injury Care Recommendation

INJURY CARE RECOMMENDATION

Name: Sport:
Date: Injury:
Recommended care:

☐ May continue regular activity
☐ Should modify activity as follows:

☐ Must see me prior to return to activity:
☐ Other:

_____
(Doctor's signature)

Chapter 9

Emergency Medical Services for Large Crowds

Chester Lloyd

Introduction

As the football crowd grows anxious during the end of the second half of the season's last game, a middle-aged spectator clutches his chest, moans and falls backward into his seat. His wife and friends attempt to revive him, but he doesn't respond—heartbeat and breathing have ceased. If he is to have a chance at surviving the heart attack trained help must arrive shortly.

When incidents such as this occur at home, we pick up the phone and dial our local emergency medical service. But when life-threatening emergencies occur in a crowd, the public is often at the mercy of the facility for providing a planned, organized and rapid response to its emergency medical needs.

Duty to Provide an Emergency Medical Capability

Numerous studies have shown that medical emergencies occur with some frequency at large gatherings. One such study reviewed injury and illness data collected over four football seasons at a stadium with a capacity of 75,000 (Ref. 1). The results showed that an average of 5.23 patients (2.83-8.00 patient range) where seen by stadium emergency medical teams per 10,000 spectators during a four-hour game. Using this data, the facility could foresee from 21-60 medical or traumatic incidents per game. In addition, the stadium or arena environment may foster more medical emergencies than those expected in the general population, because many spectators gulp down "tailgate dinners," imbibe alcoholic beverages and then rush up 100 steps to their seats. For some, this type of activity is the ultimate stress test which increases the risk for cardiac problems.

Facility managers have a legal duty to protect and warn spectators of foreseeable hazards and harms. If medical emergencies and injuries which are foreseen in large crowd situations are not handled properly through an organized emergency medical response system, the spectator may suffer additional harm. Harm results from improper emergency management causing aggravation of the acute illness or injury.

Standards and Guidelines Specify the Scope of Treatments

The American Heart Association (AHA) sponsored a conference in 1979 to update standards for emergency cardiac care that were originally developed in 1973 by the AHA and the National Academy of Sciences—National Research Council. Based upon medical research and reports during the 1970s, special recommendations were made for facilities where large crowds are regularly present or can reasonably be anticipated. In such facilities, the recommendations call for a basic cardiac life support capability to be available in 60 seconds or less and an advanced cardiac life support capability within ten minutes, preferably less (Ref. 2).

Basic cardiac life support prevents circulatory and respiratory arrest via prompt recognition and intervention in cardiac and respiratory emergencies. This level of emergency cardiac care also provides for mouth-to-mouth breathing and chest compression (Cardiopulmonary Resuscitation—(CPR)) should breathing and heart stop. This procedure keeps the vital organs alive since the rescuer acts as the victim's heart and lungs. This procedure can be learned in 4 to 12 hours.

Advanced cardiac life support includes basic life support and elements of cardiac care that require more specialized training. Doctors, nurses and paramedics may provide this type of care which consists of administration of lifesaving drugs and defibrillation of the heart in an attempt to stimulate the heart back into action.

When basic cardiac care is initiated and followed quickly by advanced cardiac care, 80% of those spectators who suffer respiratory and circulatory arrest (sudden death) may survive. This is the basis for the special recommendations. If CPR is not provided to a pulseless and non-breathing patient, after four minutes, irreversible brain death starts to occur. When CPR is provided rapidly but advanced cardiac care is delayed, survivability will be low. The 1979 American Heart Association Standards and Guidelines go on to state that "failure of a facility to provide such a readily achievable lifesaving capability (following the special recommendations) may be found to represent legally actionable negligence," It is known that standards distributed by professional societies, such as the American Heart Association, are likely to be viewed as evidence of the accepted standard of medical care by the courts.

During the AHA conference, much attention was given to "cardiac care." While fractures and other acute injuries and illnesses are important, heart disease is the number one killer in this country. More than half of these deaths occur outside the hospital and many could be prevented through a rapid emergency medical response. If the facility can respond appropriately to a "sudden cardiac death" emergency, other emergencies, many of them not as urgent, will be handled effectively as well. It is important to note that those capable of specialized training in advanced cardiac care usually have the, .capability to treat other medical and trauma emergencies.

Other Facilities and State Laws May Dictate Level of Care

Many facilities which attract large crowds have programs that provide emergency medical systems, Other facilities may be judged by the standards set by such facilities.

Some states have laws relating to emergency medical care at mass gatherings. These laws address numbers of personnel, training, length and type of the event, equipment, and crowd size. Some laws seem impractical because they do not ensure basic and advanced cardiac care according to Heart Association Standards. For example, Connecticut law requires that any gathering of 3,000 persons or more lasting for 18 consecutive hours must provide one physician per 1,000 people (Ref. 3). In addition, stadiums, athletic fields, arenas, auditoriums, coliseums or other permanently established places of assembly are exempt from this law. The law is probably never used with the exception of a state fair or outdoor music festival. On the rare occasion the law is applied, the physician requirement is not practical and is expensive.

It is important to note that whether a state law addresses emergency medical responses or not, a facility may still be held to other standards of medical care. These standards include the Heart Association's standards and those set by other large-capacity facilities nationally.

The Emergency Medical System in Action

Returning to the football game, the following scenario will suggest how a fictitious large-capacity stadium would likely handle medical emergencies,

After the victim's wife shook him with no response, she had to summon aid. She remembered reading the notice which came with her season ticket and which was announced over the loudspeaker at each event. "In case of medical emergency, please notify the nearest usher, police officer or emergency medical team." She had her friend run to the nearest usher to request medical aid.

The usher's orange vest made him clearly visible to the crowd. In addition, he was trained to concentrate on the crowd and not the game. When notified of the emergency, he knew how to react. His facility's emergency medical system had provided him with CPR training, written guidelines and practice in approaching medical emergencies.

On his portable radio, he notified the central communications center of a medical emergency in section L, row 25. He approached the victim and after a quick assessment notified the communications booth that he had a spectator who was not breathing and had no pulse. As he had learned from frequent drills, he positioned the victim across the bench with the help of another usher and provided CPR.

Central communications immediately dispatched a team of emergency medical technicians (EMTs) covering that sector of the crowd. The technicians had taken an 80 to 120 hour course covering the management of medical and trauma emergencies which was used as the ambulance training program for the state. This facility provided experienced EMTs to stabilize and then evacuate victims of medical trauma emergencies from the spectator area.

The communications center also notified the physician and both nurses in the emergency life-support station closest to that area of the stadium. While one nurse readied the station for receiving the patient, the physician and other nurse responded to the incident with advanced cardiac care equipment via a golf cart modified to serve as a "mini" ambulance.

Through the communications center other ushers and public safety personnel (police, security, etc.) were alerted for crowd control. Since all radio messages were coordinated through one central point, all facility public-safety and medical personnel were notified of the emergency and acted as per a planned, clear and concise protocol. Some responded to the incident, others filled in areas left vacant by those responding to the victim and the remaining public safety staff were alerted that resources for a particular area were busy and to be prepared to provide coverage to other areas as well as their own. The emergency medical-system coordinator, the security chief, the head usher and other administrative personnel were present in the center to help coordinate the response.

Shortly after the ushers started CPR, the team of two EMTs arrived with oxygen and a special patient litter to facilitate safe evacuation. The team continued CPR but provided ventilation to the victim now using the much needed oxygen. The team prepared the victim for transportation to the waiting golf cart just outside the section L entrance.

In order for the patient to receive advanced cardiac care as soon as possible, the physician and nurse, both proficient in emergency medicine, met the EMTs with the cart and administered the initial steps of advanced cardiac care. Basic cardiac care, now supplemented by advanced cardiac care, was continued en route to the life support station.

At the station, which offered a more controlled environment and an additional complement of life-saving drugs and equipment, the patient's heart resumed beating after a few rounds of treatment. The physician-in-charge relayed the details of the patient's condition and treatment to the local hospital via the telephone so they could prepare to receive the patient. After the victim's condition stabilized, he was transferred to the local hospital by one of the three ambulances stationed at the stadium. One ambulance was on the playing field solely for the participants, the other two were parked outside the life-support units on each side of the stadium for spectator emergencies. By having an ambulance near a station, the risk of hitting spectators on crowded walks and drives was lessened considerably.

The entire incident, from the initial call for help to hospital admission, was thoroughly documented by written reports. The EMTs, being licensed and responsible for basic cardiac care, documented their treatment which also specified that ushers were doing resuscitation. This report and the physician's documentation of advanced care were kept on file for legal purposes and follow-up evaluation.

In summary, a heart-attack victim was given a second chance at life because the facility's emergency medical system was planned and organized around the goal of rapid basic (within 60 seconds) and advanced (in less than 10 minutes) cardiac care. Coordination through experienced leadership and interagency cooperation was responsible for meeting this goal.

Planning for Emergency Medical Response

Plan on-site, emergency medical-response system by structuring the system around the following elements.

A. Public Access to Emergency Medical Aid

1. Provide and train public safety officers, ushers, vendors and other facility personnel who know how to promptly summon medical aid.
2. Place emergency medical teams strategically throughout the crowd (coverage in parking areas before/after events).
3. Clearly mark emergency life support units (medical aid stations) and place them in highly visible locations.
4. Use printed programs and season-ticket package inserts to identify locations of emergency life-support units (so those with minor ailments know where to seek aid) and briefly describe how to summon help (for medical and trauma emergencies requiring evacuation by emergency medical teams).
5. Use public address announcements such as: "In the case of emergency, notify your nearest usher, police officer or emergency medical team."
6. Install public emergency phones or video monitors on exit ramps, stairways or other hard-to-monitor areas of the facility.
7. Provide emergency signs, done professionally, and targeted to the facility and crowd characteristics.

B. Personnel and Training

1. Provide all non-medical personnel with guidelines on how to react in medical emergencies.
2. Train non-medical personnel (ushers and security) in basic cardiac life support (CPR).
3. Staff emergency medical teams with emergency medical technicians.
4. Staff emergency life support units with personnel capable of providing advanced cardiac life support (paramedics, nurses or physicians).
5. Provide an adequate number of public safety personnel based upon the size of the crowd, crowd make-up, facility lay-out, environment, event-type, general vs. reserved admission and past injury and illness experience.
6. Arrange for ambulance transportation by a competent service after patient stabilization in the emergency life-support unit; if outside ambulance service provides on-site ambulances, get proof that personnel are properly trained.
7. Utilize periodic drills to test the effectiveness of the emergency medical system and update the skills of facility personnel.

C. Central Communications Center

1. Coordinate all public-safety communications (medical, security, crowd control, etc.) through a central post allowing for rapid relay of emergency messages.
2. Link emergency medical teams to each other and a central post via portable radios or other means.
3. Develop the capability of non-medical personnel to notify the central post (via radio, intercom or phone) to request emergency medical assistance.
4. Place supervisory public safety and administrative personnel in center to troubleshoot problems.
5. Locate the center preferably in press box or other location which allows view of as much of the facility as possible.

D. Written Protocols and Guidelines

1. Make certain that all non-medical personnel understand written guidelines defining their specific roles in medical emergencies (i.e., who to call or what actions to take before medical teams arrive)
2. Provide the medical staff with written treatment protocols signed by the physician medical director covering all phases of patient treatment in the facility.
3. Develop plans that address actions to be taken when heavy patient load or simultaneous emergencies occur.
4. Coordinate mutual aid agreements and disaster plans with outside public safety agencies in case of heavy patient load or catastrophe.
5. Provide written protocols to demonstrate that the facility and its staff are prepared for medical and trauma emergencies should litigation arise.

E. Record-Keeping

1. Document all emergency treatment rendered at the facility in writing.
2. Include in the record: The patient's name, sex, age, address, next-of-kin; nature of the illness or injuries and a description or the mechanism of how the injuries occurred; location and how the patient was found (i.e., lying face down, sitting, etc.); the chief complaint or signs and symptoms displayed by the patient; vital signs; patient's past medical history, current medications and known allergies to any medications; all treatment rendered by facility personnel (treatment rendered by other persons prior to medical team arrival should be noted, too); how the victim was transported to the emergency life support unit (stretcher, walked, etc.); disposition of the patient (to hospital via ambulance, referred to private physician, etc.); and data such as time call received, date, names of team members and who made the initial call for help.
3. If possible, obtain a signed refusal of medical treatment from any sick or injured person refusing medical assistance.
4. At the emergency life support station keep a log of all patients seen by name, injury or illness complaint and time.

5. Utilize complete records to prevent or defend charges of negligence.
6. Review records retrospectively to prevent future injuries by identifying hazards as well as crowds and events at high risk for problems.
7. Review records to assess emergency medical program effectiveness.

F. Equipment

1. Provide adequate communications devices which permit clear signal reception in all areas of the facility.
2. Equip emergency medical teams (comprised of EMTs) with oxygen and other "tools of their trade."
3. Provide specialized patient litters for safe evacuation from the spectator area and provide a wheeled cart or other device for transport to the emergency life support unit.
4. Provide emergency life support units with state-of-the-art equipment for advanced cardiac life support and other medical and trauma emergencies.
5. Provide on-site ambulances properly equipped as per state and local laws.

G. Physician Medical Director

1. Responsible for all medical treatment given by a facility's emergency medical personnel.
2. Experienced in emergency medicine.

H. Administrative Coordinator

1. Responsible for the overall operation and management of the emergency medical response system.
2. Prepares written protocols and guidelines with the medical director as well as mutual aid and disaster plans with outside public safety agencies.
3. Experienced in emergency medical operations.
4. Probably the most important person in determining the success and cost-effectiveness of the facility's emergency medical program.

These eight elements are guidelines that will help assess present methods for handling medical emergencies or in constructing a new emergency medical system. Pay particular attention to items G and H. The coordinator and medical director should oversee the entire program. Specifically, the coordinator serves as the link between all agencies and should be available during events in the communications center. Whether the coordinator's position is full-time, part-time or assigned to an existing staff member depends on the facility size and event traffic.

A consultant knowledgeable in emergency medical operations at large gatherings may be used to evaluate and prepare an emergency medical system for a facility. In preparing a system, the consultant may identify community resources (personnel, equipment, etc.), evaluate local and state laws, develop training programs, review facility insurance coverage (relating to the emergency medical program), and give advice on crowd management and facility safety. A consultant can also instruct a facility manager in emergency medical-program maintenance and can be available for future planning. Using a consultant to develop a program to fit a facility may save time and reduces the chance for costly error.

A coordinator or consultant should select a physician medical director with knowledge of emergency medical response. This physician should underwrite all medical protocol and treatment given by the facility medical staff. To illustrate, a facility may request a physician from the local medical center's emergency department to serve as the director. If he agrees, for a stipend or as a service of the medical center, he and the coordinator would draw up treatment procedures addressing the scope of medical care provided in the facility. Only treatment provided for in writing, signed by this physician, may be given. Even if aspirins are dispensed by facility nurses, written protocol, signed by the physician should specifically define under what conditions and to whom aspirin should be provided. Whether the medical director attends each event or not, all medical treatment is carried out under his initial written protocol. The medical director, in cooperation with the coordinator, will want to certify that all medical personnel are competent. Should litigation arise, treatment protocol shows the courts that medical treatment provided at the facility followed the accepted standard of medical care and was given under the direction of the facility's physician medical director.

In planning a system, facility managers should use caution if they depend on outside agencies for on-site emergency medical needs. In a true account, while city ambulances and paramedics sped away from a stadium of 50,000 spectators to respond to a serious auto accident, a spectator with a medical emergency was without transportation to the hospital. Finally, a station wagon-type vehicle was used because no ambulances would be available for some time. Fortunately, the facility had an on-site emergency medical system which attended to the victim. In this case, it would have been prudent for the facility to require that the ambulance contractor commit the ambulances to the facility from one hour before to one hour after the game.

If hospitals or ambulances are next door, the emergency medical response system should still be planned as if the facility were across town. Remember that the rescue vehicles may be out on other calls and a hospital's emergency department staff usually is not available to come to the facility. Consider too that ambulance crews stationed outside the entrance may have long response times trying to get through the crowds. Only with the emergency medical personnel and the emergency life-support station(s) placed strategically throughout the crowd and the facility, along with other facility personnel knowing their roles in emergencies, can the public be assured of rapid access to emergency medical help. The days of the simple first-aid station are gone. Today, having enough people on-hand under one roof or in a confined area to populate a small city is quite a responsibility.

Liability insurance covering the facility should be reviewed when implementing the emergency medical program. Since the type of coverage depends upon the individual facility and insurance company, facility administrators should seek advice from their insurer or consultant.

Emergency medical technicians, paramedics, nurses and physicians are all state-licensed health professionals. Even though they may have liability insurance, a facility should have its own liability insurance policy. Ushers; security and other ancillary personnel who are trained in CPR or first aid will usually be covered under the facility's general-liability policy which may include an incidental malpractice clause covering personnel in the event they assist the medical teams with CPR or other basic procedure. Since it is not their specific duty to provide medical treatment at the facility, and provided they are not licensed health professionals, they do not need medical malpractice insurance.

In regard to outside ambulance companies contracted to provide transportation to the hospital or additional personnel, the facility should be named as an additional insured on the ambulance company's insurance policies. The facility should also check on the limits of such policies. All ambulance staff and vehicles should be checked to make sure they comply with state and local laws.

The argument has been made that having personnel with little or no training may be "safer" than having licensed professionals. This is not a valid argument because in court the facility with the documented and functioning emergency medical system in place will be better able to defend charges of negligence. The only loss may be that of the lawyer's fees. But without an emergency medical program, loss in the form of claims may be more because of damage done to a victim by inexperienced and untrained rescuers in an environment that called for trained professionals. Even the "Good Samaritan laws" are being challenged because victims need protection too.

In summary, plan your program around the eight guidelines to achieve a "tiered" emergency medical response; provide basic cardiac care initially using ushers or security personnel and continue with teams of emergency medical technicians who transfer the patient to an on-site life support station where advanced cardiac care may be provided under the direction of a physician.

Program Complexity

Every facility, large or small, should have a plan of action for medical emergencies and the capability of rendering basic cardiac care. The question of program complexity deals primarily with the provision of advanced cardiac care. The responsibility to provide advanced cardiac care is not clear-cut when dealing with facilities which attract moderate-sized crowds (1-10,000 spectators). Whether advanced care should be provided at these facilities or events may depend upon: event length and type (rock concert vs. musical), crowd type (age, emotion, etc.), a facility's or event's past illness and injury record, weather (i.e., warm weather often results in more medical incidents), and medical (personnel, equipment, etc.) and financial resources.

The special recommendations from the Heart Association do not define an absolute crowd size when dealing with the provision of advanced cardiac care for a "large gathering." If a facility attracts 40,000 per event, advanced cardiac care should be made available without reservation. But in planning a system for a facility with 7,000 (for example) in regular attendance, the decision to provide advanced care on-site may weigh on a facility audit addressing the factors listed above and other considerations which may surface during the investigation.

To illustrate, New York State's Mass Gathering Law requires a physician onsite at any public function with 25,000 or more in attendance. If a facility in New York was expecting 7,000 "60-and-over folks" for a "senior olympics," a reasonable and prudent facility manager would do well to exceed the law and provide advanced cardiac care. If a person suffered a heart attack and was unable to be revived with basic cardiac care alone, considering the event and the type of crowd, a lawyer might argue that medical emergencies were foreseeable and the facility should have followed the Heart Association's recommendations.

As a distant alternative to on-site advanced care personnel in small facilities, a "life-support kit" carrying some essential resuscitation equipment may be kept and maintained at the facility in the event that physicians in the crowd are willing to help. The kit would have to be checked and restocked periodically with a physician's order. Facilities should take care and make sure those who offer to provide treatment with the kit are licensed physicians.

Summary/Conclusion — Program Benefits

Although there is initial expense for such a program, costs can be kept low depending upon existing facility and community resources. At a university, volunteer student EMTs may supplement a paid local staff. Equipment may be borrowed from university agencies or local service groups, such as the Red Cross or the local disaster agency. Having all agencies sit down after events to critique and improve public safety is not expensive. A facility's emergency response capabilities can be improved greatly through education, coordination and interagency cooperation.

At facilities hosting sporting events, a spectator emergency medical system will benefit athletes by making available to them the most up-to-date emergency treatment procedures. In certain facilities across the nation, spectators receive much more advanced emergency treatment than athletes simply because the athletic field is often the trainers' and coaches' domain and, except in extreme situations, off-limits to facility emergency medical teams. An experienced emergency medical technician or emergency physician should serve not to replace the trainer or team physician, but could offer valuable advice in handling emergencies on the field. After witnessing players being removed from the playing fields with unstable fractures which did not receive immobilization, or upon reading about a marathoner who was unable to find emergency medical aid when suffering heat exhaustion during her 20th mile, it is evident that athletes would gain advantages in spectator emergency medical plans.

Through rapid detection and prompt intervention of medical emergencies, the emergency medical system helps manage crowd confusion and promotes good public relations. In addition, facility safety hazards may be decreased by thorough review of well-documented injury reports. Most important, state-of-the-art emergency medical treatment, delivered by a trained staff, in a well organized and controlled emergency medical system, will save lives aid reduce risk and the chances for liability.

References

1. T. Demetri Vacalis, Ph.D., and J. Blewett, M.D. (1981). "An Advanced Emergency Medical Care System at the University of Texas Football Stadium," *Journal of the American College Health Association* 30 (December), 145-147.

2. 1979 National Conference on Cardiopulmonary Resuscitation and Emergency Cardiac Care (1980). "Standards and Guidelines for Cardiopulmonary Resuscitation (CPR) and Emergency Cardiac Care (ECC)," *Journal of the American Medical Association* 244 (5, August 1), 453-509.

3. Connecticut Public Health Code (1980). § 19-549, Mass Gathering Law.

Part 3

Marketing Management

As more attention has been placed on the management and marketing of sport by the general public and by the mass media, new approaches to marketing sports have become necessary

Bernard Mullin

Chapter 10

Characteristics of Sport Marketing

Bernard Mullin

Introduction

Sport marketing is probably the most exciting and dynamic area in sports management because it encompasses pricing the product, scaling the house, developing full season, partial season, and group plans, full promotion, advertising, selling and public relations. It is the management function where the product meets the consumer, and as rapidly as consumer tastes change, so must marketing strategies. Given the explosion in interest in sport marketing, it is hard to imagine why so little attention has been given to the marketing of sport for so much of its history. Nowhere is this more evident than the aggressive effort put forth by the Los Angeles Olympic Organizing Committee (LAOOC) for the 1984 Summer games, contrasted with the marketing efforts of earlier games. In 1998 the Women's World Cup Soccer tournament equally revealed the changing playing field of sport marketing. The LAOOC, for the first time in the history of the Olympic Games, made a profit and presented games which did not cost the taxpayers of the host city for years afterwards, as occurred in Montreal after the 1976 Olympics. The LAOOC effort, and in particular the efforts of Peter Ueberroth, coming in on the heels of 20 years of build-up in the activity level of sport marketers and an ever-increasing involvement in the promotion and sponsorship of sport by corporations from business and industry. Over the same time period, the print and broadcast media have markedly increased their coverage of sport, and the electronic media has provided sport organizations with multi-billion dollar broadcast contracts that swamp revenue from operating income. Landmark legal cases involving franchise movement and the control of rights to broadcast sports events have totally changed normal business practices. Concurrently less publicized and seemingly less traumatic events have been occurring in the participant sport segments of the sport industry. New sports may have come and gone, but participant-sport consumers have totally changed their desires, and competition for the sport consumer's dollar has intensified to a level never experienced before. Witness the X-Games and Gravity Games concept which did not exist in the early 1990s.

As more attention was placed on the management and marketing of sport by the general public and by the mass media, new approaches to marketing sport became necessary and this was acknowledged over 20 years ago (Ref. 1). As a result a new breed of professionals entered the field, and a new discipline called sports marketing began to emerge.

Sport Marketing Defined

The term "sports marketing" was coined by the Advertising Age in 1978 to describe the activities of consumer and industrial product and service marketers who were increasingly using sport as a promotional vehicle (Ref. 2). Since that time the term gained wide acceptance. Unfortunately, the media has tended to perpetuate its association with just one small portion of sport marketing activities, marketing, using sport as a promotional vehicle.

Not only is this conception of the term extremely limited, it is totally inappropriate because it fails to recognize the dominant portion of sport marketing, which is the marketing of sport products/events and services. A further less than desirable factor is that the use of sports (plural) rather than sport (singular) reinforces the view of the sport industry as a diverse and uncoordinated series of segments which have little commonality. There is little doubt that each segment of the sport industry does currently operate independently and with minimal sharing of managerial practice. However, if standardized management and marketing practice is ever to come to the sport industry then the industry segments need to be treated as a homogeneous entity. Use of sport (singular) is important therefore in communicating this concept when associated with the terms sport marketing and sport management.

In an earlier work, the author defined sport marketing using an accepted definition of marketing as a basis "Sport marketing consists of all activities designed to meet the needs and wants of sport consumers primary, secondary and tertiary participants and primary, secondary and tertiary spectators through exchange processes. Sport marketing therefore has developed two major thrusts: a. the marketing of sport products and services to consumers of sport; and b. marketing using sport as a promotional vehicle for consumer and industrial products and services" (Ref. 3).

Primary participants are those playing the sport; secondary participants are officials, umpires, etc.; and tertiary participants are such persons as broadcasters, P.A. announcers, etc. or possibly individuals gambling on the event. Primary spectators are those watching the event in person; secondary spectators are those consuming the event via the media, (television, radio, newspaper, magazine, etc.), and tertiary spectators are those who experience the sport product indirectly (for example, verbally from primary or secondary spectators or participants). It would also include indirect association with a sport or sport franchise, such as purchasing sport merchandise and souvenirs.

Given the overall focus of this text as a guide for practitioners managing and marketing sport, this chapter will concentrate on the primary thrust of marketing sport products and services, rather than marketing using sport. First, the unique aspects of sport marketing that warrant a distinct approach from regular consumer/industrial product and service marketing are analyzed. Second, through illustrations from diverse segments of the sport industry, a case is made for treating the industry as a single, homogeneous entity requiring essentially similar marketing treatment for each segment. Such a concept should not be that difficult to accept. Simply stated it contends that whether the goal is to fill a stadium (this has been rather crudely but effectively summarized as "putting meat in the seats"), or getting more members to join a fitness or health club or to get more people skiing (the author has termed this, "getting feet on the streets"), the factors which set each aside from general business are present, yet there is enough consistency to warrant a common approach.

Finally, but of greatest practical value, this chapter outlines forgotten elements of marketing (market research and the marketing information system) which must be considered by sport. marketers before making any of the marketing mix decisions (product, price, promotion, publicity and distribution (place)). These factors provide the critical foundation in the development of any marketing strategy. In this respect both the needs of individuals possessing little or no background in marketing as well as those who have considerable sport marketing expertise should be satisfied. For the former, the chapter should serve as a "road map" for a new and uncharted trip. For the latter group it should serve as a "reference manual," reminding practitioners of the foundational stages of the marketing process and reinforcing the logic used in sound decision-making.

The Development of Sport Marketing

The majority of the factors which make sport marketing unique may not appear to be that significant when taken individually. Yet when the complete list is viewed, it is apparent that the sport product is markedly different from any other product or service. When this fact is coupled with some of the unique structural elements present in most sport organizations and the unique marketing environment in which sport marketers are required to operate, the need for a unique field of sport marketing becomes evident. Sport marketers actually face a challenge which, on the surface appears to many people to be less demanding than most other industries, but is in fact invariably much more challenging. In the light of such a challenge, it is doubly puzzling why until recently sport organizations have placed so little emphasis on hiring sport marketing professionals. A look at the most recent media guides of the major college athletic departments still reveals very few marketing positions. Reviewing most sport industry segments reveals the same phenomenon. Few organizations perform any market analysis or customer/fan research. Even fewer have market-information systems in place, or in-house advertising professionals on their staff who analyze promotional effectiveness.

Why Sport Organizations Have Neglected Sport Marketing

It is understandable that professional sport teams and high-visibility intercollegiate athletic programs have used the media's desire to give sport extensive coverage as an easy way out of spending marketing dollars. Sport sponsorship and fund-raising have often been contracted to outside companies However, there is simply no excuse for the avoidance of professional marketing approaches in so many segments of the sport industry. Too much evidence exists that professional marketing techniques are critical to financial survival and too many people close to sport have called into question the old opinion that "winning is everything" in terms of attendance (Ref. 4). Of great concern is the revelation that less than 3% of all major league professional leagues surveyed in 2000 had anyone performing the central and most critical marketing functions (market research, the development and maintenance of a marketing information system, and hard analysis of promotional effectiveness. Many of the more progressive organizations tend to be the ones with higher attendance. The major exception occurs in the National Football League (NFL) where the majority of franchises are close to full-attendance capacity and apparently believe that they do not need such positions.

When we look at industry segments that cannot rely so heavily on media exposure, we find that professionalization in marketing improves. Approximately 90% of fitness and health clubs have hired specialized marketing personnel and train their own full-time sales personnel (Ref. 5). Managers of sport programs at sport resorts such as Hilton Head in South Carolina and administrators of stadia, arenas and auditoriums have followed a similar pattern in recruiting sport marketing professionals to help them reach capacity, to attract meetings and conventions and to broaden their event mix. But, here again, such actions are often taken in a vacuum. Those being hired are invariably strong in sales and promotions rather than the careful preparation of scientifically collected market research, the effective use of a management information system, or the analysis of advertising effectiveness. One sport marketing executive with responsibility for both a major indoor facility and a professional hockey team recently said about his promotional efforts, "You have to just try things, maybe something outrageous, and then see what works for you!" It is hard to imagine how long such a cavalier attitude would be tolerated in general business and industry. The question remains, why has it been tolerated for so long in sport?

A major area of shortfall in the practice of sport marketing today is the lack of data collection and in particular, relevant data collection. Why do sport organizations fail to collect, or worse yet, ignore the valuable information which is often generated as part of the normal functioning of the business? A classic example of this is the failure to retain the names and addresses of persons purchasing tickets with a check, or the returning of checks submitted by unsuccessful play-off ticket applicants without recording their names and addresses in a prospect file. Such information can readily be merged into a Marketing Information System (MIS) and be used effectively for direct mailings, rather than resorting to expensive mass media advertising campaigns.

In participant-sport marketing, similar fundamental errors are also being made, but here the question shifts to sales techniques. "Why do the majority of court and health clubs (tennis, racquetball, fitness and health centers), still have the tendency to hire part-time students, divorcees, or senior citizens without prior club or sales experience as control desk personnel who then double as sales staff?" Surely club owners realize that the destiny (and financial stability) of the club is in inexperienced hands? In all but a few clubs, desk personnel comprise the primary consumer contact (on the phone, at the front desk, and for walk-in prospects). It seems incomprehensible that in a business subject to such high customer turnover, and one which is so susceptible to fads and trends, that the most critical marketing function for survival is held in such low regard. Yet it clearly has been overlooked in the past because of absentee ownership and in part because untrained managers have been hired from former participants and coaches.

Too many new team owners feel that sport is a simple business or one that has no significant differences from their existing businesses. All too often professional team owners are asset trackers (realtors, developers, or internet gurus) who have never run a manufacturing or service business. The major reasons they survived in the past was that demand was strong and the competition was no more sophisticated. However, once competition increased and demand dropped off it became a question of survival of the fittest. Needless to say the motivation to adopt professional marketing techniques has risen rapidly for every sport segment in the last five years.

In the high-visibility segments of the sport industry (professional and intercollegiate sport), sport sponsorship, new stadiums with club and luxury suite revenues and naming rights, plus huge broadcast contracts have diminished the need to market to the average fan. Yet with continued increases in the competition for the sport consumer's dollar, even in these industry segments, the organizations employing more sophisticated marketing approaches are much more likely to prosper. If a reminder is needed that no segment of the industry is in an impregnable position, a look at the current happenings in professional football should provide a stark warning. The once sacred "golden goose" of the NFL which has provided owners with a safe and consistent flow of "golden eggs," has been threatened by internal strife, too many player violations of moral and criminal codes, too many team relocations, and the lack of a team in the nation's number 2 market—Los Angeles! Only when all of the critical functions of marketing are performed can professional franchises expect to maintain high attendance in the face of diluted player talent and increased competition.

The reasons why sport organizations have not adopted a comprehensive marketing approach in the past are numerous, yet they are worth reviewing because they provide considerable insight into the future of sport marketing. An examination of these factors is critical both to the goal of providing justification for the existence of sport marketing as a distinct discipline, and to communicating to the sport marketer the need for understanding sport marketing concepts as a basis for marketing success. Reliance on totally intuitive judgments has never been sufficient, but in the future it will no longer be enough to get by. Simply stated, throughout the 1970s and 1980s every aspect of sport marketing underwent permanent changes. The market for the sport product, the competition, the marketing mix (product decisions, pricing decisions, promotional decisions and distribution decisions) and the marketing environment all have become more complex as the sport consumer market has become more complex

The primary reasons why sport marketing has been a neglected science in the past are, perhaps not surprisingly, also the major factors which make sport marketing unique. For the most part the impact which each factor has on making the sport marketer's role unique is on the increase; therefore, there exists a strong need for a new breed of sport marketing thought. First, the stage is set for this "new thought" and then the milestones of this "thought process," called the Marketing Planning Process (MPP) are outlined.

The Unique Aspects of Sport Marketing

Almost every element of marketing requires significantly different approaches when the product being marketed is sport. Predictably the critical differences lie in the unique aspects of the sport product, and the unusual market conditions facing sport marketers. The author outlined the various unique elements of sport marketing in an earlier work (Ref. 7). Each factor is identified under the relevant marketing topic heading, as follows:

A. The Market for Sport Products and Services

1.   Sport organizations simultaneously compete and cooperate.

No sport organization can exist in isolation. Professional and intercollegiate sports require other franchises and schools in order to have meaningful competition. Without a partner a game of tennis cannot be played. If there is only one summer sleep-away camp in a market area, camp directors experience greater difficulty recruiting campers. If Johnny's best friend decides to spend his summer at home instead of going to camp, then Johnny does not want to go away to his camp.

2.   Partly due to the unpredictability of sport, and partly due to the strong personal identification sport consumers experience, sport consumers often consider themselves experts.

Few decisions in sport go without notice or comment by the media or by consumers. Every decision is second guessed, and can affect the lives (even if insignificantly) of many people. In 1983 MLB's Baltimore Orioles, replaced the Oriole fan's favorite seventh-inning stretch song "Country Boy" with the song "That Magic Feeling." The fans booed the director of promotions, Drew Sheinman who was sport-management-trained and he was smart enough to learn from his consumers. He started a competition to see which song they preferred. Many of the promotional ideas he learned from the fans led to the Orioles drawing two million fans and his winning "The Baseball Marketer of the Year Award." Sheinman capped that year by having John Denver appear personally to sing "Country Boy" at the 1983 World Series in Baltimore. Sport marketers and managers operate in a gold-fish bowl, which on occasion can impact negatively on marketing decision making, unless the marketer knows how to "seize the day."

To reinforce this fact, consider the findings of what is amazingly the last extensive study on fan preferences, the Miller Lite Report on American's Attitude Toward Sports, (which was designed to be representative of the U.S. population as a whole), published in 1983 (Ref. 8). When asked, "Do you think you could play for a professional team if you practiced?" 52% of respondents said Yes. To the question "Do you think that you could do a better job of officiating than most officials?" 74% said Yes. To the question "Do you think that you could do a better job of coaching than the average coach?"—again the majority (51%) said Yes! No other business is viewed so simplistically and with such strong personal identification as sport is viewed by it's consumers. When a fan's team wins, he/she says "We won!"

B. The Sport Product

1.   The sport product is invariably intangible and subjective.

What each sport consumer sees in a sport is quite subjective. Few products are open to such a wide array of interpretation by the consumer. This phenomenon makes it extremely difficult for the sport marketer to ensure a high probability of consumer satisfaction. In a scenario of three fans attending the same event together, we might expect quite different views of the event. One fan may have loved the game, the second may have thought it was just o.k. but loved the entertainment, the mascot, cheerleaders, etc., while the third fan may have hated it but spent a lot of time just people watching at the crowds antics. Amazingly enough, all three attended the same game!

2. The sport product is inconsistent and unpredictable.

Spectator and participant-sport events are equally unpredictable. A baseball game played today is different from next week's game even if the same starting line-ups and pitchers play. There are numerous intangibles such as weather, injuries to players, momentum, the reaction of the crowd and the records and standings of the two teams at the time they play. All of these factors impact on the outcome of the game, and consequently the excitement and satisfaction experienced by the fan. Participant sport is no different. Even a golfer playing the same course at the same time every week, experiences a totally different round each time he/she plays.

Consumer-product marketers market consistency. Sport products by contrast, market the excitement of unpredictability! If the sport marketer had to rely on consumer satisfaction from the event alone, there would be a lot fewer repeat consumers. Fortunately there are product extensions (the facility's amenities, clean restrooms, good-quality concessions at reasonable prices, excellent in-game entertainment, etc.) to ensure consistency and provide a baseline of satisfaction.

In actual fact it is because the outcome of a sport event is not predictable that sport has so much charm as well as so much frustration.

3. A greater percentage of the marketing emphasis must be placed on the product extensions rather than the core product.

All consumer and industrial products and services stake their reputation on providing consistent product quality and service. Years ago Holiday Inns Incorporated advertised that there would be "no surprises" for guests. Every Inn worldwide offered the same standard of service. Sport operates in sharp contrast to this, because no marketer can control how well his team will play, or, for example, how much the weather impacts on ski conditions. In sport, the marketing emphasis frequently must be placed on the product extensions where consistency can be achieved.

This dilemma has often been referred to as the "Do you sell the steak or the sizzle?" controversy. The answer is not a simple one. For some consumers only the quality of the steak is important, for others the style and the atmosphere of the restaurant is the critical factor (the sizzle). For the majority, both are critical. In sport, given that as sports marketers we do not usually have any say in the product, we cannot guarantee the quality of the steak, we must sell both. But we emphasize that there will always be the "sizzle"!

There have been a few cases where sport marketers have overlooked this component of sport marketing philosophy. Perhaps most notable was the New York Mets abortive 1981 season campaign theme "The Magic is Back!" The theme attracted fans who reminisced about the 1969 "Miracle Mets" when they won baseball's World Series. After initially attracting considerable attention and inter-est, the campaign which was developed by the well respected DELLA-FEMINA Advertising Agency of New York, backlashed on the Mets organization. When on-field performances failed to live up to the promotional promise the magic faded. So did the fans! By season's end the attendance levels were far below the prior season's already low levels. The sport marketer, guided by an ad agency had made a classic faux-pas promising something he could not deliver! The long term negative impact was still being felt by the Mets at the gate in the mid 1980s until a new championship team emerged in 1986 despite a highly successful record and an exciting pennant race.

4.   The sport product is a perishable commodity; it has to be pre-sold.

Sport products are developed in anticipation of demand and are produced and consumed simultaneously. (Except for some spectator sports which are video-taped for tape-delayed broadcast.) No marketer can save a seat for yesterday's game, or yesterday's lift ticket, or the 10:00 p.m. time slot on court No. 1 from last night, and sell it at a later time. The majority of sport products are perishable commodities, requiring preselling.

5.   Sport is generally publicly consumed, and consumer satisfaction is invariably affected by social facilitation.

The loneliness of the long distance runner notwithstanding, almost all sport products are consumed in a public setting, and in the company of others. Further, the enjoyment of the activity is frequently dependent upon the enjoyment of oth-ers, or at least is a function of interaction with other people. One study showed that less than two percent of those attending collegiate and professional sport events attend by themselves (Ref. 9). Only a few sports (predominantly the eco-logical sports) can be undertaken by a single person. Consequently sport mar-keters need to recognize the role which social facilitation plays. Special programs and promotional plans need to be developed which maximize the enjoyment and satisfaction of the group, with different promotions aimed at the different demo-graphic groups which make up the group. For example, more adult or "swinging-singles" promotions will occur in the 1980s and less and less promotions aimed at children. The crowd and more particularly the size, excitement, and energy of the crowd is part of the product!

6.   The sport marketer often has little or no control over the composition of the core-product and frequently has only limited control over some of the key ingredients of the product extensions.

Most consumer and industrial product marketers have a major say in the com-position of their organizations' product mix. The industrial marketer performs consumer research and then sets about to establish a product line which satisfies needs. In spectator sport marketing, this accepted marketing practice does not take place. The coaching staff and/or the general manager are in charge of recruit-ing, player drafting, trades and acquisitions. Players with major drawing appeal may be traded without consultation with the marketing staff. One of the more ig-nominious actions in this respect occurred in the National Hockey League (NHL), where the Boston Bruins traded away superstar and fan idol Bobby Orr.

The nose-dive in Bruins attendance in the early 1970s after the trade stood in stark contrast to the decade of sell-outs which preceded it. Yet the innocent marketer was held accountable for filling the empty seats! How would you like to be marketing the Chicago Bulls in the millennium without Michael Jordan?

The other critical element of the core-product of a spectator sport organization, besides the playing staff, is the schedule. Most colleges are able to impact on their own schedules with the exception of conference and playoff games. However, all professional sport schedules are developed by the league office with limited input from the team's marketing staff. Often games are scheduled on impossible days to promote. To a lesser degree some participant sports experience a similar problem. Ski resorts, golf clubs, outdoor tennis and country clubs have no control over the weather which often is the most critical factor in determining demand for their products.

7.   Sport is both a consumer and an industrial product.

Marketing theory classifies products into two categories. Those products consumed by an end-user are called consumer goods. Those products used by a manufacturer in the production of another product are called industrial goods. Sport is produced as an end product for mass consumer appeal for both spectators and participants (a consumer good). Spectator and participant sports are also used by business and industry who sponsor events and sport broadcasts and advertise in conjunction with sport events and sport organizations as a means of reaching their own consumers. Business also uses sport figures to represent, endorse and promote their products, and many businesses also purchase tickets and private suites at sport events, in order that they may entertain their clients (an industrial good).

8.   No product evokes such a strong personal identification and such an emotional attachment as sport.

Fans of professional and collegiate sport often view themselves as being part of the team, and view their involvement in sport as a major thrust in their lives. The Miller Lite study previously quoted revealed the pervasiveness of sport in American society. Of those surveyed 95% said that they were affected by sport on a daily basis [In this study "affected by sport" was defined as playing, watching (in person or on television), listening to, reading or talking about sport]. What fan does not say, "We won!" when the team he supports wins? One study of soccer fans in Brazil (Ref. 10) revealed a remarkable association between productivity and fan morale dependent upon the fortunes of the national team. World wars have even been fought over sport, and if we are to believe the popular press, numerous divorces are the result of preoccupation with sport. The sport fan, and to a lesser yet more critical extent, the sport participant feels that the sport product belongs to him or her, and for many it is a critical component of their lifestyle. The positive side of such an emotional bond also carries a negative side. A strong backlash occurs when fan favorites are traded or when teams are moved (oh, those Brooklyn Dodgers, Cleveland Browns, and Baltimore Colts!) and when product modifications are made. Once again this factor applied to participant sport to a much lesser degree. Many tennis players have a favorite playing surface which best complements their game and get most upset if they have to play on clay, hardcourt, or sportcourt.

9. *Sport has an almost universal appeal and pervades all elements of life.*

There are several ways in which sport can be viewed as having universal appeal:

a. *Geographically*—sport is evident in every nation on the earth and has been an important part of most civilizations since the advent of man. (Interestingly, in a sport such as soccer which is played in an organized form by more than 120 countries, the national personality is often evident in the style of play.)

b. *Demographically*—sport appeals to all demographic segments (young, old; male, female; blue collar, white collar, black, white, Hispanic, Native American, and Asian). Sport has sometimes been referred to as the great "leveler" of people from different social classes.

c. *Socioculturally*—sport is associated with every element of leisure and recreational activity, along with many of mankind's more basal activities, motivations and needs. In this respect sport has been said to be a mirror of society.

Sport is associated with:

a. *Relaxation and entertainment.* It is theater, and melodrama; it is a play and according to catharsis theory it is a relief from stress.

b. *Exercise.* For participants it becomes a major part of some individuals' lifestyles. Few spectators gain any exercise value, except for "12 oz. arm curls."

c. *Eating.* Spectators invariably eat while spectating. Participants often eat after exercising in the facility where they exercised.

d. *Drinking alcohol.* Consumption of alcohol is often associated with viewing of sport. Many participants drink after playing sport.

e. *Sex.* Sport has often been associated with sexual connotations. Women wanting to watch men in shorts showing their physical prowess, and men watching women in leotards in form-sports such as ice-skating and gymnastics. While these traditional sexual stereotypes are breaking down, many traditions continue. Cheerleaders, sport team groupies, taking dates to sport events and "seeing and being seen" at high school and college sport events, are no less popular activities today than they were twenty-five years ago.

f. *Gambling.* Whether legal or illegal, dependent upon the state or the sport, gambling has a strong association with sport. In particular, a significant part of the popularity of NFL football is said to be attributable to the heavy betting on beating the point spread.

g. *Drugs.* With stronger crowd security, the drug association in sport is primarily concerned with athletes' use of drugs.

h. *Physical violence.* Both on the field, off the field and between participants, spectators and even officials.

i. *Social identification.* Association with a particular group, institution or community.

j. *Vicarious gratification.* Basking in the reflective glory of a team's victory.

k. *Economic/legal environment.* Salary inflation, contract disputes, strikes, court battles in sport often parallel similar economic and legal undercurrents occurring in society as a whole.

l. *Religion.* According to renowned sport philosopher Michael Novak (Ref. 11), sport has many quasi-religious properties.
m. *Business* and industry. Apart from the direct association (sponsorship, endorsement, etc.) already discussed, much of the language, culture and mythology of business is associated with sport. "At XYZ Incorporated we have got to put a winning team together." "When in doubt, punt!" "John will be quarterbacking this project for us."
n. *The moral reflection of society.* Violence and criminal conduct in sport mirrors the problems of our society today.

C. The Price of Sport

1. *The price of the sport product itself is invariably quite small in comparison to the total cost paid by the consumer when consuming sport products.*

One estimate of spending by fans attending Pittsburgh Pirates baseball games indicated that just one third of the total cost paid by Bucks fans to watch Pirates games actually went to the Pirates organization (Ref. 12). The remaining two thirds went in transportation and entertainment costs and related expenditures to unaffiliated organizations. There is little that most organizations can do to impact on this relationship, except to ensure that they have full control over parking and concessions rights and to offer in-arena restaurants, competitively priced merchandise, stadium clubs, etc., whenever possible.

This problem is particularly acute in the ski industry, which has undergone some marked changes in the last decade. A hypothetical situation perhaps might illustrate this point best. For a skier from St. Louis, Missouri who wishes to fly to the Colorado Rockies for a skiing-weekend, the total tab might easily exceed $2,000 per person (with only limited equipment purchases). As little as $100 might be spent on lift tickets and perhaps $50 in food, drink and ski shop purchases at the ski resort. In this example at best less than 10% of the total revenue generated by this resort's ability to attract a skier would end up in the pocket of the resort owners. Obviously any price discounts or promotions on lift tickets contemplated by the resort operators would have a minimal impact in enticing this individual to ski more often. As a result many resorts have undertaken horizontal integration and now own the hotels, bars and stores in the towns surrounding their resorts. Vail Resorts, Inc., which is now a publicly traded company is an excellent example.

2. *Indirect revenues are frequently greater than direct operating revenues.*

Each year professional and collegiate sports receive television contracts offering more and more dollars from local and national media to broadcast their games. U.S. television rights to the Winter and Summer Olympic games were recently sold for more than twice the previous fee. Each NFL team is guaranteed an almost $100m each per year share of the national television contract which is at least 300% of potential gate receipts for the largest of stadia in the league, even if it were sold out for the entire season. Concessions, parking, souvenirs and merchandising, program advertising, signage, sponsorship agreements, joint promotions, trade-outs and tie-ins all increase the organizations' non-operating revenue. Even in commercial health and fitness clubs, the indirect revenues in multi-sport clubs such as personal training, diet, and nutrition are beginning to become significant when compared to direct membership dues and court usage fees as the predominant source of income. By way of illustration the most recent industry survey places indirect revenues in multi-concept clubs at just over 50% of gross receipts (Ref. 13).

3.   Sport programs have rarely been required to operate on a for-profit basis.

As stated in point 2 above, many sport organizations can rely on significant revenue from non-operating sources. At almost every level of sport, outside financial support exists. Parks and recreation departments underwrite youth sport from tax-payer's dollars. The same dollars go to support the local school sport programs and college alumni are asked to bankroll athletic departments. One estimate (Ref. 14) indicated that less than 20 of the more than 250 major college programs offering football programs actually broke even on football. Yet football continues to be referred to as a revenue sport, as if it were profitmaking. Professional teams play in publicly subsidized arenas often at amazingly low rents.

Over the years this "open checkbook" approach led to an atmosphere in which many segments of the sport industry did not need to operate with regard to the "bottom-line." Even the media helped support this state of affairs by providing free publicity. (Public organizations receive free coverage because of the commitment to public service; and the highly visible college and professional teams receive coverage because of widespread interest.) As a result the professionalism in sport management suffered severely.

D. The Promotion of Sport

1.   The widespread exposure given by the mass media to sport has resulted in a lowered emphasis on sport marketing.

For the reasons outlined above, sport has not been forced to place an emphasis on marketing and promotion to the same degree as organizations in other industries. Sport has been able to rely upon publicity as its major promotional tool. Every newspaper has a sport section, in some cases it is the largest single section. The major papers have special supplements devoted to sport. The broadcast media devotes large blocks of time to sport coverage and approximately 20% of news time to sport. The reason why this happens is simply the widespread interest in sport! As cited earlier, the Miller Lite Study showed that 95% of Americans felt that their lives were affected by sport on a daily basis!

2.   Because of the visibility which sport enjoys, many businesses wish to associate with sport.

The exposure granted sport by the media has not gone unnoticed by consumer and industrial product marketers. Sport provides a promotional vehicle where the audience (exposure) is often sizeable and the make-up of a sport audience for any given sport can be predicted comparatively accurately in advance. In addition the quality of the audience (the demographics) is generally good. With the high use of sport tickets, the attendees are invariably higher income individuals. Each sport attracts a different audience, consequently sponsorship of an event allows a corporate sponsor to segment its audience quite successfully when using different sports. Sport audiences and participants are usually higher income, up-scale groups who provide prime targets for product marketers. In addition, the association with sport places the company's product in a favorable light, and exposes the product at a time when the audience is invariably in a positive frame of mind. Consequently the natural resistance processes of the consumer are "let-down." The use of athletes as product spokespersons is in large part due to the ability of the athlete to get the attention of the audience, thereby cutting through the "advertising noise." Not only does the athlete get attention, many are given considerable "source-credibility" by the sport fan consumer. Of course the constant transgressions by many athletes has led to an increased use of retired athletes such as Michael Jordan, Wayne Gretzky, and John Elway who are excellent role models as well as superb athletes.

Once again, sport's ability to have its promotional expenditures underwritten by corporate partners through sponsorship, tie-ins (joint advertising or promotion), or trade-outs ("quid pro quo"—reciprocal trading or bartering of services without direct payment), is unequalled in any segment of the economy. The negative side is that such support leads to a reduction in the need, and consequently the motivation, to analyze advertising effectiveness. If you are not paying for it, why bother to see if it's well spent! Despite the "bottom-line" approach adopted by most organizations in their regular business practice, when it comes to associations with sport, there has been very limited hard analysis of the effectiveness of sport sponsorship. [However, the days of huge sponsorship dollars being given to sport organizations without analyzing the actual direct increase in sales or the sponsors products that is in almost all industries except e-commerce where the dot.coms merely want to get their name on the map.]

The net impact of the increased interest in sport sponsorship is good for sport in every respect except one. Sport sponsorship provides less incentive for the sport marketer to stand on his or her own two feet and adopt a comprehensive approach to sport marketing.

E. The Sport Distribution System and the Sport Facility

Most sport products are consumed in the location where they are produced. With the exception of the sporting goods industry and sport events which are broadcast, sport produces its product at the same location where it is consumed. Apart from the entertainment, food service and hospitality industries, there is no other industry which operates in this manner.

Traditional marketing spends much of its time and effort on the physical distribution channels and networks needed to get the product from manufacturer to retailer to consumer. However, most of the time sport does not physically distribute its product. The viewing rights to the product are physically distributed via broadcast networks and ticket distribution networks, which frequently lie outside of the direct control of the sport organization, consequently this realm of marketing which deals with physical movement of a product through distribution channels holds limited relevance to sport.

The above list of the unique aspects of sport marketing sets the backdrop for the market conditions in which sport marketers are required to operate. While none by itself is overwhelming, and some factors are not totally unique, the combination of all these aspects does provide a unique challenge for sport marketers which demands a significantly different approach.

In a nutshell, a sport marketer is asked to market a product which is entirely unpredictable, inconsistent and open to subjective interpretation, and usually the sport marketer has little or no control over the core product (players and team performance). This task is undertaken in a highly competitive marketplace for most industry segments with a much lower promotional budget than similarly sized organizations in other industries. On the bright side, the media is anxious to give wide exposure to almost every move the sport organization makes, and many opportunities exist for revenue-generating associations with business and industry.

We now have an idea of what sport marketing is, and yet so little has been written on the subject. Almost no theory has been published in sport marketing and the few successful experiences which have been documented in professional journals rarely detail any fundamental concept or principles which are behind the successful application. As a result the novice is left with little more than guesswork when transplanting the ideas of the industry's "gurus" from one market situation to their own market conditions unless the individual hearing the ideas and concepts for the first time has a frame of reference or a theory base upon which to hang the information, the translation from one market to another will not be successful. In the absence of prior experience, or a framework for taking an idea and modifying it to a given market situation, the chances for marketing success are indeed slim. It is hoped that the major benefit of this article will be to help provide such a framework for marketing decision-making. Let us now take a closer look at marketing and the steps in the process of developing, implementing and evaluating marketing strategy.

What Is Marketing?

The student new to the study of marketing can be excused for naively believing that marketing is nothing more than sales. Two articles by sport industry analysis previously cited (Refs. 20, 21) would indicate that many sport organizations are equally naive about their marketing practices. To many of them, marketing is synonymous with sales and promotional gimmickry. Such an approach is almost understandable given the focus of many articles written by practitioners who laud their peers to "Promote or Perish" (Ref. 22). There is nothing wrong with sport marketers using the desire on the part of the media to provide free exposure to the sport product as a major promotional tool. Within certain limits there is nothing wrong with gimmicky promotions (especially when they get a lot of attention and when their cost is totally underwritten by a sponsor). There is nothing wrong with promotions and giveaways, as long as they do not detract from the sport itself However, there are numerous questions which go begging a response in such a simplistic approach to sport marketing.

The first and most critical stage in marketing involves the development of a comprehensive Marketing Information System (MIS). In the MIS data is generated, collected and retrieved in a form which enables the decision-maker to make sound judgments about the product, the price of the product, the facility where the product will be sold, bow the product will be distributed (if at all) and how it will be promoted. In the absence of hard data on marketing research and performance, much decision-making is necessarily heuristic (rule of thumb) in nature. The danger in such an approach was pointed out by Philip Kotler, considered to be perhaps the most influential writer in marketing. Kotler said that marketing information is the key to successful marketing strategy. In an earlier work the author reinforced this view: "making marketing decisions without market research data is like taking a trip without a road map" (Ref. 23). When it's an unknown trip, smart people simply don't do it! An MIS provides a system for performing market research, and providing continual analysis of the market for the product or service. Further it allows for the monitoring of competitive activity, along with an evaluation of the consumer's response to marketing strategies. Perhaps most importantly it collects the names, addresses, phone numbers, fax and e-mail addresses, or ticket purchases for later use in direct marketing. With an effective MIS in place the sophisticated sport marketer would demand data on such questions as:

"What days/time-slots/opponents/programs should we promote using special inducements?"

"What is the impact on total attendance or participation levels when a particular night/event is promoted over another?"

"Which opponent or program offers the greatest elasticity of demand in response to a promotion or price discount?"

"What is the average umber of games which fans attend?"

To illustrate why this data is important, let us look at an example.

"Should a National Basketball Association (NBA) franchise use a promotion which has major drawing power when the opponent is the Los Angeles Lakers or when the Los Angeles Clippers come to town?"

Such analysis is not complex for an individual trained in marketing, yet currently this type of analysis is not being undertaken except in the more successful sport organizations. To expand on this question, and make it slightly more complex we might ask, "How is this decision affected if the schedule calls for the Lakers to play on a Friday night and the Clippers on a Sunday afternoon?"

It is evident that the bulk of professional and collegiate sport promotions are geared toward marketing the least attractive event-days on a schedule. These events are known in the industry as the "dogs." [The expression "dog" is used here in the same manner as it has come to be used in the popular vernacular of sport practitioners. "Dog" refers to an event that is almost impossible to sell out, such as a game against the team with the worst record in the league or an opponent without any stars. In a court and health club, it might refer to the 2 p.m. to 4 p.m. time slot Monday through Friday or Sunday evening.] Over fifteen years ago Andy Dolich developed the concept called "Power Promotions" where the best promotion was matched with the best opponent and the best date. In fact, the more attractive event day opponents offer greater elasticity of demand (as long as the projected attendance level without a promotion is not too close to the facility's capacity limit). Therefore, promoting the better teams invariably has a more positive impact on total season attendance and hence total revenues. In almost ten years of observation and involvement as a consultant in the sport industry by the author, the effectiveness of certain promotions which are in common use was questioned. In fact many traditional promotions such as bat day, jacket day, etc., often do not increase total attendance in real terms, rather they merely redistribute the attendance pattern of fans. Joe Fan, who lives 90 miles from a ballpark and brings his family of four regularly to two games per year, simply chooses to attend the two games which offer the greatest benefits (fireworks, a free cap, bat, T-shirt, poster or rock group post-game). In economic terms, Joe Fan simply maximizes his family's satisfaction for his sport-consumer dollar! Such consumer strategy is called "cherry-picking" and has no positive benefit to the marketer, even when the cost of the promotion is totally underwritten by a sponsor. The same concern is evident in participant sports. Promotions are only effective if they increase attendance frequency by new consumers, or if they induce the existing consumer to attend more often in the future. It takes time and continual evaluation to determine whether or not a promotion is truly effective.

Consideration of the above questions, and many more issues prior to the onset of any marketing strategy is critical to the success of the sport marketing effort. Practitioners are only likely to consider such questions, and indeed find the answers to their questions, when such thinking is guided by a comprehensive framework of analysis. The Marketing Planning Process (MPP) outlined by Kotler offers exactly such a framework (Ref. 25). More than a framework for decision-making, the MPP is a flow-chart of the logical progression in marketing thought. Consequently, it forms an ideal topic outline for any discussion on sport marketing.

The Marketing Planning Process (MPP): The Only Sure Way to Meet the Sport Marketing Challenge of the Future

Kotler identified the MPP as the central thread to effective marketing. He not only used the process as a prescriptive guide to marketing decision making, he also advised that its elements should become the major stage in the marketing audit. In the marketing audit all marketing functions and activities are reviewed at least annually to determine their effectiveness. Not only does the MPP provide the backbone of marketing, it communicates the interdependencies of each element of marketing. It also warns of the futility of making decisions in a vacuum. Perhaps more than most models of a process, use of the MPP forces the practitioner to "think each marketing decision through" before it is made.

Other chapters in this text deal with the sales and promotional aspects of sport marketing found in the marketing mix. Consequently, to understand how sport organizations should use the MPP (see Appendix) to respond to the marketing challenges they face, this chapter will focus only on the elements of marketing which precede the core of marketing decision-making (the marketing mix). Not by chance, the elements of the MPP are listed in priority order of progression for marketing decision making. Conveniently therefore, the MPP can be viewed as a "road map" for the development of sport marketing strategy.

To support the proposition that it is critical to consider every element of the foundational factors of the MPP before making a decision, extensive illustration from the world of sport is provided. Not by coincidence these applications also provide strong support for the consideration of sport marketing as a distinct field of study.

Relevant issues in each of the foundational elements of marketing as they apply to sport are now addressed for the most part in the order in which they appeared in the Marketing Planning Process:

A. The Market

Any analysis of marketing must start quite naturally with consideration of the marketplace for the product or service, specifically an evaluation of the structure of the market, and the needs of potential consumers. One might easily ask at this stage, "How do you know what your market is unless you know what your product is?" The fact is that you do not know. Consequently, the first step for the marketer is to establish a preliminary idea of what the product or program concept or unique product position is. Once the market has been analyzed it may be found that the concept is not viable and needs to be amended; such modification would take place under the marketing-mix function, entitled "The Product." Given that the "position" occupied by the product in the market is evaluated in depth again under that section, it becomes evident that there are some iterative cycles to the MPP. There is no way around this duplication, you must know what your product concept is before you know what the potential market is likely to be! Fortunately such overlap and iterations are kept to a minimum.

B. The Product Concept or Position

In defining the product concept it might appear that the optimal approach would be to identify a very tightly defined market segment to which a very specific product is targeted. This is the case in some markets, and is invariably the case for a new product attempting to penetrate an established market. However, many organizations have realized the benefits of defining their product concept broadly, and offering more than one product option in order to appeal to several market segments. General Motors realized many years ago that it was not simply in the automobile market, but rather that it was in the transportation business. This realization allowed GM to diversify into many other markets, which have proven extremely profitable. In a similar fashion spectator-sport organizations widened their appeal considerably once they realized they were in the entertainment business. Rather than simply selling their sport, they opened up their market to anyone interested in being entertained by offering pre-game, half-time and post-game shows, bands, cheerleaders, etc. Not surprisingly, the same metamorphosis has hit other sport industry segments. Most single-purpose tennis and racquetball clubs in the last decade have undergone a renaissance. For the most part, the clubs which have survived the shake-down period are the ones which broadened their concepts into full-time fitness and health centers.

Dependent upon the market, and the competition, room does exist for specialized product positions. This is particularly evident in the soda and fast food industries. The Kentucky Fried Chicken (KFC) chain, in response to intense competition from its giant competitors, the McDonalds and Burger King chains who have broadened their menu by offering chicken items, responded with a specialized product concept. KFC says, "Why buy from the burger boys!" The fast-food market is big enough and stable enough to support KFC's Wendy's, and Carl's Jr./Hardees specialized strategies as they take on the two industry giants. However, most sport industry segments are often not as substantial, nor are they as stable. Athletes Foot, a national franchise chain entered into the highly competitive and saturated retail sporting goods market by specializing in athletic footwear. Their timing was excellent, as they anticipated the mid-1970's boom in the running shoe market. Once this boom peaked, they were wise to quickly diversify into the so-called "software" items of' the sporting goods industry, namely T-shirts, athletic clothing, athletic bags, etc., or else they would probably have gone out of business, in spite of the fact that athletic shoes have typically counted for approximately 65% of sales revenues in the small/medium sized sports stores. In the new millennium it will be interesting to see how these stores survive the huge switch to the "brown-shoe" market.

Reliance on a single profit-center is rarely a wise long-term strategy for any business, yet there has to be a central function to an organization's existence. For example, it is vital that sport marketers in an MLB franchise appreciate the raison d'etre of the game. As "America's pastime," baseball is inexpensive family entertainment. It is the "All-American game" and as such the aficionados of the sport feel that it must exemplify tradition and high morality. Bud Selig handed down an unprecedented suspension to pitcher John Rocker for his remarks which offended everyone. Pete Rose received a lifetime ban for allegedly betting on his own team. Baseball made an example of a player and a manager because of sports association with all segments of society, particularly its youth. This incident confirmed that baseball clearly wants to maintain its "homegrown image." While this image has a strongly positive side, the emphasis on tradition has sometimes been negative. In the past baseball's marketing strategies were too old fashioned and predictable. Baseball felt that it had to offer something for each family member at a price which families could afford. While there is nothing inherently wrong with that concept, there have been many sharp changes in the composition of the market which make such a strategy invalid.

In the modern family, Mom now works. Many families are headed by a woman. Young people are not marrying as early as they used to. There are fewer children in the average family and more and more senior citizens. With the current changes in the market for professional sport, the traditional promotional strategies aimed at children's needs to be re-thought. Promotional giveaways need to be targeted less at children. There has to be a deemphasis of the bat days, helmet days, etc., and more of an emphasis toward young adults who want entertainment and single parents who want a ticket, pizza, and a soda! The family four-pack simply does not fit the modern day family of 2 or 3 persons. The sport marketer needs to sell to Mom as head of the household to bring her children to the ballpark, and she has to be encouraged to come with a friend and her family. If necessary, the ballpark may need to have a child-care center! If senior citizens are to be attracted, the sport franchise must provide transportation and easy access to the ballpark. Senior citizens have special needs, namely ground-level entrances (no stairways), seats should have backs and cushions and need to be located in the shade, more day games need to be scheduled, and concessionaires need to frequently roam in the senior citizen section. All of these changes call for a rethinking of current marketing strategy. Interestingly enough, the attendance leaders in sport already have adjusted their marketing.

C. The Sport Consumer (Spectator and Participant)

Perhaps one of the key factors that a sport marketer must recognize is that the sport spectator and participant market has never been more volatile than it is currently. At the same time, the competition for the sport consumers dollar has rarely been more intense. Not only are consumer preferences changing, but perhaps more importantly the essential structure and composition of the market is changing. People are showing less interest in spectating and more interest in participating, as evidenced by several independent studies. They are showing less interest in watching the big four (NFL, NBA, MLB, and NHL) and more interest in X-treme sports. These are the Miller Lite Study (Ref. 26); the Perrier Study (Ref. 27); and, perhaps the most valuable of all the demographic studies, is the annual survey conducted by the Simmons Market Research Bureau of New York (Ref. 28). The sports which consumers wish to participate in most are no longer the team sports requiring heavy capital equipment, groomed diamonds or expensive goalposts. Rather they are the life sports of golf, jogging and the fitness activities such as tiabo, aerobic dancing, swimming, and weight training. The ecological sports such as rock climbing, canoeing and camping are also strong. In each case, the equipment needs and the facility demands are generally lower than those demanded in the past. For the jogger it is the open road, for the walker, backpacker or mountaineer it is the countryside, a small backpack, and a good pair of boots and for the aerobic dancer it is a tape recorder or video tape machine (VCR). All of these trends serve to make it harder for the spectator sport marketer to put "meat in the seats" unless he or she taps the trend. While it is becoming easier for the participant sport marketer to get the "feet on the streets," the competition as to the form which the exercise/sport will take has risen astronomically.

As if these sport market changes were not enough, even greater forces have concurrently come into play. Athletes committing murders, beating their wives, and driving while intoxicated coupled with huge multi-year contracts with salaries have alienated the "man on the street." Players move from team to team, student-athletes leave college after their freshman or sophomore year. Players and coaches aren't loyal, so why should fans be? The effect is felt in every segment of the sport industry, even in high school and college athletic program cuts. There has also been reduced support for public stadia used by professional teams and of course severe reduction in institutional spending on sporting goods equipment.

While these overt changes have taken place, a more subtle but potentially more impacting long-term change has occurred. The comparative demographics of the United States population has slowly but inexorably changed. There are fewer children and more "swinging singles in their late twenties." People have been postponing getting married until they are older. There are more divorces, and as a result more female heads of households. Family size has decreased steadily for the last twenty years, and the largest growth segment in the U.S. population is the over-60s age group. When these demographic changes are combined with lifestyle (psychographic) changes, the picture is complicated even further. Children have moved away from playing the more traditional American sports, the so-called "Big Three" (football, basketball, and baseball). They have instead moved into

life-time sports which tend to be individual sports, and those team sports requiring much less outlay in equipment, facilities, coaching and officiating. Soccer is
one of the few. team sports to have benefited from these market changes, while ice
hockey, football and baseball in that order have been the biggest team-sport
losers. Roller hockey and in-line skating are the new sports of choice.

The sport marketer can only keep abreast of these changes if he/she is constantly accumulating data on consumer preferences and needs. More than this,
the marketer needs to adopt an information perspective which goes beyond
his/her own segment of the sport industry, and even beyond the industry to the
economy and societal changes as a whole. Who cares where you borrow an idea
from as long as it's a good one and you modify it to meet the special circumstances of our sport and your market? The real estate business got a huge boost in
the late 1970s when it borrowed the concept of "time-sharing" from the computer industry, and successfully used it to boost sales of condominiums and resort
properties. The lesson is to look within your own industry and beyond for answers to the questions you must ask regularly about the needs of your market.
What can we learn from the boom in e-commerce and the high-tech industry? The
answer is in-seat interactive video systems, where the fan can play a video game
against an opponent on the other side of the arena, place his/her vote on what
play should be called next, check his stocks and e-mail, and order a hot dog, beer,
or merchandise which will be delivered to his seat.

Many of the specific questions which a sport marketer needs to know are listed
in Chapter 16, dealing with the development and operation of an effective marketing information system. The marketing information system provides the
framework for the regular collection, storage, retrieval and analysis of market
and fan data. A cautionary note is probably apropos here. Even with the most effective of systems designed to analyze market trends, not all of these market
changes could have been predicted in advance. However, once these changes
began to occur, a sophisticated system would have picked them up in sufficient
time for appropriate action to be taken. On the simplest level, sports marketers
need to be at the gates to see who is buying tickets or sit in the cheap seats to get
a daily dose of reality.

Summary/Conclusion

Sport marketers clearly face many unique challenges and demands. Not all of
these demands are best met with decisive and aggressive marketing action. Many
require considerable thought and a well-planned response. Yet the majority of demands do have comparatively simple solutions once all of the data is put together.
In the new millennium and beyond, sport will continue to be quite unique but it
will follow one principle experienced in all industries, without any modification.
Those sport organizations most likely to succeed will be the ones who have the
best handle on the marketplace. Such a handle only comes with the development,
maintenance and continual analysis of every function of marketing. The structure
for establishing such a comprehensive sport marketing function is the Marketing
Planning Process. The element within the Marketing Planning Process which
houses the self-evaluation and analysis of marketing functions is the Marketing

Information System which is the subject of Chapter 16. Consequently the MIS becomes the cornerstone of effective marketing.

Simply put, the best sport marketers are the ones who have adopted an information-based approach to marketing. They have a better handle on the complexity of marketing sport products, because they know their markets better, and they know their fans. They follow a simple principle, "Ask the fans what they want, then give it to them!"

References

1. C. Rees (1981). "Does Sports Marketing Need a New Offense?" *Marketing and Media Decisions* 66-67 (February), 126-32.
2. L. Kesler (1979). "Man Created Ads in Sport's Own Image," *Advertising Age* 5-8 (August 27).
3. Mullin, B.J. (1983). "Sport Marketing, Promotion and Public Relations" (unpublished manuscript), pp. 266-323. Amherst, MA: University of Massachusetts, Department of Sport Studies.
4. *National Football Guide* (1983); *Pro and Amateur Hockey Guide* (1983); and *NBA Guide* (1983). St. Louis, MO: The Sporting News.
5. McCartley, J. (1999). The International Racquet Sports Association (IRSA). Boston, MA.
6. Mullin, B.J. (1979). "A Survey of the Management Training Needs of Selected Professional Sport Franchises in the Northeastern United States" (unpublished paper). Amherst, MA: Department of Sport Studies, University of Massachusetts.
7. Mullin, B.J. "How Does the Selling of Sport Fit Into Sport Marketing?" (unpublished paper). Amherst, MA: Department of Sport Studies, University of Massachusetts.
8. Research & Forecasts, Inc. (1983). *Miller Lite Report on American Attitudes Toward Sports, 1983*, pp. 71-117. Milwaukee, WI: Miller Brewing Co.
9. "An Economic Impact Study of Pittsburgh Pirates Baseball on the City of Pittsburgh, PA." (1979), p. 34. Pittsburgh, PA: Department of Economics, University of Pittsburgh.
10. Laver, J. (1969). "Soccer: Opium of the Brazilian People," *Transaction* (December).
11. Novak, M. (1976). *The Joy of Sport*. New York, NY: Basic Books, Inc., Publishers.
12. "An Economic Impact," *supra* Ref. 9, p. 27.
13. Panel, Kerr & Foster. (1984, February). *The Court and Health Club Industry: Facts and Figures Survey, 1983*. Boston, MA.
14. Eddy, S.J. (1980, April). "A Comparison of Athletic Fund-Raising Methods of NCAA Athletic Departments," (unpublished paper). Amherst, MA: Department of Sport Studies, University of Massachusetts.
15. Bolger, N. (1984). "Sport Sponsorship: Is It Really Worth It?" (unpublished paper). Amherst, MA: Department of Sport Studies, University of Massachusetts.

16. Sloan, P. (1979). "Who Gets Endorsements and Why," *Professional Sports Journal* 21-23 (July), 48.
17. Coate, C.P. (1979). "Using Sport to Change the Beer Drinking Habits of America: Miller Lite the Champagne of TV Ads," *Professional Sports Journal* 29 (August).
18. Holmes, J. (1970). "Athletes as Pitchmen: When Riggins, Theisman and Palmer Talk, The Public Listens," *Washington Post* 113-313 (January 4).
19. Lawson, J. (1979). "Minority Celebrities Reach Beyond Target Market," *Advertising Age* S-4 (July 30).
20. Rees, *supra* Ref. 1.
21. Kennedy, *supra* Ref. 5, p. 36.
22. Hartman, P.E. (1980). "Promote or Perish," *Athletic Purchasing and Facilities* 20-24 (April).
23. Kotler, P. (1976). *Marketing Management: Analysis, Planning and Control,* 3d ed., p. 146. Englewood Cliffs, NJ: Prentice-Hall, Inc.
24. Leve, R. (1979). "An Analysis of Boston Celtics Promotional Strategy" (unpublished paper). Amherst, MA: Department of Sport Studies, University of Massachusetts.
25. Kotler, *supra* Ref. 23.
26. Research & Forecasts, Inc., *supra* Ref. 8.
27. Louis Harris, Inc. (1981). *The Perner Study of Sport and Fitness in the USA.* New York, NY: Louis Harris, Inc.
28. Simmons Market Research Bureau Reports 10 (1982). *Sports and Leisure.* New York, NY: Simmons Market Research Bureau.

Appendix

The Market Planning Process

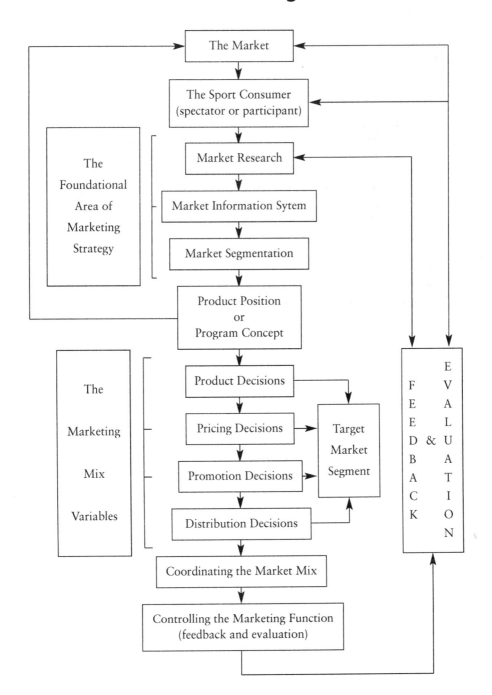

Chapter 11

Marketing Events and Services for Spectators

Frank Russo

Introduction

The sport manager is accountable for achieving a set of desired objectives and results, whatever type of facility he operates. Whether he reports to a city council, a university board of regents, a corporate board of directors or any other form of hierarchy, his professional well-being depends upon his ability to satisfy the expectations of superiors.

In most cases, however, striving to accomplish the primary objectives set for his facility is not necessarily compatible with the ever-increasing pressure to balance the budget. To come as close as possible requires considerable marketing expertise. The facility manager must know how to market a variety of services to tenants and public in a manner which produces maximum profit and results in an ever-increasing level of repeat business. This chapter is designed to help the sport manager better understand the marketing aspects of various in-house services such as scheduling, advertising, box office, concessions, merchandising (e.g., sale of programs, novelties, T-shirts, etc.), parking and television.

Importance of the Event Calendar

Most sport managers are encouraged to book a well-rounded schedule of events geared to satisfy the desires of the market. Since rental income is such a major portion of annual operating revenue, this is an extremely important process—especially considering the tremendous level of competition for quality arena events.

If the facility has a sports franchise, its home game dates will form the skeleton of the annual schedule. Basketball and hockey teams, for example, usually hold their dates at least one year in advance. Also serving as part of the skeleton will be major family show attractions (e.g., circuses and ice shows). Once these dates are confirmed, the process of booking "fillers" or "one-nighters" begins in earnest.

Fundamentals of Booking Events

To book a successful schedule of events, a good first impression must be made on tenants and the ticket-buying public. The facility should be clean, well-maintained, well-lit and environmentally comfortable. The staff should be friendly, courteous and professional in the delivery of box office, parking, concession, merchandising and other services.

Another factor that plays an important role in securing events for the facility is the level of confidence others have in the quality of services. Trust outside agency there is a responsibility to be familiar with the local media (i.e., radio and print media as well as television) so that the ads placed for an event are most likely to reach potential ticket buyers, rather than those who might be marginally interested in the event, or not interested at all.

If there is an in-house agency an -advantage is gained in that the facility can either keep the normal 15% ad placement commission as a revenue source or use it to purchase additional advertising for the same show.

It is possible to increase the advertising schedule for an event on a non cash basis if the attraction and manager are willing to allow a radio station (or, less commonly, a newspaper or TV station) to be the show's official media sponsor. For example, a concert artist whose music is in popular demand by a radio station's listening audience would make that station eager to become associated with the show. In return for some complimentary tickets which the station can give away through various contests as well as for the opportunity to have one of its disc jockey's as the show's emcee, the station is likely to provide two or three times the value of the complimentary tickets in additional advertising and promotional spots, which not only are designed to increase ticket sales for the show, but also to increase listenership for the radio station.

Never allow a media sponsorship to be construed as a sponsorship exclusive. Offer the media sponsor a promotional exclusive, but clearly retain the right to advertise anywhere else it is appropriate. Other radio stations and newspapers and very rarely television will accept tickets as non cash trade for advertising.

Media sponsorship should also not preclude an overall show sponsorship deal. For example, offer a member of the corporate community an opportunity to become involved as the official show sponsor. The Executive Director of the Hartford Civic Center secured the sponsorship for the Heublein Corporation for a Christmas concert that featured Tony Bennett and the Hartford Symphony Pops Orchestra. These two attractions, either alone or together, would not normally play a 16,000-seat arena. The funding of $15,000 provided by the sponsor was used to offset the show's advertising and promotional costs and offered Heublein the following returns:

1. Total name identification on all advertising as well as on the tickets, posters, display cards and on the Civic Center's own message center and outdoor marquee.
2. Fifty complimentary seats at cabaret tables on the arena floor.
3. A $2.00 group discount for all Heublein employees.
4. A cocktail party with Tony Bennett backstage after the event.
5. A Heublein banner in the arena as well as a program distributed to all patrons and tent cards on each table (Heublein paid for these items separately).
6. A rebate to Heublein of $1.00 per ticket sold, which Heublein in turn gave as a tax deductible donation to the Bushnell Park (restoration) Foundation. Because of this no-risk fund-raising opportunity, Foundation volunteers helped the show by working hard to sell tickets.

This sponsorship technique and variations on it may make an event possible that might not otherwise be economically feasible.

Another aspect of advertising is that which involves making potential tenants aware of your facility. Make every effort to budget funds each year for advertisements in various publications such as *Amusement Business, Variety Magazine, Aud-Arena, Billboard Magazine and Performance Magazine*. These national publications are read by people who make decisions to rent facilities such as yours for their events.

Budget funds each year to advertise the schedule of events in local newspapers in a format which people can clip out and retain on a month-to-month basis. Many facilities also publish a monthly in-house newsletter which is used as a direct-mail piece as well as a handout at the arena, the box office and other high-traffic locations.

If unable to maintain an in-house agency, it is advisable to interview and select a local agency to serve the facility and any tenant that needs such help ' Ad agencies to some managers represent 85% confusion at a charge of 15%. If an outside agency is engaged the performance must be constantly monitored in order that more than simple ad placement is accomplished. The agency should advise the facility manager and tenants of the most appropriate advertising media plan for a given event and it should have a good sense of promotion and public relations.

Depending on policy, advertising can be sold in a variety of mediums throughout the facility. The possibilities include a scoreboard system, concourse display cases, Zamboni (ice resurfacing machine), in-house publications, message centers, outdoor marquees, upcoming event display cases, ticket envelopes, ticket backs and concession product containers (e.g., soda cups, beer cups, popcorn boxes, napkins). There are a number of potential advertisers for these items within the corporate community. Concession product vendors are willing to advertise their names and products on concession containers. This coupled with discount sale promotions will increase food and beverage sales for the facility as well as its vendors.

Box Office

Booking outstanding events does not guarantee high-volume ticket sales. The key to selling tickets is good information and easy access for the ticket" buying public. How these objectives can be accomplished was the focus of a manual written by Larry Karasz for Ticket Craft, *A Complete Guide to Box Office Management* (1982).

Two basic elements of an event are the performers and the audience. The mission of the box office is to facilitate the selection of audiences. This task is accomplished by providing tickets to patrons. As a result of the service, audience and performer are brought together, with the dollars generated from the sale of tickets held by the box office until distribution of monies between those responsible for providing services (performer, promoter, agent, sponsor and facility) is determined. The box office operation also serves a public relations function, in that its personnel frequently provide the only contact between patron and facility.

A considerable amount of planning and preparation is required before the box office opens for business. The primary product of the box office is the ticket. Selection of the type of tickets and the method by which they will be sold require careful study. A number of factors must be considered, including the physical characteristics of the facility, its seating plans and the type of ticket system, pricing structure and sales incentive plans utilized.

Reserved seating is the preferred method. It assures a customer a specific seat location at the time the ticket is purchased, well in advance of the event. This will encourage early reservations and sales and the convenience of having seats together for couples or groups.

More and more facilities are introducing computerized ticket systems as a substitute for the traditional hard ticket approach. Using computerized tickets improves service to the public by providing a number of remote ticket outlets throughout the market area, usually in popular retail outlets. These outlets increase customer awareness of the facility and bring people from greater distances than normal to see events.

Many facilities have further expanded service to the public with the addition of a telephone credit-card service whereby customers simply call a special box office number and charge tickets to MasterCard, VISA, and occasionally American Express. This brings the box office into people's homes. With a "chargeline" system it is essential that each transaction be validated. Allow adequate time to process the order, pull the tickets and either mail them or leave them in the "will call" window so they can be picked up prior to show time. Such a service if properly advertised and managed can account for 20% or more of your annual gross box office sales. Consider imposing a service charge of $1.50 to $2.00 per order. This charge is not part of the box office settlement with the tenant and can produce a substantial amount of net revenue each year for the facility.

The group sales department generates volume purchases by making advance tickets available at discounted prices. It is very important that all group tickets be paid for in advance since groups have a tendency to reserve more tickets than they are able to sell and may try to return them at the last minute. This may not only result in a significant drop in the number of tickets sold, but also cause "large holes" in arena seating. This can be avoided if arrangements include either advance payment or the return of tickets in time to permit resale. Group sales account for as much as 30% of the total ticket sales for a multi-performance family show.

The box office also produces substantial revenue for the facility. Generation of monies over and above that shared by facility and promoter is accomplished by:

1. Charging on a cost plus basis for season ticketing services.
2. Charging a flat fee versus a percentage of gross ticket sales (whichever is greater) for each event. It is not uncommon for facilities to charge approximately $500 to $1,000 minimum versus three to four percent of gross ticket sales. Normally included for this fee are the box office sales staff, ticket printing charges, the group sales campaign, staffing and telephone and bank charges for your credit card service.
3. Imposing a per order service charge for all credit card purchases.
4. Reimbursement from tenants for direct printing and mailing costs for group sales material.
5. Charging a special handling fee for all mail orders. This fee is totally retained by the facility and is not part of the financial settlement with the tenant.

The amount of success realized by the box office operation is directly related to the degree that it is visible and convenient to the ticket-buying public. Box office personnel must be well-trained, courteous, friendly, knowledgeable and interested in the special needs and desires of the ticket-buying public.

Concessions

Don Meyers, Manager of the Memorial Coliseum in Ft. Wayne, Indiana, effectively spoke of the significance of the concession operations when he offered: "A well-operated concession department is more often than not the determining factor in the financial success of an auditorium or an arena. Rarely is an auditorium successful without a sound concession operation. It is an accepted fact that good food and drink go hand in hand with recreation and sports." Over a decade later, Don Jewell, author of Public Assembly Facilities: Planning and Management, made a similar observation when he stated that:

> The importance of good concessions operation to the average arena or stadium cannot be overemphasized. The role of the concessions department drops proportionately with the size of the facility to the point that it may be of only slight concern in many performing art centers. Rarely is an arena, auditorium or stadium financially successful without an efficient concession operation. If the public decides that its entertainment and recreational needs are being properly served, it will return time and time again. The total experience, however, must be consistently satisfactory. Percentages vary, but all arenas report concessions revenue as an important and vital part of total volume.

The Hartford Civic Center is an example of the revenue potential from concessions. Concession revenue amounted to $2,130,000 or 36% of its operating revenue in 1981-82.

A fundamental matter facing all event managers is how concessions should be handled, The basic choices are in-house operation or leasing the operation to a private contractor.

In-house operations offer the following advantages:

1. Management has complete control of concessions. This permits immediate response to needs that arise.
2. Management controls pricing. A fair market price can be maintained thereby avoiding customer complaints of "rip-off' or "price gouging."
3. The quality of the product can be controlled.
4. There is greater potential for generating revenue.

The Hartford Civic Center realized a net profit that was at least 15% greater than the return that any concessionaire was able to guarantee.

Concessionaires stress the following advantages of a lease arrangement:

1. Volume purchasing enables the vendor to provide quality products at reduced prices.
2. Sales will be expanded beyond anything that could be generated with an in-house system. The concessionaire can return to the facility more revenue than would be possible with an in-house operation due to its supervisory experience, efficiency, expertise and capacity.
3. Capital outlays for equipment are avoided.

4. Management, staff, purchasing, maintenance, inventory, storage, and vendor relations are eliminated.

Before making a decision regarding arrangements for concessions, information must be gathered. A survey of facilities of comparable size and profile is essential. The analysis should include such categories as profitability, purchasing and product costs, personnel and labor costs, the ability to maximize sales, accounting and controls, facility management's involvement and right of approval and capital investment. Other sources of information are national headquarters of both the International Association of Auditorium Managers and the National Association of Concessionaires. This will be one of the most important deals ever negotiated for the facility.

Information gathering is also a must if physical design problems are to be avoided. Steve Rogers called attention to the requirement in an article entitled "Avoiding Concession Design Problems," *Managing the Leisure Facility* (November/December, 1980). Rogers listed as the major shortcomings:

1. not enough concession stands to serve the number of seats;
2. inadequate kitchen location and space;
3. no installation of floor drains in kitchen and stand areas;
4. no provision for a commissary for hawking (vending) operations;
5. service elevators on the opposite side of the building from storage areas;
6. no provision for exhaust (which causes a severe limitation in ability to present an attractive menu, especially with fried foods);
7. loading docks and storerooms on different floors than needed;
8. inadequate ventilation;
9. insufficient energy and water availability; and
10. lack of wide concourse areas to facilitate traffic flow.

Geoff Older, formerly with the Volume Services Division of the Interstate United Corporation of Chicago, stated that, "You can have stands that are functionally perfect, but located in an improper position." Invariably, architects give more attention to toilets, which so often are located where the concessions stands should be. Bert Pailey, also of Volume Services, states that, "Toilets do not generate revenue and people have a way of finding them. Those prime locations should be for concession stands."

Don Jewell in Public Assembly *Facilities* Planning and *Management points* out that to be effective, stands should be conveniently located to all seats. The patron should be able to reach the nearest stand in 40 to 60 seconds. Stands should be well-organized with clear indications of where the patrons should line up for service. Equipment, food and cash registers should be conveniently located so that items can be quickly served by a single person in each selling station. This will help to minimize confusion and interference among the stand workers and also expedite one-stop service to patrons.

Concession stands should also be bright, colorful, well-lit and decorated with attractive pictures of the food and beverage being served. Menu boards should be installed clearly indicating the products and prices. The ability to generate the aroma of food such as popcorn into the concourse will also do a great deal to stimulate concession sales.

In 1982 the National Association of Concessionaires (NAC) in conjunction with Coca-Cola USA and Cornell University published a study for NAC members entitled, "Creating and Handling Buying Fever," which discussed the basic elements of a successful concession operations marketing plan such as the menu, realizing profit potential, merchandising, promotions and cutting service delay time.

The study acknowledges that concession revenue often determines whether the facility operates profit or loss. This can only be accomplished with the right products and the right packaging at the right prices provided the location is easily accessible. In order to be successful a concession stand must influence the customer to purchase on impulse. The NAC study states that "human beings experience the world through five senses: sight, smell, touch, taste, and sound. A sensation that has a positive effect on any one or a combination of the senses creates a favorable response in a person's mind. It's when that response is translated into action that the sale is made. The impulse purchase."

The smell of a hot dog cooking on a grill is often all it takes to trigger a purchase. Attractive photographs of a soft drink or popcorn will also influence a patron to buy something before finding a seat. To create *buying fever* the snack bar has to be an "attention grabber." The more senses positively affected, the better.

One of the first items noticed by a potential customer is the menu. An impulse can be destroyed if it is overcome by resistance to high prices. The pricing structure should be reasonable for the products being offered. Brand name products are easily recognized by customers thereby eliminating questions about the quality of the merchandise. The menu should include items that require minimal preparation time and have a low average unit cost. This will cut labor expenses and increase profitability while permitting reasonable prices. It is advisable for the facility manager to sample the products being offered and periodically conduct a comparative price check with competing facilities.

The NAC report stressed the value of cleanliness and employee training. People are turned off by employees that look dirty or concession stands that look unclean and poorly maintained.

In 1981 concession sales surpassed $3.5 billion in the United States. Stan Briggs, in another NAC report entitled "Concession Employee Training" published in INSITE '82, points out that the industry needs a manual which can be a real working tool and a blueprint for training employees and managing successful concession operations. Employee training is a critical aspect of a successful concession operation. Briggs maintains that management has a responsibility to train its employees. The industry is heavily dependent on young people who are starting their first jobs. This increases the importance of a training program. Employee training is also a key ingredient in merchandising concession products. Train employees to suggestively sell. For example, one out of three customers orders a soft drink in a small size. Suggestive selling is a proven technique for getting that trade up. Have your employees take the initiative by *asking* if they want a large size, The employee must act to convince the customer that all items are reasonably priced and that buying larger sizes actually results in saving money. he menu board is the main vehicle to communicate values to the customers.

Promotions and marketing are also key elements of a successful concession operation. The Hartford Civic Center introduced these elements as factors in the bid criteria for the purchase of certain resale items. For example, in the award of the hot dog contract the successful bidder was Grote & Weigel, which not only had the quality product, but also committed up to $40,000 in advertising. The basic theme of their campaign was that Grote & Weigel franks were the official franks of the Whalers (Hartford's Home NHL Hockey Franchise) sold at the Hartford Civic Center. This had a significant impact on sales. Grote & Weigel and other suppliers enhanced the appearance of menu boards and product displays. They also purchased advertising space on the scoreboard and in concourse display cases.

In general, today's suppliers are in a position and often very eager to offer the facilities promotional devices, ideas and other information to move their products. In this manner, they actually become partners in the concession operation. They will provide promotional ideas, devices and, especially with a new product, colorful promotional posters and displays which can be extremely helpful in catching the customer's eye.

The key points of the NAC's "Buying Fever Check List" are listed as follows:

1. Review merchandising and menu boards for clarity. Communicate and make it easier to order.
2. Cut down on inquiry time through effective menu board layout.
3. Use combinations of menu items to reduce the number of customer decisions.
4. Keep your equipment in good repair. Perform preventative maintenance checks regularly.
5. Locate equipment and supplies for soft drinks and popcorn adjacent to the dispensers.
6. Place the menu board so that it is easily visible to all customers.
7. Ensure that employees check supplies during slack time and that additional supplies are easily accessible.
8. Make lettering on the menu boards large enough so that it is easily readable for all customers. List all brands of soft drinks carried in their logo script and all the names of sizes and prices for all items.
9. Provide containers or boxes for customers to carry large orders.
10. If you don't have a cash register, place an adding machine or table of prices for popular combinations for the employees to use.
11. Design your stand with promotions in mind. Build in space to handle premiums such as plastic cups and posters.

Many facilities do not capitalize on another highly profitable aspect of the concession operation—having "vendors" or "hawkers" take food and beverages to the people in the seating area who are reluctant to get up and risk missing part of the event. Another contribution made by "vendors" or "hawkers" is that they relieve the pressures placed upon permanent concession stands during intermission, when customers literally swarm the concession facilities

Merchandising

The term "merchandising" describes the process of selling programs, novelties, T-shirts and other event-related souvenirs. This business has changed dramatically in the last two years, as T-shirts, jerseys and painter's caps commemorating each rock act's tour have become the fashion among concert-goers. Bands and acts, beginning with Billy Joel on July 11, 1980, are now routinely obtaining injunctions and seizure orders from federal courts to protect trade rights to their names, pictures and symbols. These rights were being exploited by unauthorized bootleggers at great loss to both the artists and the facilities in which they performed.

Because of the huge potential for the artist there is tremendous pressure on facility managers to both maximize sales and reduce the percentage rates they charge to the performers. Many managers are accused of charging exorbitant merchandising fees by representatives of the various attractions and supporting franchises. Herbie Herbert, Manager of the rock act "Journey" and Dale Morris, Manager of the country and western band "Alabama" are perhaps the most vocal crusaders against such high charges by facilities.

Merchandising seminars have proven to be the hottest topics on the agenda of various meetings and conferences of the International Association of Auditorium Managers. "Journey," for example, in 200 concerts in less than two years will gross an estimated $20 million in T-shirts and novelty sales. This is big business, and "Journey" and most other acts are looking more closely at percentages charged by facilities which usually average 35 to 40% of gross sales. While facility managers and rock artist representatives are battling one another over percentage rates, they unite to combat bootleggers. Bootleggers have a tremendous impact on merchandising sales for both the artist and the facility. The Hartford Civic Center coped with the problem in the following manner. On August 2, 1982, attorneys obtained from the United States District Court in Hartford a permanent injunction and an order of seizure permitting the restraining of the sale of counterfeit T-shirts, posters and other unauthorized merchandise at musical events at the Hartford Civic Center. The order, which was issued by the U.S. District Court Judge José A. Cabranes, was only the third such order ever issued in the United States. The other two were issued in Philadelphia and Cincinnati; however, the injunction in Hartford set a precedent since it imposed no geographical or time limitations.

The Hartford Civic Center was very active in obtaining temporary orders for most of its concerts prior to obtaining the permanent one. Concerts for which injunctions were obtained normally achieved merchandise sales of $3.31 per capita, while others only achieved $1.08 per capita. And, three major rock shows at the Hartford Civic Center since 1980 brought in average sales of $6.60 per capita. These included "The Rolling Stones" ($8.90), "AC/DC" ($5.63), and "Rush" ($5.11).

Prior to obtaining the permanent injunction, judges in Connecticut were issuing orders allowing the seizure of bootleg items sold at the Civic Center rock shows on a case-by-case basis. The new orders eliminated the need to go to court before each show thus saving a minimum of $2,300 per show in attorney's fees alone, which had been deducted off-the-top before the Civic Center split merchandising with the artist.

Because of the Hartford Civic Center's aggressive stand in obtaining the permanent injunction and because the permanent injunction resulted in significantly increased sales, there was less pressure to reduce the facility's standard 35 to 40% commission. Everyone made more money in this relatively unique approach to the merchandising wars.

Most facilities use an outside merchandising contractor rather than an in-house staff. The contractor is paid a percentage of gross sales—usually between 10 and 15%—and in turn provides and pays all sales staff, consigns over and inventories the merchandise from the artist and provides a full accounting of sales to both the artist and the facility. It is not uncommon for such contractors to invest up to

$25,000 for attractive and permanent merchandise display stands in key areas in the facility's concourse.

Rock acts, as well as family attractions and sporting franchises, are looking more and more to merchandise revenue to balance their budgets. It is vital that the facility managers create and maintain an environment where merchandising can be maximized with a minimum of friction between the facility, its tenants and the merchandising contractor. The net effect is substantially increased revenue.

Parking

Parking is always a problem, but if handled properly it can also be a very lucrative source of revenue. Virtually everyone who attends an event arrives by car, but they do not necessarily have to park in the facility's lot. Parking operations in most cases, therefore, cannot be taken for granted. Careful attention must be given to creating an easy traffic flow so cars can enter and exit quickly. The lot must be well-paved, well-lit and secured, and management should have a graphic system that makes it easy for people to find their cars at the conclusion of events. An adequate number of cashiers and attendants will improve operations.

Additional parking revenue (at least $1.00 per space) can also be achieved by offering preferred or special parking for customers willing to pay the price to park closer to the building.

In many respects, parking is a very difficult operation to manage. Having good employees with qualities of honesty and trust is a lot easier when you have tight financial controls. John Root, Manager of the San Francisco Cow Palace, presented a paper entitled, "Parking—New Sources Of Revenue" to the 1980 National Conference of the International Association of Auditorium Managers. He shared the results of a survey conducted by the Cow Palace regarding different controls in effect at other facilities. They included the following:

1. Sensors or loops buried in each entrance line.
2. A single pass lane.
3. A cashier or checker watching the sellers and authorizing passes.
4. Spot checks on sellers.
5. Different colored tickets for different events, days or hours.
6. Cash registers.
7. TV monitors.
8. Clean graphics and signs indicating special entrances.

The parking operation is second only to the box office in terms of direct contact between facility and patron. A well-designed and managed parking operation will ease crowd tension and allow for sufficient time for patrons to buy a snack and still get to their seats on time—and in a good frame of mind. There is no question that the ease of access and parking is a major factor in increased public acceptance and attendance at events.

Televising Events

Vickers, Dante Cork and Jim Millet wrote an interesting article entitled, "Cable TV—A New Day Dawns for Facility Managers," which appeared in the April 1983 issue of *Auditorium News*. The authors offer "that pay television may one day lead to crowdless games played before a cameraman and technicians. Not only will there be no fans paying for tickets, there will be no fans to park, to eat refreshments or to buy (programs) or souvenirs."

More and more events, especially sporting events, are being televised either on cable, pay and/or network television. It is still too early to properly assess the impact that televising home games will have on actual attendance levels; however, there is a clear danger that if tenants are allowed relatively unrestricted ability to televise home games, some facilities may turn into little more than large broadcast studios.

Some in the industry, such as Joe Cohen of the Madison Square Garden's Cable Network, see cable television as an opportunity. This, of course, stems in part at least from the fact that the owners of Madison Square Garden Cable Network also own Madison Square Garden, as well as its two prime tenants, the New York Knickerbockers and the New York Rangers. In such cases, televising events can be controlled so that when the teams are playing poorly and attendance is down, revenue levels can be maintained by televising the product, whereas when the teams are playing well and there is a strong demand for tickets, television can be restricted.

Most facilities are not in such a powerful position. The owner of the facility and the owner of the sporting franchise become adversaries on the issue of whether or not to allow televising of a home game. One possible compromise is to negotiate a "make-whole" clause in the agreement with the franchise whereby the franchise agrees to reimburse the facility for any drop in attendance at televised home games. For example, assume that the Hartford Whalers played non-televised home games against the Minnesota North Stars in the 1982 and 1983 seasons and the average paid attendance was 9,000 per game. The Whalers were then offered a lucrative contract by a local television station to televise the 1984 game against Minnesota. The Hartford Civic Center granted permission and the game only drew 8,000 paid attendees. By virtue of the "make-whole" agreement, the Whalers would be responsible for paying the Civic Center for lost rent and concession revenue based on the following formula:

1. The average ticket price for the Whaler's 1982 and 1983 games was $9.50. This amount ($9.50) times the difference between the average attendance for 1982 and 1983 and the actual attendance for 1984 (i.e., 1,000) produces a revenue shortfall of $9,500 for the 1984 game, which, it is assumed, was due to the fact that this game was televised. The $9,500 shortfall in ticket sales times the Civic Center's rental charge (13%) equals $1,235 in "make-whole" rent payments to the Hartford Civic Center; and,

2. The Hartford Civic Center's actual concession sales for the 1982 and 1983 Whaler games average $2.50 per capita. Both the Whalers and the Civic Center agreed that the Civic Center achieved a 55% net profit on its concession operations. By virtue of the make-whole agreement, the $2.50 per capita figure would be multiplied by the difference in attendance (1,000). This equals $2,500. This figure would then be multiplied by the 55% net profit factor (so that the Whalers would not have to reimburse the Civic Center for overhead, staffing and product costs not actually incurred), thus requiring the Whalers to pay the Civic Center $1,375 in lost concession revenue.

The total formula would result in a reimbursement penalty to the Civic Center of $2,610. There are a number of variations to this formula, but the basic intent is to ensure that the facility does not suffer lost revenue as a result of franchise's desire to televise a home game(s). With such a "makewhole" provision it becomes less risky for a facility to allow its franchise to televise home games. And there may be certain intangible benefits derived by the facility and the franchise. For example, seeing a team play well and sensing the excitement in the arena may encourage more people to buy tickets and see the action live.

Once properly protected, it then becomes time to look more positively at the opportunities that television offers. For example, while tenants have the right to televise their product, they do not necessarily have the right to provide the "hookup" for the station(s) which has been granted the broadcast rights. The actual hookup contractor should be investigated. Contractors should be charged with installing permanent cabling/wiring in the facility to make hookups more efficient and economical. They should also be responsible for providing complete state-of-the-art television, AM/FM radio and closed-circuit television equipment (including uplink capacity), as well as the personnel and technicians required for the operation and maintenance of this equipment.

The television hookup contractor must also be able to clearly demonstrate the ability to reduce the cost of originating television transmissions from the facility while at the same time providing the facility with the greatest possible financial return. Without any investment or risk a net of $500 to $1,000 per hookup can be realized.

Knowing downside risks and having the spirit of cooperation with tenants the television industry can result in considerable benefit to the facility. There is no question that television will become an ever more dominant factor in the presentation of live events. Television revenue is too lucrative to pass up and many franchises need it just to break even. While facility managers should not stand in the way of such progress, they should first protect their own interests. *Be a partner— not a victim.*

Summary/Conclusion

The facility is, in the final analysis, a sales and marketing organization. Management's primary responsibility is to satisfy the tenants who rent the facility and customers who attend the events.

A strong sales and marketing capacity is critical to success. Once an event is confirmed, there is a limited amount of time to conduct the promotion, marketing and advertising campaigns, sell the tickets and actually produce the event. How the entire package of services and functions discussed in this chapter (i.e., scheduling, advertising, box office, concessions, merchandising, parking and television) is handled will determine the immediate and long-range success of the facility. Do not forget to be ever-conscious about providing a well-run, clean and safe environment. This will add to the enjoyment of those attending the events, and patrons in a good frame of mind will be more likely to purchase food, beverages and merchandising and return to other events at the facility. Take time to review the organization, inside and out, from a sales and marketing point of view. In fact, this should be a continuous process because management should never take tenants or the public for granted.

Chapter 12

Fund-Raising Strategies

Don Canham

Introduction

Virtually all minor and major organizations are constantly in need of funds. There are, of course, many reasons why effective fund-raising is essential, but in recent years the primary one is that inflation has out-stripped the ability of organizations to be self-sufficient with the normal or usual methods of acquiring budget money. Expanded programs, recessions and changing priorities also complicate stability where funding is concerned. The end result where fund-raising fails is, of course, the elimination of activities and various teams on both the high school and collegiate level.

What Is Fund-Raising?

Fund-raising should be viewed as anything that increases revenue, including, but not limited to, concessions, merchandising, and grants.

Guidelines for Fund-Raising

It is important that the planning for any fund-raising campaign be shaped by the following factors. First, fund-raising must be program specific. For example, it is virtually impossible to raise money for general usage, while anything that directly benefits the student athlete, such as scholarship or equipment generates greater response from donors. Second, a prospect list from whom the funds will be raised must be established. Whether the organization will contact merchants, manufacturers, alumni, fans, the student body or professional people in the area are questions that must be addressed. Efforts will be more effective if contributors are able to claim gifts as tax deductions. In order for them to do so the project must meet IRS standards. Next, an accounting system must be established. Finally, an acknowledgment system has to be determined, with a complete follow-up on every dollar received. In short, a trail of paper must follow every gift. *Accurate accounting and acknowledgement must be a top priority in any kind of fund-raising.*

One of the biggest mistakes that novice fund-raisers make is to search for something new and different when, in actuality, it would be far better to adopt some program that has been successful at other institutions or other organizations. There are a multitude of events and projects that have been used successfully by others that can be adopted and used effectively regardless of the size and scope of the original undertaking. The challenge is not to originate activities but to be creative in the implementation of those things that have produced results elsewhere.

A definite *timetable* is a must requirement. There are programs that take as long as a year or more to complete, while others must be done in a very short period of time. The organization carrying out the plan must decide on a timetable to be followed. During the time of the project, constant progress reports must be filed by those involved in the fund-raising. In addition, the donors should be *updated periodically* as to the progress of the project. The reason for this is obvious. The people that have already given will give again especially if they are kept involved. The best prospects are persons who have a record of contributing to similar causes. Projects to fund athletes are a particular attraction for donors because the gift supports an enterprise that is highly visible.

In any fund-raising, the system of *checks* and *balances* must be utilized. An important caution is that all fund-raising be done through the department or the school rather than an outside booster club. One of the greatest mistakes in fund-raising is that rules of governing organizations are violated simply because outside groups are not cognizant of the myriad of rules under which school and collegiate sports are conducted.

Besides the tax exemption angle that can usually be applied when an educational institution is raising funds, we are constantly reading about outside fund-raisers who have operated out of their back pockets. Shortages and misuse of funds have occurred in every state in the union in this area. Therefore, whether one is having a pig roast, a raffle, Bingo-playing, an auction or a marathon, or whether one is attempting to sell tickets, the project must be under the firm *and absolute control of the educational institution.* Where fund-raising is done by organizations and not used for educational pursuits, it is absolutely essential that a legal binding contract be drawn and a board of directors meet periodically to monitor the funds.

Motivation of workers is essential to success. A system of rewards such as a trip to any football or basketball game, a dinner with a head coach, a free golf pass for a year, or a varsity-letter award can be used to satisfy the need.

Cautions

Regardless of what is going to be done, any fund-raising program has to evolve around *marketing* and *promotion.* The sum total of any successful program has always been the result of a good marketing program and one that dovetails with promotion. Probably the easiest way to understand the compatibility is to look at some of the things that have been done around the. country. In every case, whether it is a swimathon, walkathon, celebrity,, auction or a flea market project, the idea has to be marketed not only *among the volunteers working the projects but also among the people you are soliciting from and, of course, it has to be promoted and publicized.*

We must always remember that one cannot fool the public. Whatever you market must be of value to the potential customer. A promotion that actually cheats the public will come back to haunt the promoter many times over, and fund-raising will fail.

Fund-Raising Projects

One project that is extremely successful at schools such as Michigan and Tennessee is the summer camp. In some cases this is a day camp or a live-in camp as at Michigan and Tennessee. Camps are usually well received on the campus because they keep the dorms busy during the summer months, and food service, janitorial and maintenance workers do not have to be laid off. Secondly, summer camps provide employment and supplementary salaries for the coaches. One institution in the country nets over $160,000 each summer with a gigantic summer camp using their vacant facilities as over 5,000 campers, both men and women, go through the summer program. Many schools, both elementary and secondary, now hold day camps for anything from sports to computer learning.

Celebrity golf tournaments run by athletic departments during the summer are not only a great way to maintain relationships with alumni and community, but also provide revenue as well. Oklahoma State runs one of the most successful celebrity golf tournaments for their former athletes, and well-known alumni return to play golf and pay money to play in a foursome with celebrities. To a greater or lesser degree, most of the colleges in the country do this and many are also doing the same on the high school level using local radio, television, political and athletic personalities as the celebrities.

Several high schools and colleges put on ox-roasts and pork days or chicken fries to raise athletic funds. In this plan the alumni can donate an ox, a pig or two, or chickens, or all could be purchased at a discount. The promotion revolves around the community where entire families come to have a picnic dinner at a reasonable cost with proceeds going to athletic or other support groups. Variations of the ox-roast theme are unlimited and can be carried out in different ways.

Gabriel Richard High School in Ann Arbor, Michigan has a raffle at a "hot dog" dinner that provides a tremendous amount of money each year to support its athletic programs. Many other schools across the country use a variation of a raffle. The Gabriel Richard plan is to sell 200 to 300 tickets at $100 each and then contact merchants around town for gifts or prizes that could be purchased at cost or below. Gabriel Richard has found that often the merchant will donate the item for a tax write-off to help the program. The school has a hot dog supper and the drawing provides a prize on every tenth ticket drawn. This spreads the excitement over the evening and allows many people to win something of value. It is culminated by a drawing for an automobile. The raffle ticket sales provide between $20,000 to $30,000, making the total income from the event sizable for the athletic program.

A weekly Bingo game benefiting the athletic program, band or other causes, if properly promoted, can support more than a few needs for funds. Other progressive schools rely on concerts and such events as Harlem Globetrotters or donkey baseball exhibitions to help finance their programs.

One area that is not explored by many schools located near professional teams or large universities is the stadium cleanup. High school teams clean the University of Michigan Football Stadium and the hockey and basketball arenas after each game.

In other areas, the concession stands are manned by various high schools and church groups. At the University of Michigan we man about 50 different booths with high school groups. There are hundreds of ways that energetic teams and ambitious coaches can ensure funds.

The prime concern at most institutions on both high school and collegiate levels is the attraction of fans to the stadium and there have been literally hundreds of things tried to increase the ticket sales. One thing that should be obvious is that a full stadium or a large crowd attracts people, and that is why schools have band days where up to 30,000 band members have been admitted to the stadium free. Not only do these *band days* create the feeling that everyone is following the team, but also the free ticket brings mothers and fathers to the stadium to see their children play, and they park their cars, buy hot dogs and souvenirs and get interested in the football game and return on another day. At Michigan we have long felt that the *spectacle* is what we sell.

We also approach the lady of the house because we feel that she controls the weekend. If we can have her tell her husband that it might be a good idea to see a football game and have a tailgate picnic, we are home free. The only thing we have to do now is to make sure that they have a good time because as mentioned earlier, you cannot fool the public.

In Ann Arbor we have specialized in gigantic pre-game shows, half-time shows and post-game shows. At other institutions more flamboyant attractions have been held to get people in the stands to see the great spectacle of college football or a basketball game.

In an effort to increase attendance and thus funds, one cannot ignore group sales. Sales not only to manufacturing companies and other industries, but to churches, clubs, grade schools and high schools as well, certainly pay off. Discounted tickets are usually an attraction and when people get to the stadium, as mentioned above, they park cars, eat hot dogs and buy souvenirs. More important, if you have a show to put on you are making a fan. Cheerleading days, Boy Scout days, Girl Scout days and so forth with discounted or free tickets are now being instituted all over the country. Not only do these youngsters bring their parents who purchase full-price tickets, they all drink Coca-Cola. The special offer is almost limitless. One institution offers any student that has an "A" on their report card at either grade school or high school, a half-price ticket for a certain game. In addition to returns realized from public relations and product sampling, the half-price for an "A" promotion increased the sale of hot dogs and Cokes.

Prior to selling out the stadium on a season basis, the University of Michigan would allow a student to purchase a $2.00 ticket. In addition, we would allow an adult in free with every 5 to 10 youngsters. That way we figured the youngsters would have someone to drive the car bringing them to the game. We, of course, charge for parking. Before this practice was discontinued, we sold 72,000 discounted tickets in one year to these students. Now, 10 years later, these people are still our fans and are buying full-price tickets and no doubt one day will be bringing their own children to the Michigan football games.

One thing that was interesting in a survey Michigan once made was that weekly newspaper advertising was very cost effective. This is probably true because the paper is not thrown out each day; it is kept around the house until the next issue is delivered a week later. So, in fund-raising and promotion don't forget the weekly newspaper.

The University of Michigan is now promoting nonrevenue sports with the "Gold Key Card" where, for $25.00, an individual can purchase a card that will let him and a guest into every athletic contest on campus with the exception of football and basketball. When we sell 1,000 cards, it isn't hard to see that you are getting $25,000 for nonrevenue sports. When properly promoted by cheerleaders and athletes going door-to-door and merchant-to-merchant, the potential of the Gold Key Card is tremendous. In some situations, the "key" admission could include basketball and football. Everyone likes to think they have a pass and when the person walks up to the gate and flashes the card and walks in with his friend, without a ticket, I suppose it is assurance that he will buy again next year.

The most important factor in any fund-raising is the extent in which one gets others involved. It is extremely difficult for one individual, for instance, to raise money by phone contacts or letters, and it is virtually impossible for one person to raise any substantial amount of money for any project by personal contacts. If a letter campaign is going to be conducted, form letters simply will not do it. Personal letters directed to the individual, agency or corporation must be personalized and not mimeographed.

The same thing is true of trying to raise funds by sales of game tickets, cookies, T-shirts, coffee mugs and so forth. A group effort is essential. The most widely practiced method of involving people in a fund-raising project is by means of a team and league effort. Assume, for instance, that we are attempting to raise "Y" dollars to send our band to the Rose Bowl Parade. After having decided what group and type of people we will attempt to get the funds from, we must determine what people we have available, in the largest possible numbers, to join our organization for this effort. If 30 people, for instance, are involved in raising our funds, then our major problem is motivating these individuals to develop their own enthusiasm. By dividing these 30 people into 5 six-man teams and naming each team with exotic names (Gophers, Bench-Warmers, the Green Hogs, etc.) we have our 5-team league established. A captain is appointed for each team and a regular weekly or monthly meeting is scheduled at the outset.

The competition between the teams to see which team can be the most successful is the first small step in motivating the individual fund-raiser, as no one enjoys losing. Further, something of value must be provided for virtually all of the fund-raisers. The establishment of a campaign-closing dinner takes care of that. Everyone who does any work will receive a free dinner for himself and spouse. Beyond that, awards for the teams and individuals are unlimited. In one outstanding fund-raising campaign a university received a donation of a trip to Hawaii for two from a local travel agent who happened to be an alumnus of the University. In another case, an automobile dealer provided a free car for a year. Prizes range from seats in the press box, to a trip on the team bus, to a seat on the bench at an important game in either basketball or football, to other things such as letter awards and plaques. There should be an award set up for the overall individual and team who raised the most money. There should be individual awards for each individual on the losing teams who did the best job, so everyone who has struggled and worked will be rewarded.

At some central point (the lobby of a bank or an office building or on the campus, etc.) a visible progress chart should be kept so that others become aware of the efforts of the individuals who are doing the hard work. In addition, the individuals on the various teams must receive weekly reports via the mail spurring them on with the success and failures of the various teams in the competition. One thing not to neglect if the fund-raising project is going to be continued for more than one year is the "booby prize" and the last prize. Often the individual who failed one year is a tremendous success the next. In addition, however, it reminds everyone if they failed to perform at all, they are going to be signaled out in a humorous way. However, the point is made of this lack of effort to everyone. In one case the "booby prize" winner one year became the leading performer in a later fund-raising project and won a vacation trip to Acapulco.

There are, like changing times, certain events that are successful in a given era. Recently, with the advent of the flea market, schools across the country have benefited handsomely from properly organized flea markets. There are high schools across the country where their stadiums are used for Sunday morning flea markets almost weekly during the summer with rental fees and some profits going to the high school athletic programs.

In Ann Arbor, Michigan, celebrity auctions have been successful. The celebrity auction is accomplished by the organizers securing one item from celebrities throughout the state as a gift. For instance, a governor's tie; a famous and well-known athlete's practice jersey; a book autographed by a famous author, and so forth. The auction can be tax-exempt, and because items made available by celebrities are contributions, the celebrity receives a great deal of publicity. Of course, in that connection, the gift auction has been existence for many years. In this operation the organizing committee of fundraisers secures gifts from virtually everyone, and merchants, in general, are very generous with quality merchandise that simply hasn't moved off their shelves during the year. A general auction is held in the gymnasium or some such place and well-known auctioneers are secured to donate their time.

In the last few years in Ann Arbor, Michigan something similar has been extremely successful in that merchants hold a half-price sale extending over a two-day period. In this type of promotion, merchants are provided space in a huge indoor building and they run a big sale on merchandise that has not sold during the year. It is so successful that there is a waiting list for space on the part of merchants who are applying from various parts of the country as well as locally. It is an annual event and people know they will get tremendous bargains and the merchants know it is a way to clear nonmoving stock. The organizer makes his money in one of two ways. He can either rent the space to the merchant or can charge admission at the gate. In Ann Arbor we do both. This half-price sale has unlimited potential in small towns where it can be turned into an indoor county fair.

Many schools, of course, have used the celebrity roast and it is relatively easy to do because every school has a prominent person in town (mayor or a famous athlete). By using the local gymnasium or, in one case, a local restaurant on a Monday evening when it is normally closed, the overhead on the celebrity roast is virtually nonexistent. I think people have seen enough of them on television to understand how they are organized and run and the trick is to get the dinner donated either by the local women, the local bank, etc., and the funds from the dinner tickets sold would revert to the project.

Grants as a Source of Funds

Finally, too few schools and organizations are aware of the potential of foundations as funding sources. Virtually every town and every community have foundations of one kind or another; some individual, some corporate, some joint, and the local banks and libraries are sources to find these foundations and their purposes. Educational institutions, in particular, are the largest beneficiaries of foundation aid, and while the approach to a foundation remains a mystery with most fund-raising operations, it is one that should certainly be explored at the state and local level. National foundation aid is not as easy to come by as area aid, but to succeed in fundraising one must try everything.

Summary/Conclusion

Responsible athletic administrators can no longer view their charge as simply one of overseeing an operation that is expanded or contracted according to the size of the budget made available. The requirement today is to generate funding sufficient to meet the needs of existing programs and to provide for the establishment of new programs, The requirement introduces new dimensions to sport management. It represents both challenges and opportunities.

The starting place for a successful fund-raising effort is planning. Uses for the funds raised must be identified. A major prerequisite is carefully worked out organization, as is the careful selection of the project to be undertaken. Implementation of the project, monitoring of associated activities and careful follow-up will bring the project to a successful conclusion.

Chapter 13

Ticket Sales Through Promotion

John Moore

Introduction

There are many ways to promote a sports program and sell tickets at the same time. Dr. Bernard Mullin, an expert in sport marketing, defines promotions in the marketing sense as: "A catch-all category for any one of numerous marketing efforts designed to stimulate consumer interest, awareness, and purchases of the product."

Mullin makes a case for a sport manager with marketing training who is equally effective in "filling seats, court time in a racquet sport club, selling athletic socks and attracting people to participate in sport activities in a resort."

This chapter will consider promotions that can sell tickets. Although the emphasis is on interscholastic and intercollegiate events, the promotional ideas apply to amateur and professional sports, all elements of commercial and public sports, recreational facilities, clubs, resorts, camps and service organizations. Marketing activities include promotional planning, effective handling of ticket sales, advertising, personal selling and sales promotion.

Promotional Planning

There are numerous ways to develop fan support and sell tickets, but careful planning is essential for the promotion to succeed. Promotional efforts must be organized four to six months prior to the actual event. It is important to prepare a budget for promotions, develop objectives, establish a time frame and target dates for the completion of various items.

It is good practice to incorporate the promotional plan into booklet form with individual responsibilities designated and deadlines set so each individual will realize that a delay can hold up the entire procedure. It is helpful to keep the booklet updated as the season progresses with notes on each event. If it is necessary to make changes in the project, records will help when planning for another season. Good planning will lead to successful promotion and help create a favorable image of the program and hopefully lead to increased revenue through ticket sales.

Promotion Through Effective Ticket Handling

There are more ways to promote ticket sales for revenue sports than there are promoters, but one sure way to attract fans is to make buying tickets as easy as possible. Ticket sales can be facilitated through ticket outlets, payroll deductions, toll free numbers, Visa/MasterCards, and the use of direct mail.

A. Ticket Outlets

Some schools use a facsimile ticket program with large corporations. The University of Washington, in Seattle, works cooperatively with the Pay 'N Save Corporation with 50 ticket outlets located throughout the state. The Pay 'N Save stores are supplied with facsimile tickets for each home football game assuring the buyers that they can purchase the best seats available regardless of which Pay 'N Save outlet is used. The tickets are numbered by game with the section, row and seat number left blank. When a customer comes to the store the clerk calls the ticket office on a telephone line that is specifically installed for this program to reserve a preferred location. If there are no seats available in the preferred section, the best available seats are reported to the clerk and when the customer agrees to buy the seats, the clerk fills in the section, row and seat lines on a facsimile ticket. The ticket office at the University then "kills" the original ticket.

The Pay 'N Save Corporation receives a commission on ticket sales and has the advantage of extra traffic in its stores. The ticket outlets facilitate the purchase of tickets and the University benefits from the sale of tickets and the promotional advertising in the store.

Many small schools on both the scholastic and collegiate level may not have large corporations to set up ticket outlets on their behalf. These schools, however, can utilize banks, convenience stores or other businesses to display attractive ticket posters and order blanks. It is important when advertising season tickets to include the location of the season ticket order forms. Make the form easy to fill out and return and include a telephone number that is prominent on the envelope for persons who want to contact the ticket office with questions pertaining to certain game tickets. The order forms in the stores give daily advertisement for the sports program and convenience for ticket buyers while providing the stores or businesses the benefit of additional traffic and valuable exposure.

B. Payroll Deduction

The University of Washington promotes sales with business and industry by allowing the employees to purchase tickets through payroll deduction plans. This allows the company the opportunity to give its employees an added fringe benefit while the University receives a specialized mailing list at the same time it markets its tickets.

Boeing Aircraft in Seattle, Washington is an example of a company that works cooperatively with a university to promote ticket sales. Boeing employs thousands and the University of Washington offers them employee discounts on reserved tickets and family plans for selected games.

The University makes announcements during its games to show its appreciation to the employees of various companies that use this plan and at times its band salutes a particular company during its halftime show.

Some schools send computer cards to all the employees of a particular company and the order cards are returned to the school with mailing labels. When the school fills the order, the company sends a check to the school and collects the money through payroll deduction. The only work involved in the process for the ticket office is the task of putting tickets in envelopes, applying labels and mailing the tickets to the employees. Ticket sales cannot be handled any easier than this.

C. Toll-free Number and Visa/MasterCards

Duke University, in an attempt to facilitate ticket sales, installed an 800 (toll-free) number for use within the State of North Carolina. At the same time it added to the convenience of its patrons by allowing use of Visa or MasterCards to charge tickets. The combination of the two was calculated to increase the sale of tickets and public response was so overwhelming that a second 800 number line was installed for year-round use instead of six months. Information regarding the toll-free and Visa/MasterCard use is sent to all Duke alumni within the State of North Carolina with a small, stick-on card that can be placed on the individual's telephone.

The 800 number is easy to obtain and can be installed and charged on a monthly basis or by the number of telephone calls that are received. This helps the ticket office monitor the number of calls received for tickets and gives an indication of the usefulness of the toll-free number.

The Visa/MasterCard charge program can be arranged through a local bank. In all of the promotional material, place the 800 number and Visa/MasterCard symbol in prominent places. Tickets to all home games can be obtained merely by calling the ticket office through the toll-free number and using Visa/MasterCard to pay for them. The tickets can be mailed to the purchaser or picked up at the ticket office on the day of the game.

Once again, every attempt is made to make the purchase of tickets as easy as possible, since ease and convenience will lead to increased sales and patron satisfaction.

D. Direct Mail

Many schools and sports organizations in the sport industry use direct mail for all promotional campaigns since it is one of the best ways to reach the ticket-buying public. The cost of direct mail is relatively low when compared to the large number of people that are reached. Direct mail is flexible and can be targeted to a vast number of people or concentrated in a very small area.

Several suggestions that are helpful in planning the ticket order for direct mail:

1. *Mail third class.* Give ample time for the promotional piece and order blank to reach the public, By using the third class rate, substantial savings can be realized.

2. *Use color.* It is important that the promotional piece be colorful and attractive. The piece should be so designed that the patron will want to open and read it.

3. *Make it easy to read.* The secret in producing the promotional piece is the ease of reading. Keep the material simple, clear and concise and easy to read.

4. *Make it simple to order.* Be sure to make the order form simple so that the patron can understand the details and directions and enclose a check with the order form or call a toll-free number.

Target and direct mail to past ticket buyers of individual or season tickets. It is important to cultivate season ticket prospects by mailing pre-season publicity with comments from the athletes and coaches and information regarding outstanding performers and incoming standout-athletes. Highlight the dates of special events in the mailing.

In the spring or early summer, mail a personalized ticket order form that identifies the location of last year's seats and give the patrons the priority of retaining last year's seats. Later in the summer include the direct mail flyer to anyone who purchased a season ticket or tickets for individual games. Give previous season ticket holders as many opportunities as possible to order season tickets.

After the promotional flyer and ticket order have been mailed to past season ticket holders, members of the booster club, alumni within the state, those on the waiting list and others who for any reason have contacted the ticket office, decide who should receive the remaining flyers. Many schools mail the promotional flyer to every household in the county in which the school is located. This type of mailing list can be obtained from firms who specialize in such lists at a reasonable cost.

Coordinate the advertising campaign and other promotional plans around the direct mail flyer. Prepare the public for the direct mailing with advertisements in media, visible means such as billboards, posters and order forms placed in local businesses. The "blitz" type campaign keeps the school's sport program in front of the public and gets the public's attention toward the upcoming season and ticket sales. Two weeks after the "blitz" campaign place the direct mail flyer in the local newspaper as one final reminder.

The University of Michigan maintains sell-out crowds of over 100,000 for all home football games by using direct mail to reach over one million patrons each year. Michigan defers the cost of the direct mail flyer by advertising items sold in the University's school store. The list of items is included along with the ticket order. The public can order tickets (when available) but also purchase items bearing the school's logo from the school store. Don Canham, the former Athletic Director at the University of Michigan, reports that the sale of coffee cups alone has paid for the direct mail campaign and furnishes additional revenue for the athletic program.

Code the mail order to monitor the returns. Some institutions use a system of dots to record where the returns come from. One dot is used for alumni, two dots represent former ticket holders, three dots indicate residents of certain areas while four dots signify those who respond to newspaper advertisements. This method enables the school to determine the value of the direct sales flyer to the various target groups. It may also provide an answer to the question of whether the first mailing is sufficient or if a second mailing is required. Utilize the ticket office staff to compile the location of the direct mail to make the marketing system work. This information will target potential ticket buyers for the following season and give directions for the use of funds to promote future ticket promotion.

Advertising

The goal of advertising is to develop interest in a particular sport program and use this interest to add revenue to operate the program. Effective communication is essential in addition to careful decision-making regarding which media to use in the advertising campaign.

It is necessary to develop an advertising budget to determine the amount of funding available for the promotional effort. Each of the media has sales representatives who will explain the types of advertising available and fee structures. After an amount is determined, divide the percentage of advertising to be used for the pre-season ticket campaign and individual game advertising. Include the amount of funds apportioned to radio, television, newspaper and billboard promotion.

Trade outs. One of the most economical ways to advertise is through a process known as trade outs. By this method a school offers a certain number of tickets or reciprocal advertising in its publications to the various media. In return, the media allocates advertising for the dollar amount of the tickets or advertising. The process is simple. For five individual tickets at eight dollars each or a total of $40 for the entire season ticket, the media allocates $40 in free advertising. It is possible to furnish $5,000 in tickets and add another $5,000 and receive $10,000 in valuable media publicity and guarantee a good advertising base. It is never a good policy to simply trade out advertisement without purchasing advertisements. Good public relations with the media dictate a balance in trade outs and paid advertisements. Trade outs make an excellent supplement and strengthen the advertising budget.

Assistance From Business and Industry

Business and industry can often provide valuable assistance in the promotion of ticket sales. Some of the more common ways it can help is through sponsorships, visits to shopping centers, group ticket sales at discount prices and help in promotional events at particular contests.

In planning for the sports year, remember that businesses often sponsor promotional items enabling a sport program to pay for the cost of a project or add revenue for the program.

Schedule cards are an important item to any sports program and this item can be sponsored by a business. Some organizations distribute over 100,000 schedule cards for their revenue sports and the cost is paid by a business that finds it a valuable means of exposure. The business usually puts its name on the card and through the distribution to large- numbers of patrons receives tremendous publicity.

Other items that can be sponsored include posters, flyers and special days at games. Local businesses are often willing to assume the entire cost of promotional items and consider it an inexpensive venture that pays significant dividends. This is an economical way to reach the public and gives the organization and business an opportunity to reach many people and potential ticket buyers.

Elon College, a liberal arts institution in North Carolina with an outstanding sport program, faces a perennial problem in its attempt to operate an intercollegiate sports program through revenue derived from ticket sales. While its athletic program is highly successful and nationally prominent, the college is located in an area in which spectator interest is centered around the Atlantic Coast Conference and particularly the Big Four (Duke, University of North Carolina, North Carolina State and Wake Forest).

Elon College's athletic director, Dr. Alan White, actively promotes the sport program through vigorous and often innovative ways. According to White: "We have tried about every type of promotional idea that we can think of, some have been successful, some not so successful." He points out that he tries various ways to promote the sale of tickets that include:

1. Season ticket sales for basketball and football;
2. All sports season tickets;
3. All sports family season tickets;
4. A family basketball plan; and
5. A family football plan.

Of the plans listed above, White reports that the family all sports plan and the season family football plan are the most successful.

The College utilizes other promotional plans that can be adopted by high schools, small colleges, large universities and other segments of the sport industry.

A. Corporate Sponsorships

A corporation puts up front money for a particular event. A fast-food corporation, for example, sponsors a Friday and Saturday basketball tournament and distributes coupons that provide free admission to the games. In return the University gives radio advertisement to the corporation, provides advertisement in its program and features the corporation by putting up signs in the arena. The corporation receives tickets which it distributes through its restaurants. This sponsorship is offered to many other corporations in the area.

White notes that many corporations support his sport program in other ways that include:

giving funds for advertisement, not only in the program, but also on the back of tickets with the usual coupon for a reduced price on various items. Tickets are sold to the corporation for the employees on a two-for-one basis or in some instances the employer makes the tickets available at a reduced rate. Some corporations give away items at half-time on a free drawing-type basis an provide sponsorship as well as the give-away prizes.

Many sport organizations encourage group sales at special discount prices to attract fans.

B. Group Sales

Elon College invites junior and senior high school pep bands, marching bands, and cheerleading groups to its sports contests. Many parents come with these groups and, in many instances, return if they like what they see.

The sports department works closely with the admissions office to promote tickets for high school students. The admissions office purchases a block of tickets for a particular sports event at a reduced price and invites prospective students and parents to visit the campus and attend the event.

C. Shopping Centers (Mall) Visits

In most communities the majority of ticket buyers live in suburbs rather than in downtown areas. In like manner shopping is located in the suburban centers (malls). Malls are ideal locations to promote ticket sales. The businesses located in the malls are often eager to sponsor promotional visits from sport programs to increase attendance and sales.

One of the best ways to promote the sale of tickets is to get athletes and coaches into the community through special visits to the malls. Such visits give added support to the businesses in the malls who may also be supporting the sport program through advertisements or by being outlets for ticket sales. Duke University utilizes the shopping center visit to promote its program and sell tickets at the same time and recommends the following:

In communities with more than one shopping mall, plan several visits to the various malls. Visits can be scheduled by contacting the mall's manager who is usually interested in promoting events that attract people. It is preferable to schedule a Saturday afternoon in August for football or soccer or a week night for basketball or ice hockey. The week night activity should be scheduled at an hour that young children can attend.

The promotional visits should include cheerleaders to create a festive atmosphere and last for two to three hours. Many schools distribute general information about their institution and sports program and give out season ticket flyers, bumper stickers, pens, buttons and other promotional items. This is an excellent time to sell posters or yearbooks which the athletes and coaches can autograph for the purchasers.

During the mall visit, it is helpful to set up a game that will involve participation for the public with the athletes. This works very well in basketball and soccer. In basketball set up indoor goals, provided by a local sporting goods store, and sponsor a free-throw shooting contest with the athletes. The public is encouraged to kick a soccer ball into an indoor goal or participate in a dribbling demonstration with the members of the team. Small prizes are awarded the winners. Some schools receive a good response to sport clinics conducted by the athletes.

Encourage the athletes and coaches to wear game uniforms during the mall visits so the public can identify with uniform numbers as well as faces. Attempt to schedule the mall visits annually.

External Promotional Events

A. Special Days

After plans are completed for promoting season tickets, look at each game on an individual basis and identify the games that will not sell out. Plan special day promotions to attract fans. These days can include helmet day, jersey day, parents day or celebrity day. The type of day will be influenced by the location of the school and particular interests of its fans.

B. Autograph Day

One of the most successful promotions at many schools is an autograph session at the school where the public has the opportunity to personally meet the athletes and coaches. Many schools invite the public to their campus prior to the start of a particular season to meet the athletes and coaches dressed in game-day uniforms. Autograph days can be publicized through the media by featuring various athletes and coaches personally inviting the public to attend. The public is encouraged to bring cameras and take family pictures with the athletes and coaches. Some schools obtain soft drinks from the vendor who has the refreshment rights and provide them at no cost to the public. Autograph sessions are popular with the public and particularly children who love to meet athletes and coaches in the arena in which they play when they are dressed in game uniforms. Autograph days can be used for any sport.

C. Youth Day

Youth Day is successful at many schools and a popular annual event. Several suggestions are as follows:

Select a day for Youth Day well in advance of the event and schedule it for a game that will have seats available. In football, for example, the day is scheduled in early spring. Avoid cold or inclement weather by choosing an early game. After a date is selected, contact various youth and church groups for names of the youth leaders and mailing lists. After the mailing lists are received, do an early mailing in May in the form of an announcement so youth groups can place the event on their calendars and plan to attend. The early mailing is very important for a good response.

Follow up the early mailing with another mailing in the fall after school has begun with final details of Youth Day. The details should include a time schedule for each event, name the speakers and provide directions to the sports arena. Enclose in the letter order cards for tickets to the game with special ticket discounts for youth and adults to encourage attendance at the game.

A typical Youth Day program format may include:

10:30 a.m.	Sing-A-Long (to give youth a chance to gather)
11:00 a.m.	Youth Day officially begins with a welcome from a school official (principal, president, or representative of the school). The welcome can be followed by several brief speeches by athletes, coaches, cheerleaders. Some schools feature an athlete or coach who can sing or play a musical instrument.
11:30 a.m.	Main Speaker. Select an inspirational speaker who relates to young people.
12:00 p.m.	Lunch on campus (opportunity to see campus).
1:30 p.m.	Football (Soccer) Game.

D. Celebrity Day

Some schools have successful days when outstanding celebrities are invited to be honored or attend the game. In some instances, former athletes who have achieved special honors attract fans and alumni.

The Greensboro Bats, a Class-A baseball team affiliated with the New York Yankees, experience sell-out crowds twice a season by featuring the San Diego "Chicken." The appearance of the San Diego "Chicken" is an annual affair and one that attracts tremendous fan support.

Many special days are possible. Boy Scout and Girl Scout Days are popular while Future Farmers of America Days are popular at schools with strong ties to agriculture. Some schools encourage statewide and regional meetings of youth groups and offer their facilities for displays. Discount rates on tickets encourage attendance by the youth groups, parents and friends.

The area of the country and the nature of the school dictates the type of special days that can be successful. Special days have an important place in the sport program's attempt to promote a favorable image and sell tickets.

Alan White, the Elon College Athletic Director, sums up promotions and its attempt to sell tickets when he says "We are constantly trying new things and it's more-or-less a hit and miss basis. We look at what major institutions are doing and try to adopt those things that are applicable to our situation. We also feel that we have created a few things on our own that tend to work for us."

Summary/Conclusion

There are more ways to promote the sale of tickets than there are promoters. Promotion is part of a marketing effort designed to develop interest in a program that results in the sale of tickets or product. Techniques that sell tickets on the interscholastic and intercollegiate sport level also are relevant for all elements of the sport industry.

Careful planning should precede any promotional effort and plans should begin early in the process. Incorporate the promotional plan in booklet form and use it as a guide and a future reference.

Effective ticket handling encourages the sale of tickets. Ticket sales can be promoted by the use of ticket outlets, payroll deductions, toll-free numbers, Visa/MasterCards and direct mail.

Advertising can effectively aid the sale of tickets and valuable media publicity can guarantee success in promoting the program.

Business and industry offer many ways to promote the sale of tickets. Sponsorship for various events can often attract fans. Group sales provide a means of promoting sales as does visits to shopping centers. Many sport organizations promote special days to attract fans. These include special days such as parents day, autograph day, youth day, and celebrity day. There is no sure way to promote ticket sales but each segment of the sport industry should try various promotions to find the ones that succeed for that particular sport program.

Chapter 14

Internal Marketing— A More Effective Way to Sell Sport

Bernard Mullin

Introduction

When launching a new sport product there is little choice but to attract first-time consumers. A common sport-marketing strategy in such situations is to focus a majority of the promotional effort on mass media advertising designed to attract a broad market base. However, when dealing with established products many sport marketers forget to change their tactics. They get locked into the "new-consumer" mentality. This mentality is prevalent whether the product is a professional or collegiate sport team attempting to attract new spectators, a retail sporting goods store, or a ski resort attempting to attract new participants. Yet the data show that the more mature a sport organization is, the lower the impact of new consumers contributing to total attendance or total participation figures. This phenomenon occurs both in terms of the number of new consumers as a percentage of the number of' existing consumers, and more significantly in terms of new consumers' total purchases as a percentage of total purchases by existing customers. Existing consumers usually consume at higher rates (they attend more games or visit a store or the slopes more often than new consumers). Simply put, existing consumers are more likely to be medium/heavy frequency users.

The "new consumer" myopia is understandable in those segments of the sport industry where demand is low and where there are high attrition rates, such as the high pressure sales approach used in some fitness clubs. This phenomenon also applies to certain franchises of the National Basketball Association (NBA), and the National Hockey League (NHL) and the Major Soccer League (MSL) in most of their markets. However, it is in these very sports (as demonstrated in the Pittsburgh Pirates data shown later), because of a high supply of the product (the MSL has no home dates, the NBA and NHL have more than 40 home dates, and Major League Baseball (MLB) has 81 home dates), that there is considerable room for increasing the attendance frequency of existing consumers. In fact, when increases in attendance/participation does occur, it is invariably due in large part to increased sales to existing customers. The same experience would be the case for virtually all segments of the sport industry.

Perhaps the only explanation for the widespread ignorance in sport marketing is that little if any market research is conducted by sport organizations. Any sport marketer who has collected data on attendance or participation frequency by his/her sport consumers realizes this phenomenon. The so-called 80-20 rule of marketing (where 80% of all goods consumed in a particular product category are consumed by 20% of all persons consuming that product) does apply although the percentages are not equal across all sport segments. The impact of the so-called heavy, medium and light users will vary greatly from sport to sport, dependent upon the supply of events and the demand for the product. National Football League (NFL) franchises invariably have a much higher percentage of heavy users than MLB franchises, for example, because with fewer home games, games predominantly every second Sunday, an NFL season ticket holder can attend most every game.

A few years ago at the MLB's business meetings, attendance frequency data for a National League club was presented in a marketing seminar. Many marketing personnel from the major league clubs were not only surprised by the analysis made of the data, they were surprised that the data had ever been collected in this form. The data presented was taken from two studies. The earlier data came from the University of Pittsburgh study on the impact of baseball on the City of Pittsburgh (Ref. 1) and the later data came from a study commissioned by the Pittsburgh Chamber of Commerce (Ref. 2). While the data may seem to be very old and out of date, it is worth noting that the same principles apply today, and regrettably nobody has taken the time to update it.

The data provides a most dramatic illustration of the fallacy that new fans account for the majority of increases in attendance. For the Pittsburgh Pirates (known as the Bucs), a 17% overall increase in the number of fans attending games resulted in a 57% increase in total attendance, quite clearly because the average number of games attended by all fans increased 35%. In fact, a simple calculation (assuming all 1978 fans returned) indicates that just 200,000 of the 580,000 increase in attendance was attributable to new fans. Of course, it would be easy to assume that the team's success at the gate was largely due to victories on the field. While there is little doubt that it is a lot easier to market a winning team, winning simply is not the only thing, and it is not everything! Several people who have analyzed attendance (Refs. 3, 4, 5, 6) indicate that many other factors have an equal and sometimes bigger impact. They also warn against the adoption of a "winning is everything" attitude because it can easily become a convenient excuse for explaining away poor marketing performance. The Chicago Cubs been a prime example of a team which has drawn well despite poor performance.

Internal Marketing — Getting Existing Customers to Buy More Is Easier and Much Cheaper Than Selling to New Customers

Given that existing fans are usually already "sold" on the product, and that many of them are known by name and address, it would appear obvious that the simplest and cheapest method (direct mail and telemarketing to a high-response probability group) for increasing attendance or participation rates is to market to existing consumers. Marketing programs designed to target existing con-

TABLE 1

Attendance Requency Distribution at Pittsburgh Pirates Baseball Games for the 1978 and 1980 Seasons

Attendance Frequency Category	Number of Fans in Category			Average Number of Games Attended			Total Attendance		
	1978	1980	% Change '78-'80	1978	1980	% Change '78-'80	1978	1980	% Change '78-'80
Heavy Users (mostly season ticket holders)	11,000	10,000	+ 10	20	24	+ 20	200,000	264,000	+ 32
Medium Users	17,250	16,500	+ 4.5	13	16	+ 23	214,000	276,000	+ 28.7
Light Users	278,000	235,000	+ 18.2	2.5	3.75	+ 50	587,500	1,042,500	+ 77.4
TOTAL	306,250	261,500	+ 17.1	3.83	5.17	+ 35	1,002,000	1,582,500	+ 57.9

Source:

a) *An Economic Impact Study of Pittsburgh Pirates on the City of Pittsburgh, Pa.* 34-37 (Pittsburgh, Pa.: Department of Economics, University of Pittsburgh, 1979).

b) *Pittsburg, Pa. Chamber of Commerce,* 1980.

FIGURE 1

The Staircase Approach to Sport Marketing

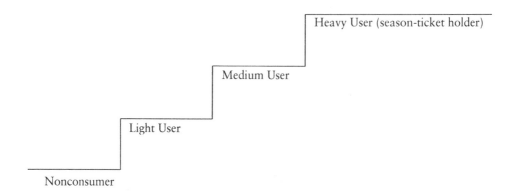

sumers to increase their frequency of usage and designed to get them to bring their friends has been called "internal marketing" by this author (Ref. 7). Such marketing programs need to be organized systematically. "Sport Marketing," a book written by the author proposed that a "stepping-stone approach" be used to target existing customers, where light, medium and heavy users would be targeted in sequence (Ref. 8). In the same time frame, in totally independent thought, Bill Giles (now owner of the Philadelphia Phillies) proposed what he called the "staircase approach" (Ref. 9), where the marketer would attempt to move fans up the stairs from being a light user to a medium user to the "ultimate"—a heavy user. Giles' analogy of the staircase seemed much more appropriate than a stepping-stone approach and it formed the germination of the concept presented in this chapter.

While the staircase analogy is an excellent foundation, it has limitations. First, it assumes that each step in the process involves a distinct and perhaps difficult movement. Second, it implies that all light users are on the same step. Observation of attendance-frequency distribution shows that this is not the case. Sport consumers are distributed in terms of their attendance or participation frequency across a continuum which runs from 1 through N, where N is the maximum number of events, contests or days that a consumer can consume. (N in professional sports varies greatly, the NFL has 10 home dates (8 regular season and 2 pre-season games); MLB has 81 home dates; the NBA has 40 dates; N for other sport industry segments also varies greatly from the 125 or so days that the Vail Ski Resort is typically open each year to the 363 days that a typical YMCA is open each year). In fact, the frequency distribution is better represented by an escalator, which has many steps, all of which appear to run into one another. The step between a heavy-light user and a light-medium user is just one extra game attended or just one more visit to a ski slope. When viewed in this manner, it becomes apparent that the marketer can make fluid the movement of a sport consumer up the frequency escalator, by better promotions or improving the benefits to full membership or a full season ticket or pass.

TABLE 2

The Levels of Non-Consumer Readiness to Purchase

Unaware Nonconsumer	this individual is unaware of the existence of the sport product, and consequently does not attend.
Aware Nonconsumer	this individual is aware of the sport product but for whatever the reason he/she does not choose to attend. Presumably the product does not offer the benefits this person is looking for, or this person has no need for this type of product, at least at this time.
Media Consumer	this individual is aware of the sport product and although they do not consume it directly, they do consume the product indirectly through the media. This is not limited to spectator sports but includes participant sports which receive media exposure.

The Attendance/Participation Frequency Escalator

In fact, the distribution of existing-consumers' attendance frequency is invariably a continual series of steps on an escalator which runs from 1 through N. However, before the consumer even gets into the ranks of the existing consumer, there are clearly 'Several stages through which he or she passes. Bill Giles used the generic term "nonconsumer." But it would appear that there are several forms of nonconsumption. In one article discussing consumers it was suggested that as many as 50% of all people who consider themselves sport fans never attended a game (Ref. 10). In a survey of Boston Red Sox fans it was revealed that although almost 40% of all fans watching the Red Sox on TV were female, just a little over 20% of those attending games at Fenway Park were female. We can therefore construct three levels to the nonconsumer hierarchy.

The promotional effort and expense required to move consumers up steps on the escalator is usually considerably less than that which is necessary to move consumers onto the escalator. But more importantly, unless the consumer is already satiated, the response to get an existing consumer to consume one extra game/event is likely to be considerably greater, cheaper and easier than it is to get an unaware or disinterested consumer to consume one game or event for the first time. Further support for the approach of targeting existing consumers first comes from the well-known fact that existing satisfied consumers are an organization's best salespeople. One estimate is that 70% of all consumers are referred by word of mouth from existing consumers. This "bottom-line" for repeat business is outlined in Chapter 16, entitled "An Information-Based Approach to Marketing Sport." Using the multiplier effect it is shown that the total multiplied impact of word of mouth is 3.33 additional consumers from each existing member assuming that 70% of new consumers come from word-of-mouth referrals (.7 + .7 x .7 + 3 x .7 x .7, etc.).

It is suggested therefore, that sport marketers who are in mature markets with a solid base of existing consumers focus their promotional efforts initially on attracting higher frequency of attendance and participation by existing consumers —not on attracting new customers. Once the response from these efforts has been assessed, then attention can be turned toward attracting new consumers. This

FIGURE 2

The Frequency Escalators for Sport Attendance and Participation

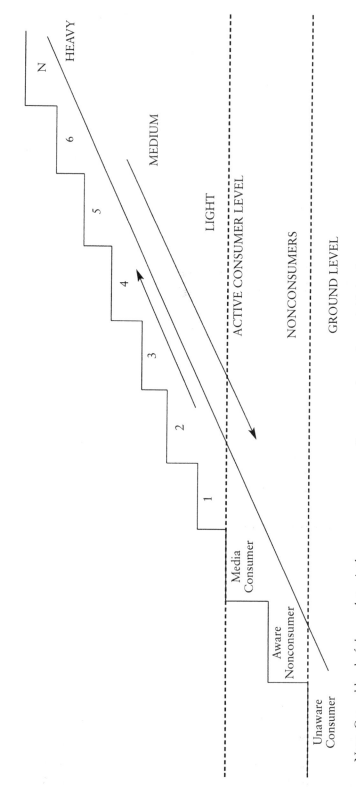

Note: Ground level of the escalator is the unaware consumer. Because each step beyond this level represents a movement toward attending or participating in the sport product, it represents a progressive step *on* the escalator.

strategy does not assume that the two efforts are mutually exclusive. It is clear that certain promotions and advertising efforts (such as direct-mail promotions to existing fans only) are mutually exclusive. It is clear that certain promotions and advertising efforts (such as bat days, Fireworks Nites, post game concerts, etc.) will reach both existing and potential consumers. It is also evident that organizations with adequate resources will be able to design promotional campaigns aimed at both groups which will be put into effect simultaneously. Most sport organizations, however, experience limited human and financial resources for marketing and consequently the following time-ordering recommendation is made. Given that the increase in frequency is most dramatic with the light users, and is probably the easiest to accomplish (assuming medium and heavy users are closer to their satiation point), the suggested program for starting a "one-way escalator ride" of increased consumption is outlined in order of priority to increasing total attendance frequency or total participation levels in a sport organization.

Moving Consumers Up the Escalator — "The One-Way Escalator Ride!"

The programs outlined in this section include promotions used in sport settings which have been successful and some untried strategies which would appear to have considerable chance of success.

A. Increasing Light-User Frequency

The light-user would *prima facie* appear to be the easiest of all consumers to "move on up" the escalator. Given that by definition they attend or participate in the sport product at the lowest frequency level, they would appear to have the greatest room for improvement. The experience of organizations who have applied "increased-frequency" programs has shown that this is in fact true for most light-users, although a hard core of consumers cannot be moved.

1.   Special Attractions and Give-Aways

The most common strategy used for decades is to offer special sales promotions such as product give-aways (hat day; bat day; water bottle giveaways, etc.) or *quasi-price promotions* (2 for 1's, half-price days; four tickets, four pizzas, four sodas, etc.) or special attractions (rock concerts, fireworks shows, etc.).

The popularity and frequency of usage of the above methodology is testimony that these techniques do increase attendance. However, the lack of data on the true effectiveness of promotions is a great concern. In one study which analyzed the effect of promotional days on total attendance frequency at the Boston Celtics regular-season NBA games, it was shown that the increase in attendance at promotion nights was often at the expense of other dates. This phenomenon can be called "cherry-picking." Cherry-picking occurs when the fan merely redistributes his or her attendance preference away from one event day to the best nights (the cherries), and does not increase total attendance frequency. Several strategies which are designed to reduce cherrypicking are outlined in the section entitled "Theme Promotions." If the promotion cost is underwritten by a sponsor this may not be a major concern to the sport marketer. However, regular fan surveys are warranted to check that this is not occurring when promotions which result in expense to the sport organization are offered.

In fitness and health centers, where a complete listing of members is readily available, and with the use of computer-based marketing information systems complete member-usage frequency tracking has become possible, significant improvements have been made in increasing light-user participation frequency. Special programs have been designed to meet light-user needs. In an excellent study (Ref. 11) performed by Weston Racquet Club Owner/Operator Dick Trandt, the former Harvard University MBA analyzed why light users either quit his club, or failed to play more often. First, he found out that there was a direct correlation between playing frequency and playing-skill level. Better players played more often, and players who could not improve their skill became frustrated and quit. Second, he found that the major resistance to increasing playing frequency was that the light users did not know of players with similar interest and skill who were available at compatible times. His response was first to offer free clinics and lessons, a concept unheard of by most tennis pros. Then through his member tracking program he was able to follow up personally on all members who did not increase their frequency. He also offered a game-arranging or matchmaking program which offered participants a guaranteed match with a comparably skilled opponent at mutually convenient times. As an incentive, the member got a free assessment of his/her playing skill level first. The result was an increase in court occupancy rates in excess of 90% for the last four years' 36-week winter season in his 14-court tennis club. This is by far the highest level attained in North America known to anyone in the court club business.

2.   Theme Promotions

Theme promotions use a particular theme to attract consumers over a period of time. This strategy was first employed by Andy Dolich, who at the time was Executive Vice President and General Manager of the now-defunct Washington Diplomats of the NASL. He developed the theme "Year of the Uniform" where young fans would receive different parts of the "Dips" uniform depending upon the game they attended (shorts, shirt, socks, ball, etc.). The promotion was very successful for the youth-oriented soccer market. A similar approach was used by Dave Whaley, Director of Advertising for the Colorado Rockies of the NHL (now the New Jersey Devils) who modified the theme to meet their "swingles" (single, twenties to thirties) market. The Rockies' "Year of the Cowboy" theme featured coupons good for significant discounts on various aspects of western wear offered at a local store (boots, belt, buckle, jeans, etc.). Here again, market research revealed that the program was successful in increasing attendance frequency. In both cases it was academically trained sport managers who collected data first, and then developed the appropriate marketing strategy. In recent times the themed give-away has gone out of fashion by sport marketers, but not necessarily by the fans.

The theme promotions described above are what may be called "soft" approaches to frequency increase. A harder approach might be to modify the Rockies' discounts such that for each additional coupon collected, an added discount (a multiplier) would be available to induce higher attendance. Another example comes from Britain, where soccer clubs for years have always experienced a high percentage "walk-up" of cash admission on the day of the game. When games of special interest have occurred (local rivalries, or Football Association Challenge Cup (FA Cup) games) the games have often been made "all-ticket admission" with advance purchase required. Several clubs have successfully capitalized by selling the tickets only at the club's home stadium on the day of a prior home game, so that the fan would only need to make one trip to the stadium and be asked to line up on one occasion only. (Of course, they would also attend that day's game!) This latter technique is generically similar to using "coupon multiplier-discounts," and falls under the category of contingent promotions.

3. Contingent Promotions

These are promotions which are tied to repeat purchases. Retail trades have used these very successfully for many years but to date they have received limited attention in sport. An ideal application of this technique would be to capitalize on what might currently be a deterrent to sales. Many sport organizations offer give-away promotions with the number of give-aways being limited (usually to the first 5,000 or 10,000 fans entering the stadium or arena). By offering rain-checks on the promotional item, redeemable at a later game, fans could be induced to return when they might otherwise not. Similarly contests and drawings where fans are asked to complete surveys or fill-in name and address blanks as entrants are disguised methods for obtaining basic demographic data, and provide valuable information for the mailing list. Completion of the form is tied to winning a prize having significant value (a car, color television, vacation, etc.). The drawing should always be held at a later game, and redeemable only if the person whose name is drawn is in attendance. This is a cheap way to increase frequency of attendance or participation.

B. Increasing Medium-User Frequency

While many of the programs already outlined under light-user strategies may have a potential impact on medium users, there are some strategies which can be targeted specifically to medium users.

1. Half-Season Plans

Many professional teams and some sport facilities (ski resorts and indoor tennis facilities, etc.) offer half-season plans designed to attract a light user who cannot afford a full-season plan, or whose time schedule or budget does not fit the demands of a full season.

There exists ample evidence from several organizations that this approach works quite effectively in attracting the light user. However, the big fear of sport owners and managers is that there will be sales erosion from the full season ticket plan (the heavy user). There can be no doubt that if the benefits of the half-season plan are too close to the benefits of the full-season plan, such erosion will occur. For example, the Boston Bruins offer first-half and second-half season plans. For many fans the first half of the NHL season prior to January is not that important because it is too early in a very long season (80 games running from October until May), and many people view hockey as a winter sport belonging in a time frame that comes after Christmas. In this situation, many season-ticket holders are tempted to give up the first-half plan. When introducing this plan it is evident that the sport marketer must collect data on the increase in revenue from light user "trade-up" and contrast this with the loss in revenue from "season-ticket holder erosion." If the balance is positive, then the overall increase in fan satisfaction is well worth the introduction of the plan.

2.   Contract Time or "Pick-10," "Pick-20" Plans/Flex or Coupon Plans.

Many professional sports having a high number of home contests per season (baseball with 81;basketball with 40; and hockey with 40) have adopted this approach which has proven to be well-received. Under this plan consumers are given the choice of either buying a fixed portion of a schedule (booking courts every Thursday evening at 7:00 p.m.; or having every second home date; or seeing each opponent once in a season); or they are given a fixed/variable combination plan. Under the Pick 10 plan offered by the New Jersey Nets of the NBA, fans are given three contests against top-rated opponents; three contests against opponents with poor won-loss records and a choice of the balance of four contests. The Nets allowed total freedom of choice for their Pick 20 plan when their games were played at isolated Rutgers University Arena in Piscataway, N.J. The flex plan or coupon book gives even more flexibility. A ten coupon book can be used by two people to go to five games or five people to go to two games or any combination thereof.

C. Maintaining Heavy-User Frequency — Rewarding Customer Loyalty

By definition, the heavy user is at the pinnacle of the frequency escalator and it would appear impossible to move him or her any higher. The concern then becomes ensuring that the consumer does not "drop off" the escalator or move back down to a lower frequency of consumption. In fact, this concern is not limited just to heavy users. Data from court and health clubs (Ref. 12) indicates that non-renewal rates are well distributed across all members, although it is usually highest in the light-user category because these members are not as committed, and there are many more of them as a percentage of total membership. While the distribution of light, medium and heavy users will vary greatly from sport organization to sport organization, it is likely that those industry segments having the highest supply of available event days open to the consumer will have a higher percentage of light users, and consequently a higher percentage of nonrenewing members. (This means that baseball with its 81 home dates per season will have a much higher percentage of its fans being light users in comparison to football with its 10 regular-season home dates, and college football with just six home dates having an even lower percentage of light-users.)

Preventing Defection and Reducing Attrition Rates

The nonrenewing sport fan has been termed a "defector" by Matt Levine, senior executive with the San Jose Sharks (Ref. 13). The defector can be viewed as an individual who is going in the reverse direction on the escalator, or who has fallen off the escalator. This "reverse escalator" can be illustrated graphically, as a basis for identifying programs which would be effective at reversing the trend of defection.

FIGURE 3

The Downside of the Frequency Escalator for Sport Attendance and Particpation

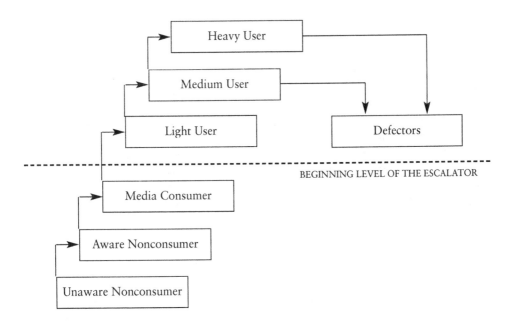

Techniques for Reducing Attrition of Existing Consumers

It is apparent that two broad categories of approach to anti-defection strategies can be developed. First, those programs designed to stop the consumer from defecting -preventative strategies. Second, those programs designed to get a defector to return to consuming the product— "Come Back to the Fold" strategies.

A. Preventative Approaches

It has been said that you cannot please all of the people all of the time. There is little doubt that this is true. However, with good marketing and a good product, people who have been consuming the product on a regular basis should not defect unless something goes wrong or unless they naturally grow away from it (they get too old, they have a change in financial status, or leave the market area). Reducing membership defection on the front-end requires a good management information system, which may be somewhat unwieldy and very expensive for organizations with large number of consumers. For example the Philadelphia Phillies have over 500,000 different persons who have purchased tickets in the last three seasons, and an estimated additional 500,000 persons who call themselves fans because they "follow the team" via the media (Ref. 14). The Phillies have most of these fans identified by name in their computerized file. In court and health clubs, computerized information systems have been in place for many years and club managers have been able to track the frequency of participation by all club members and even guests and prospects. In the mid-eighties programs were introduced for clubs to monitor frequency of attendance, and automatically print a list of names of those members who constitute potential defectors. (Ref. 15). The program has three components:

Red Light — Defector for more than three weeks/or three games no show
Yellow Light — Defector for two weeks or more/two games no show
Green Light — Defector for a week/one game

Club owners can choose a strategy for each group, but typically form letters are sent automatically via the word processing capacity of the computer. The essence of each is as follows:

Green Light — "We miss you, hope to see you soon"
Yellow Light — "We still miss you, have a free drink on us next time you visit (coupon enclosed)" and "let us know if anything we have done is keeping you away"
Red Light — A telephone call to find out "Where did we go wrong? What can we do to help you? How can we get you going again?"

As might be expected, the results have been very favorable. Members felt needed and were impressed with the club's efficiency and interest in them. Of course, a few members felt that their privacy was being intruded. On average, for ten clubs using the system in the first six months of its introduction, annual membership nonrenewal rates dropped from over 50% to just over 30%, resulting in an average increase in annual revenues of 18 to 25%. While such a system is more difficult to install in spectator sport marketing, it is possible to develop systems which do provide early warning of member defection. Of course, bar coded tickets and intelligent "reader" turnstiles make it an easy task to identify "no shows."

B. The "Come Back to the Fold" Approach

Sports Illustrated offers a personal letter from subscription director, Bob Mc-Coach, in which he invites nonrenewing *S.I.* subscribers to immediately put them back on *S.I.*'s active roster!" *Sports Illustrated* and all magazine companies have long realized that the sooner a defector can be identified and approached, the more likely that individual is to renew. Once again, much in the same manner as for preventative approaches, a solid market-information system is the key to any anti-defection efforts. Season ticket holders and members who are nonrenewing are readily identified once that have failed to meet the renewal deadline. An immediate telephone response is justified in such cases, followed by active efforts (letters, special offers, discounts, etc.) to encourage renewal or at least a trade-down to a medium-user plan. When all else fails a good rule of thumb is to keep the person on the active mailing list for 12 months (send them member's newsletters, fan information, special event information, etc.). After 12 months these individuals should receive renewal information and appeals for medium and light-user plans for the second year. After this time period they should be removed from the active list.

Where possible, the sport marketer should attempt to remove the "nonrenewal option" by programming an automatic renewal. The same "assumptive" approach should be used in playoff ticket sales for minor league and emerging sports. Health and fitness clubs, perhaps because of their high nonrenewal rates, have been developing antidefection programs much more rapidly than most other segments of the sport industry. Originally, most clubs offered a flat membership fee and per-court hour usage payments. Under this schedule, members were actually discouraged from high frequency of play because of additional cost. Successful clubs soon switched to a flat initiation fee plus monthly dues; this encouraged high frequency of play because the fee was already paid. We might call this, "The All You Can Play Plan!" An offshoot of this approach was to have members pay by direct payment electronic fund transfer (EFT) transferred from their bank account to the club's bank account, and the natural extension was to remove the idea of a renewal date. Once a member, you were always a member, until you went out of your way to tell the club that you no longer wanted to be a member. Once a new season had started the member was locked-in to paying for a full season), and they usually kept active as members. Spectator-sport marketers could easily offer monthly time-payment plans where payment is guaranteed by EFT and renewal is in the contract as being automatic, unless the fan notifies the organization in advance of a certain date. Some professional teams have even had their banks provide loans for fans to buy their tickets so that the team can get their cash-flow up front.

C. Maintaining Fan/Member Loyalty

A major part of any anti-defection plan by a sport marketer must include concrete rewards to the consumer for being loyal to the sport organization. Unfortunately, sport organizations' loyalty to their fans has not been in the mainstream of management thought. There are many Dodgers fans whose lives are still affected by the Dodgers' move from Brooklyn, New York to Los Angeles, California. If loyalty to a sport organization is to be expected, then loyalty to the fan/member by the sport organization is a prerequisite. There are many ways in which fans can be rewarded for loyalty:

1. Season Ticket Holders or Full Membership Plan Consumers

1. Each year, full members or season-ticket holders should be given first choice at improving their seat location, or the contract time they have. Where possible, this choice should be in direct relationship to seniority as a ticket holder or member (through the priority number).
2. Certain milestones should be established, for example:
   (a) After one year's renewal, consumers could receive free programs at games, or free locker rental, or a discount on pro shop/souvenir merchandise.
   (b) After five years, consumers could receive free membership in the stadium club, or free seat-backs, or free dinner specials, or a certain number of hours of free playing time, or even larger percentage discounts on pro-shop/souvenir items.
   (c) After ten years, consumers could receive free car parking at a location close to the stadium gate through which they enter, etc., or even larger

discounts in the stadium club or on merchandise purchased. Of particular value to long-term season ticket holders are monogrammed apparel with "10 year season ticket holder."

2. Medium Users

A similar set of rewards could be offered on a scaled-down basis for the loyal medium user.

D. Light User

There are many light users who, for whatever reason (geographic distance, young children, lower incomes, etc.), cannot increase their attendance frequency. For these consumers some special efforts might also be appreciated to reward known loyalty.

1. Admission to a designated picnic area after a certain number of years on the club's active mailing list.
2. Special invitations to meet players when the "travelling caravan" visits their home town.

Maintaining a Healthy Balance of Light, Medium and Heavy Users

The balance between light, medium and heavy users is an important one. Unfortunately, sport organizations with inexperienced or untrained sport marketers have a tendency to go for as many heavy users as they can. This is a serious mistake; when an arena is filled only by heavy users many potential consumers are excluded from the product, and the long-term effect can be disastrous. In the late 1960s the Boston Bruins allowed their success at the gate to create a situation from which they are still suffering today. In the 1960s Boston Garden was sold out for years to only the season-ticket holders. However, once their superstar Bobby Orr left Boston, attendance declined rapidly and a whole generation of fans who might have received their initial exposure to the Bruins as light users was lost. Even though these fans watched their team via the media, many did not go to games at Boston Garden even though seats were now available because they were not in the habit of going, and because they did not conceive of being able to buy a ticket for home games. No ideal balance can be developed, because the dependence and the need for heavy, medium and light users varies widely across sport-industry segments. Given the lower number of home dates in the NFL, and the fact that most games are played on Sundays (apart from the very occasional Monday, Thursday or Thanksgiving game that an individual club may play), it is comparatively simple for a fan to attend all home games of an NFL team in a season. By contrast, the Pittsburgh Pirates data shows that less than one percent of baseball fans see every one of their team's home games.

Once the situation has arisen where a high percentage of fans are heavy users two problems occur. In tennis and racquetball clubs, all the prime-time hours are clogged up by just a few members. Discontentment occurs on a wide scale. In spectator sports, it becomes impossible to buy season tickets, and as in the case of the New York Giants of the NFL, a very long waiting list occurs. Ticket holders who die bequeath their tickets to descendants who rarely notify the club of change of ownership for fear of losing their tickets. In the late 1970s the Buffalo Sabres of the NHL had a 10,000-name waiting list, and were able to offer 400 nonrenewed tickets each year. Even when they offered half-season and quarter-season splits, few of their waiting list could be satisfied.

Although in the short term, a waiting list appears to be a nice headache to have, in the long term the over-demand problem may be as devastating to an organization as under-demand. Many tennis and racquetball clubs have gone out of business because they had reputations for being "clubs where you can never get a court!" The Denver Broncos of the NFL have recently tried to get control of their season tickets from scalpers and individuals selling their seat location rights. The Broncos lost in a court battle. Other teams are wise to include "succession and transfer rights" written in the season ticket holder policy manual. This policy also provides the opportunity to collect data on the individuals who are sharing season tickets. The Colorado Rockies (MLB) limit transfers to blood relatives and those named as sharing tickets—what this does is provide an excellent mailing list for play-offs, etc.

The Added Benefit of Internal Marketing

Once all the strategies aimed at increasing existing consumer attendance frequency have been exhausted, then it is time to turn toward attracting new consumers. Most sport organizations have adopted professional marketing techniques to accomplish this goal, but many have not fully capitalized on internal marketing strength. The common practices used by all segments of business and industry have been borrowed by sport organizations to generate leads and prospects, and professional sales-closing techniques have been employed. Spectator and participant sport marketers have moved away from using expensive mass-media advertising to direct mail and personal sales approaches which are now targeted at specific groups. It is not uncommon to find a professional team which has several sales personnel, each with a different specialty, having one doing corporate sales, one advertising sales, a third selling season tickets, a fourth selling to groups and a fifth involved in telephone sales to the general public. However, much of these sales efforts may be wasted by targeting toward one-time group attendees. The success of group sales, sales promotions and special events is entirely dependent upon two factors: first, how much did the promotion cost? If it was entirely underwritten by a sponsor, the long-term impact is of less concern. If it was an expensive promotion which the organization underwrote itself, then the long-term effect is of primary concern. Second, how many times did the consumers attracted into first-time attendance by the promotion attend for the balance of the season or year? If the answer is zero, then the effort probably was not worthwhile.

One informal study performed by one of the most professional sport marketers in the country, Andy Dolich, Executive Vice President of Marketing for the Oakland A's and a prime influence behind the A's "Billy Ball" success of the early

1980's, revealed that the probability that a new attendee would become a loyal A's fan increased each time they came to the ballpark and had a positive experience. Dolich latched onto a magic number of three visits. When he was selling to groups for the NASL Washington Diplomats (now defunct) and when his current staff sells Oakland A's baseball, they attempt to get the group to visit three times in a season rather than once as most organizations attempt to do. As a result a higher percentage of group fans, become loyal fans of their own volition. While no empirical data exists to support this contention, it is reasonable to assume that the impact of repeat trials of a product would follow a logarithmic formula, or an exponential (continually increasing) function. Namely, each time you come, the higher probability that you will come again. The author's research in sales-consulting for court and health clubs has led to the following findings. Each successive product trial which results in positive satisfaction (represented by a + sign below) will increase the repeat purchase probability logarithmically, and consequently a graph would show an exponential probability that a trial consumer will become a loyal consumer. For example, the repeat purchase probability which may hold true for group attendees who are drawn to attending or participating in a sport product is shown in Figure 4 below.

FIGURE 4

Probability of Repeat Attendance after a Postive Experience

One trial	(+)	=	20%
Two trials	(+ +)	=	40%
Three trials	(+++)	=	70%

Consequently fitness centers should allow guests a free trial, not a paid trial, and in fact they should allow up three free trials per person!

Summary/Conclusion

Sport marketing is continually advancing in terms of the techniques it is using. However it has been much slowed in its adoption of professional market research techniques. It is inconceivable that sport marketers can spend several thousands of dollars on mass media efforts without solid market information which supports the use of the media vehicle, or indicates the target market to which their message is aimed. Matt Levine (whose work has received high acclaim, including a feature article in *Sports Illustrated*) exclaimed: "Professional baseball marketing is where consumer product marketing was in the 1930s, and that's just the good teams!" (Ref. 16). Things have drastically improved in the MLB in the last twenty years, but MLB is still way behind in it's use of e-commerce and one on one marketing techniques.

This chapter made the case for gathering information on the attendance or participation frequency of sport consumers as a prerequisite to all marketing efforts. It has proposed that considerable room exists for increasing bottom line attendance and participation figures purely by increasing the attendance frequency of existing consumers. The technique of focusing marketing efforts on existing customers first has been called "internal marketing." Internal marketing has been shown to be cheaper and more effective at increasing total attendance and/or participation levels. In turn, more satisfied existing consumers attract more nonconsumers so that internal marketing has added benefits.

While every recreation director of an intramural program on a college campus would prefer to have five students, each participating in one sport, than one student participating in five sports, the bottom-line figure presented to the university administration is usually one and the same thing. In the long run, the heavy user intramural participant should become a good product salesperson to increase the number of new consumers, 3.33 at a time for a much lower promotional dollar and less sales effort. The same phenomenon occurs in all segments of the sport industry when internal marketing techniques are employed. Internal marketing is cheaper, easier and more effective in the short and medium terms. Of course, long-term efforts are needed to attract new fans but incentives given to existing forms (such as free guest passes, reduced ticket/membership prices when friends are referred, etc.) invariably are more effective and are much cheaper than most mass media campaigns.

References

1. "An Economic impact Study of Pittsburgh Pirates Baseball on the City of Pittsburgh, PA" (1979), p. 34. Pittsburgh, PA: Department of Economics, University of Pittsburgh.
2. "Update: An Economic Impact Study of Pittsburgh Pirates Baseball on the City of Pittsburgh, PA" (1980). Pittsburgh, PA: Chamber of Commerce.
3. Canham, D. (1979, May 10). Speech given at the First Annual Sport Management Art and Science Conference (SMARTS 1). Amherst, MA.
4. Giles, B. (1980). "Special Efforts Needed to Attract New Fans," *Athletic Purchasing and Facilities* 16-19 (October).
5. Kennedy, R. (1980). "More Victories Equals More Fans Equals More Profits, Right, Wrong, Wrong, Wrong!" *Sports Illustrated* 52 (April 28), 34-41.
6. Mullin, B.J. (1981). "Sport Marketing, Promotion and Public Relations" (unpublished manuscript). Amherst, MA: Department of Sport Studies, University of Massachusetts.
7. Id., p. 251-57.
8. Id., p. 138-40.
9. Giles, *supra* Ref. 4, p. 17.
10. Rees, C. (1981). "Does Sports Marketing Need a New Offense?" *Marketing and Media Decisions* 66-67 (February), 126-132.
11. Trandt, D. (1982, June). Unpublished study of participation frequency by members at the Weston Racquet Club, Waltham, MA.
12. Bannon, J. and P.E. Rose (1980, January). "The Court Club Industry: A Nationwide Assessment," pp. 36-39. Champaign, IL: Department of Leisure Studies, University of Illinois.
13. Levine, M. (1978). *Sport Marketing Review* 8 (May), 3-4.
14. Montgomery, D. (1980, December 10). Personal conversation with B. Mullin held at the Winter Meetings of Major League Baseball, Dallas, TX.

15. *COURT-SPIN,* The Court Sport Information System, National Sport Management, Inc., P.O. Box 911, Amherst, Massachusetts, 01004.
16. Kennedy, *supra* Ref. 5, p. 38.

Chapter 15

Corporate Sponsorship of Sport

Nancy L. Lough

Sponsorship Defined

Sport offers many unique attributes that are attractive to any business that seeks association with a winner or an effective addition to their communications mix. Sponsorship has been defined as "the acquisition of rights to affiliate or directly associate with a product or event for the purpose of deriving benefits related to that affiliation or association" (Mullin, Hardy, and Sutton, 2000). As a unique element capable of cutting through the clutter present in traditional advertising and promotional approaches, sport sponsorship has grown dramatically throughout the 1980s and 1990s.

Sponsors use their relationship with a sport property to attain established marketing objectives. Typically, a sponsorship agreement will be utilized by both the corporate partner and the sport property to contribute to the overall marketing mix. Product, price, place and promotion comprise the four primary elements of the marketing mix. Manipulation of these four elements, to meet the target market's needs in an ever-changing environment, is the job of the sport marketer. By implementing a sport sponsorship agreement, a sport marketer can integrate components of all four elements to effectively meet the established marketing objectives.

The average person is exposed to more than 5,000 selling messages each day. Thus, separation and retention of information is difficult for most consumers. By utilizing sponsorship as an alternative channel for communication, many companies have found that they can achieve new levels of exposure. Additionally, sport sponsorships are often positioned at a much lower cost than traditional advertising mediums. Costs for television and print ads have consistently been on the rise with no apparent change on the horizon. As an example, a 30-second television ad spot during the NFL's 1998 Super Bowl cost $1.3 million. This was more than triple the cost 10 years prior. By 2000, a 30-second television spot during the Super Bowl averaged $2.2 million. Values such as these point to the extreme desire many companies have to associate their product or brand with a "winning" sport property. The Super Bowl represents the two top teams in the U.S. competing for the title of World Champions. It also represents the largest single-event television audience available, not only in the U.S., but also internationally. For sponsors involved with this sport property, the association translates to awareness, image enhancement and possibly increased product sales.

On the opposite side of the equation, sport managers and marketers have come to rely so heavily on the monetary support provided through the sponsorship medium that many believe sport as we know it today could not exist without corporate sponsorship (Irwin, 1993). How pervasive has sponsorship become in sport? At present, the relationships between companies seeking the sport affiliation and sport properties willing to sell those opportunities extend beyond professional and intercollegiate sport to interscholastic and youth sport teams, organizations, events and facilities.

As one recent example, the New Mexico Activities Association (NMAA), the governing body for high school sport in the state of New Mexico, signed State Farm Insurance to the association's first recognized sponsorship deal. State Farm will benefit by being the exclusive sponsor of the most recognized and most influential sport organization in the state. Potential exposure to consumers extends beyond high school student athletes, to include their parents, grandparents and extended family members. (Any who may value the association of State Farm with high school athletics enough to consider the insurance company in future insurance decisions.) The NMAA benefits by receiving money for organizing and implementing championship events, while also establishing the value of that association for additional sponsorship endeavors.

Sponsorship growth in the U.S.

The 1984 Olympic Games in Los Angeles have been recognized as the catalyst for modern corporate involvement in sport. Prior to the 1984 Olympic Games, host cities lost money and many incurred debt that lasted for decades beyond completion of their last Olympic competition. To prevent such an occurrence to the city of Los Angeles, Peter Ueberroth, president of the LAOOC (Los Angeles Olympic Organizing Committee), initiated a corporately subsidized Olympics. The number of sponsors was limited to 30 to avoid clutter and provide product exclusivity. This limitation allowed Ueberroth to develop corporate partnerships, suggesting that both parties would achieve benefits by working as partners to create desirable results.

Following the enormous success of the 1984 Olympic Games, corporate sport sponsorship began to flourish. By 1990, a 15% growth rate was predicted for each subsequent year. In terms of millions of dollars, this was a staggering prediction. Yet, by 1997 the figure was up to $5.9 billion spent by North American companies. The growth has yet to see any significant slowing, as the $6.8 billion figure for 1998 revealed a 15% increase over the previous year.

As more companies become interested in sport sponsorship, and as more sport manager's have sought sponsorship dollars, sport properties previously non-existent or overlooked, have become increasingly attractive to cut through the clutter of more traditional sport sponsorships. As an example, in 1992 sport sponsorship for women's sport was at the unprecedented level of $285 million in the United States. By 1997, that figure had more than doubled to $600 million in only five years. Previous to 1997, the majority of sponsorship money spent on women's sport was allocated to golf (LPGA), tennis (WTA) and figure skating (Lough, 1996). However, following the 1996 Olympic Games, which effectively served as the catalyst for women's sport sponsorship, new women's sport properties such as the Women's National Basketball Association (WNBA) secured corporate support through sponsorship that established the sport property as viable and valuable.

Yet, sport sponsorship is often considered to include considerable risk for the corporate sponsor, as certain elements of sport can not be controlled. For the organizers and event promoters of the 1999 Women's World Cup Soccer Tournament in the United States, securing sponsorship was not easy. For the sponsors who jumped on the World Cup Soccer bandwagon when the U.S. men's team played host, the elimination of the U.S. team translated to a poor return on their investment. However, the success of the U.S. women's team in 1999 became a tide of emotion that was transformed into enormous financial success for event organizers and sponsors. In the case of the Women's World Cup, the risk that some corporations were not willing to take, turned into valuable benefits for those who were willing to commit.

Why Corporations Buy into Sport

Three of the most significant reasons that corporations buy into sport have already been discussed. First, the cost of advertising will undoubtedly continue to escalate along with the number of companies competing for consumer dollars. Additionally, the number of media outlets will make the competition even more fierce as internet use becomes increasingly sophisticated and mainstream. Second, the use of sport sponsorship as a component of the marketing strategy that can help a company cut through the clutter and media "noise" will only enhance the third rationale, that strong brand equity can be achieved through association with a winning sport property.

One important attribute that is somewhat unique to sport is the element of emotion. When the home team wins, the fans feel that they are winners, and as a result often enjoy celebrating the victory. Sport fans and sport consumers have strong emotional ties to teams, athletes and specific sport properties or events. Corporate sponsors seek emotional ties with consumers that will translate to brand loyalty. As a prime example, consider the National Association of Stock Car Racing (NASCAR). Spectators for these auto races not only buy tickets to attend the events, they also buy merchandise with sponsor's logos prominently displayed to support both the driver and the sponsors who support the driver. Fans acknowledge that without corporate sponsorship their sport could not exist. Many fans even admit to changing brands if sponsorship changes for their favorite driver. The strength of this association is unlike any other. In this example, sponsors can count on a degree of brand loyalty, simply by maintaining sponsorship of a specific driver.

Yet, sophisticated sponsorship decision-makers consider many aspects before committing to a specific sport sponsorship. Identification of a market segment that the corporate sponsor needs to reach provides a significant selling point. Target market demographics of sport consumers suggest a viable avenue for corporate sponsors to communicate with specific groups that are most likely to purchase their products. As an example, the WNBA focuses on a family demographic inclusive of kids, parents and grandparents. While in typical demographic terms this is actually a combination of several specific segments, the family approach has appealed to ticket buyers and corporate sponsors. By providing a wholesome, fun, exciting sport experience in an exceptional arena, the WNBA has been able to provide access to an audience that sponsors such as *Sears*, are willing to pay to reach. For *Sears*, who sells a wide variety of products to service a family demographic, the sponsorship fit with the WNBA has proven to be successful. In WNBA cities, fans can get player autographs by visiting the local *Sears* store on scheduled appearance days. The WNBA players effectively drive traffic into and through the *Sears* stores where fans will be exposed to the many products that *Sears* sells to this target market.

Sponsors Rationale

Sport properties and events can offer opportunities that extend beyond simple advertising and reach consumers at the point of experience. This attribute is one of the many aspects corporate sponsors seek in relationships with sport. Extensive research has been conducted to determine the objectives sponsors most often utilize when making sponsorship decisions. Objectives as identified in research are provided in the revised sport sponsorship proposal evaluation model presented in Figure 1 (Irwin, Asimakopolous, and Sutton, 1994).

The objectives most often utilized in decisions to enter a sport sponsorship agreement include:

- To achieve sales objectives
- To generate media benefits
- To secure entitlement or naming rights
- To increase public awareness of the company, the product, or both
- To alter or reinforce public perception of the company
- To identify the company with the particular market segments
- To involve the company in the community
- To build good will among decision-makers
- To create an advantage over competitors, through association or exclusivity
- To gain unique opportunities in terms of hospitality and entertainment

As an illustration of how many of these objectives can be achieved simultaneously for companies involved in a specific sport sponsorship, consider the case of the ESPN X Games. Sponsorship of this unique sport event created by ESPN allows companies such as *Mountain Dew, Volkswagen, Nike, Taco Bell,* and *AT&T* to reach the specific demographic group of teens and Generation X. Through guaranteed quality exposure on multiple media outlets including ABC, ESPN, ESPN2 and EXPN.com, the sponsors message and image will be communicated to the target market they are seeking to reach. Image enhancement for these companies will be achieved through association with the ESPN property that has been the leader in showcasing extreme and alternative sport competition, in both winter and summer venues. The association includes on-site exposure through use of a jumbo-tron screen that continuously provides coverage of the ongoing event along with repeated play of sponsor's advertising spots for the several thousand spectators milling on the event site. Additionally, the interactive village allows sponsors the opportunity to meet potential consumers (spectators) face to face for product trial and demonstrations. Product is also provided to many of the people involved in running, staging and producing the event through "shwag." Typically, a sponsorship package inclusive of all that has been described would be sufficient. Yet, additional aspects X Games sponsors find appealing include the hospitality provided for sponsors and the opportunities for trade networking with other corporate representatives that include companies such as Disney and ABC.

Win–Win Strategies

The creation of symbiotic relationships, ones that are greater than the sum of the separate entities, often provides the best strategy for establishing long term, successful sponsorships. In the case of intercollegiate athletics, establishing win-win sponsorship relationships with community businesses often prove to be the best source of consistent revenue. In 1991, "70% of NCAA Division I athletic programs lost money, continuing a trend in place for several years" (Associated Press, 1). While new initiatives have increased to address the growing costs for remaining competitive in intercollegiate athletics, the most significant avenue for many athletic programs to generate new revenue has become development of sponsorship programs. Although NCAA Division I football and basketball typically generate more revenue each year, the two sports also continue to demand a bigger share of the overall athletic budget to continue to remain competitive. Thus, to sustain current programs, more financial resources are required each year. With this significant need for revenue, athletic administrators have increasingly hired sport marketing personnel to develop revenue streams such as corporate sponsorships. "The college demographic is one with which all national corporations wish to have involvement" (Milverstedt, 1989). A successful relationship between college sport and corporate sponsors can be established with athletics serving as the vehicle. Corporations are seeking a means for communication with the college-age target market because they comprise one of the largest groups of potential consumers and should soon have significant purchase decisions to make.

Recognizing the value in a sport property that sponsorship is being sought for, begins with the sport organizers. In the case of intercollegiate sport, the NCAA has led the way by establishing value in the Division I men's basketball championship tournament known as March Madness. The most recent media deal signed by CBS and the NCAA established the overall value of the men's national championship basketball tournament at $6 billion. For corporate partner's associated with the NCAA, this figure translates to considerable value added to their established relationship. Thus, the sport organization benefits by selling the media rights to the highest bidder, while the NCAA sponsors benefit by being associated with a property that has increased in value exponentially in recent years. Yet, the "wins" in this situation also include benefits for the fans of men's intercollegiate basketball since sponsors and event organizers have teamed together to provide a high quality, easily accessible, televised event. This exposure also allows corporate messages to be communicated to a wider audience. Associations that provide benefits such as these rarely experience difficulty in renewing sponsorship deals simply because the "wins" are measurable.

Creating a Match

All of the examples provided are products of what was once a sponsorship proposal. Initially, the concept was merely an idea that was then translated into a working document. To take these ideas and actually develop a successful sport sponsorship plan, several key steps need to be accomplished.

Identifying Potential Sponsors

First, consider specific business relations of your own institution or organization. There may already exist some natural relationships that would be strengthened or enhanced through a sponsorship agreement. Additionally, businesses that do business with you often have a vested interest in your success. Considering a sponsorship agreement with a business that is already a supplier can be readily altered to include more benefits for both parties. Another consideration involves examining the business interests represented among your participants, parents, or other individuals closely associated with the organization. A parent that owns or manages a business may find a sponsorship option to be very attractive, as a means of further supporting the team or sport opportunity. Good inside contacts can be very beneficial when initiating sponsorship interest. Even if a contact within a business is not known, make sure to do the necessary research to determine who is the correct person to approach, who will in fact make the decision and what is the best time and method for reaching these individuals.

Sponsor's Needs

One of the most pervasive problems in sport marketing has traditionally been the myopic focus that sport tends to create. When securing sponsorship, the problem is manifest by the failure to consider what the sponsor's need in a sport relationship. Typically the focus is on what the benefits of the sport are. While sport is often a unique opportunity with elements that are not easily attained in alternative options, those seeking to develop sponsorship relationships must also consider what the business who becomes involved in sponsorship needs to achieve. Wilkinson (1988) was one of the first to classify corporate objectives into various categories. Overall categories often include sales objectives, image objectives, awareness objectives, and employee motivation. The objectives discussed previously can easily be placed into one of these categories. When sales objectives are sought by a sponsor, aspects that they are desiring may include increasing the sales levels of certain brands or getting people to sample a product. Floor traffic, meaning the number of people who come into the store, and product-sponsorship related displays are also common elements of sales objectives. Ultimately, this objective has proven to be the most often sought. Research has revealed that a return on investment is the key for most sport sponsors (Lough, Irwin, and Short, 2000).

To achieve this desired objective, a number of tactics have been employed. Event-themed coupons can be made available in the sponsor's place of business or event tickets can be redeemed as coupons at the sponsor's stores. At certain events, product sampling can be provided through special displays on the event site. Coupon related tactics have been utilized effectively in intercollegiate sport sponsorship. In one example involving a mid-west NCAA Division I university, points scored at a winning football game translated into a percent discount at a sponsor's business if the game ticket was brought in on the following Monday. At a separate university, basketball tickets were printed with a sponsor's coupon on the reverse side to be redeemed as entry into a contest awarding a shopping spree to winners at the conclusion of the season. In each example, sponsors achieved the objective of driving traffic into their store via the sport-sponsor relationship.

Image objectives can be enhanced through sport sponsorship when a logical link is made between the sport property and business sponsor. Community related businesses such as banks or financial institutions often utilize the image of a university association such as a basketball team or tournament to communicate their image as "supporting our community." Companies also seek to alter their image via sport sponsorship. By becoming linked to a specific sport property or event, the image associated may be assimilated by the sponsoring company. *Mountain Dew* has recently gained significant presence as a brand, do to their image as an "extreme" beverage that has been furthered through sponsorship of the ESPN X Games.

Awareness objectives are often abused by sport marketers. For years, signage at an event or on a t-shirt was enough to secure financial backing from sponsors. Yet, as more companies have become involved the sophistication of meeting sponsors needs has increased. Awareness of a brand is most often crucial when that brand is being introduced or altered. Consumers now have exposure to so many forms of advertising that simple awareness often will not suffice alone. Combining the opportunity for awareness with additional objectives may prove to be a more effective strategy for meeting sponsor's needs. For example, extended media coverage that includes saturation of the market through television, print and internet would be viewed as more valuable than simply providing signage at the venue. Providing exposure for the sponsor through multiple outlets can be one of the advantages of sport sponsorship. The cost to sponsors for newsprint publicity is free, which is difficult to compete with when advertising rates for the same publications are considered.

Employee motivation as an objective of sport sponsorship can be achieved by providing opportunities for employees that may not have existed or may have been too expensive for individuals. Tickets to events are often provided to sponsors who then can reward employees by dispersing the tickets for specific reasons. A sport organizer can enhance this objective by creating a special "meet and greet" the athletes and/or coaches after the game or during a pre-game meal. The cost to enhance this experience for sponsors is minimal to sport organizers, but may prove quite valuable for employee motivation and sponsor satisfaction.

Criteria for Sponsorship Evaluation

Considering how businesses can best evaluate their sport sponsorship agreement is a key element to securing successful sponsorship deals. Companies often have an established list of requirements for becoming involved in sport sponsorship. The abilities of management, the sport organization's status and reputation along with the sanctioning body are often key factors in sponsorship decisions (Stotlar, 1993). Corporations only want to be associated with high quality organizations run by competent and stable management. The number of events and the geographic representation also need to be considered. Securing a sponsor that has no presence in the primary market(s) will not provide positive feedback during evaluation, unless the sponsor is primarily seeking awareness and has an additional plan for gaining a presence in that market. Securing sponsorship will undoubtedly be more difficult for first time events or organizers that do not have an established history or developed reputation. In these circumstances, gaining the support of a sanctioning organization, such a National Governing Body or similar established club can assist in insuring potential sponsors that the event will be run well and managed efficiently. Specific criteria cited by Ensor (1987, 40-43) can be found in Figure 2.

Recognizing Why Sponsors Drop Out

Considering all of the time and effort that must go into securing a sponsorship agreement, it would seem that sport organizers would be concerned with keeping sponsors once secured. Yet, one of the primary reasons that sponsors will drop out or not renew a sponsorship agreement is the lack of attention and service paid during the agreement. Feedback should be provided to allow the sponsors to determine whether their investment is paying off, or may need to be altered. However, when no feedback is provided, the most often realized conclusion by sponsors is that the relationship is not worth the investment. Commonly cited reasons for dropping out include lack of service, decreased market value of the event as determined by reduced attendance or a drop in television ratings, or a change in corporate direction.

Providing attendance figures, crowd demographics and copies of newspaper clippings of the event can be simple means for giving feedback to sponsors. Interpreting these elements relative to established corporate objectives may be the extra bit of service that will enable a sport organization to retain a sponsor. Yet, too often sport organizers fail to simply provide feedback. Communicating with the sponsor throughout the agreement is crucial to continued success. Taking proactive measures to prevent a perceived decrease in value or ineffective strategy can go much further than being reactive when change may be too late. The value that corporate sponsors involved in both general sport sponsorship and women's sport sponsorship place on key objectives may assist in the formulation of new strategy to better meet sponsor's needs (Lough and Irwin, 1999).

Another common rationale for dropping out of a sponsorship agreement is a change in corporate direction. In many instances this rationale is simply a reflection of a dissatisfied sponsor. However, in certain circumstances the fit between the new image the company is seeking and the established image of the sport event or property is too distant to be remedied. The best strategy for sport marketers in this circumstance is to maintain positive relations with the business, in case the corporate direction changes some time in the future. The most effective approach to take in preventing sponsor drop out is to work the relationship to meet the sponsor's criteria, provide service and data to justify their continuation, and help them establish the measures for a successful sport sponsorship.

Summary/Conclusion

Developing a successful sport sponsorship plan requires attention to five primary areas: (1) the description of the sponsorship, (2) the plan objectives, (3) the plan components, (4) the budget and (5) evaluation/relationship management. The initial document developed to create interest and motivation for potential clients to review the entire proposal is the executive summary. In this short, often one page document, the major points of interest are clearly provided for the potential sponsor. Once interest is created, the proposal should illustrate objectives that sponsors can achieve by becoming associated with the sport opportunity. The section that presents plan components should establish the unique opportunities available through various levels of sponsorship. Typically the top level or most expensive opportunity will include aspects such categorical exclusivity and rights to use of specific marks protected by and belonging to the sport property. The fourth section outlines the investment required to achieve specific levels of sponsorship. Finally, the concluding section provides the evaluation measures that will be implemented and feedback that can be anticipated to maintain a strong working relationship between the sport property and the sponsor.

Creating successful sport sponsorship relationships requires skill, creativity and attention to detail. If all of the above areas are researched prior to engaging a corporate client, and a professional document that includes these components is presented, the likelihood for achieving success will be greatly enhanced. Securing sponsorship for sport properties and/or events is a crucial element in today's competitive sport landscape. By incorporating the ideas discussed you will be capable of competing for and establishing successful sport sponsorship agreements.

References

Associated Press. (1991, August 30). "It's all a matter of money." AP wire service, Slug/9704 3144.

Ensor, R.J. (1987). "The corporate view of sports sponsorship," *Athletic Business* (September), 40-43.

Irwin, R.L., M. Asimakopolous, and W.A. Sutton (1994). "A Model for screening sponsorship opportunities," *Journal of Promotional Management* (2), 3-4, 53-69.

Irwin, D. (1993). "In Search of Sponsors," *Athletic Management* (May), 11-16.

Lough, N.L. (1996). "Factors Affecting Corporate Sponsorship of Women's Sport," *Sport Marketing Quarterly* 5(2), 11-18.

Lough, N. and R. Irwin (1999). "The Objectives sought among sponsors of women's sport: Do they differ from general sponsorship?" Research paper presented at North American Society for Sport Management conference, Vancouver, CA.

Lough, N., R. Irwin, and G. Short (in press). "Corporate Sponsorship Motives Among North American Companies: A Contemporary Analysis," *International Journal of Sport Management*.

Milverstedt, F. (1989). "Colleges courting corporate sponsors." *Athletic Business* (March), 25-26.

Mullin, B., S. Hardy, and W. Sutton (2000). *Sport Marketing*. Champaign, IL: Human Kinetics.

Stotlar, D.K. (1993). *Successful Sport Marketing*. Dubuque, IA: Brown & Benchmark.

Wilkinson, D.G. (1988). *Event Management and Marketing Institute*. Willowdale, Ontario: Sport Marketing Institute.

Part 4

Media and Information Management

Public relations in sport management is not a luxury—it is a necessity.

Jeaneane Williams

Chapter 16

Public Relations

Jeaneane Williams

Introduction

Public relations in sport management is an all-encompassing term. Taken in its simplest form, it means the positive relationship of the organization/institution and its *total* personnel complement with *all* of its public constituencies.

In many respects, the sports manager's role must be considered one in which public relations is a major key. Nowhere is this more obvious in recent years than in college and university athletics. A coach who "shoots off his mouth" at the wrong instant may find himself looking for a new job. Even major league owners are not immune to the power of the public perception.

The best way to rally public constituencies to an institution or organization is often through its sports program. College and university presidents are very aware of this—athletic "booster clubs" have become even stronger assets to college and university sports than in the past. Their growth has not been wholly positive—as their members have gained a significant toe-hold, their power is often more excessive than the academic administration finds comfortable, but as potential heavy donors, they are likely to be tolerated.

Youth clubs and other service agencies running athletic programs must handle public relations very carefully. PR is likely to be the component third in importance for them—behind actual participation and the recreational/physical fitness value. YMCAs running organizational sports are likely to find, like high school and small-college programs, that local citizens examine first their team sports programs and successes and second their value to people on an individual basis.

Knowing Your PR Audience Is Vital

The role of good public relations may be somewhat less significant in some sport management positions than others, but every operation's success depends on some part of the public for its existence. The way in which bad PR plays itself out may vary enormously, but in many instances a single poor PR move can nearly destroy an otherwise perfectly good operation. Take a new health-spa owner, whose building adjoins the property of a crotchety 85-year-old widow; if some of his clients rile her with their noise in the parking lot, she may take her complaint to the mayor—who happens to be her son-in-law. Take a minor sports program in a public high school where just one set of parents can spread innuendo about the volunteer coach and, even if the gossip is proven to be untrue, the program—and the school administration as well as the reputation of the coach—may be damaged almost irreparably. Take a college athletic director who has to acquiesce in the decision to drop the football program after several of the players have pleaded guilty to gambling on the games; it may be the AD who loses his job if the college's largest benefactor has a passion for football and is determined to find a scapegoat for his aggravation. Take a Boy Scout sports camp director and stretch him to the limits of his patience with the neighbors across the lake who don't like the midnight "good, clean" (but noisy) fun that roused them out of a sound sleep and let him make one ill-timed comment and see what wrath he can bring down on the entire organization. Take the new local "farm" pro baseball team and find out how much of a problem the manager's life (and possibly, his job) can suffer if the local media and the newspaper sports editor "don't really like baseball all that much."

Such instances take all the positive public relations that can possibly be created. While smiling and listening to complaints is always necessary, that's not all there is to it. The best key in good public relations is always going to be proactive PR. That means trying to cover all bases *before* something gets to be a problem, explaining and getting approval in advance, not *after* being called on the carpet by a City Councilman or an irate neighbor. People who have been consulted in advance, who have met the kids in the program, who have been recipients of good deeds from the team—in other words, who have "bought into" the sport in some way—are much more likely to be willing to resolve problems in helpful, and not hurtful, ways.

There are two important categories of public relations: internal and external. If you don't have the first, it is nearly impossible to have the latter.

Internal Public Relations

Good internal public relations means communicating openly and often with personnel in the organization. The best promotion for an event can be negated if one of the employees gives a disgruntled response to a television report. The new health club members will be furious if they are not advised by the receptionist taking court reservations that the raquetball court is temporarily under water because of a plumbing leak. If students are taken out of an English class to make the extra practice that's just been called, count on losing credibility with at least the English teacher (and maybe the student, the parent and the school board too).

Make it a habit to communicate with the staff and support personnel in weekly planned meetings. Sessions need take no more than 30 minutes, but they are essential, even if the total staff component equals two people. Pre-plan an agenda by jotting notes on a handy desk pad or your computer. This will ensure that even minor events with major implications for an employee will not be overlooked. It may be possible to lengthen one of the sessions every few months and use it to sketch out long-range plans for the organization. No one, from the janitor to the bookkeeper, likes to be surprised with the rewiring paraphernalia hanging from the front door on a Monday morning.

If your sports program is part of a large organization (college, school, etc.), make sure that communication with the other parts of the internal organization is maintained. If there is an internal newsletter, e-mail or even a central bulletin board, be sure to publicize changes that will affect other areas well ahead of time.

Try to plan schedules that will not be a burden, not simply for the staff or players, but for others who must schedule other events.

External Public Relations

Communicate with the external public both directly and through the media. Be aware that these are two very different kinds of communications — yet they ultimately reach the same people who can become either supporters or non-supporters, often totally dependent on how you deal with the local media.

Dealing with Negative Public Relations

The truth is that negative public relations is most often practiced unwittingly. Its result can be, in many instances, devastating and, even when the initial effect appears to be positive, one has to ask what the long-term effects might be. What effect, for example, did the widely publicized tiffs of Billy Martin have on his team's overall image to the public? How has George Steinbrenner permanently affected baseball? Has Dennis Rodman made pro basketball more supporters among the youth? Has the conservative stand of the Boy Scouts of America in its court case related to homosexual orientation made a difference in local BSA troop recruitment? Was the University of Nevada-Las Vegas academic program compromised by NCAA and court findings against its basketball program? For every fan out there who applauded Martin's spirit or Steinbrenner's idiosyncrasies, how many baseball fans were permanently turned off the sport?

It is inevitable that a sports-related organization will have problems from a public relations standpoint. The very nature of the work means someone is going to get hurt sometime and it is going to have an effect on the program. Don't try to avoid publicity about accidents; respond openly, quickly and honestly to their occurrence.

A. *Accidents and PR.* Accidents need not produce adverse publicity. In order to avoid it, planning is essential. If a player gets hurt, be sure your coaches and other employees react promptly, not simply by getting proper medical treatment taken care of, but by also advising those who saw the accident about its seriousness or its nature. Public address systems are often the best way to take care of such incidents. If the game is being announced, see that someone gets an accurate explanation to the announcer. If there is no PA system, ask school officials to help pass the word. If an injury occurs in a public facility such as a YWCA, be sure to ascertain the seriousness and cause of the accident. If equipment is at fault, know about it before the media descend or before the insurance claims-adjuster appears. For a stadium manager or a pro team manager, the first people to deal with are the media. Know the facts.

B. *Words to Avoid.* In most instances, the worst public relations words are "No comment." Use them only as an absolutely last resort. It's generally just as easy to say, "We are investigating the incident and we have already asked the staff to check this out, but we reallly don't know the exact details just now and will have to get back to you." Most often, that kind of response is really accurate and it shows greater concern for the interests of the television or newspaper reporter than "No comment."

C. *You Make the Call.* In really serious instances, when something major has happened and it is certain the media will pick it up, don't wait for a call. Do the organization, public, and media a service by reacting *proactively.* "Control" of the media is impossible and should not be attempted. The worst thing that can happen following an accident is to refuse to see or talk with the media and leave them in the dilemma of trying to serve the public (i.e., readers, viewers) without proper information. If a reporter must resort to interviewing anyone available for on-the-spot comments, don't expect an accurate account to appear in the media.

D. *Marketing and Licensing Are PR Bad News Bears.* Colleges and universities with top athletic programs have found a new way to make money in recent years by registering or patenting their logos and their names. While portions of the funds paid in for licensing fees generally make their way back into athletic budgets, entrepreneurial fans and others are often irritated at the way in which athletic paraphernalia — t-shirts, hats, etc. — may be sold at a higher cost to offset the licensing requirements. Usually only pro sports and big-time college programs are apt to have this problem. Make sure that you make an effort to keep the public aware that the fees collected are used for scholarships or other student purposes. An article in athletic programs would not be remiss, and it may be possible to focus a local TV interview toward something the funds have paid for.

E. *Time Switches Madden the Fans of Successful Teams.* In recent years, highly successful football and basketball teams at colleges and universities have created big PR nightmares by catering to television demands for setting game times. Some university football games are now played on a weekday in locations away from *both* campuses primarily to please networks. Fans who buy tickets to a home game may not know until the last minute when to arrive for the game if television coverage is an option. The nonchalance with which TV networks or ESPN give a last-second nod to what games they will televise leaves sport management personnel scrambling, especially those in charge of publicity. Personnel should be clued in to explain the realities of TV coverage — it's big bucks and it generally pays enough to fund minor sports for both male and female athletes which would otherwise be left out. Again, articles in athletic programs and other mention of this reality should be attempted.

F. *Make an Effort at Political Correctness.* Sports organizations bring a great deal of fury down on their heads by not looking ahead to the consequences of some of their actions. Especially in recent years, team logos and team mascots have come in for a lot of criticism from ethnic groups and from feminists and other supporters. Understand that keeping an ethnically-offensive mascot is going to lose you some supporters — as well as gain you some — and you have a chance to choose which ones. If you are in the planning stages of choosing an emblem or a mascot, set up a committee to advise you. Be sure you've looked at every angle for potential criticism before making your final choice. You have enough hoops to jump through in the rest of your job, without setting up another one laced with fire.

G. *Equipment Contracts May Anger Supporters.* Yet another recent attention-getter for successful college and university athletic teams is the corporate equipment contract and the understood endorsement that comes with the signing of the contract. Brand-name shoes, helmets, caps, headbands — whatever the successful sport can accommodate — have become advertising and marketing directors' targets for selling related goods. Of course, Little League teams and employee leagues have used this kind of "sign board advertising" for many years as a reliable way to share matching shirts or equipment. Then professional athletes began to endorse specific items of equipment for big contracts, and it wasn't long until the more successful college and university athletic programs got in on the act. Now even top-rated high school teams are being approached by corporations hoping to establish their brand name equipment in the minds of young people with years of buying ahead of them.

Think long and hard before you ink a contract with a corporate entity for sports equipment. Question the company thoroughly about its product and its production. Don't get surprised in front of a TV camera when you are asked if you know that child labor in a third-world country was used to produce the item. If that turns out to be the case in your initial fact-finding interview, try to make a difference by making your views known, at the very least. Who knows? You may be able to make a difference in getting the company to change its ways!

Understand that many of your supporters will be suspicious of equipment contracts—in most cases, the team coach as well as other personnel will get a percentage of the endorsement money which comes along with the contract, in addition to that allocated directly for the institution or organization. Make every effort to be honest about the contract's details because the media will find out anyway. Try to explain how the contract money will be used; if any of it is being given to charitable organizations by coaches or others, be sure to say so. If it will be used for minor sports not otherwise funded, make it known. Always use honesty as the best policy, but never refrain from putting the best light on the subject.

H. *Youthful Infractions and True Crime.* The popularity of sports has spawned an impression, in the eyes of many, that athletes are high crime committers. Though statistics do not bear this out, it is true that the media—and therefore, the public—do focus an undue amount of attention on both major crimes and petty misdemeanors attributed to athletes. Part of the reason is no doubt rooted in the hero mystique which surrounds many athletes and the way in which the public seems to expect higher standards of athletes. In some cases, the athlete's star status, nationally or locally, has caused him to be "fingered for" the crime—even when he is not guilty—because he was recognized from among many—his face, his size, height or bulk made him an easy mark. Whether local or national, football and basketball players seem to take the brunt of criminal accusation.

College and high school sport management programs suffer the most embarrassment from allegations against players. It is to coaches and athletic directors that the first calls come when the media get a tip about a criminal infraction or an arrest warrant.

If you get one of their calls, be judicious in your comments. Again, avoid "No comment." Remember that everyone is innocent until proven guilty and also remember that you are dealing with young people's lives. Try to impress both these facts on reporters. Voice your support for the student, but avoid absolutes—you cannot *know* for sure the student was not at fault unless you were there—but express an intention to stand by the student through the legal process and to withhold final decisions until all sides are heard.

Numerous athletic programs have lost public confidence by allowing youthful offenders to continue playing on teams even after it is obvious they are guilty of at least some minor infraction of the school, if not the criminal justice system. If you are involved in the decision-making about such a situation, try to assess it very carefully. Is winning one game—or even a winning season—worth the confidence that has been placed in you to mold young minds and bodies for the future?

Is your job at risk, dependent on which way you decide? What will be the cost to your financial support from the booster club, whichever way you choose to go? What will your decision mean to the rest of the team? To the ethical teachings for the student body as a whole? To your colleagues? To your school's adminstration?

Be sure you have answered all the questions in your own mind before you make a decision—and make sure it's a decision you can live with for the rest of your life.

Essentials of a Good Print Image

Written communications are some of the most essential proactive PR tools that can be used. They are a visible image of the program and the operation. They must be, first and foremost, accurate and clean, with correct spelling and grammar. They must be clear and carefully thought out. They must project a coordinated image of the operation.

Perhaps more than any other organization, a sports program seems to have a problem coordinating its image. Often it is because too many possibilities are floating around. The group may have a nickname with a logo (usually a distinctive alphabetical type face of some sort), and it may also have a team mascot that may or may not have some direct connection with the logo. Or there may be an institutional or team emblem that is part of the insignia of the sports program. In too many instances, an effort to try to incorporate every possible symbol may make, at best, a busy-looking and, at worst, a trashy and garish visual product for the organization. While often passed off as a cute idea, too many sports organizations tie themselves irreparably to some insignia that will give them an inappropriate visibility for the remainder of their existences.

A great deal of care should be put into everything to appear in print about an organization—its letterhead stationery, its logo for banners, uniforms, activity buses, scoreboard, billboards, brochures—anything to be seen by the public. Every printed piece should have some continuity with the overall image.

If the organization can possibly afford it, hire a reputable design firm to provide a logo and guidelines for its use on your printed materials. If the organization has an established logo, make time immediately for some careful thought about it. Questions that must be addressed are:

1. Is this the kind of image around which I want to structure my job?
2. Does this image meet the current and perceived future program offered?
3. Is this the kind of logo that will attract the clientele (customers, players, supporters, members, fans) we want? (Quality tends to attract quality. A "red neck" image can easily come across from a tacky design and gaudy colors. A "trite" logo can detract from the qualtiy of an organization. A "cute" logo can subtly belie the seriousness of a program.)
4. Does the logo do justice to the scope of the program? (If the sports program has broadened since the logo was designed, it may no longer be appropriate, especially if a female team sport is now included.)
5. Can the logo be used properly in a way that will produce the desired res-sults within the framework of the budget? (If the logo was designed for color printing and you are stuck with a one-color brohcure, problems will arise.)

All of these questions are important because the printed materials of the organization will reflect, to a great extent, on the quality of the job being done, as perceived by the public.

If a design professional cannot be hired, check the volunteer network. It is possible a parent, a supporter, or a member who is in the advertising or design business will be available. Ask for advice and help.

If the organization is of a size to afford someone to write and design publications on a full-time or part-time basis, choose that person carefully. Make sure that the organizational image being sought can be translated into printed pieces through the skills of the employee. Look at writing or design samples in detail; if unsure, ask a volunteer professional for advice.

In recent years, the proliferation of computers and desk top publishing has made it possible for even very small organizations to produce their own publications. Easy computer access also makes it easy for just one employee to give your program a black eye. Make sure that the person who is in charge of products going out to the public has good taste, good grammar and good sense!

When you don't have your own publishing ability and the budget is small, it is still possible to find a good printer who can be relied on for design and formatting of the work your staff has written. It may be necessary to pay a little more for the total job with a full-service printer who has complete production facilities, but it will be worth it. And it may save time and money in the long run if your staff is inexperienced in print media.

Written communication takes on even more importance than usual if your organization relies on fund-raising for its existence. Studies show a direct correlation between the quality of a fund-raising brochure and the dollars it brings in. Even the texture of the paper in your brochure will subliminally affect the potential donor; a smooth-finish paper generates fewer dollars than a quality rough-texture; and off-white textured paper will generally produce more money than a stark-white sheet. *Anything* will produce more money than a poorly photocopied sheet. Ask your printer's advice, but do not always ask him to do the job in the least expensive way possible. It is not just *his* income that will be affected.

Communicating with the Public through the Media

Good media relations can make or break an organization in many instances. Three cardinal rules stand out in the area of media relations:

1. Think carefully before you speak.
2. Try to let your voice fall *only* when you are at the end of a sentence, and put everything needed for a complete thought sequence into a single sentence. Media types have been known to splice or disconnect several sentences and have you say something you never intended—so be crafty!
3. Honesty is the best—*and only*—policy.

Because of the national interest in sports and physical fitness, it is often relatively easy to attract local media attention to a winning team (or even a despairingly losing team), to an outstanding athlete, an unusual sports event, a special piece of sports equipment, a unique physical-fitness device, a record-breaking winner, an offbeat record-breaker. The everyday, run-of-the-mill events may require some ingenuity and perseverance.

A. Newspapers

Especially in small towns, it may take nothing more than making a telephone call to the local newspaper to get good sports page coverage. Today, many daily and weekly papers in small towns and cities or counties have gained much of their readership by covering local high school competitions. Because their advertisers are interested in attracting local buyers, these papers are eager to cover not just educational teams but many club and athletic events of all kinds. Often, media coverage for such teams and sports grows increasingly difficult as the size of the town or city (and the newspaper circulation) grows. In larger venues, sport management professionals may find they need an extra helping of creativity to try to get publicity or coverage for their activities.

B. Radio

Radio coverage and publicity have much in common with newspaper coverage —they depend on size. If the sports operation is in a small city with a locally owned AM radio station, audiences can be reached simply by providing station announcers with appropriate information. Written news releases, originally designed for print media, can be edited and shortened for radio stations. If the sports organization has its own information officer, it's possible to get much more publicity than merely reports of final scores on the radio with just a little creativity. The same is often true for FM radio stations, although more of them have stricter programming formats and your coverage will therefore be less frequent.

C. Television

Television is a medium in a place by itself. It is the least likely medium where regular coverage of events other than those staged by large university or major pro teams will occur.

The reasons are obvious: Programming is far more standardized, in stricter time segments, with less opportunity for local information. And TV costs are expensive. The most likely spots for media attention are the local early and late evening news segments or the community affairs programs (often morning or early afternoons only). Again, forethought in electronic media relations is important: do not waste time with a point that is too complex for spot coverage—remember their time is in spoken segments measured in seconds, not column inches. And it is generally considered newsworthy only if it makes a good picture.

Do not be disdainful of what may appear to be a TV reporter's or cameraman's excessive interest in some off-beat aspect of the sports program; media disdain is a habit too often practiced by those in public or media relations. The result is that same cameraman or reporter may be the one to cover the "really big event"—and give it less than his best because you have offended him earlier. Media personnel are just like everyone else: they respond to courtesy, to helpfulness, to friendliness. And they remember where they got them—and where they did not.

In recent time, local TV stations have become more likely to show highlights of local high school games, especially football and basketball, due to the attractiveness of these sports events to their viewers. Some stations even provide ten or fifteen minutes of special coverage on Friday nights in an extension following the late evening news. While this is cursory coverage, it is priceless PR for high school athletic programs—coaches and students alike—and is a valuable educational tool for savvy principals and school boards when it comes to budget time.

Media Relations and Media Realities

Never try to play one medium against another when you're trying to get coverage for your sports program. While this may seem like a good idea if your town or city has several radio stations or more than one newspaper, don't do it. It's a losing game. Understand what is unique about each station or paper, and then play *to* that strength, but don't try to set up a competition.

For example, if one radio station plays contemporary or mainstream jazz, a look at the listener profile would likely indicate a middle-aged, moderate-income audience. Suggest or create a news feature that focuses on some aspect of the sports organization that will be of interest to listeners, and the station may use it. A predominantly country and western music station would not be interested in a feature on a comparison between ballet and football moves, and a classical station will not likely announce the dates for a YMCA jump-rope competition.

Be realistic in efforts toward the media; do not offend them by treating them all alike and sending them mass-packaged material via "snail" mail or e-mail. A personal visit to the newspaper office or broadcasting station is not inappropriate on occasion, but do not do it too often. Make an appointment when planning to stop by with an idea or a news release; remember their time is valuable too. In many instances, business may be transacted over the telephone or via the Internet or mail, but be sure to keep up the personal one-on-one approach every once in a while.

One word about reporting sports scores for teams: it's amazing how often newspapers or radio and even TV will report them if the information is made available. School and college sports directors should recruit student assistants to be directly responsible for e-mailing or telephoning scores to the media immediately after a game. Coach the student in performing this task by giving him proper credentials, a title and seeing that he gets basic information clearly and concisely. Even if he has to use his own computer or home phone for low- or no-budget programs, you'll be surprised how much more visibility can be obtained on a regular basis.

A. Media Aids

Do not be hesitant to contact newspaper, radio or TV reporters with an idea for a story or feature segment. Often they will ask to have it in writing (it's always good to have a brief outline already in hand), and be sure to give them plenty of planning time. Even in big city media operations, it is often impossible to assign on-the-spot coverage without several weeks' notice, and the talk show sequences are often planned several months in advance.

If your sports program is part of a non-profit organization, it will be less difficult to secure publicity for events. The media, perhaps even subconsciously to an extent, often seem to think in terms of revenue and advertising and will therefore avoid giving "free ads" to potentially paying customers. Under current federal regulations, some broadcast media still are required to provide "public service announcements" (PSAs)—many of which are subtle "advertisements" for non-profit organizations. Offer ideas for PSAs, however, even if you are part of a profit-making organization. Many stations automatically allot a certain number of hours or minutes each year to PSAs out of a spirit of community involvement. The PSA on physical fitness can as easily be filmed in a health spa as in a university athletic clinic.

Don't overlook the proliferation of computers and the Internet in the hands of many of your students, clients or customers. One of them may be able to set up a striking web site for your organization, which can be updated from time to time and used as an advertising vehicle. Layouts in full color, advertisements in eye-catching formats and big type are at the fingertips of more people than ever before. If you can establish a network of capable volunteers who are computer-savvy, you will have yourself and your organization a ready—and inexpensive—publicity department at your beck and call.

B. Using Volunteers in Media Relations

If at all possible, hire an expert to handle media relations, even if it is only on a part-time basis. The work is time consuming and sometimes the pay-offs are a long time in coming—often too long to keep the attention of any except a professional. And it is a field in which expertise and inside information are valuable—a novice can commit a faux pas and never even know what went wrong.

But if the budget simply won't cover another salary and especially if the organization is small, consider asking for volunteer help. Often, the mother of a Girl Scout or a Boy Scout has some writing talent on which you can capitalize. In many cases, a parent may have an affiliation with one of the local media that can be very helpful to a non-profit sports manager. Be careful not to overstep the ethics of the media profession, but seek advice and counsel from those who know the answers.

For instance, the father of one of the students on the high school's soccer team may be the arts editor of the local newspaper. Do not ask him to try to get the sports editor to write a feature about the Brazilian twins who have just moved to the school district and have joined the team. Consult him about the story idea instead; try to get him interested in helping to write the story lead which can be marketed to the sports editor. Ask the mother who is the television producer for advice on some community-affairs time for the team because it has managed to sell enough chocolate bars to buy its own uniforms, but don't ask her to intercede with the sports reporter. The mother can help with an outline, she can help you visualize the photographic aspects of the idea, but she may be unwilling to use her influence directly. If she can help with the strategy and the name of the person to contact, that may be all that is needed. Or she may be willing to "put in a word" —sometimes a word from the right person will suffice. But be properly grateful for it, and be sure to follow through on the contact she helped you make.   Think about a media relations effort from the time you are hired or from the time you begin a sports operation: determine immediately what resources are available, both in financial terms and in human terms. Find out which students have parents who are journalism or other media professionals. Solicit the "pros" for help, advice and ideas for publicity. Managers of physical fitness centers or health spas should make it a practice to find out if any of their members are media employees —try out publicity ideas on them or ask them for advice about features. If affiliated with a YMCA or YWCA or other similar organization, check the board of directors for media professionals. In the case of a city recreation department, seek out any media-connected parents of the children who use the facilities. They may be able to help you directly with feature ideas. Find out which adults or teenagers are computer savvy in whatever organization employees you. They can be of inestimable help in preparing everything from team rosters to batting averages to PSAs or colorful posters to advertise your events.

Summary/Conclusion

The importance of public relations to an organization is often overlooked. Many people feel that good public relations is easy—that anybody can do it. And it *is* true that everyone within an organization does public relations—good or bad. From the receptionist who answers the phone to the trainer, the coach, the team doctor, the ticket taker, the activities coordinator, the star quarterback, the promoter, the mascot, the manager—the public is building an impression of your organization based in part on the people who work within it.

In Search of Excellence: Lessons from America's Best-Run Companies was one of the best-selling nonfiction books ever after its publication and release in 1982, and its sales in paperback and audio cassette have continued in the decades to follow. The book's authors, Robert H. Waterman Jr. and Thomas J. Peters, defined the qualities that make large companies successful. The book's impact made them popular authors and speakers in much demand all over the world.

One of the common threads they discovered in their search for excellent companies was something they defined as *simple courtesy*. In its most basic format, public relations *is* courtesy—courtesy to all segments of the population or the constituency, both internal and external.

When *In Search of Excellence* first appeared, some of its detractors complained that much of what it described was obvious. The fact is, however, that authors Peters and Waterman were able to find only a few large companies that regularly practiced the obvious.

So it is with public relations. Everyone seems to know what it means; too few seem to practice it.

Public relations in sport management is not a luxury—it is a necessity! Its value can be measured in the success of the program and the way in which it is viewed by all its constituencies.

Chapter 17

An Informative Approach to Marketing Sport

Bernard Mullin

Introduction

The case for the development of an information-based approach to marketing was made extensively in Chapter 10. In this chapter the elements of the data storage system [called a marketing information system (MIS)] are outlined. In addition, the types of data which a marketer needs to collect are discussed, The major contribution of the chapter is to highlight the use of the data in determining the most appropriate target segments which marketing strategy is later developed to reach.

An MIS can be as simple as a system of index cards, or it can be as complex as a fully integrated database, stored and retrieved on a computer. Obviously there are many alternatives in between these two polar extremes, and just where an organization chooses to make its stand depends upon the following factors;

1. The size and geographic dispersement of the market for the organizations product or service:
    The larger the market, and the more geographically dispersed the market, the larger and more complex the AUS,
2. The availability of data on consumers and potential consumers.
    The more data available, the larger the MIS.
3. The budget allocated to the development and maintenance of the MIS.
    The larger the budget, the more sophisticated the MIS.

Whether the index card system or a computerized system is chosen makes no difference in the type of data needed to be collected, nor to the analysis and manipulations to be performed with the data. However the access to data and the level of sophistication will be much greater with computerized systems and with the ridiculously low price of PCs and integrated cash registers there is really no reason not to computerize.

The difference between manual (paper) and (electronic) systems is that electronic systems permit storage and analysis of much greater volumes of data, the data can be analyzed much more quickly and accurately, multiple departments in the organization can access the data at the same time, and data from various sources can be integrated. While the differences are significant and permit much more powerful marketing data to be generated in electronic-based systems and hence more sophisticated marketing strategy to be developed, the time taken to maintain a simple index card or paper file system is still worth the effort, Even for the sport entrepreneur working in the smallest of organizations the payback is considerable. The problem with manual systems is that they require long hours of tedious work, and this often deters all but the most ardent of sport managers.

Below, the characteristics of an effective MIS are developed, along with some guidelines of how the system should be used, and the potential benefits which can accrue for those taking the time to develop and maintain an MIS.

Characteristics of a Marketing Information System (MIS)

An MIS should have the following characteristics:

1. It must be centralized. An organization needs to have all of its data located in one centralized database system.
2. The various data bases (consumer files, accounting records, sales records, etc.) need to be fully integrated so that, the data from one source can be contrasted and/or combined with data from another source.
3. The data must be retrievable in a form which the marketer can use for decision-making.

Only if all three of the above conditions are met, does an MIS reach its full potential. As a simple rule, the MIS must contain only the information that will be used by the marketer, yet it must contain all of the information that the marketer needs to make effective decisions. One caution needs to be offered at this time, many marketers fall into the trap of feeling that the only data which is relevant is that which they collect themselves about their market, and their own consumers (called primary data). In almost all industries there is a wealth of data which has already been published (called secondary data), which is invaluable to the marketer. Much of the secondary data used by marketers comes from federal, state or county government sources (such as population demographics); or from public sources (such as local chamber of commerce data), or from trade and industry associations and publications (industry averages, profiles and standards performance and cost ratios). Additional information from independent market research agencies such as the A.C. Nielson Co., Simmons Market Research Bureau, and Louis Harris, Inc., all of whom collect data on consumer preferences, viewing and participation habits, product purchases, etc., is extremely valuable but can be expensive. Data from all of the above primary and secondary sources should become part of the overall MIS, and should be updated at least once a year.

For many sport industry segments, external secondary-data sources provide the sole "yardstick" by which the organizations' own data can be contrasted. For example, several years ago a major New England college contacted the author to perform market research for them concerning their intercollegiate football program. The team had suffered significant and continual declines in paid attendance despite a steadily improving win-to-loss record. One of the most relevant pieces of information which the athletic administration had ignored was the fact that their attendance decline rate was significantly lower than comparative schools throughout New England, and far below the drop-off in interest being experienced at

New England high school football games over the same time period. While this information did not solve their problem per se, it did provide a most critical backdrop in deciding which media alternatives should be employed to boost sagging attendance, and particularly in estimating the probability of favorable advertising response,

The author stated in an earlier article that "Marketing without a marketing information system (MIS) is like taking a trip without a road map!" (Ref. 1). Simply put, smart marketers do not do it! Every marketing decision should be made only after the impact on all of the key elements of marketing have been fully considered and after the program concept, price, or promotion has been "test marketed" with existing or potential customers. A list major information needs of a marketer is given below, broken down under the headings of the key elements of marketing.

Informational Needs of the Sport Marketer

The first thing that a marketer needs to do is to define the extent of his market area. A concept which has been used in the retail industry is that of the "critical trading radius" (Ref. 2). The critical trading radius was initially conceived as a system of concentric circles of mileage using the facility location as the center and 5-, 7- and 10-mile radii as milestones. The concept has now been refined as a series of nonconcentric radii based upon consumer traveling time to the sport facility rather than straight mileage. The size of the critical trading area varies with each segment of the sport industry. Commercial recreation clubs (racquet sports and health clubs, etc.) usually have a 20-minute driving time radius from the facility in which 80-85% of members and potential members reside; retail sporting goods stores in urban and suburban areas have a similar trading area to the health clubs. In rural areas, the radius naturally expands considerably. The trading radius increases as the degree of competition decreases for professional sports teams; intercollegiate, athletic events; and coliseum, stadium and arena events, 80% of the market usually resides within a one-hour driving or traveling time radius, (longer for weekend afternoon events). Baseball (MLB) and football (NFL) draw from a larger area. For small ski resorts near population areas, the radius will be an hour or less. For all destination resorts (the more popular ski resorts; sport resorts such as Hilton Head Island in South Carolina and Disney World, in Orlando, Florida) the trading area is almost unlimited. The concept of traveling time rather than straight mileage reflects more accurately the decision criteria of a consumer, and consequently *is a more* accurate predictor of potential demand.

The data which is critical to be kept on hand concerning the nature and extent of the market is as follows,

1. Size of the market (total number of individuals living within the critical trading area).
   This outlines whether or not the market has sufficient size to support the product.
2. The target demographics of individuals residing in the critical trading radius. Specifically, the major factors are:
   a. Total population within trading radius (year round residents and commuters).

b. Breakdown by age, sex and income relevant to the profile of target consumers, e.g. college educated males aged 18-35.

From these data, the marketer is able to make predictions on total market potential. When industry averages are available, it is possible to predict quite accurately the total demand for a particular product, For example, in the bowling business, it has long been an industry standard that one bowling lane is demanded per 10,000 population, Similar "rules of thumb were used for court and health clubs but are modified because racquet sports and fitness aligns to a younger market.

3. The purchase behavior and consumption patterns *of* those living and residing within the market.

    Where possible, data on the spending patterns of consumers are helpful in determining potential market demand, Marketers have found demographics to be extremely useful *in* determining the profile of potential consumers, and yet demographics have their limitations. For example, a 3.5-year-old college educated, white professional male living in Iowa is simply not the same "animal" to a marketer as the similarly-profiled individual residing in New York City, The major difference is life-style characteristics. Lifestyle characteristics *are* called psychographics and are usually captured through A10, (activity, interest, and opinion studies (Ref. 5. Psychographic studies tend to be expensive and they are difficult to undertake. Data take much more effort to solicit and respondents are not always forthcoming in offering opinions and attitudes. Consequently, many decisions are made in the absence of such research. *When* no hard demographic data are available, or when the data bear no relationship to the product being marketed, it is essential that at least a "quick and dirty" pulse-check 9f consumer attitudes be performed concerning key product attributes. Illustrations of this latter process might be a verbal sampling of opinion of participants in a road race as to certain aspects of the race's total organization, form and marketing. Or a more comprehensive study might *be* to ask individuals to complete surveys on their attitudes concerning running shoes, where several products are compared. As a last resort, the sport marketer should stand at the gates/doors of his/her arena, stadium, or facility and see who is using his/her product. The first series of questions would concern the product attributes which the individuals felt were more critical in their choice of shoe. The second would deal with their subjective ratings of each shoe on each of the attributes they identified.

    From these data a strong idea of key product attributes can be developed which determine product choice. The strength of one's own product can also be "guesstimated," along with the areas of weakness according to consumer perception. Similarly, some general ideas about the competitors 'strengths and weaknesses can also be developed.

4. The level of spectatorship and/or participation level by sport(s), broken down by demographic categories.

    This identifies the profile of the target consumer of any given sport. All promotional strategies and advertising media choices are then designed to reach this target market segment.

One of the founding fathers of sport marketing, Matt Levine, once said that all marketing boils down to how well you know the market (Ref, 4). There can be little doubt that knowledge of the market is critical to marketing success, even if there are other important factors impacting on success.

A. The Consumer

The ideal situation for a marketer is to be able to identify all of his consumers by name, address, phone, fax, and e-mail address, so that they can be contacted by one on one marketing. In private clubs, this is quite easily accomplished, and yet the author's research has revealed that the majority of sport clubs which have more than 1,000 members at any one time have only a superficial idea of their demographic breakdown of the membership, and often only a "guesstimate" of the total head count. Of course those with computerized membership databases are able to keep completely accurate information (assuming that the database is kept current!). Comprehensive consumer information is often collected by sport organizations as a regular business practice, but much of this data goes unused. One major market, the baseball franchise that regularly reaches the play offs and the World Series still throws away the names and addresses of unfilled ticket applications when these individuals clearly should be added to the fan database. Most retail sporting goods stores ask for customers' names and addresses when they fill out the sales receipts but these names and addresses are rarely recorded in an MIS for marketing use; instead they lie in an accounting or tax records file.

The data on existing customers which are most critical to be kept for marketing decision-making are as follows

1. The name, address, e-mail address, phone and fax numbers of consumers.
    Used for communication and correspondence, and for direct mailings.
2. Frequency of purchase/use of the product; type and quantity of product purchased/when purchased.
    Used for tracking usage frequency, targeting low-frequency users, and upgrading existing consumers from lower-priced products to higher-priced products, and from partial plans to full season plans.
3. Method of payment/location where purchased/purchase lead time.
    Used in determining price, distribution outlets and lead time in promoting events and ticket distribution.
4. The media read/viewed or listened to; which media/message led them to purchase the product?
    Used to determine promotional effectiveness and lead analysis.
5. The pattern of consumption—Does (s)he consume alone, with family, or friends? What does the consumer do before, during, and after consuming the sport?
    This information is extremely valuable in marketing planning, particularly in deciding such strategies as what promotional items to offer (is a particular event-day more likely to attract families, couples, business groups or friends?). Should this package be four tickets, four pizzas, four sodas or any number more than three persons? What

*kind of concessions would be best? Is a post-event disco party likely
to succeed? Should we promote more to the father, mother, single female, etc.?*

In short, the major goal of a marketer in establishing an MIS should be to
know the name, address, phone and fax number, e-mail address, sex, occupation
and income of all consumers, along with information about what product(5) they
buy, when and in what quantities, and with whom they consume the product. If
possible, additional information on what media they view, read or listen to is extremely valuable, as well as any information on which promotional message or
media helped to attract the consumer.

B. Competitors

The MIS should contain up-to-date information on competitors which would
include complete price list(s), product line(s) offered, promotional strategies, sample advertisements, promotions strategy and special promotions, etc. Any organization offering a similar product or service whose critical trading radius overlaps
more than 25% with your own trading radius is to be considered a competitor.
Usually this means that the competitors' facility or retail outlet will be located
within 30 minutes traveling time of your own facility.

One strategy which the author uses in sales-training seminars for court, health
and fitness facilities is to require all sales staff to visit all competing facilities and
to critique competitors' strengths and weaknesses.

C. Future Trends

No organization can exist without strong consideration being given to the future. In sport the ability to project future trends may be even more critical than
in other industries. Sport continues to operate in a highly volatile., marketplace,
with fads coming and going. With sport trends historically running in seven-year
cycles, the industry is not one which can be taken for granted. Perhaps the most
vivid illustration in this regard is the fitness and health club business. The majority of facilities in this industry segment started in the eastern USA 20 years ago as
indoor tennis clubs. New trends started in California and spread east as clubs
added bars and lounges; weight rooms (later Nautilus centers then personal
trainers, then the return to free weights, plated and variable resistance machines), racquetball courts, aerobic dance studios; cardiovascular fitness centers;
pools, saunas and jacuzzis; multi-purpose rooms; day-care centers and pro
shops. The more sophisticated clubs then moved into stress management, diet
and nutrition education classes, cardiovascular risk screening, and preventative
medicine so that they are now really "Wellness Centers." Few other industries
have experienced such marked changes, in such a short period of time, and yet it
is clear that evolutions in this segment of the sport industry still have some way
to go! Other sport industry segments have not changed their concept quite as
drastically; however, changes in the market for their product have been equally
volatile. Who would have thought that almost all of the football, baseball stadiums built in the 1970s would be torn down and replaced in the 1990s and early
2000s.

Integration of the Data Sources

Invariably, the full value of an MIS is realized only when data from various sources are integrated into a common database. For example, a small, retail sporting-goods store as part of it's existing procedure collects the customer's name, address, item(s) purchased, the amount purchased and date of purchase. Currently this information is written onto the multi-copy sales slip (receipt) given to the customer at the time of the purchase. All that is required for the development of an effective MIS is to organize these receipts by alphabetical order and hire a student intern to load them into a database.

When the sales slips, data from telephone inquiries and information on institutions/groups, etc., in the market area are all logged into the database, integration can then occur.

Application of the MIS

Even the smallest of sport organizations, such as a sporting goods retailer, can use a simple computer system quite effectively. Each customer record (an index card) would contain a customer's name and address and the marketer would log the purchase date, item(s) purchased and amount of purchase on the columns beneath. Sophisticated systems would maintain a running total of the amount purchased broken down by product categories. Perhaps a coding system would be used (football = 1, tennis = 2, swimming = 3, etc.). The data would then be scanned at regular intervals. Prior to the fall football season, any record showing a check in the football column, indicating that the customer made a purchase of football equipment, would then be selected and that person's name and address would be automatically printed on a mailing label or on a letter to receive a football equipment catalogue, or a flyer announcing a sale on football equipment. For those customers who spent say, more than one hundred dollars in the store over the preceding six months, a personal invitation could be mailed to them for a special pre-sale evening at the store. These "heavy spenders" would have first choice of sale merchandise, would be allowed to invite a friend, and might be treated to a floor show of next-season's merchandise, hot hors d'oeuvres and beer/wine. Inviting a friend makes the consumer feel like a "bigshot," gives them greater satisfaction and, more importantly, attracts new customers.

A. The Advantages of Electronic Systems

It is self-evident that any MIS is useless unless it is well-maintained, and readily accessible. If the maintenance of the system becomes too costly compared to the return, then marketers will not maintain it. Consequently, computers offer the only truly effective alternative whose ease of maintenance is comparatively low and whose return is great particularly if the data can be captured by the computer in the first place via integrated cash registers, optical scanners, smart cards, etc. The price of computers has dropped into a range where no sport organization can afford to be without one. The most significant impact of computerized MIS, however, is their ability to integrate data from a variety of sources to provide the most telling and useful information. For example, a court and health club with a computerized MIS can identify members who are available to play in the low-occu-pancy hours that the club is open, by analyzing the demographics of these members they can then tailor-make a program which appeals to this specific group. Such data has revealed at several locations tremendous demand in the early morning and at lunchtime for aerobic classes for working married women. The timing of such classes is critical because of the need or desire of the mothers to be home with younger children as soon as possible after the work day. By purchasing take out lunches, the clerical or administrative worker on a fixed lunch can work out, shower, and take lunch back to the office.

Although integrating and using the information for marketing purposes is more difficult without a computer, it is not impossible, though it is unlikely that any such integration on a manual system will be relatively simple. Inspecting index cards to select recent purchases and cross-tabulating this list by zip code to determine market penetration in an area not previously advertised to, is a simple but laborious task, yet the value of the effort can be immense. As one sport executive recently said, "Half of our advertising budget is totally wasted! If we ever knew which half, we could save a lot of money." Without an MIS it is almost impossible to identify just which dollars are being wasted. Perhaps the most telling factor is that organizations with a well-kept MIS invariably spend less of their promotional budget in advertising than their non-MIS counterparts and their direct sales efforts are so much better!

B. The Impact of MIS on Promotional Budget

The smallest of sport organizations allot four-figure budgets on advertising to attract individuals who are not currently consumers; the larger organizations allot six-figure budgets. A sport industry rule of thumb for the promotional budget is five percent of total annual expenses for an on-going organization and 10% of total annual expenses for a start-up organization, or one needing to increase its market share. Another rule is approximately $10,000 per game or event. While advertising is critical to attracting new consumers, all mature organizations can usually obtain a much better return by giving incentives to existing customers to purchase more of the product or to promote the product more to their friends. This latter strategy has been called "internal marketing" (Ref. 5). Internal marketing strategies can usually be achieved at much lower cost and with greater returns in sales volume than the majority of mass media campaigns designed to reach non-users. Consider the following questions: What do professional sport teams do to reward the loyalty of a season-ticket holder who has held a season ticket for several years? What does a tennis or country club do for the member who has been there ten years? Unfortunately the answer too often is, Very Little! Marketers have known for a long time that satisfied customers generally spread positive word of mouth and attract other customers. One estimate (Ref. 6) projected that 70% of all sales in many segments of the sport industry come from word of mouth from existing customers. For many sport industry segments the figure could be even higher. If we take this relationship to its logical extension, then we can see that the total positive impact of word of mouth from just one satisfied member/customer would be as follows:

Satisfied customer A refers .7 additional customers
Those .7 additional customers refer another .7 x .7 = .49 customers
and those customers in turn refer .7 x .7 x .7 = .34 customers

The total impact of this relationship can be calculated using a simple geometric progression as .7 + (.7 x .7) + (.7 x .7 x .7) . . . . + N or more simply using the economic multiplier formula (6), below:

$$\text{total impact} = \frac{1}{1-(\text{W.O.M.}\%)}$$

total impact = 1 ÷ (1 − .7) = 1 (.3)

The *total impact* of 70% W.O.M. = 3.33 total persons referred by one person's positive word of mouth.

If the W.O.M.% is higher, then total impact is much higher. In fact, the relationship is a logarithmic function. For example, at 80% the multiplier is 5.0. The impact of the multiplier can be used as a most powerful tool for motivating personnel, particularly when sales staff realize that if they sell to one person, they will refer five others on average. Similarly, for service personnel they must be made to appreciate that, if they turn off one person at 80% W.O.M., the organization loses five customers.

Despite the power of this relationship, too many organizations ignore the importance of tracking the purchase frequency of existing customers. In this respect, two major relationships need to be tracked: first, the breakdown of low-, medium- and high-frequency users, in order that programs and promotions may be established to increase attendance frequency; and second, the tracking of consumers whose frequency of usage is dropping. This latter group is obviously getting ready to quit. As stated previously, many organizations do not even collect the names and addresses of customers when they have been "handed them on a plate." Such information is available on checks and letters. Valuable information can be easily obtained from credit cards, phone calls, and walk-ins. For example, it would be interesting to know how many collegiate athletic departments maintain a database of the names of those purchasing student season tickets for football and basketball games. Of greater interest is how many of these schools stored that information in a retrievable form for later use? There is little doubt that students who bought tickets while in school comprise a high-probability response segment for alumni season ticket mailings, particularly when cross-tabulated by an address inside the critical trading radius. It would also provide a high probability response group for alumni fund-raising for athletics when cross-tabulated by their current income and cut down greatly on wasted mailings and phone calls to low probability individuals. There simply is no way to go back and recreate this information at a later time, you have to collect it right there and then!

In multi-purpose sport clubs for the last four years, the better-managed clubs have been tracking attendance of members on a member-by-member basis using software programs custom-designed for the industry (Ref. 7). The information obtained allows the club manager to develop special programs (tournaments, ladders, aerobics classes) and promotional ideas (free racquetball lessons for aerobic class participants, guaranteed tennis game arranging with a compatible partner, etc.) designed to increase usage frequency or deter member attrition in the low-usage member. It also reduces overcrowding at peak-times by limiting the frequency of participation of heavy-users, (members cannot hold more than one court reservation at a time). Such computer based MIS for clubs have helped reduce attrition rates from an industry average of approximately 35% of membership lost per year down to 20-25% per year. This translates, for an average-sized club, to maintaining $250,000 of revenue per annum which would otherwise be lost (based on an average sized club having 2,000 members with average revenue per member of $500 per annum. Such a club would normally generate 50% of its revenue from membership dues and court-time fees (approximately $1,000,000) with anywhere from an additional $500,000 to $1,000,000 from product extensions such as bar and lounge, pro shop sales, lessons programs, aerobics classes, etc. For a $2,000 to $3,000 investment in a totally integrated computer system, the club could expect a 1,000% first-year return on savings from the reduction in membership attrition alone). The benefit does not include the savings on promotion costs (advertising) and selling costs (commission, sales training, etc.) which would have been incurred to replacement membership. To say the least, a computerized MIS justifies itself on that statistic alone.

C. How MIS Fits In to the Marketing Process

The MIS provides the link between the market and the marketer, and it is therefore the lifeline of marketing. Perhaps the most critical facto, of marketing success is the ability to collect accurate and timely information about the consumers and potential consumers, and to use this data in the formation of marketing plans which are specifically targeted to meet the needs of specific consumer groups (known as target-market segments). Marketing-mix decisions must be based upon accurate and comprehensive data on the market, the competition and how the market views the product, its pricing structure and the promotional messages transmitted about the product. Simply put, anything short of a complete MIS leaves the door open for competition to erode the organizations product position and to eat into its market share.

In reviewing the data generated in the MIS it becomes readily apparent to the marketer that not all consumers have the same wants or needs which they expect to have fulfilled by the sport product. The recognition that consumers have different aspirations, needs or wants, and the grouping together of consumers based upon certain characteristics common to a group is called market segmentation. The process of segmenting consumers into several target-market segments is a necessary pre-condition to any marketing strategy development. In order to maximize consumer satisfaction and therefore maximize the chance of marketing success, a different marketing strategy (called a marketing mix) requiring a unique blending of product, price, promotion and even place (seat location, access to certain amenities) must be developed for each target segment. Without a doubt, identification of the key target-market segments is the single-most important output of the MIS.

Market Segmentation — Targeting for the Marketing Mix

There are four common bases upon which market segmentation (grouping by similar characteristics) are usually performed. They are:

1. *Demographics*—Such characteristics of the consumer as sex, age, income, geographic location, occupation, etc.
2. *Psychographics*—Lifestyle characteristics of the consumer such as activities they engage in, interests such as being sport-oriented, outgoing, healthy, etc., or opinions/attitudes they hold.
3. *Benefits*—The specific benefit(s) the consumer is looking for. For example, weight-loss, relaxation, entertainment.
4. *Usage rate/frequency*—The purchase frequency or frequency of product usage. This is usually broken down into heavy/medium and light users—single game ticket purchaser, partial or full season ticket holder.

Most segmentation has traditionally employed demographics. There are several reasons for this. On the simplest level, demographics appear to tell us quite a lot about differences in purchase behavior. It is self-evident that men and women generally have different needs that they wish to have satisfied from a sport product. Also, the needs of young and old are invariably far apart. Demographics are generally readily accessible from government or other publications and most consumers do not mind giving out their demographic information (age and income are sometimes sensitive but most people are happy to give a range). However, demographics have their limits. Two individuals having identical demographics yet who have different lifestyles may differ widely in their purchase behavior.

As a result of the limitation of demographics, marketers became interested in psychographics which measure activities, interests and opinions, which would go beyond where demographics leave off. The reason psychographics are not used more extensively for segmentation is that they are not as readily available, and are therefore expensive to generate on an individual basis.

Benefit segmentation has increased in its usage in recent years because of its simple effectiveness. In fact, many sport marketers have practiced benefit segmentation for many years without recognizing the term. Examples of benefit-segmented sport products are suites, club seating, padded seats with backs and arms, stadium club membership, and court and health club membership plans such as the Gold Plan (total club usage with a nicer locker room), Silver Plan (fitness only) and Bronze Plan (pool amenities only).

The final basis for segmentation is product-purchase frequency or product usage frequency. This method is widely used throughout almost every industry and has been used most effectively in sport. Examples are season ticket plans, mini-season plans, contract-time rates in court clubs, family or individual season passes to ski resorts, etc.

In reading down the list of methods for performing segmentation, it no doubt became apparent to many readers that these bases were not mutually exclusive. In fact, combinations of demographics and benefits abound, along with the combination of usage frequency and benefits. The critical questions for the marketer in deciding whether or not to choose the market segment, whether employing single or multiple-segmentation bases are as follows:

1. Can the segment be identified? It is all well and good to say that the consumer of a product is "sport-oriented" but is it possible to identify sport-oriented people? For example, can you purchase a mailing list of Sports Illustrated readers? Is the S.I. reader likely to be a soccer fan anyway?

2. Can the segment be accessed by a particular media which the majority of the segment views, listens to or reads? If there is no way to reach the segment, then there is little point developing marketing messages targeted toward this group.

3. Is the market segment big enough in size and potential response (sales) to warrant spending time and money developing a targeted product and promotional strategy just for this group?

If the answer to each of the above questions is "Yes," then the marketer needs to identify significant clusters or groups among consumers and potential consumers for the product or service being marketed. This is done by reviewing the demographic, psychographic, benefit and usage-rate data available on consumers. Much of this data is already available in published form from secondary data sources such as government population data, industry publications and several excellent studies exist. Publications such as Sports Business Journal and Team Marketing Report provide critical data for sport marketers. The A.C. Nielson data on viewership and the Simmons Market Research Bureau's statistics on demographics of sport participation, spectatorship and viewership provide invaluable data on the media which each market segment views, reads or listens to.

Once the clusters/segments have been identified they should then be placed in priority order based upon size of potential response. Shrewd marketers identify just the top two or three untapped segments to be targeted at any one time. In mature sport-marketing departments, where there exists a strong existing base of consumers, it may well be possible to run marketing and promotional plans targeted at more than three distinct segments, but this is rare.

The days when consumer needs were satisfied by a single product are long gone. Henry Ford's insistence that the consumer could have a Model-T Ford in any color that he liked as long as it was black, simply would not hit the mark in today's marketplace. At the same time you cannot be all things to all people, and "niche marketing" is clearly the smart way to go.

Not all of the segments identified in a market need to be targeted. Dependent upon the product concept as outlined in Chapter 9, it is perfectly possible to specialize in a single segment, at least in the initial introduction of a product. In the long term, more than one segment invariably must be targeted. For new products and mature products the early target segments are likely to be the opinion leaders among the larger, target segment groups. These opinion leaders would then spread word of mouth to other members of the group, thereby reducing the sales response time to the advertisements considerably. The marketing-mix for opinion leaders is likely to be a direct approach rather than a mass-appeal approach. An illustration of this technique would be a marketer of a new Major League Soccer (MLS) or National Professional (Indoor) Soccer League (NPSL) franchise who might first target opinion leaders in the soccer community and ethnic groups traditionally playing soccer in the market area, along with targeting the coaches and officials of local soccer leagues at all levels. At the same time owners and managers of retail sporting-goods stores, radio stations and other media having influence on the target populations would be contacted with specialized appeals designed to raise the level of consciousness about the sport and the franchise. This strategy is particularly effective in sports where marketing staffs are small. Often these opinion leaders can be harnessed to help sell the sport product. In this way each opinion leader is given incentives to sell to their groups. The author has called this technique "positive pyramid selling" (Ref. 8).

Summary/Conclusion

The return on investment on the sport promotional dollar is directly proportional to the marketer's ability to accurately segment the market and target the appeal to that particular group. The ability to segment is directly related to the sophistication of the MIS. A distant second is the creativity of the message. Remember that Clara Peller's "Where's the Beef?" commercial for the Wendy's hamburger chains may have received lots of attention and creativity awards but the research showed that too few people remembered that it was a Wendy's commercial, and even fewer increased their consumption of Wendy's products. Who remembers what any of the dot coms were advertising in the latest Super Bowl?

Without an information-based approach to sport marketing, at least half of the promotional budget is likely to be wasted. The only problem is that without an MIS the sport marketer will never know which half is being wasted. With an MIS the marketer knows who the consumer is, what he or she needs, and if he or she has slowed down in consumption frequency. Promotional efforts can then be specifically targeted toward an "internal marketing" approach to selling sport which is the topic of Chapter 14 where direct mail and telemarketing programs can be used to greatest effect. Internal marketing is a method of using existing consumers to sell on behalf of the organization and includes marketing strategies designed to increase consumption frequency and to reduce the attrition rate among existing consumers. This latter strategy is only possible with a sophisticated and up-to-date information system, with data collected now for immediate and long-term use. Paraphrasing an old television commercial, "You can pay a little now (to build an MIS) or you can pay a lot more later (for expensive mass media advertising)."

References

1. B.J. Mullin, W. Sutton, and S. Hardy (1999). *Sport Marketing*. Second Edition. Champaign, IL: Human Kinetics Publishing Co.
2. M. Levine (1977). "Increasing Attendance By Knowing Your Market Better," *Auditorium News* 810 (October).
3. H.H. Kassarjian and T.S. Robertson (1983). *Perspectives in Consumer Behavior*. Glenview, IL: Scott Foresman & Co.
4. Levine, *supra* Ref. 2.
5. Mullin, *supra* Ref. 1, at 180.
6. Panel, Kerr and Foster (1983). *The Court and Health Club Industry: A Nationwide Assessment*. Boston, MA: International Racquet Sports Association.
7. Mullin, *supra* Ref. 1, at 198-201.

Chapter 18

Technology for Sport Managers: Trends and Innovations

David K. Scott
Todd L. Seidler

"In these days of expanding programs and decreasing budgets, it is essential for managers of sport and recreation programs to keep up with the latest trends and innovations in the field. New procedures, design ideas, or tools that may allow for an increase in efficiency or productivity of staff can be invaluable and may prove to be the difference between success and failure. Perhaps the most important of these trends and innovations are advances in electronic technology and the increasing use of computer applications in daily operations. Computer technology is advancing rapidly. Faster, more powerful and less expensive computers and specialized software applications are being introduced almost daily. Computers, used properly, are tremendous tools and can have a positive impact on cost reductions through increased staff efficiency and productivity as well as increasing revenue generation. Not only can computers help with the streamlining of daily operations but they also provide almost immediate access to updated information which can enhance the decision making process. Computers can assume many of the day-to-day operational tasks, thereby freeing up staff for other responsibilities and are finding their way into such diverse applications as marketing, recruiting, automated building control systems, security, access control and energy management systems. From simple word processors, spreadsheets and data base programs to specially designed computer and software packages developed for specific management applications, the options are increasing rapidly. This chapter presents a selection of these trends and innovations and briefly describes what potential impact they may have on today's sport manager. It is by no means a comprehensive look at technology and computer use in sport management but merely an overview of several areas that today's sport manager should be aware of. Many of the more widely used applications such as e-mail and mail merge programs will not be discussed here. The focus will be placed on some of the more recent methods of using new technology. It should also be noted that changes in technology are occurring so quickly that much of the information in this chapter may be out of date soon after it is published. However, this information is valuable for establishing a base or building blocks for future trends and innovations.

Every sport manager needs to become familiar with how computers and related technology can be beneficial to their operations. The following are a few examples of how this technology can be used in various capacities related to sport management. For those readers who would like a brief explanation of some of the basic terminology used in many computer and internet applications, please see the Glossary of Terms at the end of the chapter.

Technology and Ticketing

Nowhere is the technology revolution more evident than in the event ticketing industry. In what seems like overnight technological advances, ticketing for sport events has gone from "standing in line at the ticket window" to fully automated electronic ticketing services. These advancements now provide sport venues with the equivalent of a 24-hour open box office. However, it is now virtually a requirement for a sport organization to have a "webmaster" on staff to manage the integration of the athletics department or team web site and its internet ticket distribution provider.

Currently, any individual with access to a computer and the internet can place online orders for tickets to almost every professional sport event as well as most major collegiate sport events. The tickets can generally be purchased several weeks in advance and are paid for through online credit card transactions. At the present time, processing fees are relatively small and it is likely that most customers appreciate the convenience of not having to stand in line. The actual tickets can be received in the mail or they can be picked up at Will Call on game day.

Several advances including new software developments and insightful business agreements have been responsible for changing the face of event ticketing. For example, in early 1999, Paciolan Systems, Inc. (PSI) made a move toward enhanced customer service by establishing an agreement with Ticketmaster that would allow PSI customers to expand their ticket distribution network. This agreement allows venues using the PSI system to interface with the global network of Ticketmaster's internet site. Similar agreements have been developed with various sport organizations and the Tickets.com Network.

In addition, other recent software developments (e.g., CyberSEATS™) provide customers with the opportunity not only to select their seats online, but also to see the view of the court or playing field from those seats. Another approach that has surfaced recently offers automated ticketing to consumers through a "ticket machine." ETM, a ticket solution company, has introduced electronic ticket machines (similar to ATM machines) complete with interactive touch screens and graphic, video, and audio capabilities. These machines can be placed in strategic, high traffic, locations and can provide sport organizations the opportunity to communicate directly with potential customers.

Advances in "ticket distribution technology," such as the ones mentioned in the preceding paragraphs, have optimized customer service for many professional and collegiate sport organizations. As more people purchase or rent home computers and utilize the Web, it is likely that online ticket sales will continue to grow. User friendliness and consumer satisfaction with at least this part of the sport entertainment experience is certainly enhanced by these recent technological developments. Perhaps the day will come when an individual can pay online for a "ticket" to a sport event and then be able to print out a verification and seat number that can be punched in on a keypad or scanned for admission at the gate.

Conjoint Analysis, Data Mining, and Knowledge Discovery in Sport

The power of the most recently developed computers allow enhanced methods of market analysis that were previously unattainable. In marketing for competitive sports, there are a number of uncontrollable aspects of the "product." However, such things as ticket price, parking services, facility design, security, and general customer relations have various attributes that can be manipulated.

One approach that can be used by marketers to better understand and predict what consumers choose as the best combination of attributes for a product is conjoint analysis. Although the procedure of conjoint analysis has been around for approximately 20 years, only recently has software been developed that will allow mathematical analysis of large numbers of subjects with hundreds of combinations of product attributes. For example, a professional team might want to study what their fans prefer relative to types of game promotions, half-time entertainment, styles of seating, concession offerings, and various arena or stadium amenities. A sample of subjects can be chosen and a variety of methods (e.g., questionnaires, prop-cards, attribute rankings, and virtual experiences) can be used to collect data for conjoint analysis (Green, Krieger, and Vavra, 1997). In sport, the resulting analysis of the data can provide insight into what the most preferred combinations of attributes are for a particular product. This information can then be used to develop the "controllable" aspects of a sport product that are most likely to satisfy existing fans and attract new customers.

Another approach that has potential to increase knowledge relative to customer satisfaction management is "data mining." Recently, data mining has been introduced as an inductive process that uses a variety of data analysis tools to discover patterns and relationships in data that may be used to make valid predictions (Edelstein, 1999). While the collection and organization of data has become a common administrative tool for most sport organizations, actually using the data for strategic decision making is not as common.

In sport organizations, data are housed in various database software programs and provide sport administrators with what is hopefully an efficient way to manage large amounts of information. In the mid to late 1990s, technological advances in data management have made it possible to uncover significant information contained in data that might otherwise be unknown. In addition, advancements in onboard memory and processor speeds now allow many computers to process information that can range into terabytes (1 trillion bytes) of data.

From a sport business perspective, the information uncovered through data mining has the potential to increase revenues and reduce costs by contributing to insightful decision making at the management level. Currently, data mining applications provide both simple and complex statistical computations and may require the use of a consultant or in-house specialist to set-up and prepare data for mining as well as analyze the results.

The applications of data mining and knowledge discovery in several aspects of sport business are numerous. However, it may be that sport marketing depart-

FIGURE 1

Data Mining Decision Tree for Athletics Fundraising

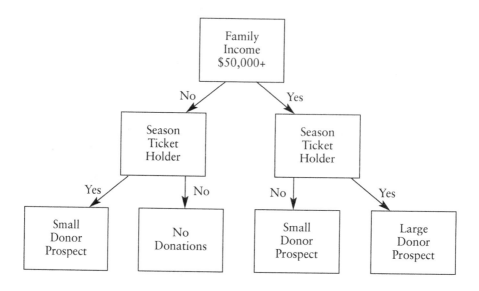

ments have the most direct benefit. For example, a collegiate athletic department can collect information from season ticket holders, boosters, students, and even fans at the game regarding such things as seating preferences, ticket packages, preferred merchandise, facility offerings, etc. This information can be systematically entered into a database that can be "mined" using a data mining software program. The program will examine patterns in the data and identify categories of consumers relative to their demographic profiles and their product preferences. This information can then be used to target future market segments and develop or enhance products to fit their desires. In this sense, data mining allows a sport marketing department to answer market research questions and build both demographic and psychographic profiles of current and potential consumers. Ultimately, this may allow marketing and promotional efforts to be directed toward the most likely consumers for the sport product. Although marketing departments in collegiate and professional sports are, or should be, identifying their most likely target customers, data mining can uncover patterns in enormous amounts of data collected over several months or years. This can allow the marketing department to make strategic decisions based on patterns in the data that provide predictive information about potential customers.

Another example of how data mining could be used is to classify likely donors for collegiate athletics fund raising programs. This can be accomplished by obtaining some relatively simple information from alumni, boosters, season ticket holders, and fans. Then, using data mining "decision tree models," which generally split into yes/no branches for each criterion, the department could analyze results and focus specialized fund raising efforts on those individuals and/or businesses who fall into different prospect categories (see Figure 1). Data mining can also be used in athlete recruitment efforts and will be discussed in the next section.

Data mining is relatively new and is being used by more and more corporations to assist in decision support and customer relationship management. It appears that amateur, professional, and commercial sport organizations can also benefit greatly from this technological advancement.

Technological Advances in Athlete Recruiting

As the need to reduce costs continues to be a priority especially in collegiate athletics, sport administrators in this environment can, or should, look to the advancements in recruiting technology. While most coaches will be at least cognizant of the latest trends, administrators should be aware of what is really on the cutting edge and what will be cost effective. Two of these areas are: (a) use of the internet for recruiting and (b) the recent introduction of digital video.

Most, if not all, collegiate athletics departments have a web site that provides pictures, statistics, schedules, and other insightful information on each of their athletics programs. While very important to the recruiting process, there are a number of innovative ways that an internet site can be used to facilitate and enhance recruiting efforts. With the advent of digital video, departments can now develop their own highlight tapes for each sport that can be viewed by recruits on their school or home computers. Presentations and electronic brochures can be developed that can be e-mailed to recruits. In addition, Fielitz (2000) presented several components of how the internet can be used for athletics recruiting. These components were based on suggestions from Dysart (1999) and include the following: (a) web site search engines, (b) interactive questionnaires, (c) E-mail autoresponders, (d) mailing lists, (e) chat rooms, and (f) data mining.

A brief summary of these areas will be presented here. However, the reader is encouraged to read the article by Fielitz (2000) for more in-depth information on applying these concepts in athletics recruiting. Regarding web site search engines, it is now possible for universities to place search engines on their own web site so that potential student athletes can gather important information about the university's academic and athletics programs, as well as social activities and the general community environment. In addition, web-tracking software allows institutions to monitor who is visiting their sites and track the type of information being searched. This knowledge can be very valuable to a coach who is trying to learn everything he or she can about a potential recruit's interest in the university.

Interactive questionnaires can be developed and posted on an athletics department's web site that allow information to be gathered on prospective athletes without the traditional mail costs and delays. This, in itself, reduces expenditures and provides coaches with an opportunity to add, modify, or delete questions as necessary.

Although basic e-mail has become a convenient and efficient way of communicating with recruits, there are at least two other advances in this area that should be utilized. The first of these is the use of E-mail autoresponders. This technology allows individuals to request information from an organization, via its web site, and then receive a computer generated response automatically via e-mail. In addition, autoresponders can send follow-up e-mails to recruits with updated information. The second is the use of e-mail "mailing lists" that allows an athletics department to send out personalized electronic form letters. Several relatively inexpensive software products have been developed that can allow an athletics department to greatly reduce the long-term expense of developing and mailing traditional form letters.

Electronic "chat rooms" are another advancement where coaches can communicate in real time with prospective athletes. This can be a very helpful tool in answering questions for several athletes at one time. Chat rooms can also be used for prospective athletes to carry on conversations with each other. Of course, it should be noted that communication with athletes is a policy concern of the NCAA and must be monitored closely to ensure compliance. New policy is being developed and will likely change periodically in order to address issues with technology and recruiting. For current updates relative to NCAA legislation or recruiting issues the readers can visit <www.ncaa.org/databases/internet_and_recruiting.html>.

Finally, the insightful functions of data mining can also be used in athlete recruiting. Data mining, as described previously, can be used with student/athlete databases to look for patterns and trends that may provide valuable information and predictions for future recruiting efforts.

Another important technological advancement that impacts athlete recruiting is digital video. After evolving from eight or 16 mm film to videotape and super VHS (high quality video), athletics departments now must enter the age of digital video. From a recruiting perspective, teams can develop digital highlights that can be produced on videotape, on compact disc CD-ROM or Digital Video Disk (DVD), or, as mentioned previously, the highlight video can be accessed directly on the web site. High schools, who have the hardware and software, can produce and deliver digital highlight videos of their college prospect athletes to interested collegiate programs. Even athletes, with their own equipment or through a recruiting service, can market themselves online to colleges or universities who may be interested in their athletic talents.

Other Recent Technological Developments in Coaching and Sports Information Management

Advances in computer technology are in the process of dramatically changing the way in which coaches, event directors, and sports information directors do their jobs. In coaching, recent technology allows coaches to use computers to analyze players, game video, scouting reports, and ultimately teach movements and strategies to their athletes. Advancements in computer and video technology allow coaches and/or athletics staff members the luxury of digital video and data analysis all in the same package. Coaches can now edit their workout or game video from a desktop or laptop computer. They can create video sequences to show or to send via e-mail to other coaches or players. And, they can create scouting reports, workout scripts, and training video clips for players. Coaches, recreation administrators, and event directors have a plethora of software products that offer numerous time saving features from season scheduling to tournament bracket development and seeding.

Computer technology also has a tremendous impact on the job of the sports information directors. Recent advancements allow information to be automated so that game results and statistics can be electronically forwarded to the necessary media outlets and to conference offices almost instantly. This can be a valuable tool for saving both time and money within an athletics department.

Sport managers who may not be directly involved in using the technology described above should be aware of its existence and be prepared to make budgetary decisions that will allow their programs to remain competitive in a high-tech sport environment. Interested readers are encouraged to see the suggested resource list at the end of this chapter for related websites.

Marketing and Sponsorship

Virtual Signage

The use of virtual signage is increasing quickly in the world of sport. Recent computer technology allows a sport marketer to digitally place a company logo or advertisement into a television picture and make it appear to be real. A grass field, a blank wall, the side of a building, anywhere within a television picture can now be made to look as if a sponsor's logo were really painted on it. As an example, virtual signage is often used in baseball. The wall behind home plate is typically a solid, dark color so that the white ball can be seen against this backdrop. To the fans in the stand and the players on the field, it is only a blank wall. At home, however, computer technicians can insert a sponsor's logo with such realism, that viewers cannot distinguish the difference between it and a real one. Another advantage is that different logos or messages can be inserted for different viewing areas. Take the broadcast of a match in the World Cup Tournament. A different sponsor's logo can be inserted for each different region or country receiving the broadcast. Instead of event marketers having to sell one huge sponsorship package to a company that wants to gain exposure worldwide, it is now possible to provide opportunities for many smaller sponsors to have their message seen only in the area that is important to them.

Access Control

Controlling access to sport, recreation and fitness facilities is often an important duty of facility managers. Legal liability, deterrence of vandalism and theft, and member safety and satisfaction are a few of the reasons it is necessary to deny access to those who don't belong. A properly designed and equipped facility along with the use of computer controls and a well trained staff can make access control relatively easy to deal with (Seidler, 1999).

When designing a facility it is often advantageous to plan for one control point through which everyone entering or leaving the building must pass. This control point is usually staffed during open hours so the appropriate fee is paid, ID card checked or permission is given to those who are eligible to enter. If a higher degree of control is desired, a door, gate or turnstile can also be used.

In the last several years, many computer software programs have become available to help with access control. If the clientele are issued ID cards such as in a club, school or corporate setting, systems with magnetic strip, integrated circuit or bar code readers can be used to quickly check a person's status. In systems designed for high traffic flow, the computer is often connected directly to a turnstile. If, after scanning the ID, the computer determines that the person be accepted for entry, it can send a signal to release the turnstile and allow the person to enter. This, however, does not prevent an unauthorized person from using someone else's ID. For increased security, picture IDs are desirable to ensure that the person using the card is the legal owner. Other systems of access control include software programs that display a picture of the patron on a computer monitor. This photo can then be compared to the person requesting entry. More sophisticated systems can actually scan a patron's fingerprint, palmprint or retina and compare it to those in the computer memory. These are typically used where high security is a priority. These systems can also be used to track each member's attendance and provide information for marketing or retention programs. Furthermore, they can determine patrons attendance habits and set staffing levels to provide services at the proper times of the day.

Another aspect of access control that is improving with advances in technology is the replacement of standard door locks and keys. Systems now exist that place an electronic card reader at each door. Instead of a key, each authorized person is issued a card that can be passed through any of the card readers. With "proximity cards," a card only has to come within a few feet of the reader in order to be verified. A central computer then receives the information from the card and compares it with the information stored in memory. The computer determines if the person who was issued that card is authorized to open that particular door and either unlocks it or refuses access.

There are many advantages to this type of system. The computer can be programmed to allow access only to certain areas of the facility for each individual card holder. A part-time employee may have a card that works only on a few certain doors while the facility manager's card can be programmed to open them all, like a master key. Also, the computer may be programmed so that certain cards only work during specified hours.

In the case of regular locks, if someone loses a key it is often necessary to re-key many or all of the locks in the building. New keys must then be issued to everyone, often at great expense. With the card system if someone loses an access card, that card can simply be turned off on the computer and a new card issued to the owner. The old card becomes useless.

Another feature of the card access system is that each time someone uses a card to open a door it is recorded on the computer. For example, computer records may show not only that a certain door was opened on Saturday night at 12:21 but also whose card was used and if the person went in or out through the door. This information can be extremely valuable for facility security. The system can also be connected to the fire alarm and programmed to automatically unlock any or all of the doors when the alarm is triggered. Though it may be initially more expensive to install the card reader system than standard locks, it will usually pay for itself in increased efficiency, convenience and long-term cost.

Another innovation in facility security that is seeing increased usage are Closed Circuit Television (CCTV) systems. A well designed system can allow a supervisor in one location to visually monitor many diverse locations, both in and outside of the facility. Often these supervisors are equipped with a two-way radio in order to stay in constant communication with attendants on duty throughout the facility. If a problem is spotted on the CCTV monitor, the supervisor can order an attendant to respond immediately.

Both black and white and color monitors are available for CCTV systems. Color is nice but many users still prefer black and white for improved clarity, especially in low light situations. For security in dark areas, night vision cameras are also available.

New developments include digital technology which is now becoming cost effective. A properly planned system may allow for a smaller staff than would otherwise be required while actually increasing supervisory coverage of the facility.

Building Controls

In order to improve building and staff efficiency, many facilities are being designed with most of the building controls located in one central location, often near the check-in desk or in the main office. A centralized lighting system might include a panel with a schematic drawing of the floor layout of the facility with indicator lights and switches that control all of the major lighting systems in the building. Instead of having to physically go to an area to see if the lights are on or off, a quick look at the panel will indicate the status of the lights and allow staff to make changes if desired. This also eliminates participants from turning off the lights in a given activity space and then possibly making the next person wait five or ten minutes for them to warm up again.

A centralized high-quality sound system may be beneficial to consider. This allows for announcements to be provided to individual areas or to the entire facility. A multiple channel intercom can greatly improve staff communication and can be extremely valuable in emergency situations. The ability to pipe music, other audio, or even video to any area of the facility and possibly several different channels, each to different rooms simultaneously, is not difficult with today's technology. This could allow for soft music to be played in a relaxation class, fast invigorating music for an aerobic dance class in another room, and possibly general announcements or sports scores in a lounge area. Internet connections in specific or all rooms is also worth consideration. A new generation of exercise machines that allow the user to surf the internet while working out are now on the market. Planning for such equipment now is essential.

Energy Efficiency and Air Quality

As we continue to build our facilities to be more energy efficient, we add more insulation and make the building tighter. One of the side effects of this trend is that fresh air exchange is being reduced and the quality of the indoor air is becoming more of a problem. Computerized indoor air quality (IAQ) control systems allow for easier and more precise control of the heating, ventilation, and air conditioning (HVAC) system and can also be designed for minimal energy consumption.

It can be a very expensive proposition to try to remedy a facility with poor air quality. For those fortunate enough to be planning either a new facility or an extensive renovation, a proactive approach should be taken by communicating concerns about the indoor environment to the project architect and mechanical engineer involved. Sport managers must explain the unique requirements of certain areas within the facility so that the corresponding mechanical systems can be properly designed. Activity areas such as weight rooms, aerobic dance studios, and combatives areas require an upgraded HVAC system to handle the high-humidity environment. Sensors designed to monitor temperature, humidity, occupancy load, noxious gases, etc., can control ventilation in individual spaces within the facility. This not only improves air quality but also energy efficiency. The manager also has the capability to "put the facility to bed" at night with occupancy sensors based on participant loads in the arena, gymnasium or pool. It is extremely important that sport managers get involved in the planning process of any new or renovated sport facility. It must be stressed that along with a highly energy efficient building, the quality of the indoor air must be addressed.

Online Video Conferencing

Another advance in technology that is becoming more commonplace is the use of online video conferencing (OVC). With the advent of digital video, OVC is rapidly finding new uses for sport managers. It is now possible to hold meetings by computer in "real time" with several other people, each located at a different site anywhere in the world. With broad-band, high speed internet connections, a video camera at each terminal can transmit to each of the other participants with only an extremely brief delay. It is like making a conference call by telephone but with the advantage of seeing the others involved and without the corresponding long-distance charges.

Another aspect of this technology makes use of recorded video that can be accessed by computer from anywhere. An example of how this may be used is if an athletics administrator has a question about the interpretation of a league rule. The administrator may go to the league's website and select a video on the particular rule in question. The video would then be played online, hopefully answering the administrator's question without having to talk to anyone. This could be a real time-saver for both the administrator and the staff in the league office.

OVC can be very useful in many situations by saving time and travel expenses. The down side to its use is the lack of intimate contact and socialization between participants. As our technological capacity continues to increase, this is bound to become more of an issue in our society.

Planning for High Tech Applications

It is extremely important to consider all future needs and desires when planning a new facility. It is much easier and less expensive to plan a new facility with the necessary accommodations to support future trends and high-tech applications than it is to add them to an existing structure.

One of the primary considerations when planning facilities for the future is to design an easy method of connecting all of the associated computers, networks, sensors, switches, lights, etc. that may be needed later. Even if these high-tech systems are not installed at the time of construction, planners should realize that they are becoming more important every year. If, in a few years they need to be added, planning now for ease of installation will save many headaches and much money in the future. These systems are usually connected by wires and electrical or fiber-optic cables. Designing and constructing the pathways, such as tunnels, conduit and access panels costs little up front and will make the eventual installation simple and inexpensive.

One recent example of a technically advanced public assembly building is the Portland Rose Garden. Owned and operated by Paul Allen, co-founder of Microsoft with Bill Gates and owner of the Portland Trail Blazers of the NBA, the facility is controlled by a command center that operates and monitors the building's lights, security and event cameras. All of the doors and elevators are operated by a card key system in an effort to make the facility keyless.

Events are planned and tracked on Event Manifest using Microsoft Word to access and produce a computer assisted design (CAD) drawing for event set up. All management personnel have a computer on their desk and e-mail, rather than paper, is used extensively. There are no menu boards at concessions as TV monitors flash the menus, promote upcoming events and show the game or event activities in progress. Even the suite holders can use the internet to order food and drinks ahead of the event. The Rose Garden is even perfecting an automated crew calling system to schedule the over 200 employees needed for an event. The program will enable the computer to call all part-time employee and leave a message as to their schedule and also receive incoming calls confirming availability to work a designated event. This will save a lot of management time and, when perfected, will make the Rose Garden truly a facility at the peak of the information and technology curve.

Summary/Conclusion

The job of managing sport and recreational programs is becoming increasingly complex. With budgets being reduced, customer preferences constantly changing, innovations in technology, and many other factors affecting the job, it is becoming more difficult to maintain, much less improve service and productivity. There are not many professions that demand such knowledge in so many diverse areas. Many jobs in sport and recreation management are changing rapidly. The job of Sport Information Director is evolving quickly with new high-technology skills required. These continued advancements in the use of technology may also lead to the need for new positions in sport organizations. It soon will be commonplace to see job titles such as webmaster, director of technology or data analyst to complement traditional management positions.

Continued education for sport and recreation managers is becoming more important every year. Recognizing the need to stay up with the changes in the field is the first step in remaining competitive. Joining professional organizations, subscribing to professional journals, attending appropriate conferences, networking and communicating with other sport managers are all effective methods of keeping up with the latest information in the field.

As we enter the new millennium, computer technology will continue to create new opportunities for sport managers to operate their programs more efficiently while communicating and marketing their programs and services to a knowledgeable and demanding world. Staying up with and making use of the latest in modern technology makes good sense for managers of sport and recreation programs.

Glossary of Terms

Client—your computer and software

Download—transferring a copy of a file from a remote computer to your computer's memory

FTP (File Transfer Protocol)—allows the transfer of files from one computer to another

HTML (Hypertext Mark-up Language)—the "language" used to develop and manage websites

HTTP (Hypertext Transfer Protocol)—the "language" used by client and server computers to communicate with one another

ISP (Internet Service Provider)—the Internet company that charges you and/or your company for the network connection.

Listserve—e-mail discussion groups categorized by special interests

Search engines—programs that allow you to find information on the web through key word searches

Server—a remote computer that houses text, audio, video, and software files that you want to download

TCP/IP (Transmission Control Protocol/Internet Protocol)—connection needed in order for your computer to interface with the Internet

Telnet—a text-only protocol that allows you to issue commands to a remote server, an example would be update commands for changes made to a website that is hosted on the server

URL (Uniform Resource Locator)—the internet address for a file located on a server computer

www (World Wide Web)—the most user-friendly segment of the internet that allows communication through text, audio, video and advanced graphics capabilities

Related Web Sites

Due to the fact that websites are constantly changing as technology and business evolves, the following websites are recommended. Most of these act as a "clearing house" of other sites that are related to a particular area of interest. They each do an excellent job of staying current and may be searched for particular needs or interests.

Access Control & Security Systems Integration Magazine
　http://www.securitysolutions.com

American School & University
　http://www.asumag.com
　http://www.schooldesigns.com

Athletic Business Magazine
　http://www.athleticbusiness.com

Coaching Technology
　http://www.avidsports.com

Data Mining
   http://www.dataminers.com

Fitness Management Magazine
   http://www.fitnessworld.com

Sports Information
   http://www.sports.mediachallenge.com

Ticket Technology
   http://www.ticketmaster.com
   http://www.tickets.com
   http://www.etm.com

References and Suggested Reading

Dysart, J. (1999). "HR recruiters build interactivity into web sites," *HR Magazine* 44(3), 106-110.

Edelstein, H. (1999). *Introduction to Data Mining and Knowledge Discovery*. Potomac, MI: Two Crows Corp.

Fielitz, L.R. (2000). "Using the Internet for athletic recruiting," *JOPERD* 71(2), 13-15.

Green, P.E., A.M. Krieger and T.G. Vavra (1997). "Evaluating new products," *Marketing Research* (Winter), 12-21.

Linio, R. (1995). "Technology and marching orders," *Facility Manager 11*(6).

Seidler, T. (1999). "Planning Facilities for Safety and Risk Management," in T. Sawyer, *Facilities Planning for Physical Activity and Sport: Guidelines for Development*, 65-73. Ninth Ed. AAHPERD. Dubuque, IA: Kendall-Hunt.

Stotlar, D. and M. Walker (1997). *Sports Facility Management*. Boston, MA: Jones and Bartlett.

Part 5

Facility and Event Management

The development, design, construction and eventual operation of a public assembly facility can and often has been the most dramatic and at times traumatic experiences ever undergone by any community.

James Oshust

Chapter 19

Management of Joint Venture Spectator Facilities

James Oshust

Introduction

During the past several decades, college campuses have become the site for development of structures once considered primarily the province of cities and counties. These structures are more commonly referred to as public assembly facilities. A "public assembly facility" is any structure, building or complex of buildings used for the viewing of or participating in spectator-oriented events and activities. More simply put, it includes those facilities most often referred to as auditoriums, theatres, arenas, coliseums, exhibition halls and a myriad of other names which will be discussed later in this chapter.

The word "public" does not itself mean the facility is necessarily publicly owned or controlled by any particular governmental entity. It does define the structure in question as one which is open to public use, for rental, and promotional enterprise as compared to a school building used just for class work, a church or the private auditorium of a fraternal organization used only for the benefit of that group's membership.

In the early 1960s, the University of Illinois, at Champaign-Urbana, constructed a 16,000-seat arena to house its basketball program and certain elements of its major college theater series each year. The University of Illinois recognized the need to provide a forum for the entire community. The Illinois "Assembly Center" was a forerunner in a development that resulted in the construction of public assembly facilities on college and university campuses across the country. It represented a dramatic departure from the past.

The purpose of this chapter is to describe the various strategies employed by colleges and universities to obtain spectator facilities. It should be remembered that, as with all situations, time quickly changes certain parameters and there is nothing within this chapter that should be considered without potential for measurable change unless it be the basic principles of sound management, fiscal reliability and consistency in operational practices.

Reasons for Building Public Assembly Facilities on University Campuses

There were three principal reasons for building public assembly facilities on campuses. First was the need to house those activities very much a part of the university or college schedule. They included the performing arts, various campus dramatic societies, and musical organizations. More often than not, they included athletic facilities for various team sports and in some parts of the northeast, even hockey was favored to the degree that it merited its own structure.

Secondly, schools felt there was a need to maintain a high degree of sensitivity to the academic community and a closeness of administration with the student body through the provision of spectator-event facilities on campus. In many cases, the campus was a captive community. At many universities, from 10,000-30,000 attendees could easily support the several dozen events held during a particular building's scholastic schedule year.

To some observers, possibly one of the greatest impetuses for such development was the ease of acquiring special grants, federal moneys, state and community subsidies. And there was always the alumni association coffers which seemed to prosper or decline according to the success of a particular athletic program each year. Money literally flowed from a number of sources and thus it was not difficult for universities or colleges, whether publicly or privately endowed, to raise the two to four or more millions of dollars necessary for a center for the performing arts, a large arena, or whatever other such facility fit the then-considered primary needs of the school, This was not true, however, in communities that bordered and often surrounded these campuses. In the tax-supported community, prices were rising, inflation was beginning its heinous upward spiral again, and "keeping the cost of government down" nearly sounded the death knell for many proposed public-assembly facility bond issues.

There were of course, those instances when federal grants, the famous, or to some, infamous "revenue sharing plan" or other such money exchange devices did provide needed seed money for funding one or more facilities or ancillary developments in a city.

Then the great surge of interest in professional sport franchises, particularly in the late sixties and early seventies, added fuel to the fire of competition for potential patron dollars. But mainly, it was academic institutions that had the initial ability to construct facilities for their own uses during those years.

Funding Plans

The methods of acquiring these collegiate facilities started, as do most community projects, with an approach to primary funding. In the case of state controlled institutions it would be initiated in the state legislature as a seed funding grant supported further by guarantees of revenue potential from alumni and athletic fan-support organizations. This, coupled with federal entitlement grants, arts foundation grants, and various other such funding sources would quickly fill the "war chest" necessary for a particular project and many such buildings were conceived, designed, constructed and implemented in far shorter time than it took to change a particular course of study or develop an academic field of endeavor at that same university or college.

During the mid-1970s colleges and universities found their funding sources drying up. Federal grants and "in kind" fundings had vastly diminished and in some cases, ceased to exist. Alumni, faced with their own personal and business financial problems, had to diminish their input into athletic department coffers. Universities were no longer able to put together funding packages for the construction of needed facilities. At the same time the demand for bigger and better arenas for athletics and other campus activities continued to increase. The answer to the problem was found in joint ownership. Academic institutions united with their home communities to subsidize the construction and operation of a large facility to be used in part by the university and for the revenue potential needed to sustain the facility, as a public assembly center for the entire area. Examples of this merging of interests can be found in the Tallahassee-Leon County Civic Center in Tallahassee, Florida; the University of Florida Facility in Gainesville, Florida; the Lexington Civic Center in Lexington, Kentucky, more commonly referred to as Rupp Arena, named after the legendary University of Kentucky coach Adolph Rupp; and the University of New Orleans arena in New Orleans, Louisiana. There are numerous others of course, but it is hoped that the examples mentioned here will provide the broadest spectrum of approach and involvement so as to reflect the best "average" situation faced by such ventures.

Management requirements for facilities constructed under the new arrangement are identical to those for any public assembly facility. Although the ownership, and thus the resultant control, was dictated by who has paid the price of construction and who has supplied the necessary funds for operation, it should be remembered that once the doors are opened to the public for whatever purposes, the facility must maintain a posture similar to that of others in the industry. The public must feel it will receive a consistent and sufficient mode of event operation. Regardless of the ownership of the facility in question, its methods of funding, administrative source or other such particulars, certain basic requirements must exist in developing an operational technique in keeping with industry needs and standards. Unless the facility conforms to established practices for the public-assembly facility industry it will be viewed as unstable. Such a label will result in an erosion of its capacity for conducting business.

Elements of a Standard Operational Policy

A standard operational policy concerning any public assembly facility, regardless of ownership, funding source or unique characteristics, should have a consistent schedule philosophy; a consistent event operational policy; a clear and monitored recognition of purpose; and active promotion of the facility and its services to those groups vital to the facility's success.

A. Consistent Schedule Philosophy

Often a facility is designed and implemented with one set of highly publicized and vocally espoused schedule concepts. Unanimity of thought and almost magnanimous attitude toward any and all in the community who would wish to make use of the facility becomes the basis for which the project is promoted and eventually comes to fruition. Nevertheless, once the facility is in operation, certain pressures begin to build. Certain factions form and there then develops the division as to who should use the facility, who should have prior right of domain, and in the most basic sense, "who actually runs the building?" Regrettably, this invariably leads to the demand by certain local groups that they, as part of the funding community or membership in the tax body that ostensibly supports the facility, should have use of the facility for little or no payment. If this agreement prevails, then no method of additional funding, rental charges or usage fees can ever truly provide a realistically valid financial picture.

In the case of athletic facilities, too often the athletic department, particularly through strong alumni-support activity, seems to hold sway. It is well-recognized that a basketball arena is of primary importance to the basketball team from late November to approximately the first weekend of March in each school year. Yet, there are facilities that have been literally taken out of the marketplace during that period by the insistence of a coach or athletic director that the facility during that same basketball season also serve as the practice floor for the team, With this in mind, there are many days that the facility goes unused because of the desire of the coach to keep the building sacrosanct to one and only one type of event.

In certain cases, the student government or student affairs office becomes very involved in the facility's operation and particularly that of scheduling. Contemporary music concerts are aimed toward the student body and thus, theirs might be the only sponsorship or involvement permitted.

When summer arrives, many schools or combination facilities feel the market period is over and it would be more economically viable to keep the facility closed. Ostensibly, some building administrations contend that this is the time for normal seasonal maintenance. Others feel that very little staff is available, and with the college or school out of session there is no potential audience. This may be true in some small communities. In the normal sense, however, it should be recognized that when students leave a campus there may be a number of other students in the overall trade area returning home from other distant campuses.

A consistent schedule philosophy must be developed in advance of the facility's completion. It should be administered and controlled by management personnel with professional expertise, and should not be countermanded at whim by other administrative officials unless there are definitive and eligible considerations that might preclude certain types of bookings. There is also a very shadowy legal question regarding the rental facilities and freedom of access.

Once a facility has been developed and put into operation to serve a multitude of public interests, both academic and community, the facility's ownership is under the legal obligation to provide a consistent access to the facility. If there are any precluded events, they should be addressed prior to a facility's opening. If there are activities which take preeminence over others, then they should become part of the predetermined schedule allocation. If there are inconsistencies in the schedule philosophy or there are those items which come within the academic and/or cooperative community that the administration feels are offensive or contradictive to the best interests of either group, then those items should be discussed fully and such action, if found to be legally allowable, can be taken to preclude such events. It should be emphasized time and time again that in any such discussions, there is no such thing as preclusion of liability under the first and fourteenth amendments to the Constitution. These amendments particularly refer to freedom of speech and due process.

The university or college, as with any governmental entity that comprises the community administration, cannot set themselves apart from those jurisdictional controls with which any private business would have to comply.

If a certain event is part of standard entertainment industry fare, it cannot be precluded if other such acts have been allowed to perform and there are no clear cut and constitutionally allowable prohibitions that can be exercised. Artistic judgment is not one of the criteria provided the owner of a facility in selecting which act shall perform and which shall not, so long as the facility is operated in a manner so as to entice, lure, invite and induce various spectator activities to use its facilities.

B. Consistent Event Operational Policy

Just because a facility may be student-oriented in the tenor of a great number of its activities, when the general public enters the facilities to attend any event, they should expect a certain consistency in treatment. That includes trained event-staff, medical personnel, security, and administrative personnel. Even if a student activity is to be controlled by the students and thus they are responsible for staffing and other event-oriented services, the facility owner may have placed the professional requirements to meet public needs in the hands of those who are not trained to provide such services. Such students can provide a basic work force if they are guided by professional administration. In many cases, facilities on university campuses or in a cooperative academic/community arrangement can be excellent teaching tools for students and provide a certain sense of involvement heretofore unavailable in most campus/community activity formats.

The same is true with a system of maintenance for the facility and provision of certain vital services, including the access by the public for uses and attention to public inquiries, complaints, and so forth. To have one policy for one group and a different policy for another is, in most simple terms, discrimination. For example, the student government association wishes to have a concert with a certain contemporary music group. The student government will provide the ushers, security, set up the staging and do whatever else is supposedly requested by the act or group. They will guarantee the act or group and sign any and all contracts. The school realizes that the cost is as great or even more so than any revenue potential and in fact the concert is being "subsidized" by student fees or other such budget allocations.

Several weeks later an outside promoter or separate organization from off campus wishes to use the facilities for a similar activity, and within the scheduling philosophy this is allowed. Yet the rental figure is much higher, there is a requirement for certain amounts of staff, security, medical personnel, even to the extent of requiring certain unionized service groups such as stagehands (International Alliance of Theatrical and Stage Employees). When queried, the facility's management or administration states that the previous concert was "promoted" by and for the students. Not only will this affect the credibility of the facility but is totally indefensible if litigated within the context of overt selectivity without conscious regard for constitutionally required criteria for access of all similar groups.

Access to the facility by user groups and tenure of those groups in the facility, provision of services and supply of appropriate material must be the same for all parties concerned. True, there are differences in the level of needs and there may even be some differences in charges. Yet, if a facility in itself becomes actively engaged in presenting a spectator event and its rates and fees and provision for normally expansive services create an economic hardship for a competing community facility elsewhere in the area, another sensitive issue arises. Can one governmental entity—a state operated university for example—actively compete with a city-owned and operated public assembly facility or a privately owned facility in the same community? In some cases, both are governmental entities and enjoy their existence through a sustaining tax base; in the latter example of the private facility, an unfair competitive factor can be claimed.

C. Recognition of Purpose

Although somewhat similar to Items A and B, this area is often more clearly articulated by complainants than are the first two factors. What appears to be criticism of certain scheduled events or complaints about inconsistency in event-operations policy could be better stated as a contention that the school or combined academic/community authority no longer recognizes the original purpose of the facility. Is the facility developed strictly for an on-campus and interdepartmental relationship and to provide services for a very restricted and predetermined user group? Or, was the structure built and is it operated to serve the overall community while at the same time filling certain needs of the school where it is located? The Rupp Arena situation in Lexington, Kentucky is an excellent example of where the needs of the University of Kentucky not only are fulfilled by providing the beautiful facility that now exists in the city of Lexington but also, they provide a certain financial base in an activity area that a lot of buildings do not enjoy. Yet, the purpose of the facility was and still is to provide a community and consumer trade area-wide forum for a multitude of activities.

Recognition of purpose is so important because it is an emotional issue at best. It is the very fiber of certain community and/or academic institutional concepts. The arts theater that is used by more groups off-campus than on campus often created hard feelings among certain school officials, particularly those closely allied with the workings of the school's theater department. In retrospect, there are those avid alumni who, supporting their college athletic programs, will find that the intervention of a certain event, thus precluding their favorite team's constant access to a particular arena floor for practice, strikes at the very heart of the school's tradition and time-tested values in their personal viewpoint.

D. Promotion to Those Groups Vital to the Facility's Success

This section is directed to the facility that particularly needs the community's involvement so as to make the building fiscally viable. Or, in those cases where the services to the community were a very necessary part of the original funding request, there continues to exist the need to direct the attention of that consuming public to the advantages and facilities available at the building in question. Alumni groups are very close-knit organizations that can be reached by direct mail. Often, many of them live in the trade area, or if not, are extremely attentive to each and every mailing, telephone call or public announcement concerning their alma mater. The university community itself is a close-knit entity due to the proximity of one person to another. Dormitory living, close in-campus housing, mutually attended classes, and the traditional atmosphere of the scholastic community make advertising and promotion of events and recognition of needs of a facility far simpler.

But there are those many thousands of individuals in the trade area who are not connected to the school in question. They may accept the school for what it is, and be happy with the advantages of having a particular academic institution in their community. They may even feel there is a benefit in having the number of individuals residing in town even if only for a nine month period each year. Yet, it is to these people that a facility must direct certain promotional aspects. An ice show or noncollege-oriented activity in an 11,000-15,000 seat facility may require an audience factor made up of from 50-80% of nonschool people. Thus, if there has not been a consistent and strong approach to achieve rapport with this trading area even before the facility is finished, there can exist, as regrettably does in a number of communities, a greater gulf or separation between the school's efforts to promote the facility and the acceptance by the community that this is a structure and an activity schedule designed with all of them in mind.

The pronouns "I" and "us" must be couched in the more broader term of "we." The community should not be cut off from the operation of the facility either by access to the events or promotional mediums. Once a division of opinion concerning a facility appears then a chasm begins to form. It can take years to correct, and has in some situations, and there are certain situations where this division of opinion between the consumer area and the academic community in question has never healed properly. The separation of the two entities and the philosophic and emotional distance between these two groups is but the proverbial tip of the iceberg and could very often be merely a reflection of a deeper and greater split that may have existed long before the facility was ever constructed.

The unique quality of any spectator facility is its normal unsuitability for any other type of use other than that for which it was originally designed. An auditorium is an auditorium and a basketball arena still remains a large open space structure suited primarily for spectator usage even after the seats and playing court have been removed. In recent years, restorative techniques and architectural ingenuity have turned some abandoned department stores and other large retail sales facilities into fairly acceptable convention and exhibition areas. This ability to be transformed rests primarily in the structure's similarity to the standard exhibition hall or convention center configuration -that of a flat floor, four wall structure divided by movable partitions into meeting, exhibition and banquet space.

This is not the case with auditoriums, theaters and larger arena-type structures. Once a facility is constructed for these specific purposes it serves little good to attempt using it for any other purpose radically apart from that for which it was originally built. With this in mind, the owners and operators of such facilities must quickly determine the most practical and efficient method of operation within the building's basic design.

Size is not as important a factor in operational stratagem as one might think. The large, multi-thousand-seat facility has more area to be cleaned, more seats to be repaired, more lighting instruments to be replaced, and more space to be heated and air-conditioned. But on the other hand, it also produces a larger amount of revenue during most usages thus allowing for a greater allocation of support funds or event receipts to budgeted maintenance categories.

There is a strong operational similarity of any such structure to many small businesses. As with such businesses the product line is somewhat limited by the type and size of structure involved, the permanent staff is not overly large, and the level of specific activity costs are related directly to the size and type of event scheduled. Although the structure may appear unique, practical fiscal policies, efficient maintenance techniques and sound personnel practices coupled with innovative and aggressive promotional programs still form the basis of any successful facility operation.

Importance of Organization, Cooperation and Discipline

To operate with the highest degree of efficiency and productivity under existing circumstances any such facility, however large or small, must emphasize three basic tenets. They are organization, cooperation and discipline. The organization must be well-defined, simple, clear in its goals and objectives and yet flexible to meet changing times. State-of-the-art is an expression that has been coined for the modern day computer world. It should also be remembered when dealing with any organizational structure. New conditions, changes in market potential, fluctuations in the local as well as regional economy, and the increasing development of managerial techniques can all have bearing on the basic structure of any facility's management system.

Cooperation in any facility, regardless of size, is imperative. It begins with the desire of the owner-operator to provide a consistent and unfettered support of its management staff. That cooperation then must pervade all staff activities. It is carried forth into the community through a sincere desire to be of assistance in fulfilling not only what the owner-operator and management feel are community needs, but what the consuming public themselves feel the facility can do for them as potential users.

The last of the three-part concept, discipline, must be both individual and organizational. An unbending attitude is not a reflection of discipline but of an overly rigid management personality. An unquestioning obedience to every request, every demand and every desire for change by others is also not reflective of discipline, but rather of insecurity and insufficiency in the needed professional approach to the management responsibilities required in operating any public assembly facility.

If you have organization, cooperation and discipline in their appropriate forms and degree of sufficiency to meet normal management challenges, you then can safely assume you have "control" of your facility's operation. Control may be the most important element in any successful facility operational technique. By control we mean that the various aspects of facility operation are within the authorized domain of the facility management and its owner/operator. Any changes, additions, or deletions are developed by, implemented by, and the responsibility of that same management/owner-operator combination.

Every facility must control its own scheduling procedure and booking authority. Although there may be some scheduling limitations, particularly in the case of athletic facilities where practice time is provided, or community oriented centers where certain traditional or periodic activities take precedence, once those limitations are recognized and parameters set, the scheduling must then remain within the province of the facility's management.

Extremely important is control of finances which includes accounting procedures, collection and payment of funds as well as management of any and all contracts that might deal with franchises such as leased concessions, labor service contractors and parking service operators among others.

Management of any facility requires control of all individuals who make up the facility's permanent and temporary staff. The selection procedure may necessitate involvement of a personnel department somewhere else in the overall organizational set up. There are, of course, numerous regulations, procedures, techniques and limitations for indiscriminate hiring and firing that are very much a part of current Affirmative Action programs, Equal Employment Opportunity and other state and federal regulations regarding the acquisition and disposition of personnel. But after the personnel forms are completed and the individual joins the facility's staff, he or she has come under the direct authority of the facility management and its authorized agents both in the performance of the individual's assigned responsibilities as well as application of appropriate personnel discipline and merit evaluation procedures.

Public Relations

" 'Public relations" means many things to many people. Most important to any spectator-oriented facility is the direct concern that the facility relates to its consuming public, their wants and their needs. Without direct involvement with such promotional and public relations programs, a facility management team has little or no control over its own merchandisable potential.

As in the case of any physical structure, preventative maintenance is the least expensive and most effective method of ensuring continued physical plant operation at peak efficiency with a minimum of continuing deterioration in both structure and plant equipment. Preventative maintenance, repair procedures and equipment replacement are essential parts of every annual budget consideration. They are the direct responsibility of the management team and thus, that same management team must have full control over these appropriate measures necessary to successfully carry on an effective maintenance program in the facility.

On the horizon or in the "tomorrow" of spectator facilities are some fascinating and challenging new concepts that may in time totally revamp the entire image of public assembly and spectator facilities so long considered impervious to change. Those new features just coming into view include renovation of facilities for multi-use where once they were considered suitable for only a limited type of activity. These renovations can encompass collapsible seating, electrically operated folding walls and partitions to divide floor space into smaller use areas, special floor coverings to provide additional styles of court services for such activities as indoor tennis and soccer, along with increasing seating capacity or in some cases, reducing cavernous buildings to more intimate, energy-efficient and operationally functional structures.

A combination of operational styles with the merging of community with academic institutions, various departments of the same government, quasiprivate authority and governmental involvement have created a myriad of management structures and funding approaches that dazzle even the most veteran facility observer.

Private Management Arrangements

With this introduction of innovative funding and operational combinations has come the element of private management. Numerous facilities throughout the United States are now operating under what is generally referred to as private management contracts even though the facilities themselves may have been originally designed, funded, constructed and operated by governmental entities before entering into an agreement with a private management firm. Many advantages appear available through this type of management contract, not the least of which is the elimination of the traditional political squabbling and controversy that has plagued many city, county and state-operated facilities as well as the internecine institutional politics that even affects some academic institutional facilities. The subject of private management versus public ownership and operation, as further augmented by variations on the same theme, is a subject far too complex and broad to be covered in this chapter. The reader may wish to contact the International Association of Auditorium Managers, 500 North Michigan Avenue, Suite 1400, Chicago, Illinois 60611, whose membership includes a diversified group, of ownership and operational combinations. A list of their membership would be a starting point for examination of the multitude of "operational arrangements" as currently exist.

Trends

Automation is an expression perhaps ill thought of in certain industries where it may have meant a decrease in the number of individuals utilized for certain functions. But in the spectator facility industry, automation in plant operations as well as the management and administrative services field may be the answer to what is the constant spectre of large overhead costs during a budget year that features a fluctuating and often capricious schedule potential and activity level.

In the plant operational field, computerized heating, ventilating and air conditioning controls, as well as devices for the shedding of excess energy demands and the conservation of fuel supplies has become an inevitable consideration during every building's annual budget review. Most recent has been the introduction of management programming, schedule consolidation, financial "spread sheets" and operational planning guides provided through the magic of "in-house" computer systems. These systems, whether several terminal units with limited data base or the more expansive and all encompassing "mainframe" configurations, present management personnel with far greater access to operational and financial data than ever enjoyed before.

This, coupled with the proliferation of automated or "computerized" ticketing systems allows a facility to literally and figuratively reach out to the consuming public with their most visible product identification—the event ticket. Where once the use of hard tickets to an event limited the number of agencies or "outlets" that might provide distant customers access to an activity, today a number of buildings have either developed their own system or are part of national computer ticket chains that can provide almost instantaneously tickets to a popular event hundreds of miles away from the facility in question. In addition, existing software provides quick retrieval of sales data as to where, when and how often tickets are sold. This is an invaluable tool for the advertising and promotion sections of any facility but even more importantly, to management itself. It is this type of recorded customer demand that indicates scheduling possibilities for future events.

Summary/Conclusion

The development, design, construction and eventual operation of a public assembly facility can and often has been the most dramatic and at times traumatic experiences ever undergone by any community. Whether the structure was built and is operated by the city in question, or is county owned, or privately built and operated, or part of the neighboring academic institution servicing that community, or the facility is a part of the total community recreational system, it is important to recognize that man is a gregarious creature. Man has gathered in urban conclaves for centuries, and will continue to seek the company of his fellow man; in doing so he will desire to be entertained, edified, educated, inspired and more directly stated — emotionally fulfilled by the presentation of events and involvement in activities at structures and facilities designed for these specific purposes.

Chapter 20

Event Management: A Practical Approach

David R. Maraghy

Introduction

Since the early 1980s when I began my involvement with the Greater Greensboro Open, one of the oldest stops on the PGA TOUR, I have reveled in the process of marketing, promoting, and operating all manner of events-from golf tournaments to polo matches to rock concerts and even a softball world series. It is most satisfying to sit back after such efforts and reflect on all the many pieces which came together to make the event successful.

A sure sign of the individual who thrives on the frenetic pace and chaos which usually at the center of any event is the pure enjoyment received m', vii one problem to the next and finding solutions knowing that while things are unsettled, the spectators, participants, and guests at the function think all is well. Now that deception is really fun!

If you have ever been involved in any event you can identify with the above feelings. While you may be normal, and therefore not thrive on the feeling of being "in a kind of "war," you also realize that controlled commotion is inherent to every activity which brings together large numbers of people in one place.

With experience and planning you should be able to minimize greatly the risks involved with staging an event. Much of the planning process involves identifying risk areas, and then formulating the right questions related to such risks. Another key to success is to reduce the potential for surprises and the attendant risks which follow.

In writing this chapter the term "risk" is sometimes viewed broadly to cover not only physical injury and potential litigation, but also financial loss. In fact, risk can even mean failure in terms of not fulfilling the expectations of the spectators and/or participants—maybe even the simple fact they did not have fun. Therefore, the event was not successful, money was probably lost, and the event will not be supported in the future.

The purpose of this chapter is to provide some practical advice on avoiding risks. The actual solutions for each challenge you face will vary depending upon the particular event and nature of the risks. Therefore, this chapter emphasizes developing the ability to ask the proper questions as opposed to providing any general panacea.

The patient lying exposed on the surgical table never wants to hear the attending physician utter the word "oops." Hopefully, this chapter will aid you in avoiding use of that same dreaded word in caring for your "patient"—the event.

Planning and Organization

There is an old adage: "Plan your work, and work your plan." The crucial element in striving to reduce risks associated with operating an event is careful planning.

In the proper planning of an event, there is no substitute for experience. Therefore, when facing your first few projects do not be shy about seeking assistance, knowledge, and advice from experienced sources. If live mentors are not available, or experienced individuals are too competitive to lend assistance, then do your research. A trip to the library will reveal articles on planning most anything: a golf outing, conference, marathon, or car rally.

As you gain experience in this area, you will find that your expertise transcends any one specific field. While the particulars of marketing the event will change based upon the demographics of the target audience, the logistics will be very similar. I find this rule to run true in my dealings with successful event managers for all different sports and activities.

Accordingly, the Organizational Chart provided below was developed through the years primarily in designing and implementing golf events. Nevertheless, it has also been used quite successfully to plan and operate many other events by gearing the questions raised towards that particular sport or activity.

Your concept of planning needs to move beyond thinking in terms of simply following any outline or chart. Instead, sit alone with a pencil and large sheet of paper, computer, (or whatever creative tools you find comfortable), and run through all aspects of the event from the very first stages to the desired conclusion.

For me, this process results in an outline containing many sections and sub-sections. Also key to this process of analysis is a narrative or editorial comments on those sections where necessary. This exercise also results in an added back-up checklist to the Organizational Chart used to structure and plan the event.

The narrative and comments are such a crucial ingredient in my recipe for success because they reveal the "what ifs…." Again, careful planning like this helps to eliminate risks. More often, events fail, people are injured, or money is lost because the promoter did not anticipate well the risks inherent to the activity or event.

Organizational Chart

Through experience, trial and error, you will develop the form of chart which works best for you as a planning and operational tool. In the meantime, this section will offer some general considerations for you. The suggestions will be geared toward the issue of avoiding, or at least reducing risks of injury/liability or financial failure.

In planning any event my organizational structure takes the form of a schematic skeleton. This chart usually results in ten major sections with an average of ten sub-sections or sub-headings of more specific areas of responsibility.

Those sub-sections will vary with the kind of activity, but the ten primary headings seem to cross-over very effectively. Therefore, those ten sections are enumerated below, with only those sub-headings pertinent to risk issues being discussed. You will note that some key considerations such as crowd control, security, and transportation, actually extend beyond just one section and will be addressed in several places.

Sales — Ticket Sales

Plan for the procedures related to sales of tickets at the event site. How will you monitor sales, and enforce spectators' purchasing? Provide necessary security for locations with cash.

In terms of crowd control and possible risk of injury, formulate a well-conceived plan for sales, avoiding long lines and frustrated spectators. Walk through the actual process of selling the ticket, picking up the ticket, adequate staffing, cash versus credit card services, and ingress and egress through narrow entrance areas. Uniformed officers in the area provide a calming effect on customers waiting In line, thereby deterring pushing and possible jostling or injury of others.

Do you need to allow for bilingual or multi-lingual ticket sellers to speed the process and render it more effective? Similarly, will your ticket sellers need to convert money? If so, find bright people and provide them the necessary conversion tables, charts, calculators, etc.

Clear, simple, easy to read, large signs can also quicken the sale process. Prices of tickets, available seating, cost of goods or concessions, can all be grasped and the appropriate money made ready while customers wait in line. Again, consider whether the signs need to be in several languages, and prices in more than one currency.

Do you need to allow for "Will Call" where spectators can pick up tickets left for them or purchased in advance? Where will such an area be best located to avoid confusion, and the clogging of lines for ticket sales?

Similarly, do you anticipate a large number of individuals with special status for discounted prices, or perhaps free admission: military, students, seniors? If so, the process will be smoother if you provide special lines to accommodate them.

Sponsor Services

Most sub-headings here address the area of promotions and hospitality functions for large dollar sponsors as opposed to any real risk issues. When considering financial risks, however, you better take care of these folks!

Actually, in caring for your sponsors you will face many vital areas of event management, but they are all addressed elsewhere herein. Such issues will be transportation (valet parking?), planning and maintaining a safe hospitality area (seating, special tents, etc.), security and credentials, and crowd control.

Contestant Services — Special Consideration of Accommodations, Security, and Transportation

What special arrangements need to be made for your contestants, performers, artists, players, or drivers? Consider not only issues of comfort, but also safety.

If you are dealing with a bona fide superstar do you need to find very secure, private accommodations? Will you reserve an entire floor of the hotel? How much of an issue is security at each stage of the event? Do you need to assign security guards to the individual 24 hours a day?

Is transportation an issue? Do you need to provide for reception at the airport? How many cars, vans, limousines are necessary? Think through every transportation need—air and ground—from start to finish of the event.

How will the contestants get to/from the event? Is a special traffic lane necessary? What about getting to/from a stage, field, track, course?

What security will be required during the actual performance, race, match, concert, tournament?

With the disturbing increase of terrorism, and other senseless acts such as the victimization of Monica Seles, one of tennis' brightest stars, where is the event business headed in terms of liability? How much planning and security will be sufficient, both in terms of protecting the contestant, and protecting you from financial ruin through legal actions by an injured performer? You will have to balance carefully your risk of exposure to liability for injury to a contestant versus the potential prohibitive costs of obtaining necessary security, and special expensive accommodations and modes of transportation.

Hospitality — Liquor Liability

Most sub-headings here concern entertaining of guests, sponsors, and special VIPs. Nevertheless, for all social functions you must again consider all the relevant questions posed in other sections herein: access, ingress/egress, security, traffic flow, crowd control, and other thoughts relating to large numbers of people.

One additional key area of concern is the ever-growing body of law on liability for an event or function serving alcohol. I offer this caveat with a few examples of how others have attempted to prevent problems. Be aware of your very high exposure to potential liability when serving alcohol to someone who is then injured and/or injures others as a result of those actions taken while under the influence, especially driving.

When hosting an event seek legal consultation on the prevailing law in your jurisdiction. Sound advice on this subject will be worth every penny. Discover if case law or statute offers guidelines to be followed in such circumstances which may help insulate you from liability.

Some examples of preventive measures being employed at events are suggested below. *Nevertheless, nothing contained herein is to be taken as a guarantee that such measures will relieve you of liability in such situations.*

Many stadiums now cease selling alcohol prior to the end of the game. This strategy provides two benefits: it shortens the amount of time spectators can drink, thereby hopefully reducing the number of intoxicated persons; and, also lengthens the time between the last drink and when the spectator climbs behind the wheel of a car. You certainly can consider such a time control device in your event.

Common at many functions is the stringent check of age identification for the purchase of alcohol. Attendant to that process is a manner of identifying legal aged individuals throughout the duration of the event—hospital-type wrist bands, etc. Again, uniformed officers with power of arrest in the jurisdiction can be quite a deterrent, as well as very useful in case a scene becomes disorderly.

Many events now offer services such as free soda or other non-alcoholic beverage for designated drivers.

Another strategy is to provide access to designated driver services — whether hired by the function or paid for by the user. Some of these services will actually follow you home in your car so it will be there in the morning when you wake up.

Ready access to traditional cab service can also be effective.

Whatever route you choose, know that you are very vulnerable on this point.

Operations — Crowd Control

This area naturally is the heart of any event. Sub-headings, therefore, are many and varied depending upon the type of event. In my organizational chart, however, one sub-heading cries out for consideration in terms of concerns for risks: crowd control. Some of the relevant questions have been posed above and should be reviewed by you as they relate to this issue. A new, very pertinent consideration in avoiding liability, however, is where you place your spectators.

Incredibly, there is a body of law that hints a golf tournament might be liable to a spectator hit by a golf ball straying into the gallery area as marked by gallery ropes. Some courts have indicated that by placing gallery ropes behind which spectators must remain to observe golf action, the tournament has somehow implied that those areas are safe. Actually, I always thought the gallery ropes were intended to protect the players from the crazed fans!

More seriously, whatever happened to the legal theory of "assumption of risk"? That theory holds that whoever attends a golf tournament or baseball game or car race, should be presumed to know that balls go out of play and cars run off the track. Therefore, the event should not be capable of being held liable providing it exercises reasonable efforts to allow for the safety of the spectator.

Beware. This area of the law may not be working in your favor as much as it once did. Once again, therefore, consult legal counsel for the applicable rule in your geographic area, legal jurisdiction, and your particular event. Standards may well differ for a highly dangerous sport like auto racing as opposed to the professional badminton exhibition of India vs. Korea.

What level of precautionary measures are sufficient? Should the netting behind home plate extend all the way down both the first and third foul lines to prevent injury from one of those wicked foul line drives? How high should the protective glass be in a hockey rink? Is it reasonable to lower that glass on the sides of the rink, but extend it to the ceiling behind both goals where errant shots fly? What areas for the viewers at an auto race are safe from flying debris, tires and flames when a tragedy occurs?

Assess your event carefully, try to envision the worst thing that could happen no matter how remote or unlikely it may seem, and plan accordingly.

Site Management — Construction, Electrical, Maintenance, and Signage

This section involves several areas of potential risk: construction, electrical, maintenance, and signage. Legal analysis on the duties imposed on you by the first three items would constitute a voluminous treatise on the law of business invitee. Lacking such space, suffice it here to raise real warning flags for you in organizing your event.

You are inviting onto your business premises-be it arena, stadium, golf course, or race track-potential litigants in large numbers. Are you building or providing bleachers for them to sit? Do not assume the competence of anyone erecting such structures or the soundness of any provided. Take reasonable, necessary steps to ensure the safety of fans using those seating areas.

Once everything is in place, you will bear the responsibility of maintaining the facilities and grounds in a safe manner. Your actual standard of care under the law may vary in different Jurisdictions, but be aware of common hazards: water on the floor, holes on the golf course, loose steps, dead tree limbs.

Are you providing power? If so, has the electrical work been performed competently? Are there exposed power lines? Is the proper current provided where necessary? Are the heaters in the corporate hospitality tents a fire hazard?

Signage is the final sub-section to be considered for purposes of risk. Place warning signs in areas where errant golf balls, baseballs, flying cue balls, if applicable, may somehow come into contact with spectators. jurisdictions vary on the, efficacy of such signage in insulating the event from liability. Nevertheless, risk consultants strongly recommend such signage as a useful piece of evidence when presenting your side of the case.

Provide information plainly, clearly and often on what to do in case of emergency, lightning, or other dangerous inclement weather. What is the procedure and where should the spectator go if a warning siren screams of approaching lightning?

Exit signs should be clearly marked.

If effective in your area, signs disclaiming any responsibility or liability whatsoever for anything should be displayed.

If you know of the existence of a dangerous condition you cannot rectify, then rope it off and surround it with bold warning signs. If necessary, consider assigning security personnel to the area to prevent entry.

Concessions — Licenses, Taxes

Most of the risks here are financial.

Know the various licenses you may need, and applicable taxes for sales of any kind. Regarding food and beverage, what are the county, state, and ABC licenses or permits needed? What, if any, is the governing tax associated for such sales for which you will be accountable?

If merchandise is the issue (souvenirs, the ubiquitous event T-shirt), again what licenses and taxes apply? Is there a legal way to avoid such taxes: nonprofit status, 501(c)(3) status under the Internal Revenue Code, charitable, church, other?

If you are selling items on a consignment basis, know how stringent the accountability will be on you to return either the product or the equivalent in cash.

The bottom line here is to ensure you are not assessed a fine, penalty, tax, or other invoice you were not expecting.

Be aware of freshness of food/beverage products where that is an issue. Are there any special requirements for preparation of certain foods? You could also be liable to consumers at your event who become ill through bad food.

Finance

If you undertake the sale of tickets on behalf of 'someone else, be clear regarding your accountability at the end. Too often I have seen situations where someone felt he was acting more as a favor to the promoter in helping to distribute tickets, but at the end of the event a dispute arose regarding an unreal expectation of strict accountability for such sales.

What measures need to be taken to reduce your financial risk? Some events use scrip tickets instead of cash for the purchase of food and beverage. It is easier to control the sale of scrip. You need fewer people to handle the money. You also have an easier accounting system because a quick tally of tickets compared to cash reveals any discrepancies.

Do you have adequate security for people and areas handling large amounts of cash? Are the proper systems in place for dealing with credit card sales? How will you safely transport cash and make deposits? Who will do so?

Establish a sound system of controls for tickets, merchandise and concessions products. What is your system for monitoring all spectators to ensure display of proper tickets or credentials, and of enforcing sales to those individuals lacking such items?

Insurance is a vital issue failing under this section. Because of its importance, however, it is separately discussed below.

Support Services — Health and Safety, Communications, Traffic Control, Transportation, and Parking

With the litigious nature of society the topic of Health and Safety deserves special attention from you in your planning. You must guard against any failure to provide reasonably adequate medical care for your spectators and contestants. Certainly at every event site you are not expected to provide a fully-equipped medical unit equivalent to a transportable Mt. Sinai Hospital. You will, however, be expected to provide for some measure of medical care that is reasonable under the circumstances. Anticipate.

What you provide will be dictated by the distance from the nearest medical facility, the size of the crowd, the nature of the event, the demographics of the crowd, and the inherent danger in the event or of the site. Example: an outdoor event in the summer in the South can expect sunburn and dehydration. Take steps to protect against such conditions—water stations, shade areas—and to provide treatment when they do occur. Example: a surfing contest will add to the first example the need for expertise and personnel to provide rescue services in large seas and surf. Example: the medical problems to anticipate will differ greatly-by worlds in fact-if you are hosting a croquet championship in Newport, Rhode Island, as opposed to being involved in a NASCAR event in South Hill, South Carolina.

While the examples are endless, you should allow for at least an acceptable level of on-site care: EMTs, volunteer doctors/nurses, transportation for such personnel, adequate supplies, and satisfactory treatment area. The key here is to anticipate, do your research, and respond to the data appropriately.

The next sub-section is an essential tool not only in preventing risk situations, but simply for ensuring smooth operation: communications. Have a sufficient number of radios, walkie-talkies, cellular phones, whatever it takes to keep key personnel in contact with each other. You or your designate should be capable of communicating with and monitoring conversations of all necessary department heads. By monitoring you can anticipate problems and defuse the situation. You also want the proper personnel to be able to react quickly to emergencies of any kind and magnitude: medical, parking, traffic, security, inventory control, even running out of ice in the title sponsor's hospitality tent.

In your advanced planning be cognizant of potential traffic control and parking problems. Snarled traffic can mean lost revenue in tickets and concession sales. Moreover, are you allowing a hazardous situation which might result in injury? Has your lack of attention to detail in this area created a dangerous intersection somewhere? Because of your failure to plan for an orderly departure from crowded parking lots are your spectators engaged in a spontaneous demolition derby?

Do you have adequate security to control traffic and provide safe parking areas? Is your signage directing traffic sufficiently clear and well-placed?

The final pertinent issue hereunder is transportation. In nearly every event of any kind transportation issues tend to be the most bothersome.

Shuttling large numbers of fans brings about images of long lines at shuttle stops, uncomfortable buses, and generally a miserably inconvenient experience.

Transporting a small number of VIPs—sponsors or celebrities—can also be a nightmare. Nothing will lose a key sponsor faster than when its CEO stands cooling his heels on some sidewalk waiting for his/her ride. My experience is that such little things cost you sponsorship dollars more often than major catastrophes. Therefore, spend plenty of time in planning for these details.

A couple of hints should be most helpful to your planning in this area. Drive the routes to be taken to confirm actual time and distance. Be sure all drivers know the directions well, and even practice driving the routes! Do not laugh. While it is incomprehensible to me, I have seen significant events where the hired drivers show up for work and have no idea of the location of elemental destinations: the airport, the host hotel, even the site of the event. This was a source of criticism during the 1996 Olympics in Atlanta.

Educate your drivers on rush hours to be reckoned with during the event. Discover reliable short-cuts and alternate routes.

Convey all this information in writing to the drivers. Provide simple maps. Provide accurate, detailed, written schedules to everyone. Place a cellular phone in each vehicle.

Realize, too, your tremendous potential liability in hiring drivers and providing transportation. Be a smart consumer. Is it ultimately cheaper and wiser to hire a transportation or destination company with large umbrella insurance coverage, than to try to manage transportation yourself? Under the circumstances, can this step insulate you from disastrous risks?

If you insist on hiring drivers, be aware of a range of issues: obtaining adequate insurance, and screening drivers by running Motor Vehicle Records for DUIs or similar severe violations. Otherwise, you could be held grossly negligent in a legal action. Do your research on this issue in your venue, jurisdiction, and with your insurance advisor and legal consultant.

Advertising, Promotions, Media Relations

Unless you assault an esteemed member of the paparazzi for snapping a photo of you in a compromising position, your likelihood of risk for injury under this section is slight. Nevertheless, several angles are worth considering.

First, you may open yourself up to ridicule and some risk of financial liability if you are not careful with your advertising. While you may be desperate to promote your event and increase sales, do not declare that Michael Jordan will be coming when it is actually Vernon Jordan. As a rule, under-promise and over-deliver, and you will be a hero with your sponsors and spectators. By performing well under that guideline you are assured of a long and successful event career.

Be careful around the press. I enjoy working with the media, and have been fortunate to enjoy a good relationship for any event or individual client I was promoting. Remember, nonetheless, the media always has more power, ink and videotape than you ever will, so do not go to war with them. Off-hand remarks, or "off the record" comments made to members of the press you do not really know can end up as headlines. Derogatory comments by you which are broadcast or published can result in your calling yourself by a new name: the Defendant.

Also, use the press to help you. The media may not always cooperate, but often they will aid you in disseminating information. Do not limit their assistance to trying to sell tickets. Use the press to help control traffic by providing a map, and designating alternate routes to your event. Provide necessary information about parking, shuttles, and transportation.

Insurance

To paraphrase an old real estate formula for success: "There are three factors which will reduce your exposure from risks associated with organizing and operating an event: (1) insurance; (2) insurance; (3) insurance." While it is preferable to head off problems by all methods and considerations, such as those contained herein, I am an advocate of insurance. This is not the area in which to cut corners financially. Thus, the issue is important enough to justify dedicating this brief section to offer a few general comments and principles.

Find a good insurance company specializing in the area of your event. Assess its track record in terms of providing service, and any pertinent history of paying off on losses when necessary. A good insurance representative with experience in this field is a useful tool in your planning efforts to reduce your exposure. Find one who has handled similar event business.

Determine a sufficient amount of insurance coverage for your event. Do you need an umbrella coverage for liability of $1,000,000 or $5,000,000?

Moreover, establish a minimum requirement of insurance for any subcontractor who will work on your event. Require such proof of insurance before they are allowed on site. Be certain you and your company are named insured on the policy. Identify the other individuals and entities who also should be named insured.

A good insurance group will serve as a clearinghouse for all certificates of insurance which need to be collected from the various subcontractors for your event: caterers, transportation company, golf course, arena, stadium, parking service, contractor, electrical, sanitation company, etc.

Discussed above was the risk associated with hiring drivers. For a fee the insurance company can run the motor vehicle records of your potential drivers to determine past serious violations.

Together with your legal counsel your insurance representative can advise you on the dangerous area of liquor liability. The representative will want the certificates of insurance covering that risk from the caterer, the site, and any entity serving alcohol at your function.

Over the years the experienced representative I use has been very helpful in creating a trusty checklist of risk factors in a particular event. Find your insurance advisor who can perform the same valuable service for you.

Be cognizant of the specialty insurance coverages which are available. Although somewhat expensive, you should at least consider the viability of event cancellation insurance whenever you conduct an outdoor event. Determine exactly the conditions under which you can recover. Also, define what items you will recover: expenses only, lost profits?

Even narrower kinds of coverage are available. In golf, American Hole In One will insure prizes to reward a hole in one at your golf event. The standards will be very strict as to the yardage required on the hole to be covered under the policy, the number of players participating, the permitted number of shots, the sequence of shots, officials necessary to observe and verify, and whether or not professionals are eligible (this will increase the premium). Naturally, the premium amount will fluctuate depending upon the value o the prize.

We have been very successful creating excitement and promoting a major event with ancillary contests such as a Hole In One for significant cash amounts or a Mercedes, etc. It also is a good way to bring in sponsors who can gain exposure by taking title to the contest. Do not forget to build into the sponsorship package the cost of the premium.

I suspect you can find insurance—for a price—to cover most any promotion you want to stage. Consider creative incentives when examining ways to market your event by adding excitement. Is it financially feasible to offer a bonus for winning three races at your steeplechase race? In your series of Monster Truck Races the tension will be unbelievable by providing a $1,000,000 bonus for winning two races in a row.

A client of yours may want to enhance the value of its title position in several events by offering a similar kind of bonus. Example: a company is the title sponsor of two or three tournaments on the golf or tennis tour. It wants to ensure the highest caliber of the field of participants. As your client, that company may call on you to devise some bonus program to encourage the stars to play all the titled events with a big reward for winning two or more. You will want to be able to respond to that inquiry by seeking the consultation of your trusted agent in the field of specialty insurance.

Waivers

As mentioned above, there is a vast body of law on the issue of waivers. The advice here is simply to obtain the opinions of your legal counsel and insurance representative on the most effective form of waiver for your jurisdiction and event. Incorporate that waiver into your entry process. Be sure every participant has signed such a waiver with the entry blank.

Also, know the law in your area regarding validity of such a waiver. What are the age requirements? Is every participant 18 years of age or older? Is parental consent necessary? If so, is such parental consent evident on the waiver?

Many events include a waiver of liability somewhere on the ticket purchased to gain entrance to the event. Again, how binding such a waiver is will depend on the law of the jurisdiction and circumstances. Nevertheless,, it certainly cannot hurt to place that waiver on the ticket. Such language could be one more piece of useful evidence for your side in case the worst happens and you are dragged into our legal system.

Contingency Plans

A solid contingency plan can reduce risk of physical injury, perhaps even save lives and also affect the other aspects of the term "risk" as contemplated herein considerations of finances and fun. Once your planning and organization has revealed a potential problem, then you must be creative and flexible to design the appropriate and effective contingency plan.

Anticipation

One of the best examples of the many benefits of a solid contingency plan involves the greatest fear of any outdoor event: dangerous inclement weather. For purposes of this example we examine the most difficult outdoor activity to control, the golf tournament.

Golf tournaments are uniquely difficult because unlike an auto race, tennis match, concert, or ball game, you have many spectators spread out over a vast geographic area watching the athletic activity unfold over that same area. Neither your contestants nor the spectators are concentrated in any one place. Accordingly, all the usual problems associated with those outdoor activities are magnified greatly.

In recent years golf tournaments, especially at the professional level and the knowledgeable level of the United States Golf Association, have become more sophisticated in protecting players and spectators. It was not long ago, however, that various professional players were injured when struck by lightning, and a spectator was killed by lightning at a major golf tournament.

Naturally, the first defense against such disasters is advanced warning. Modern radar and related weather technology now supply very accurate and timely progress reports on approaching bad weather. Be sure to do your research and make the arrangements to take advantage of that technology. Use all such tools available to you.

Do not panic, you do not have to purchase expensive electronic wizardry to render your event headquarters a NASA station. Such services are available for a reasonable fee on a per event basis which will provide you up to the minute reports on approaching weather during the event.

Now, suppose you have determined there is a problem of advancing dangerous weather conditions, what next? In golf, a horn or siren signals play shall stop because of lightning. Nevertheless, both players and spectators remain at risk out on the course. So, you now engage the evacuation plan you devised when you were planning the tournament.

First, the signal is given in ample time for the spectators to seek shelter. Limited space in the clubhouse has resulted in tournaments providing alternative safety areas out on the golf course, facilities equipped with lightning rods.

Both for considerations of safety and comfort, the players and caddies quite often are treated differently. At the Virginia State Open we have large utility vehicles parked out on the golf course. When play is stopped for lightning the volunteers serving as gallery marshals or scorers near those vehicles are designated to drive the players and caddies back to the clubhouse in those vehicles. Remember, this plan works only if the car keys are accessible to those designated drivers. Do not laugh! It happens. Nothing is quite so frustrating and scary as observing very irate players abusing a poor volunteer as standing in the pouring rain outside a locked evacuation vehicle as outlined against a backdrop of a black sky streaked by lightning flashes.

Unforeseeable

Inherent to the term "unforeseeable" is the inability to guard against such circumstance with any contingency plan because you could not possibly know it was going to occur hence the concept of the term. Nevertheless, when the unforeseeable does occur you may still be held accountable, no matter how unfair. Accordingly, you better work on your seer imitation.

In that regard you can prepare for the "highly unlikely," and better do so. As an example, I am very proud of a contingency plan developed for a wonderful golf experience titled "Fantasy Golf Camp."

The Fantasy Golf concept is to allow amateurs to spend five nights/four days with PGA TOUR stars in a very close environment. Not only does the amateur receive daily instruction from the TOUR players and then play 18 holes of golf, but at night everyone gathers for drinks, dinner, and camaraderie. The experience far surpasses a one day pro am where the amateur may barely hear a word from the pro for 18 holes.

The socializing with the pros after golf and the intimate access to the TOUR players really make the Fantasy Golf Camp special. Add to that experience the venue of Las Vegas, and everyone involved really had the unique opportunity to become friends.

As you can imagine such an event requires significant financial underwriting for the hotels, meals, and most of all the fees for the TOUR players. Imagine the investment it takes to assemble the Fantasy Golf "staff" of true luminaries who attended such as Tom Kite, John Daly, Curtis Strange, Davis Love, III, Lanny Wadkins, and Payne Stewart. Therefore, it was crucial to ensure the participants had the fun expected, or else financial failure could result to the organizer.

I go to such great lengths to describe the experience because this particular Camp took place in early November in Las Vegas. Everyone, especially the Las Vegas contacts, assured me that the weather would be acceptable. We might need sweaters and windbreakers, I was told, but it never rains that time of year. Fair enough, I thought. It did not occur to me, however, to inquire about the likelihood of...SNOW!

Yes, the very first day of the Camp with expectations soaring, and grown men and women acting like children in the presence of the TOUR stars, it snowed. It was so cold I wanted to weep. But wait...

The day would be saved because of a contingency plan. I mentioned earlier I was so proud of this plan, and it is because we ignored all the assurances of pleasant, if not balmy, weather. In fact, the day turned out to be the best possible kick-off for the Camp.

Many months prior to the Camp arrangements were made with a local golf shop to have indoor golf practice equipment ready, and on standby. A large ballroom was reserved at the host hotel for a practice facility. Within one hour of the first camper facing cold weather we were set up inside with Tom Kite offering full swing instruction to campers hitting off a moveable practice tee into a net. Noted teaching instructor, Scott Davenport of the famous Golf Digest Schools, was providing swing analysis with the aid of the latest technology. Other PGA TOUR stars were working one-on-one with campers on putting mats.

The biggest hit of the day was TOUR player Peter Persons organizing a chipping contest into nets. Peter was also collecting the bets while he cajoled the campers into competing, wagering, and verbally abusing each other. They were having a ball! Cocktails and food were plentiful, and the entire atmosphere reeked of camaraderie.

We finally had to drag people out of there in time for dinner. No one wanted to stop having fun. From that first makeshift day, many friendships were made, and a fantastic tone was set for the rest of the Camp.

Summary/Conclusion

Assess the potential problems applicable to your event, and formulate contingency plans accordingly. Be creative and flexible. Do not let yourself be bound by thinking in terms only of the usual or normal. While precedent and experience are very helpful, also take the time to envision those things "unforeseeable" to other, less successful event managers. Accumulate all the information you can from all sources on ways to organize and operate an event. Speak with experienced individuals. Assemble all the written materials available. Use that research to create your own Organizational Chart which you trust.

Make a solid attorney and insurance representative a standard part of your event team. Seek advice before the problem occurs. Preventive legal advice is much cheaper than bringing in the attorneys to defend you later in litigation.

Chapter 21

Activity Centers

Geoffrey Miller

Introduction

There are hundreds of variables which make each manager's job different and unique in the area of facility management. There are certain characteristics and problems, however, which are common to all facilities. Budgeting pressures are forcing the owners and managers of activity centers to be much more creative on how the facilities are used. The days when the term "down time" was used are coming to a close. Increased traffic and use of the facility lead to the need for more efficient scheduling, security, supervision and maintenance. As facility management becomes more of a science and the emphasis is on efficiency, the trend is to give responsibility for the building to a single individual, the facility manager.

Policy development, planning, scheduling, personnel management, supervision, security and maintenance are areas which need constant attention by the facility manager. In addition, a brief examination of the shared facility in a collegiate setting can serve as a guide for what appears to be an indication of things to come.

Policy Development and Implementation

The activity center manager, whether he is opening a new facility or taking over one already in operation, is at an extreme disadvantage if operational policies have not been developed. If there are no policy guidelines, and decisions are left to the facility manager, it will lead to inconsistencies and inequities in the manager's decision-making process. For example, if there are no policies relating to the length of court time or reservation procedures for racquetball, the manager will inevitably make subjective decisions as disputes arise. Clearly, 95% of these disputes could be eliminated if established policies are widely publicized.

Although fair and equitable policies take time and energy to develop, they are the basis of the activity-center manager's administrative operation. Once a policy is developed, the manager has something concrete to work with and also develops a rationale which can be explained to the public. If the policies are not in place, or if the policies are creating difficulties in the operation of the facility, it is imperative that a policymaking body be created to formulate new policies or change the existing ones. All too often these policies are decided upon without the input of the manager. It is important that the manager, who will be implementing these policies, have input and be involved in all policy decisions affecting the activity center.

Operational policies do not guarantee a problem-free facility, but it will improve the decision-making procedure. Administrators often fail to see the long-term ramifications of allowing exceptions to be made relating to policy. Once an exception is made for one facility-user, other users will inevitably be seeking the same treatment and beseeching the manager to go even further. *Take the time to formulate fair policies and then enforce them with no exceptions.* If users complain about a specific policy, ask them to formalize the complaint. Take the formalized complaint through the established decision and policymaking process. It is easier to change a policy than it is to deal with the complaints and issues associated with making exceptions.

Scheduling and Planning

Planning and organization are two of the central characteristics necessary for success. Although the routine duties of day-to-day operations may dominate the activity center manager's time, short-term and long-range planning can make the scheduling process less stressful and the job more enjoyable.

When preparing a schedule for the activity center, the manager must be organized and must establish (and be prepared to defend) priorities that allow one group to have access to the facility over another. In the case of the purely recreational facility, this prioritization process may not be as essential. However, most managers are dealing with a number of different program offerings. Either way, policies need to be established which clearly define the priority structure. For instance, Guilford College owns and operates the Physical Education Center, but leases time to the local YMCA. The college has requests for physical education classes, varsity intercollegiate practices and contests, and intramural offerings. The YMCA has class offerings and its membership has need of open recreational space. It is obvious that a need exists for a set of priorities that the manager can use to schedule each of the areas in the facility.

Once the priorities are agreed upon and set, the logical way to proceed is to obtain requests for space from each constituency. If communication is poor between the various groups competing for space in the facility, the more difficult it becomes for the manager to schedule efficiently. Every effort must be made to encourage communication and the meeting of scheduling deadlines. See the Appendix, at the end of this chapter for a form that is color coded which must be submitted two weeks in advance of the date for which reserved time is being requested. Depending on the number of spaces available (i.e., pool, racquetball courts, weight room, gymnasiums, seminar rooms, etc.) and the number of requests received construct an activities calendar board on a monthly and yearly basis. The board, displayed in a prominent place in the manager's office, can be a tremendous help in answering spontaneous questions relating to new requests for space and for rentals, particularly those that come in by phone and need immediate answers. A computerized grid, accessible by staff who need the information, is an effective way to maintain the monthly schedule. A display board, preferably with three months posted, is also an effective way to display a schedule of activities. A master calendar notebook should also be kept close at hand so that the whole year's calendar is always at the manager's fingertips.

Ultimately, it is up to the manager to implement the priority system and schedule available space. Inevitably, there are conflicts or request overlaps, and it is important that the manager detect these as soon as possible and inform the respective groups so they can adjust and make alternate plans. It is also important to save the original request forms to avoid misunderstandings about what was originally requested.

Once the schedule has been developed based on the request forms, open space can then be determined and opened up for recreational space or rentals. Whenever possible, one area is kept open at the PE Center for recreation to accommodate the large number of students and YMCA members who use the facility. As a way of helping the "spontaneous user" of the facility, devise a recreation sheet which lists when spaces are open for free play on a monthly basis. This sheet is available at a check-in or equipment desk, or sent in the mail or via e-mail to all the individuals who use the activity center. This sheet is particularly helpful during the busy months for activities such as basketball (December, January, and February), and minimizes ill will that is associated with patrons coming into the facility and finding no space open for recreation and exercise. Communication is essential when gathering the information to put together a schedule, but it is imperative to communicate that information to the various constituencies who use the facilities.

A final concern of the manager in the scheduling process is rentals. A decision must be made by the policymaking body, about rental requests. Who can rent the facility? What about liability insurance? What fees will be charged? What kind of staffing arrangements need to be made for the rental period? These are valid questions and need to be handled.

In theory, all rental groups should have equal access to the facility. It may be prudent, however, for your policymaking body to define the qualifications for rental. If there are restrictions, they need to be made very clear. For instance, many nonprofit activity centers are reluctant to rent to groups who plan to use the facilities for a fund-raising activity. It is important to issue a contract to rental groups with specific terms regarding the nature of the request and the fees to be charged. The rental group must furnish proof of suitable insurance to indemnify the activity center, against any liability arising from the use of the facility. In this day and age of multi-million dollar lawsuits, the manager must pay close attention to adequate and suitable insurance for all rental groups. A rate schedule should reflect the real costs that include utilities, labor, and the "wear and tear" of the facility. It is prudent to charge on an hourly basis for one half day use and add a full per them charge. It is important to make necessary arrangements for adequate staffing which is well-trained to supervise the rental activity. It is a mistake to allow the rental group to provide staff, because control of the facility is lost.

Personnel Management and Supervision

Many factors influence the manager's leadership style, but no role is more important than that of the organizational leader. In any situation, qualified individuals must be chosen who have a sense of pride and responsibility for their job and the facility. An administrator's behavior and use of authority in directing employees are critical factors in determining the effectiveness of the leadership style or pattern. Heinz Weihrich points out, in his article in the April, 1979 edition of *Management Review*, that a leadership pattern is a function of balance between the "use of authority by the manager" and the "area of freedom for subordinates." Many managers, particularly those in collegiate environments, are required to handle a number of diverse areas of responsibility. This balance becomes crucial in those situations in which the facility manager needs to rely heavily on his subordinates.

Individual managers ultimately decide upon a leadership pattern or style that depends upon the number of employees and the structure of the organization. Beyond "style" there are a few steps which are critical to effective personnel management. It is imperative to formulate accurate and sufficient job descriptions for each of the positions on the staff. A job description not only provides a means of evaluating an employee's performance, but it prevents disagreements or misunderstandings that undocumented conversations frequently create. Since the job description is discussed by both parties, communication will be enhanced, and a pattern will be set for future discussions on job responsibilities and performance. As a job description changes, it is essential to update and share these alterations with the employees. It is helpful to use a job description with student and work-study employees, For those in facilities where student employees are a possibility, or necessity, a detailed job description is very helpful. Students are frequently preoccupied with other matters and the way to gain attention is through a contract or job description, signed by both the employee and manager, outlining duties and responsibilities. The development of job descriptions for each position is tedious, but time well-spent at the front end of the facility operation. It will effectively reduce the number of misunderstandings between the manager and the employees.

Another essential element of personnel management is the supervision of a facility and its operations through the permanent staff. If the activity center includes a pool or natatorium, supervision is a high priority. A pool can be a dangerous place or an "attractive nuisance," as well as a health hazard if it is not staffed adequately and professionally. The activity center manager cannot take responsibility for the day-to-day operation of the pool and maintain other facets of the managerial duties. The obvious key to safety and efficient management of a pool is the selection of a qualified and conscientious individual to run it. The pool manager should have flexibility to perform pool maintenance, schedule lifeguards, establish rules of operation, and order essential equipment without the burden of constantly clearing everything through the manager. Weekly or biweekly meetings with the aquatics director to review and discuss any particular items which may arise is recommended. It is through these meetings that emergency procedures, lifeguard regulations and maintenance procedures can be defined.

The supervision of the other areas in the facility may not be as vital as the pool, but it is still important to the day-to-day operation of the facility. It is important to employ a staff member in the building at all times who is mobile (not tied to a desk or phone) who can handle the spontaneous problems which inevitably arise. An activity center locker room can be a prime area for abuse and/or theft. The wrong kind of shoe or equipment can easily damage a synthetic or wood floor, racquetball court, tennis court, or other areas in the center. In addition, there are times when certain kinds of free play or activity are not acceptable because of a class conflict. These problems need to be handled by the facility manager or someone on the staff to maintain the facility and keep it attractive for people to come and enjoy.

Security

The kind of security the activity center chooses is largely dependent upon budget and the facility's design. The activity center manager must make the decision about security early in the operation of the facility, keeping in mind the experience preferred by the user of the facility. In the planning stages of a facility, get advice from security experts and incorporate their suggestions into the building design. Whatever the system agreed upon, the public's experience is a vital consideration.

For instance, an outside service can be hired, but the manager must weigh the pros and cons of the impact of a uniformed attendant versus a nonuniformed individual to perform the security. Frequently, a non-uniformed employee can check I.D. cards for admittance and also lend a warmer and more hospitable greeting to those who come to use the facility. In addition, this individual can perform other administrative functions which support the operation. If an electronic system for check-in is affordable, the manager must also decide before purchasing whether there will be personal contact with the user of the facility.

If a receptionist is used, consider the requirement of photo-I.D. cards instead of ones with only the name, address and expiration date. Although the choice of photo-I.D. cards results in greater capital expenditure at the front end of the operation, the cards will clearly pay for themselves in the long run as they diminish abuse and therefore ensure that the only people using the facility are those who have a right to do so. With the receptionist system, it is essential that all other entrances be closed off and that emergency exits be secured so that they are only used during emergencies. This is particularly relevant when the facility includes a pool or natatorium. Depending upon the situation, the frustration of keeping up with exit doors may be a continuous hassle. However, the chances are good that your facility is something people want to get into and, as the cliche states, "where there's a will there's a way." The public is going to try to enter your facility in any way possible. As manager, do everything possible to direct all traffic through the main entrance and past the building's receptionist.

Give keys only to those who absolutely need them for opening and closing, or equipment check-out. This is sound advice and will prove to be helpful. The manager needs a set of master keys, as does his assistant and possibly one other staff member. If a receptionist is present during the hours of building operation, it is possible to set up a key check-out system where other staff members, instructors, and maintenance personnel can obtain a set of master keys. By keeping tight control of keys, the activity center manager can more efficiently control the facility. Whatever system you decide upon, be conscious of how little time it takes for "lost" keys to be copied and subsequently require the changing of all locks.

Maintenance

The maintenance and upkeep of the facility is a vital part of the activity center manager's job. The way a building looks and the standards that are set for its maintenance have a great deal to do with the public's total experience in the facility, and, in many cases, has a large bearing on whether the public decides to continue to use the facility. In fitness centers, spas, and racquetball clubs where the operation is contingent upon the selling of memberships, the maintenance considerations become even more critical.

A well-chosen janitorial and maintenance staff can add to the success of the manager. It is important for the manager to take daily tours through the facility to note any problems or potential trouble spots. Many managers carry a small hand-held tape recorder as they inspect the facility and make comments as they go. The items can be listed afterwards into immediate or long-range project categories and then shared with the maintenance staff. Take into consideration any "down" periods when traffic in the facility is limited, so that major maintenance or painting operations can be scheduled during those periods. Also, periodic meetings with the maintenance staff can assist in developing preventive maintenance schedules which will help to avert major problems or shut downs which might interfere with the smooth day-to-day operation of the facility. In situations where the maintenance is performed by an outside group or a college maintenance staff which has other responsibilities besides the facility, the manager needs to keep accurate records of work that is requested and be flexible in making preparations for the work. Regardless of the particulars of each individual situation, the activity center manager must be sensitive to and involved with the maintenance and efficient upkeep of the facility for which he is responsible. Anything less than a conscientious effort in this area can soon result in not only the rapid deterioration of the facility but also in deterioration of the relationship between the building staff and those who use the facilities.

General Operations

In summary, create a checklist for the everyday operation of the activity center. This checklist cannot encompass all the particulars of each manager's situation, but it can be a helpful guide for those who are willing to pick up on general suggestions. The items include the following:

1. Be visible, accessible, and willing to deal in a prompt and professional manner with problems that come up.
2. Make certain at the start of each day that the receptionist, maintenance person, or the staff member responsible for opening up has checked on the operation of the essential equipment that affects space temperatures, hot water in the showers, pool temperature, and similar duties. Two-thirds of the complaints a manager receives are related to things which directly affect the public's experience at the facility. A routine check every morning will enable the manager to prevent potential problems or address them in a timely manner.
3. Each morning, check the daily building schedule for special events or anything that could potentially alter the normal routine. On Mondays, check the whole week's schedule in similar fashion. If the facility is used as a back-up in inclement weather, there will be times when it will be essential to make a decision about going to a "rainy day" schedule. This is particularly relevant when there are outdoor tennis courts, programs

that are taught outdoors, or athletic teams which need to have space indoors for practice in bad weather.

4. Check on phone messages, mail, injury report forms, or particular problems from the day before and prioritize and follow up in the appropriate manner.

5. Set aside a period of time according to the day's calendar, without the interruption of the phone, to complete paperwork. Failure to discipline time and keep up with the paperwork associated with administrative duties can be problematic. A part of this time should be devoted to updating current schedules and working on long-range scheduling plans, particularly if the facility is used by a number of different constituencies who need some advance notice of changes and/or alterations. Establish scheduling deadlines and enforce them.

6. In the morning, set up appointments that are necessary during the day with staff, maintenance people, aquatics director, sales representatives and other publics. Keep enough time between appointments to pick up on any spontaneous situations that may develop which need immediate attention.

7. Before leaving the office at the end of the day, communicate with the person(s) on the staff who will be remaining until the facility is closed. Be sure to advise them of any special changes in the schedule or areas that need attention. Also, advise them how you can be reached until the time the facility is closed.

The Shared Facility

Cooperative-based facility which was planned and built with consideration for several constituencies is an example of shared arrangement that is becoming common throughout the United States. Guilford College, a four-year liberal arts institution, and a local branch of the Metropolitan YMCA of Greensboro, North Carolina, entered into an arrangement for cooperative use of a facility.

The "town and gown" athletic center was conceived when representatives from the college and the local YMCA realized that each was considering building its own separate facility within a four-mile radius of each other. The College had decided to construct a new building to supplement its forty-year-old gymnasium which was inadequate and failed to meet the needs of the students. The Guilford College Community Branch of the YMCA, operating out of an elementary school, with little equipment and limited programs, also was trying to meet pressing needs for a building to house its operations. Conservative estimates predicted that it would take the YMCA close to 10 years to schedule and carry out the capital fund drive necessary to finance a $2.5 million structure. The' initial contacts from college administrators answered the YMCA's needs and it marked the beginning of years of research and planning. Both groups realized the waste of resources for the community to build two expensive sport/recreational facilities with two separate administrative staffs, since the buildings would be vacant part of the time.

The careful planning which followed helped create a structure that is both unique and functional in design. In addition to renovating the old gymnasium and creating additional locker room space, a $4 million structure was constructed and connected to the old facility. The 64,581-square-foot structure includes a 25-meter, six-lane pool with a separate diving tank, a weight room, locker and shower facilities, four handball and racquetball courts and a field house with three regulation basketball courts that can be converted to use for tennis and volleyball. There is seating for 2,500 persons.

The end result is a contractual situation where the college owns and operates its Physical Education Center facility, and then leases time and space to the YMCA based on 40% of the operating cost. The rent includes all utilities, maintenance, equipment and a percentage of the salary of staff people who serve both institutions such as the building director, front desk receptionists, lifeguards and equipment desk employees.

In similar situations, a full commitment by both institutions, particularly the staffs, is an absolute must. There is little chance for success if anyone is not fully committed to the belief that the decision to share the facility is best for both institutions. With this in mind, all parties involved in the relationship need to maintain sensitivity and flexibility necessitated by the uniqueness of the situation.

Secondly, there is a distinct need for planning and putting everything in writing. The planning process includes asking the endless list of "what if' questions and establishing specific guidelines for priority usage. Putting everything in writing helps to keep all the related boards and committees informed and ensures that all policies are correctly interpreted before becoming effective. This includes the drafting, development and eventual signing of a contract between the two groups which covers the specifics of budget, budget review, staff, insurance and payment schedules.

Finally, it is important to employ a building director to oversee the operation and scheduling of the facility. The facility director is necessary to provide an objective approach to scheduling, and he or she can eliminate possible conflicts, ensure a more functional use of the facility, and administrate the operation of the building and its staff.

The joint utilization of the Physical Education Center has not been without its scheduling, security and coverage complications, but the cooperative arrangement has unquestionably resulted in the following accomplishments:

1. The center, open for 92 hours per week, is fully staffed and utilized with very little "down" time. The building is open a great deal more than either group could afford through separate staffing.
2. The joint utilization serves to bring the community and college into closer contact through a variety of scheduled programs and intercollegiate events. The citizens of the community come onto the campus and therefore feel a part of the college through the YMCA. For example, the YMCA is encouraged to enter teams in the college intramural leagues, and the college offers football and basketball season tickets at a reduced rate to YMCA members.
3. Although it is difficult to assess the actual cost savings, each group is undoubtedly saving a great deal compared to the cost to operate separate buildings. This is accomplished through the sharing of the daily operational costs (staff, pool maintenance, utilities, housekeeping supplies, work-study student labor, athletic equipment and towels).
4. The YMCA is able to offer and supervise summer programs in which college students and the college community may participate without

having to supply a full complement of staff. Due to the operation of these programs, many summer jobs are available to students in summer school and those living in the area.

Both the college and the YMCA not only endorse this concept of shared facilities, but also highly recommend it to any groups where this type of cooperation might be feasible. With the rising cost of construction and maintenance of athletic facilities, it is expedient for all to work together to reduce costs. To the YMCA, the cooperative agreement is vital as it provides a home for its members and programs. To the college, the arrangement is a way of providing expanded hours and a first-class facility to its students, staff and community. This situation is the first example of a cooperative venture planned from the beginning. The practicality of the venture represents a possible option to the traditional use of sports facilities in the past.

Summary/Conclusion

Budgeting pressures and increased use of activity centers place additional burdens on the facility manager, necessitating greater efficiency in planning and overseeing total use.

The facility manager must formulate or have a strong voice in formulating a fair policy as to use. Once in force, the policy must be adhered to by all users. Complaints must be formalized before policy changes are considered by the manager.

While the manager must deal with day-to-day matters, careful long- and short-range planning is essential to a smooth, ongoing operation.

The scheduling of space is critical, with priorities clearly defined and followed. An excellent way in which the manager can both demonstrate to a client and give quick answers to requests for space is to maintain master sheets and a large chalkboard in his/her office for easy referral. Once legitimate requests for ongoing space needs have been plugged into the schedule, and time and space are allotted for the "spontaneous user," that information should be printed and made available to all users of the facility. The facility's policymaking body must sharply define qualifications and fees for rental of space. The facility manager must provide adequate staffing for events staged by rental groups; this insures control of the facility.

The facility manager must, by his/her actions, set a "style" of leadership which should filter down throughout the staff. Job descriptions for subordinates should be written out and discussed with potential employees to avoid misunderstandings as to expectations of either party. This is especially true when a manager in a college setting hires students.

Since it is impossible for the manager to personally supervise all activities in the facility, he/she must employ extremely capable and dependable persons for key areas. This is particularly true if the facility has that "attractive nuisance," a swimming pool. Also, it is important to employ a staff member who, is not tied to a desk or phone and who can handle problems as they arise.

A facility's budget and design should determine its security program. In planning security measures, get advice from experts, and incorporate their suggestions into the building design. Consider pros and cons of uniformed versus non-uniformed security personnel. Choose identification or membership cards which best suit your budget and physical layout. Keep close reign on keys for efficient control. "Lost" keys can be copied quickly and may necessitate the changing of all locks.

The activity center manager must be sensitive to and involved with the maintenance and efficient upkeep of the facility. If the facility is not clean and well-kept, it will neither attract nor hold users. Plan ahead for upkeep such as painting and refurbishing. Remember that the use of outside maintenance firms will require scheduling well in advance.

The effective manager must be accessible to deal with problems that arise; check with employees about "comfort" items such as space and water temperatures; be prepared for special events and the eventuality of putting rainy days schedules into effect; check messages and calendar of events; make appointments with staff and other publics; before leaving for the day, check with staff who will work until they close the facility for the night.

Before entering into a venture in which a facility is to be shared by two organizations, proceed with caution. Visit a facility such as the one at Guilford College, where the college owns the facility and leases time and space to the YMCA. From the beginning of talks, get everything out in the open, and when there is agreement as to sharing and operation, have everything in writing. Then, chances are excellent that a successful cooperative venture awaits.

Appendix 1

P.E. Center Space Request Form

Date of Request:_____

Name of Sport or Group: _____

Person Representing Group:_____

Dates Requested: From _____ To _____

Times Requested: _____

Space(s) Needed:_____

Number of Participants: _____

Spectators: Yes___ No ___ Estimated Number _____

Special Details: _____

_____

_____

Laundry Needs: Training Room Needs: _____

Person(s) Responsible for Take Down and/or Clean Up: _____

_____

_____

SPACE MUST BE REQUESTED AT LEAST TWO WEEKS IN ADVANCE

Chapter 22

The Facility Manager as Co-Promoter of Events

James Oshust

Introduction

The expression "to promote" or "to co-promote" is often used incorrectly. Any facility that charges a percentage rental, or that derives the majority of its business from a percentage of event ticket grosses is in fact a "semipartner," in a manner of speaking, with the lessee. The facility and its management are in fact involved in the event. They are, along with the promoter, striving for the greatest amount of gross ticket sales possible. The only difference appears to be in the attitude and awareness of the lessor in the lessee (promoter) expense side of the ledger.

Contractual Relationships

Among the possible contractual relationships between lessor and lessee are the following types.

A. Co-promotion

In co-promotion, most often, a larger rental percentage is garnered by the facility, and within that larger percentage the facility's management has agreed to bear certain costs. Reasonable examples could be a 15 to 20% rental, with the facility charging no additional monies for box office services, purchase of tickets, stagehands or maintenance, etc.

True, there is some gamble, since the show's attendance might be disastrously poor and the additional percentage may turn out to be well below what it cost to provide those previously guaranteed services. Yet, there is the other side of the coin when a show does very well and the three to eight percent margin gross is far more than normally would have been charged the lessee for these services, leaving management with an appreciable amount of additional revenue.

B. A Promotion or Promoted Event

In a promoted event the facility actually engages in guaranteeing or purchasing outright the event in question. Possibly a 60-40, or 50-50 split is incurred, but the facility may actually have to put some of the money up in advance for deposits for the act's services, or during the settlement finds itself paying more out than its incoming share of the gross ticket receipts might have been. Like any business gamble, however, these are the alternatives, win or lose.

C. Buying or Creating Events

It is possible for a facility to buy or create an event which utilizes no middle person or has no involvement with the promoter, where the relationship is directly with the act or service or agency. A facility may also develop events such as a large "flea market" in an exhibition hall where the partners of the facility, private citizens, actually do the physical work and utilize their expertise. The facility provides the back-up service crews, utilities, space and fiscal guarantees. Then the two groups share all surpluses above all in preagreed expenses. In certain cases, where the facility provides all the personnel to operate an event it in fact becomes the lessor and lessee, one "in toto."

The facility manager must accept this fact: the arrangement agreement determines the role and thereby the responsibilities. He or she gives up certain prerogatives as the pure "lessor figure," and must accept some of the responsibilities, the difficulties, complexities, work level and efforts of the promoter or show booker. Details that previously were never the concern of the facility manager now become part of the required list of things to be done. The evening of the event there is no "guaranteed rent" or lack of liability. The bottom line of the settlement becomes extremely important for it truly indicates whether the facility has "won or lost."

It is vital that once the manager agrees that his facility will co-promote, or promote, or in some other fashion risk monies or possible revenues, that the manager understands that he has assumed the role of a partner, producer or promoter. One should not be overly impressed by the fact that some buildings will often "co-promote" or be recognized as management known to "promote" many events. To do so is to assume a role and an obligation that may not be desirable. Such a role assumption is to join into a very close relationship with another individual, organization or activity. An observer once remarked that in his hometown it was often said that certain marriages were made in heaven but what confused him was that the divorce court was still located on the first floor of the courthouse. Such is true with any partnership for it is necessary for anyone entering into such a relationship as an event partner to recognize that too often the expression friendship is confused with or considered to be synonymous with partnership.

A partnership is a legal entity created by joining, according to the law, two mutual interests. The law says nothing about the two groups or individuals being compatible, likable, capable of being friends with one another or having anything other than a legally endowed relationship. So be careful when selecting a partner.

Cautions in Co-Promotion

The following things should be considered before entering into co-promotions.

Determine if in fact a partnership with another individual or entity, company or building is a possibility. State statutes or local ordinances may preclude such a relationship. Many facilities are owned by cities which are in themselves municipal corporations and as such are creatures of the state. Such entities may prohibit one department of the city from enter in type of agreement with another non-municipally controlled entity outside the jurisdiction of the government in question.

Before asking the city attorney or assigned legal representative about this matter, prepare a "brief" of sorts. It should explain in concise terms what is being proposed, how many such activities, the extent of such possible involvement, the desired end results, and how such involvement would vary from your current practices or procedures.

Participate in the writing and developing of any agreement between management and another entity. It is not necessary to be versed in the "legalese" of modern contract law, but it is important to assure the document will not expose you to the unexpected. If the arrangement is to promote an event, will the relationship be as the buyer of the product and/or artist and/or service; or as the distributor of that talent or service to the general public; or is the role one of a vehicle for the artist and/or act, service or promoter to appear or to be used in the facility?

Develop an atmosphere of mutual understanding between management and your staff as well as other pertinent governmental agencies or individuals essential to security endorsement for such "involvement." Make certain they understand the purpose for the involvement and the benefits to be realized. Perhaps a small-scale involvement would be best, serving as a sample of the type activity, rather than a large promotion that could lose several thousands or more dollars, and thus ruin any future participation in such activities. Make each and every member of the management staff an integral part of the "co-promotion" or "promoting" effort.

Regardless of the type of facility, its structure or organizational design, a co-promotion or partnership exists both in the sharing of loss as well as the sharing of any profit. Be cautious of those very "nice terms" wherein 50% of all the proceeds are offered. It is possible that the contract contains provisions that are contrary to assumptions. The difference between reality and expectancy can be expensive.

For example, a young building manager signed a "promotion agreement with a small family-styled show." The terms were excellent inasmuch as they reflected a 50-50 split after agreed-upon advertising costs, facility costs and other items. In his desire to do well, the young manager exceeded the advertising budget by some $1,500 but felt that surely the increased business generated by the sixth performance justified the action. What the young manager found was that he had actually committed himself for payment of at least three meals for the company of some 30 persons, engagement, and the $1,500 additional advertising expense. The promoter had not agreed to share the costs.

Furthermore, the "co-promotion" contract called for certain standard fees to be paid by the building-partner, which included not only local stagehands, but all technical and nonperforming personnel in the company—far greater than the so-called "heads of departments" as might be charged by the ice show or circus or other such major sustaining family events now on the road. When the final settlement was computed, the young manager recognized that although he had received 50% of the revenue, he had in fact absorbed some of the costs, almost a third of which were actually show-related costs and should have been paid by his partner. In this fashion the partner may have received a lesser amount than he might have on a "standard contract" rate, but his partner acquired a contract where the building picked up almost 50% of the show's ongoing operational costs. The net available to the show was far higher than the building's standard contract deal.

It is possible to give an appearance of having been co-promoters of an event when actually serving as a highly skilled professional and comprehensive specialist in the handling of certain details for the lessee. In this role a facility can perform all of the advertising and much of the promotion and publicity duties for the show and be paid for the services. Also the facility arranges for all staffing, stagehands, special material requests, catering if desired and will even handle certain financial arrangements such as submitting necessary artist's payment checks, divisions or split of the revenue to the pertinent parties concerned, including sound and lighting company billings. It is possible to provide extended services like stage and production requirements and other special needs of the event. In this way the facility is very much involved in the event, desires its success greatly and still reaps the greatest amount of revenue for the least amount of risk. This system has been quite popular with a number of promoters since it lessens their initial out-of-pocket expense, modern-day credit requirements and particularly their personnel's time to "work the city."

In any such arrangements, however, the needs of the lessee should be carefully spelled out. Facility management should address itself to responsibility for certain tasks and the methods of reimbursement and compensation, particularly in the case of event cancellation. If the facility has systems or procedures for the fulfilling of lessee needs, management is in a much better position to write those types of terms necessary to protect the facility from unnecessary loss or imprudent acceptance of liability.

Need for Guidelines

Although there is no sure formula for success in the fields of partnerships and co-promotions, the following cautions might be of assistance when dealing with the obstacles of inference, irrationality, emotion, public pressure, economic concerns and the very nature of the facility business—that of providing a forum for the presentation of increasingly popular spectator events.

A. Know the Proposed Associate

Such firms as Better Business Bureau, Dun & Bradstreet, fellow facility managers, various legal authorities, police departments, governmental investigative agencies, the trade journals and court records are all sources of information concerning who or what you are being asked to join with on a particular venture.

B. Require the Prospective Partner or "Associate" to Submit Information Concerning His or Her Background

The use of an application for lease form is proper since it allows you the chance to review pertinent data which constitutes the entity who wishes to join with the facility in partnership or co-promotion arrangement.

C. Take Sufficient Time to Consider and Implement a Partnership

Schedule the proposed event eight, ten or more weeks in the future and longer if possible. Don't accept the ploy, "You've got to move now or you will lose the event." Instead of making a hasty decision, offer to rent the facility at a standard card rate, and adopt procedures that allow for the normal introduction and implementation of such an event. If the event is so good, the procedure is more than adequate. Don't trade proven practice for "opportunity" represented to you by some individual of unknown quality.

D. Seek Legal Advice

As has often been stated, "The value of law lies not in the happiness it creates but rather the misery and the suffering it prevents." This is even more substantive in this instance because a partnership, co-promotion or promotion agreement constitutes a legally acceptable tie between two parties in the eyes of the court. Any resulting litigation will be fought in the courts, and by attorneys and all the data and information will be submitted in compliance with existing codes, ordinances, statutes and within the framework of judicially-required procedure and practice.

E. Participate in the Formation of the Contract

This is absolutely necessary so as to clearly define for the local legal counsel, those things that should be addressed. Once such an agreement has been developed and practiced, and procedures have been tested by time and situation, agreements without constant attendance by your attorney are possible. Yet, if a potential partner suddenly decides to vary from an accepted norm, contact your legal advisor.

F. Insistence Upon Communications with All Parties Involved in an Event Is Imperative

If building A is contracting with promoter or individual B to co-promote or partner with or assists in promoting an event featuring individual C. who may be represented by agency D, who may be working through the artist's personal representative individual E, make sure all those individuals or companies with whom the facility is, in fact, sharing the responsibility for possible loss, perform their functions properly by defining each party's role and detailing such understanding in writing.

G. Remember the Thin Line That Divides the Permanent Position as Facility Manager and the Assumed Role as Partner or Co-promoter or Promoter, or Agent of an Event

Most importantly, do not try to wear two hats at the same time. Particularly, do not try to be all things to all people and to "have it your way" regardless of what happens. If it is necessary to act in the capacity of a facility manager in certain instances, then so define those areas in the agreement. Furthermore, let the staff know that obligations accepted under the agreement must be fulfilled.

It is important to develop guidelines for all such relationships. Institute "stop guards" in the event plans go awry. Set fiscal limitations as to how much money may be drawn from the box office, who is to pay what portion of the performer's salary, when, and who is to be billed for or responsible for certain activities and materials or supplies, and what shall be the framework and sequence of time regarding the settlement of the show. It is impossible to maintain all the prerogatives of facility management and not be liable for any criticism and/or financial obligations that are inherent in co-promotion, promotion or partner arrangements for any event.

Special Event Promotion

Finally, there is the "special event" promotion that actually refers to one of the most important roles building management may assume. Aside from all the discussions of the traveling concert tours, "road shows," "major star events," there is often a very strong need for your involvement in those events that cannot muster or do not have the type of direction and/or impetus to allow them to be successful on their own.

The facility manager is an entertainment leader, director, expert and developer as well as activity implementer for the community. Groups, civic clubs, officials of government, novice promoters and others will seek advice, consultation and assistance. One important service is to help local groups resist the challenge and lure of promoting an event in the entertainment field for fund-raising purposes if such promotion is totally impractical, destined for failure, or totally out of character with the abilities of the group in question. The truly enjoyable part of the job is to help various groups acquire, develop and implement events within their fiscal resources, their promotional abilities and organizational needs.

From a selfish standpoint it is simply good business to provide such assistance. Expertise and encouragement can give the facility another event—one which is oriented to the community and can prove very successful not only from a revenue standpoint but from "polishing" if not increasing the professional image of the facility.

Summary/Conclusion

Like all such complex activities the facility manager must determine the ground rules acceptable to both parties. He must document the ground rules in writing. And, most important of all, he must adhere to the ground rules on a continuing basis. Inconsistency is the fatal flaw that will ruin any good promotion. There is no such thing as allowed inconsistency under the law. The law views inconsistency as the fault of one party or another in failing to meet his/her part of an agreement.

Co-promotions, promotions, partnerships and the development of certain events in the name of the facility should be approached as the most exciting and exhilarating part of the facility management profession. Despite the potential returns to be realized, cooperative ventures should be selected with great care.

There are times when either the knowledge of certain event is insufficient, or financial odds are relatively in favor of the facility. At times the undertakings would become too great a burden. The number and kind of special arrangements to be entered into should receive very careful consideration. If you know your facility, understand your market area and have the confidence of your employer, the involvement in promoted or co-promoted events offers a challenge and a sense of accomplishment for all concerned.

Chapter 23

Event Management: Tools of the Trade

Frank Russo

Introduction

There is a phenomenon that causes managers of public event facilities to recognize the importance and specialized nature of the role of the event manager. Each event must be managed; if not, it will assuredly mismanage itself. At one time the event manager simply coordinated activities prior to, during and following an event to ensure that equipment, physical setups and personnel were provided to meet all contractual requirements. Now, however, the event manager must become involved in many, if not all, of the following important tasks:

1. Scheduling and directing event, admission and crowd control staff, including ushers, ticket takers, security guards, private-duty policemen, firemen, and emergency medical service personnel;
2. Ensuring that tenants understand and comply with house policies and rules and regulations;
3. Making tenants fully aware of all that is involved in staging an event in the facility to avoid surprises, hidden costs and arguments. This is usually best handled at a production meeting with the tenant;
4. Developing, implementing and monitoring emergency operations and evacuation procedures; and
5. Ensuring compliance by all tenants of federal, state and local fire, building, and life safety codes.

During an event many things occur simultaneously that must be coordinated and managed. The box office, which is often the only contact many patrons will have with a facility, is open and in full operation. The concessions department sells food, beverage and merchandise. Security concerns itself with admission and crowd control and the ushering of people quickly and safely to their seats. The facility crew puts the final touches on the event setup and keeps all public areas free of debris, trash and obstructions. The engineering department makes sure that the Heating, Ventilation and Air Conditioning (HVAC) system is working properly so that everyone is comfortable, monitors the life-safety systems and also responds to such mundane tasks as repairing a plugged toilet or leaking faucet. Meanwhile, stagehands and other technical crew members are tending to a variety of details necessary to successfully stage the event.

Since the coordination and management of a facility is complex, a clearly established liaison between the tenant, the public and building management is critical. This responsibility often falls on the event manager.

The event manager is responsible for the protection of the per well as the physical plant and, most importantly, the well-being of the attending public. The balance of this chapter is an attempt to provide practical information for developing a comprehensive plan that will cover all these areas of responsibility. The emphasis will be on how to manage events rather than constantly reacting to one crisis after another.

Radio Communication — A Critical Tool of the Trade

A key to successful event management is a properly functioning radio communications system since total and instant communication, in certain situations, may mean the difference between life and death.

If a radio system is not available, it is advisable to contact local police, fire or civil preparedness department for guidance.

In an operational radio system, there are basic radio usage rules that should be followed:

1. Radios and pagers should be for business use only.
2. Since the number of radios and pagers being used by various personnel places limitations on air time, transmissions should be concise and any unnecessary conversation should not be tolerated.
3. Because Federal Communications Commission (FCC) regulations govern all language on the air, use of profane and/or obscene language and derogatory remarks should be strictly forbidden.
4. Because they are very costly to replace or repair, radios should be placed in holsters and not carried by hand. Microphones connected to the radio make this easy and very convenient. Also, earphones make it possible to hear even during a loud concert.
5. A code system to communicate critical information should be developed and all security personnel should be required to memorize and use it. Such a code system should be developed for the following types of situations:
   Fire (specify location)
   Bomb Threat (discussed in more detail later in this chapter under Security and Emergency Procedures Manual)
   Medical Emergency (specify location)
   Engineering Emergency (specify kind and give location)
   Elevator Emergency
   Telephone Fire Department
   Telephone Police Department (specify need, i.e., police or ambulance)
   Accident (specify location)
   Disturbance and/or Breach of Peace (specify location)
   Assistance Needed (specify location)
   Return to Headquarters
   Telephone Headquarters or Other (specify)
   Try to Locate (usually a person)

Assignment to a Certain Area or Check of a Certain Area
Discovery of Something of a Suspicious Nature (specify location)
Stand by for an Announcement (emergency pending)
Resume Normal Activity
Sign on the Air
Sign off the Air (give location)
Testing Radio Equipment
Break

Architectural and Physical Considerations

Thomas Minter, currently the Manager of the Lexington, Kentucky, Civic Center, stated to the International association of Auditorium Managers that "security begins on the drawing board." He observed that many problems can be avoided by proper design and planning of public facilities. This notion is supported by Don Jewell in his book, *Public Assembly Facilities: Planning and Management 124* (New York: John Wiley and Sons, 1978), when he states that "safety begins with good architectural planning." Jewell correctly points out that while such considerations are well covered by governmental building and fire codes, to some extent management's need to guard the entrances and exists to restricted or ticketed areas may be in conflict with rapid evacuation in emergency circumstances. Careful planning by the architect in cooperation with your management team and state and local fire officials as well as the facility's insurance representative (risk manager) will do much to prevent serious operational and public safety problems. But, the process does not end here.

Because you are morally—and legally—responsible for public safety, ensuring public safety is an ongoing process which requires constant inspections of the physical plant to make sure that all hazards and potential hazards are eliminated before the public arrives.

Another architectural/physical consideration is Thomas Minter's recommendation that a facility be zoned into "activity areas" as follows:

1. The "public area" is where the public may move about freely and have access to all public facilities, concession areas, first-aid services, restrooms, drinking fountains, facilities for the disabled and public telephones. These public accommodations should be available without requiring access by the public into other zones within the facility. They must also be provided in sufficient number so as to discourage public demand to exit and return through admission areas.

2. The "performance area" includes backstage and dressing facilities. These areas require separation from the audience and service areas as much as possible. Such physical separation greatly enhances the ability to provide privacy and security for the performers or athletes. The use of backstage passes for those persons necessary or desired in the back-of-the-house is mandatory if effective control is to be maintained.

3. The "service area" includes workshops, custodial and concessions supply rooms, the shipping and receiving entrance, utility rooms, and equipment storage areas. The service area can most effectively be secured when performer and public access is restricted. Employee theft

can best be reduced and general order and inventory control maintained if this area is further restricted to only those persons actively employed by your facility.

4. "Support personnel areas" include police and security offices and the first-aid station. These areas should be adjacent to public areas but have access to the back-of-the-house entrance in order that those persons who serve the public may enter and leave without public surveillance, as well as allowing for removal from the facility of those who require medical attention or police detention.

Admission and Building Access Control

Only persons who have purchased a ticket or have been given authorized passes should gain entry to the facility.

Admissions control actually begins in the box office with the ticket itself Tickets must be clearly printed on a type of safety stock to prevent counterfeiting. The ticket must allow the staff to quickly check the event, date and performance time, as well as the section, row and seat number(s). Admissions-control personnel should be trained to spot strange-looking tickets. Tickets should obviously be printed by a reputable and bonded ticketing company that ships them with the audited manifest directly to the box office to be counted, racked and distributed under direct control. An alternative to this, of course, is computerized ticketing, which may offer even greater control.

Most admission-type events fall into two basic categories: "general admission" which permits a person to sit in any available seat on a first-come, first serve basis, and "reserved seating" which provides patrons with a specific seating location.

It is advisable to open the doors to the facility approximately one hour and fifteen minutes prior to the scheduled starting time. This will allow patrons adequate time to find their seating location, go to the restroom, purchase a snack, socialize, and get settled before the event begins,

It is important to constantly monitor the size and mood of a crowd in the lobby and outside the facility before the doors are opened. Have an adequate number of ticket takers and turnstiles to allow the crowd to enter in a quick and orderly fashion. Prior to opening the doors, however, the event manager should conduct a radio check to ensure that the performers and the house staff are ready for the public. The ticket takers should be supported by a supervisor, a "customer relations representative" to handle problems, and adequate numbers of security guards and policemen to handle trouble and/or to supervise a search and seizure operation. The duties and responsibilities of the admission control staff are discussed in more detail later in this Chapter.

There should be a system for admitting people to the facility that do not have tickets. Many facilities use a photo ID system which provides one of the best means of identifying persons with legitimate business. Employees, show personnel, and service contractors do not have an inherent right to be at an event. A system of IR's and backstage passes designed to restrict entry is absolutely critical to building security and safety.

Crowd Management

In any crowd situation a risk to public safety is inherent and cannot be totally eliminated. While no facility can anticipate all the situations which might lead to disorder, cooperation between the facility management staff and promoters, agents, performers, admissions control staff, security, police, fire and government officials will do a great deal to minimize risks.

Crowd management requires *always* being prepared for the worst. The worst happened at Cincinnati's Riverfront Coliseum on December 3, 1979. Thousands of patrons were awaiting admission to a concert to be played by the "Who," a very popular rock group. General admission with festival seating had been established for the event. The anxious crowd (which was held outside the building until just before the concert was to begin) mistook the sounds of musicians warming-up as the opening of the concert and rushed the door. Eleven people died and eleven more were injured. The situation was not riotous or out of control and the deaths were senseless. But this, more than any other occurrence in recent memory, graphically shows the need for advance planning, precautions and sensitivity to people who buy tickets for events. Regardless of the size of the crowd, proper management is essential to minimizing and hopefully preventing unsafe situations. The tragedy promoted a careful study by the City of Cincinnati. Recommendations presented in *The Report of the Task Force on Crowd Control and Safety* are given below.

1. There should be clearly defined and published house policies which should be followed for each event. The facility management staff should be clearly in charge and ensure compliance with all laws, house rules and regulations, health standards and common sense practices.
2. Carefully evaluate the effects of the sale of alcohol. If necessary, place a security person, or preferably a uniformed policeman, at the sales outlet.
3. Clearly define the chain of command and the duties and responsibilities for the event manager, as well as all policemen, security guards, ushers and usherettes, ticket takers and first-aid personnel. Be sure they are constantly trained on how to properly react in an emergency situation.
4. Encourage patrons to report dangerous and threatening situations.
5. Avoid general admission ticketing and seating if at all possible.
6. Carefully plan the sale of tickets, especially when the demand will greatly exceed the supply. Develop a fair and equitable distribution system. Control your lines. Treat the crowds well and courteously. Do not allow line cutting. A wristband ID system works well here. And if necessary to ensure fairness, establish a maximum number of tickets each customer may purchase. And if it appears that some people in line will not reach the box office before the event is sold out, let them know as soon as possible and do not allow any more people to stand in line.
7. Conduct search and seizure to confiscate bottles, cans and other items which may be used to injure others.
8. Establish legal attendance capacities for each event setup, and obtain the written approval of the fire marshal and building inspector. Also, designate handicap wheelchair-locations in a manner least likely to cause them to serve as obstructions in case of an emergency evacuation.

9. Pay close attention to the architectural plans and designs of your facility. Do not allow illegal and dangerous obstructions. Be careful where you place your turnstiles. Make sure your graphics system works to your advantage and to the crowd's advantage by helping them get to their seats and other conveniences and exits as quickly and safely as possible.
10. Develop an emergency evacuation plan.

Some other comments and observations by the Cincinnati Task Force worth noting here are:

1. A clean, well-maintained building and a hassle-free atmosphere will do much to reduce crowd tension.
2. Be in control of the stage and the attraction. Do not allow the attraction to overly or dangerously excite a crowd.
3. Before and after an event and during intermission, play soft, soothing music.
4. Do not turn the lights off completely. Allow at least three foot-candles of light to illuminate aisles and emergency exits.
5. Keep people without floor tickets off the floor.
6. Keep aisles clear.
7. Make sure the public address system works and that its volume and clarity are adequate.

The International Association of Auditorium Managers (IAAM) established the IAAM Foundation. The first major project to be undertaken by the Foundation will be a crowd management study. The project is an outgrowth of years of behind-the-scenes planning and research on the part of Dr. Robert Sigholtz, the Foundation's first Chairman, and Dr. Irving Goldaber, an internationally known sociologist, specializing in the study of social violence.

The first phase of the project calls for a comprehensive review of crowd control literature, supplemented by the combined field experience of facility managers within the IAAM.

Goldaber recently stated that:

Crowd management encompasses all that is undertaken by professional personnel in the public assembly field to facilitate the comfort and safety and lawful nature of crowd gatherings so that those in attendance may have satisfying experiences. Crowd management activity occurs in both the inner administrative office and the outer public parking lot. It focuses, for example, on aspects of executive decision-making, managerial expertise, supervisory responsibility, public relations, patron services, traffic regulations and safety and security. It includes among its concerns such matters as architecture and interior design, food and other items either provided or vended to those present, and the sociological capability to read "the mood of the crowd." An effective crowd management approach begins with the first blueprint for the event or assemblage and ends when the last patron has vacated the area. For this reason, crowd management deals with planning, preparing, conducting and taking remedial action. It is the sum of all that is undertaken to obviate the need for crowd control action involving forcible restraint.

Crowd Violence

A growing problem in facilities throughout the United States is that of crowd or spectator violence, especially at rock concerts which attract large numbers of young people. Often there is a metamorphosis that occurs when certain fans go through the turnstiles. They virtually abandon the constraints normally placed upon them by society and feel totally free to act in an uninhibited manner, including the physical destruction of property, physical threats and other antisocial behavior.

Contributing factors to crowd violence, according to Goldaber, involve a number of low-level sources of tension including close and involuntary contact with strangers, abnormal physical discomfort, and competition for space, goods, services and information. These tend to frustrate fans and make them more irritable and belligerent than they are when they are alone or in smaller groups. Crowds also provide a degree of anonymity which encourages troublemakers to act more irresponsibly than they might in situations where they can easily be identified and punished.

Everything possible should be done to make the facility hassle free and comfortable. A fact of life is that large public assembly facilities—and sport facilities in particular—when compared to those offered to other crowds, are often somewhat inefficiently designed, uncomfortable and unattractive. This atmosphere and the fast and easy flow of such basic emotions as elation, anger, panic and vengeance are contagious within a crowd and may create so-called mass hysteria. Moreover, sporting events regularly draw the largest crowds of any public event.

People lose control when they identify so fully with an athlete or a team that they begin feeling physically aggressive. Crowds at sporting events regularly respond by cheering, booing, hissing, stamping their feet, waving their fists, screaming, and threatening and yelling at officials.

One problem in particular offers facilities a serious dilemma. Because competition for events is becoming greater and facilities are forced to offer overly competitive rent deals, the facilities must exploit their concessions and other ancillary sources of income in order to make a profit. The sale of alcoholic beverages unquestionably contributes to fan violence and crowd disorders. Yet, beer, wine and cocktails are perhaps the most profitable items a facility sells. The facility manager must therefore exercise close and constant care in the monitoring of the alcoholic beverages sales and be prepared to call them to a halt when necessary—even if it means giving up an extremely lucrative source of revenue.

Another problem which complicates your ability to manage a crowd is violence on the part of professional athletes. Richard B. Horrow is the author of *Sports Violence—The Interaction Between Private Law-Making and The Criminal Law* (Carrollton Press, Inc., 1980), in which Horrow emphasizes the alarming trend toward excessive violence in all professional sport. The well-known comedian, Rodney Dangerfield once quipped that he "went to a fight the other night and saw a hockey game break out." As athletes become more competitive and as the pressures to succeed become stronger, the possibility of violent conduct during a game increases, and this causes a spontaneous reaction with the crowd. Athletes are taught to be aggressive and to be tough because one of the skills of sport is violence. The fans expect and demand violence, and the players themselves accept the fact that many less talented players must be more violent to compensate for inferior talent.

If violence erupts on the playing surface, the security team should be prepared to respond. For instance, they should be watching the crowd and not the event. They should be polite but firm with any troublemakers who, if uncooperative, must be ejected.

One way to effectively manage a crowd and contain violence is to conduct an advanced assessment of the anticipated audience. This will help decide on the necessary level of security staffing. The event manager must bear in mind that security requirements are not the same for all events. Each event has its own particular personality and should be considered separately from all others. Obtain as much advance information as possible about the audience and the performers and then plan and be prepared. Good sources of information are counterparts at other facilities where the event was already held. They can describe the nature of the crowd and how it reacted during the event. The box office is also a good source of such information, since it has already had contact with part of the crowd during the ticket-buying process. The local police department should also check with its counterpart in other cities to determine what type of criminal activities and disorders occurred.

Security and Emergency Procedures Manual

There is no substitute for well-trained security staff. The most basic training tool for security personnel is a written manual covering as many pertinent topics as possible in plain and simple language. Use the manual to welcome and indoctrinate your security personnel. Emphasize that they are there to provide professional service on behalf of the facility. The manual can provide security personnel with guidelines and help them be alert and safety conscious.

The manual should contain a clear written outline of the chain of command in your facility. Moreover, it should describe what is expected of the security staff. For example, security officers should:

1. Be able to handle any normal situation which they may encounter and know how or where to get help if required.
2. Be alert at all times while on duty. Always be on the watch for activities, conditions or hazards which could result in injury or damage to activities, conditions or hazards which could result in injury or damage to persons or property.
3. Have an attitude that reflects proper human and public relations.
4. Be helpful. When fans arrive at an event they are usually confused. The location is unfamiliar and they are often late and do not know where to go or what to do.
5. Be courteous but firm at all times.
6. Properly obey and execute all orders given by superiors.
7. Take pride in their duties and maintain a keen interest in their job. This will show in the manner in which they perform their duties and will be recognized by all who come in contact with them.
8. Act without haste or undue emotion. Do not argue with visitors, fellow employees, or supervisors. Present a calm friendly bearing.
9. Remember that courtesy earns respect, knowledge gets results, patience receives cooperation, service increases good will, and the total application of these qualities gets the job done well.

Written procedures are one thing, but if they are not read, understood and carried out by the people on the front line they are meaningless. Such service will be exemplified on their part by the use of tact, friendliness and courtesy while maintaining a professional attitude in the performance of their duties. Let them also know that they are important members of your professional crowd management team.

Given these general expectations, the manual should also contain a section on the specific duties and responsibilities of each job classification:

A. Usher Supervisor

The usher supervisor should supervise, not usher. This means that he or she will be free to respond to problem areas. Each event should have an appropriate number of supervisors assigned according to the total number of ushers being used and the anticipated size of the crowd. Supervisors should be alert for any problems or unusual difficulties encountered by any usher under his or her supervision and offer assistance and advice if needed.

B. Usher

An usher, on the other hand, has the primary responsibility for making certain the patron is assisted to the proper seat. In addition, an usher should:

1. Be certain that each patron is properly greeted.
2. Check each ticket completely for event, date, performance time, as well as section, row and seat.
3. Offer clear directions to seating locations and service accommodations.
4. Act on customer complaints. If necessary, refer complaints to the Usher Supervisor.
5. Keep aisles clear at all times.
6. Ask patrons to surrender any bottles or cans in their possession. If necessary, refer such a problem to the Usher Supervisor or a policeman.
7. Try to anticipate problems and act before they become serious.
8. Enforce house policies such as "no smoking."
9. Use a flashlight to assist patrons to their seats when the lights are down.
10. Be sensitive to the needs of mobility-impaired people such as senior citizens and handicapped persons.

C. Event Security Officer

The event security officer is a key figure in the safety of each facility. He or she is a figure representing authority and safety to the various patrons and visitors of your facility. Their professionalism and courteous attitude will make your patrons feel they are in good hands. By an officer's presence alone, potential trouble situations may be avoided. Specifically, the security officer is responsible for the following:

1. Reporting on time and ready to work.
2. Wearing the proper and complete uniform.
3. Following instructions by reading and memorizing post orders.
4. Remaining at an assigned post until relieved.

5. Exhibiting proper courtesy at all times.
6. Not eating, drinking or smoking while on duty.
7. Being alert to minors possessing alcoholic beverages.

Another key element of the manual is the section on emergency procedures. For this portion of the manual you should solicit the input and written approval of the state and local fire marshal, police and civil preparedness departments, and your contractual medical and ambulance services.

The most common form of emergency is the bomb threat. The manual should, therefore, describe the role of employees, as well as the overall emergency evacuation procedure. Employees should be instructed to cover assigned areas carefully when requested to make a search, noting any unusual package or item. If one is found, they should be instructed not to touch it, but to notify the supervisor immediately.

In case of the necessity to evacuate the facility, event security officers should follow any instructions given very carefully. They should always remain calm and in command of their area, never using any panic-producing language such as "bomb," "fire," or "explosion." Many lives may depend on their calm and efficient actions.

Many facilities use the Phase Coding System which was designed as a safe method of conveying to event personnel the type of problem, location and action to be taken without alarming any members of the general public that happen to overhear radio transmissions, phone conversations, or person-to-person communication. The purpose of this coding is to prevent the greatest of all threats—panic.

The Phase System is an escalating and compartmentalized plan to help prevent another great threat—overreaction, while simultaneously informing all necessary personnel of the type, location and current status of the problem.

Phase 1A indicates smoke, water, a small crowd disturbance, or an equipment or lighting failure. Descriptive information should be provided on the location, size, seriousness and nature of the problem. Security should clear the immediate area until the problem has been controlled.

Phase 1B indicates a bomb threat has been received and all staff should immediately conduct a search for an explosive device. Notification should be given when the search is completed.

Phase 2A indicates a serious fire, flood, crowd disturbance, equipment failure or other problem. Security should be posted at the location of the problem and control access to the area.

Phase 2B indicates that a suspicious package or device has been located. The fire department and police bomb squad should be dispatched to investigate and decide whether or not a full or limited evacuation is necessary. Ambulances should be called for standby.

Phase 3A indicates the need for an orderly evacuation due to failure of the regular power system. This will most likely result in the cancellation of the performance. An appropriate pre-recorded message should be activated over the public address system and ambulances should be called for standby.

Phase 3B indicates the need for an immediate emergency evacuation. Appropriate alarms must be sounded and pre-recorded messages activated. Ambulances should be called for standby and the security/usher staff should begin to calmly but firmly evacuate patrons. Security should also be sure no patrons re-enter the building, regardless of the reason.

The Facility Manager must take great care to clearly establish the chain of command when it comes to emergency evacuation. It must be clearly understood who has the right and responsibility to call for an evacuation. In most cities this responsibility is that of the ranking on-site member of the police bomb squad.

A way to ensure that proper procedures will be followed is to have a telephone bomb report form. If any member of the house or security staff takes a call during an event, this form or one very similar to it should be used and as much pertinent information as possible should be recorded and immediately conveyed to the event manager or police department.

Most people who actually put a bomb in a building want to be caught or want the bomb found before it goes off. If possible, keep the person talking because he/she may disclose the location of the bomb. Having the phone operator trained by the police bomb squad would be very helpful.

Preparation for emergency evacuation is absolutely critical. Drills should be conducted on a regular basis. A standardized routine should be developed for each type of event. Once the routine has been set, it should be typed and posted in strategic locations such as the office, the security room, the usher's locker room, backstage, lunch rooms and refreshment stands. The facility and its patrons are always vulnerable. The best defense is a plan carefully evolved to fit the facility and the organization. Being able to evacuate a facility in an emergency with a minimum of injury or loss of life is one of the greatest challenges and responsibilities.

Search and Seizure

The issue of search and seizure is a complex but important aspect of security and crowd management. Most facility managers believe the procedure is necessary in order to keep people from bringing beverage containers and weapons into facilities. But, each facility manager must be very cognizant of the requirements of the fourth amendment of the United States Constitution.

Normally, the event manager in conjunction with the facility manager and chief of police decide if a particular event (usually a rock concert) will draw a crowd of unruly patrons, many of whom will likely be in possession of bottles, cans, and other containers as well as assorted weapons and drugs. In such instances the facility's own security force and ticket takers must be supplemented by additional personnel to prevent these items from being brought into the facility. This relieves tension and protects people from being injured by objects used as missiles. But be sure to obtain sound legal advice from your attorney before you establish any procedures for search and seizure.

The September 1982 issue of Auditorium News (the official monthly publication of the International Association of Auditorium Managers) contained a very interesting article by Jerome O. Campane, a Special Agent of the FBI Academy, entitled "Amendment IV, The Fourth Amendment at a Rock Concert." The Article provides an enlightening update of the issue and offers some guidance on how to conduct a legal search and seizure operation. Campane indicates that the courts agree that civic authorities are entitled to take certain steps to prevent injury to the public and to provide protection for those who attend events by prohibiting the introduction of contraband and dangerous items. However, this cannot be done in a manner which violates a person's rights under Amendment IV, which states that 't It1he right of the people to be secure in their persons, houses, papers, and effects, against unreasonable searches and seizures, shall not be violated, and no warrants shall issue, but upon probable cause, supported by oath or affirmation, and particularly describing the place to be searched, and the persons or things to be seized." Therefore have an attorney provide you with written search and seizure guidelines—and perhaps even occasional on-site supervision.

Campane offers some practical advice on how to cope with the problem. For example, a notice on tickets and signs at your entrances will give the impression of voluntary consent. The availability of checkrooms for the deposit and safekeeping of large packages will also help, as will the elimination of festival seating which will avoid the rush through the turnstiles as doors first open, thus giving the security force a better opportunity to observe the patrons. When items are seized or arrests made, mass media publicity of the fact may help convince. patrons not to bring such prohibited items to future events. Above all, Campane states any procedure should be uniformly applied. It should not be employed only at rock concerts and only against teenagers. The facility manager should carefully document any incidents of violence and unruly behavior and apply this screening procedure at all events where such conduct is likely to take place. These procedures are obviously not all inclusive and again you are urged to meet with an attorney for specific guidelines regarding search and seizure procedures.

Summary/Conclusion

This chapter has provided the facility manager with a considerable amount of practical information that can be directly applied to his own operation. Because the business of facility management is exciting and because it is therefore, easy to get caught up in the "glamour" of the events hosted, it is sometimes possible to lose sight of the most important responsibility—protecting the lives of patrons. By preparing for the worst, the facility manager will make each event a professionally managed, safe and enjoyable experience for the public and the performers. This, more than any other factor, will enhance such a manager's reputation and assure the success of a facility.

Part 6

Legal Management

The most important task for sport administrators may be the most overlooked—legal management that includes the implementation of risk management strategies.

Herb Appenzeller

Chapter 24

Risk Assessment and Reduction

Herb Appenzeller

As we enter the 21st Century, litigation continues to plague the sport industry. Troublesome sport-related issues so common in the 1980s and 1990s continue to end up in court with enormous awards and damage to the reputation of an institution and its personnel. Today the issues are no longer just contract disputes or allegations of negligence in personal injury cases. There is a trend toward more diverse issues that have a tremendous impact on the sport industry and all who are associated with the multi-billion industry.

The authors of *Sport Law* observe that:

> One need look no further than the morning sports section to realize that law now has a rather profound influence on the world of sport. With labor law issues, contract issues, issues regarding the regulation of amateur athletics, antitrust issues regarding compensation for injuries and many other legal issues in the sport context, attorneys and judges are more than idle spectators at sporting events (Schubert, Smith and Trenadue, 1986).

Sport litigation involves athletes, administrators, athletic trainers, physicians, coaches, equipment manufacturers, officials, facility operators and even unsuspecting spectators. It seems that no one is immune from litigation today. It has been said that anyone can sue for anything. As a result of the escalation in sport-related lawsuits, the sport administrator (manager) has added a new responsibility to a growing list of duties. The sport administrator has the responsibility of meeting the challenge of risk management and risk reduction. The most important task for the sport administrator may be the most over-looked; legal management that involves the implementation of risk management strategies.

Risk Management Defined

Risk management has been described as asset management, asset protection and asset preservation. It has been associated with business and especially the insurance industry for many years. Loss control, exposure to loss, pre-and-post loss objectives, risk management strategies, and risk management techniques were common terms in both the business and insurance industry prior to the 1970s. In the mid-1970s and especially in the late 1990s and today's litigious world, risk management has become a "hot topic." Risk management became a familiar expression of a program designed to meet sport litigation head-on.

In simple terms, risk management is the practice of assessing the risks inherent in a sport program by the implementation of a safety audit. After the risks are identified, the sport manager should correct or eliminate the risks that exist in the program. A final step is to transfer the risk by acquiring medical or liability insurance to protect the participants, the institution and personnel of the program.

Sport Publications Reveal Trends In Litigation

The Society for the Study of Legal Aspects of Sport and Physical Activity (SSLASPA), an organization of legal scholars, attorneys and sport law professors, published a list of legal publications in the field of sports (SSLASPA, 1995). SSLASPA listed only five sport and law texts published in the 1970s. These texts included 1970 *From The Gym To The Jury*, H. Appenzeller; 1975 *Athletics and the Law*, H. Appenzeller; 1977 *Professional Sports and the Law*, Lionel Sobel; 1978 *Physical Education and the Law*, H. Appenzeller; and 1979 *The Law of Sports*, John Weistart and Cym Lowell. These books were published in response to litigation in sport begun in the 1960s. In the 1980s, when the number of lawsuits increased dramatically, publications in the field of sport and law increased to 43. In the 1990s, 38 texts were added to the profession. By 1995 the list of authors had grown from four in the 1970s to 117 who produced 89 texts. Statistics by SSLASPA revealed that by 1995 there were a total of seven sport law journals, 22 sport law newsletters, 12 professional periodicals and over 18 videos on a variety of sport law issues. The growth of sport and law publications was an attempt to meet the escalating litigation. It was and is today a desire to meet the needs of those associated with sport by reducing injuries and subsequent lawsuits against all who participate in the sport industry (SSLASPA, 1995).

With the increase of risk management in the sport industry, risk management texts became a reality in the 1990s and appear to be on the rise in the 21st Century. At the SSLASPA Conference in 2000, 80 presentations were scheduled and the majority dealt with risk management issues. The increase of risk management publications is predictable and will continue to dominate sport and law publications in the 21st Century.

Importance of Risk Management

Risks are inherent in sport and even the safest program will never avoid accidents and injuries. The fact that someone is injured does not automatically mean that someone is liable. The law does expect, however, that sport managers develop and implement loss control and risk management programs to ensure a safe environment for all who participate in sport activities.

Dr. Betty van der Smissen, a legal scholar and pioneer in sport law, explains the importance of risk management in the sport industry when she writes:

It becomes imperative that managers and administrators as well as policy boards of entities offering leisure and educational services affirmatively and aggressively give attention to the management of financial and programmatic risks to effectively reduce costs and enable desirable programs and services to be continued (van der Smissen, 1990).

Risk management is as important as budgeting, financial management, eligibility, scheduling, equipment control, insurance coverage, contracts, transportation, medical services, due process, facility management and other duties.

Ronald Baron, a sport law authority and Executive Director of the Center For Sports Law and Risk Management, sums up the importance of risk management when he writes:

> Risk management should help those who direct the sport program comply with their legal duties, provide safe programs and enable sport personnel to defend themselves and their programs in the event of a lawsuit (Baron, 1997).

What Is The Problem?

"An ounce of prevention is worth a pound of cure" still holds true and people recognize the importance of implementing a risk management plan. However, despite the need for such a plan, sport managers too often assign it a low priority. For example, a facility manager admitted that the implementation of a risk management plan could reduce the cost of her insurance premiums and save substantial money. She stated that while such a plan is a good idea, she would not spend money to save money. Her response, unfortunately is typical of others in the sport industry who understand the need and value of risk management but fail to develop a plan thereby exposing their program to financial loss. In all too many instances, safety audits and risk management plans are put in place only after severe injuries occur or a damaging lawsuit is filed. We react to the crisis rather than being proactive or creative in preventing catastrophic injuries and subsequent lawsuits. The key is prevention.

Areas of Concern

John Weistart and Cym Lowell, writing in the *Law of Sports*, point out that:

> The area of the law of sports which has received the most frequent analysis and which has received a correspondingly large body of decisional authority, is the liability which may result from injuries sustained in sports activities. The issues that are raised by the liability cases are actually broad, and the question presented by any given case is likely to fall within a very narrow applicable legal principle (Weistart and Lowell, 1979).

On the basis of numerous cases, it is safe to conclude that areas of concern for the sport administrator are (1) a lack of supervision, (2) incompetent instruction, (3) defective equipment and (4) unsafe facilities. Legal experts have added additional areas of concern since the publication of *Law and Sports* and consider the following as factors in risk management that involve litigation: insurance, medical, student rights and constitutional issues, transportation, discrimination and employment.

Dr. Gary Rushing, a legal scholar and risk management authority, developed a legal liability self-appraisal instrument for sport administrators to evaluate their sport programs. Rushing comments that:

the purpose of this self-assessment is to provide school personnel with a means to identify safety and legal liability problems related to the operation of the school's athletics program (Rushing, 2000).

He notes that:

an auxiliary benefit is the act of performing the assessment that should make the evaluator aware of problem areas and therefore less likely to neglect them (Rushing, 2000).

The self-appraisal instrument with its 188 objective statements is designed to reduce the risks in a sport program. The instrument is available in Chapter 25 of the text and is a practical method for a staff to test their knowledge of the areas of concern in a sport program. It creates an awareness of problems and an opportunity to correct them.

Diversity of Lawsuits

A look at a few captions of cases reported in *From The Gym To The Jury*, a sport law newsletter, indicates the diversity of today's lawsuits and enormous awards:

- Pool Drain Case Settled For $30.9 Million
- College Student Rendered Quadriplegic Receives $9,000,000
- Accident At Pool Results In Four Million Dollar Settlement
- Fall Off Jungle Gym: $500,000 Settlement
- Deaf Lifeguard Sues For $20 Million
- Failure To Warn Results In $3,500,000 Award
- Defective Railing In Gym Results In Wrongful Death Award of $1,400,000
- Collegiate Swimmer Crippled From Injury In Practice Settles For $7,600,000
- Injury On Mini-Trampoline Leads To Award Of $6,800,000
- Jury Awards Over $18 Million To Student Injured Before Volleyball practice
- Injured Student Sues For $52 Million: Awarded $23 Million (Appenzeller and Baron, 1997).

The suits are diverse and the awards have skyrocketed in the past few years. No one is certain how much awards will continue to escalate. A recent study of awards as reported in *From The Gym To The Jury* by the University of Houston Law School indicates that the average injury award is over $1.5 million (Fried, 1999).

Center for Sport Law and Risk Management

In 1987, I joined Ronald Baron and The Center For Sports Law and Risk Management (Center) as a special consultant. After 40 years of involvement in sport as a coach, athletic administrator, professor and director of sport management, I had the opportunity to actively put into practice, risk management strategies. This valuable opportunity to conduct risk reviews at all levels of sport gave me insight into the problems confronting all who are involved with sport at every level.

I now realize the importance of risk management on a first hand basis. The Center conducts risk reviews across the United States for elementary and secondary schools, colleges and universities, professional sports, venues, and municipalities. These clients have similar problems that we have seen over the years such as:

- Exit doors locked in sport arenas while events are in progress.
- A lack of policy dealing with potential catastrophic events such as fire, tornado, earthquake, or bomb threats.
- An absence of proper signs in swimming pools, weight rooms, playing fields, racquetball courts, bleachers, and other areas.
- A lack of informed consent agreements for participants in many schools
- A lack of emergency medical response plans for participants and spectators at sport events.
- Accident and injury reports worded in such a way that they cause problems in litigation.
- People with disabilities denied access to facilities in violation of federal law.
- A lack of expulsion policy for unruly spectators. Ushers, not security personnel, often mistreat spectators.
- Open drains and irrigation heads on playing fields.
- Participants playing on overlapping fields in sports such as softball, soccer, football, baseball and track.
- Areas where water and electricity mix that lack ground fault interrupters (GFIs).
- Inspection of facilities and equipment is often overlooked and not documented.
- Schools often lease facilities without requiring a certificate of insurance from the lessee. In many case, the lessee is not required to indemnify the lessor in a facility use agreement.
- Insurance contracts often contain exclusions regarding sporting events, resulting in the facility or program having inadequate coverage.
- Glass doors and windows located under or near goals.
- Lack of due process procedures.

These are just a few situations observed during risk reviews that can plague a sports administrator. A risk management program is necessary as well as essential in today's litigious society (Appenzeller 1993).

Five Steps in the Process of Risk Management

George Head and Stephen Horn II, writing on risk management said:

Risk management occupies an important place in the broad definition of management—that devoted to minimizing the adverse effects of accidental loss on the organization.

The authors of *Essentials of Risk* list five steps in the risk management process as:

1. Identifying exposures to accidental loss that may interfere with an organizations basic objectives;

2. Examining feasible alternative risk management techniques for dealing with these exposures;
3. Selecting the apparently best risk management technique(s);
4. Implementing the chosen risk management technique(s);
5. Monitoring the results of the chosen techniques to ensure that the risk management remains effective (Head and Horn 1994).

Risk Assessment and Risk Reduction

United Educators, a risk retention group and a leader in risk management devised guidelines to reduce injuries and loss of property and reasoned that:

Safety risk and liability exposures are inherent in sports activities. Policies and procedures carefully communicated and enforced lessen the likelihood of injury and potential liability of the institution, faculty or staff (United Educators, 1992).

United Educators write that attempts at managing risks often fails to meet our expectations due to the lack of "certain key components that are either not present or not totally integrated with the others." It lists as essential components of a risk management program six essential parts that include the following:

1. *Policies and Procedures*. Those in authority must provide policies and procedures directing and governing all activities sponsored by their athletic departments, including intercollegiate, intramural, and recreational activities. The guidance must clearly direct those who are supervisors to manage risks which are reasonable foreseeable. Policies and procedures must be developed, codified, disseminated, and enforced with sufficient documentation at every step in the risk management process.
2. *Training*. Traditional ad hoc "on the job" training is no longer adequate. Some formal training should be given to all personnel, especially concerning the institution's policies and procedures. Substantive training must be given, and updated periodically for those assigned higher risk tasks like trainers and bus drivers. In each case, the institution should document the training.
3. *Supervision*. Every level of supervision must be actively involved in "looking over" rather than "overlooking" the actions of their subordinates. Failure to properly supervise should be treated as a serious shortcoming.
4. *Corrective Action*. When supervisors are aware that policies and procedures are not followed, the corrective action must be timely, relevant, and progressive. Some form of remedial training might be required; reprimands, suspensions, or possibly terminations might be necessary in the case of more serious performance shortcomings.
5. *Review and Revision*. Administrators must use the management data available to them, including: incident reports of injuries; deficiencies on the part of staff; inspections and audits; possible claims or lawsuits; new statutes; and even court decisions that will affect the performance of duties. The review should be followed by consideration whether to revise policies and procedures or conduct training.

6. *Legal Counsel and Support.* To reduce the chances of lawsuits, corporation counsel must be actively involved in providing direction, reviewing policies and procedures, and giving proactive guidance to the staff. Thoughtful advice before the institution is sued is always superior to advice after the fact.

Risk Management Strategies For Sport Administrators

The athletic administrator should develop a risk management plan that assesses and reduces the possibility of risk. Implementing a risk management plan includes the following strategies:

1. Organize a Risk Management Committee and appoint an assistant or associate athletics director as Risk Manager and chairperson of the committee. Add representatives of maintenance, security, finance, Title IX, ADA, student(s), and facilities. This committee can identify the risks of the program and accountability for the various areas of risk.

2. Implement an Agreement to Participate for all athletes that informs them of inherent risks of participation in sports and safety measures to follow.

3. Develop an emergency medical action plan and put the plan in writing. Discuss the plan with the coaches and emphasize their role in the emergency plan. Have the coaches sign off that they understand the plan and their role in it.

4. Develop a Catastrophic Injury Protocol to respond immediately to such an injury. Know immediately who informs parents, becomes the point person, arranges travel, lodging, meals for the parents on site. Know the proper procedure to follow in notifying the media, campus officials, athletes, attorney and insurance carrier. Know the proper way to follow up with the injured athlete and parents and how to deal with a subsequent lawsuit.

5. Comply with Title IX and ADA mandates. Recent court decisions have clarified the position of the courts. An active plan must be developed to comply with the legislation not avoid it. Have the Risk Management Committee assess Title IX and ADA compliance.

6. Implement procedures for transportation. Know how to write a contract with transportation carriers to ensure safety as well as economy.

7. Set up a regular routine of inspection of equipment and facilities. Devise forms that meet the needs of your program and document the inspections.

8. Review your insurance coverage to ensure proper coverage for your institution and personnel.

9. Make certain due process is extended student athletes and other personnel in your athletics program.

10. Computerize your program so that equipment is not issued for practice or games until insurance, eligibility and pre-participation physicals are checked and cleared.

11. Have a plan for student disruption that can go into affect immediately when a confrontation or protest occur.

12. Check signage in all areas of the sports program, such as the weight rooms, swimming pool, stadium, field house, locker rooms, gymnastic areas. Make the signs readable, attractive and positive.

Trends in Risk Management

1. Today's average citizen is better informed than ever before of individual rights and the law. There is a prevailing attitude that every injury should be compensated by insurance companies, manufacturers and school systems that society believes have endless financial resources. This attitude and awareness of the law leads to litigation and a future that legal authorities predict will be the most litigious ever.
2. Enormous damage awards are the rule today and million dollar awards are common.
3. All 50 states have reportedly modified the doctrine of governmental immunity with exceptions, such as insurance, tort claim acts and claim procedures that do not go through the judicial system to resolve conflicts.
4. There is movement toward acceptance of the doctrine of comparative negligence rather than contributory negligence; a majority of the 50 states have adopted comparative negligence, and others are expected to adopt it in the future.
5. Lawsuits dealing with individuals with disabilities continue to escalate along with cases based on race, religion or sex.
6. Lawsuits for injuries involving alleged negligence continue to be taken out of the negligence area in favor of the constitutional law arena. Legal authorities report that lawsuits are now filed under the Civil Rights act of 1871 when governmental immunity is claimed as a defense by state and local governments.
7. Sport managers will be held to a higher standards of care in the operation of their programs than ever before as the court is placing added responsibility and accountability on the sport manager.
8. More and more legal authorities, scholars and practitioners are publishing books, periodicals, journals and newsletters in the area of risk management. This information will be available to all who work in the field of risk management.

Summary/Conclusion: Recommendations for the Reduction of Risks in Sport Programs

1. Keep abreast of current trends in the law as they relate to sport. Attend workshops that deal with risk management, sport medicine and injury prevention.
2. Organize a Safety Committee (Risk Management Committee) to address the problem of risk.
3. Designate a safety officer to conduct and assume the responsibility for a safety audit of the sport program. Develop a clear, written policy for identifying and correcting potential risks.

4. Transfer the burden and cost of risks in the program by acquiring medical and/or liability insurance to protect participants, personnel and the program itself.

5. Know and obey the rules, regulations and the law as they apply to the sport program.

6. Do not wait for an accident or crisis to act. Act now and be prepared by careful planning and preventive action to provide a risk-free program.

7. Warn participants in the program of all potential dangers and risks.

8. Provide competent personnel to direct and supervise the sport program. Determine the number of supervisors by the activity, size and age of the group. Work closely with inexperienced or less qualified personnel. Eliminate high risk activities until qualified personnel is available.

9. Consult with a qualified attorney in planing the operation of the safety audit and overall program.

References

Appenzeller, H. (1993). *Managing Sports and Risk Management Strategies.* Durham, NC: Carolina Academic Press.

Appenzeller, H. and R. Baron (1980). *From The Gym To The Jury.* Greensboro, NC: The Center For Sports Law and Risk Management.

Baron, R. (1997). *Risk Management Manual.* Dallas, TX: The Center for Sports Law and Risk Management.

Burling, P. and G.P. Gallagher (1992). *Managing Athletic Liability: An Assessment Guide.* Chevy Chase, MD: United Educators Risk Retention Group, Inc.

Fried, Gil (1999). *Safe At First.* Durham, NC: Carolina Academic Press.

Head, G.L. and S. Horn, II (1994). *Essentials of Risk Management.* Malvern, PA: A Insurance Institute of America.

Rushing, Gary (2000). *A Safety and Legal Liability Self-Appraisal Instrument for Athletic Programs.* Mankato, MN.

Schubert, G.W., R. Smith, and J.C. Trentadue (1986). *Sports Law.* St. Paul, MN: West Publishing Co.

Society for the Study of Legal Aspects of Sport and Physical Activity (1995). Terre Haute, IN.

van der Smissen, B. (1990). *Legal Liability Management for Public and Private Entities.* Cincinnati, OH: Anderson Publishing Co.

Weistart, J. and C. Lowell (1979). *Law of Sports.* Charlottesville, VA: Bobbs Merrill Co.

Chapter 25

A Safety and Legal Liability Self-Appraisal Instrument for Athletic Programs

Gary M. Rushing

Purpose of the Self-Appraisal Instrument

The purpose of this self-assessment is to provide school personnel with a means to identify safety and legal liability problems relative to the operation of the school's athletic program. An auxiliary benefit is that those performing the assessment become more aware of problem areas and, therefore, less likely to neglect them. The ultimate goal of the assessment is to rectify the identified inadequate areas of concern and, thereby, improve participant safety. This should have the corresponding effect of reducing the likelihood of a lawsuit.

This instrument contains 188 objective statements which represent established standards and practices against which a secondary school's athletic program may be compared. These standards are grouped into seven different categories with each category representing a major aspect of the operation of an athletic program. The categorical grouping is significant because it enables the evaluator to see more specifically where problems exist.

Who Should Use the Self-Appraisal

Only one knowledgeable and conscientious person is needed to adequately perform the self-evaluation. However, the ideal method of assessing a program is to have a number of people perform the evaluation (preferably a risk management committee) and then compare the scores. This method provides a variety of viewpoints and produces a more accurate profile of the program. A risk management team composed of people most familiar with all aspects of the program would be ideal.

As mentioned above, one of the benefits of this assessment is that it provides the evaluators with an increased awareness of the safety and legal liability aspects of the program. For this reason, those most directly involved with the operation of the program should be selected as evaluators.

The following is a list of possible candidates:

> athletic director/activity directors
>
> head coaches
>
> assistant coaches
>
> safety officers
>
> risk managers

Directions For Evaluator

The evaluator should consider each statement carefully to determine the extent to which his or her sports program conforms (complies) with the standard or practice listed. Then using the following rating scale, circle the corresponding number which best represents that opinion. Answer each item based on personal judgment; however, should the evaluator lack familiarity with an item, that item should be researched in order to make an accurate rating. Should an evaluator believe that an item does not apply to the evaluated program an "N/A" (not applicable) is provided.

The following rating scale should be used to measure extent to which your school conforms to the recommended standards and practices:

N/A: **Does not apply**—this practice does not have any application to this program

4: **Completely**—conforms to the standard without exception

3: **Extensively**—meets the standard with a high degree of conformity but with exceptions

2: **Moderately**—meets the standard with a low to medium degree of conformity

1: **None**—standard is not met at all

After the items in each section have been rated, a total possible score and a percentage of the possible score for each section should be calculated. A calculation formula is provided at the end of each section. When all sections are completed and percentages calculated, the percentage score should be placed on the "profile" table found on the last page. This table will provide the evaluators with a cursory profile of how well the athletic program complies with recognized standards and practices. The profile is a measure of the level of safety and legal responsiveness of the evaluated athletic department.

Personal Data Sheet

Name:

Name of School:

Position Held:

Years of Experience in Position:

Number of Years Employed by the School:

Insurance Standards and Practices

	N/A	1	2	3	4
1. Insurance coverage for accident and general liability is purchased by the school or is available to all persons involved in the athletic program, including athletes, employees, volunteers, and school boards.	—	—	—	—	—
2. There is a person or group of persons delegated to explore insurance policies, and after developing a set of criteria, to purchase the best possible coverage.	—	—	—	—	—
3. The school utilizes a cooperative plan with other schools on a county or other basis to obtain competitive group rates.	—	—	—	—	—
4. Catastrophic lifetime medical liability plans are available to your athletes.	—	—	—	—	—
5. Dental injury benefits are included in the school athletic insurance coverage.	—	—	—	—	—
6. Administrators have a clear understanding of what claims the insurance company will and will not pay.	—	—	—	—	—
7. The school insists that all athletes are enrolled in some form of athletic insurance program.	—	—	—	—	—
8. The school has a liability policy which has generous excess medical, rehabilitation, and work loss benefits. It also provides lifetime benefits for permanent athletic injury.	—	—	—	—	—
9. The school has a comprehensive plan for insurance to protect itself.	—	—	—	—	—
10. The school has a comprehensive plan for insurance to protect its personnel (all coaches, administrators, and trainees, etc.).	—	—	—	—	—
11. The school seeks good advice from qualified persons (broker, lawyer, agent, etc.) concerning its insurance needs.	—	—	—	—	—
12. Athletic personnel know the difference between liability and accident insurance coverages.	—	—	—	—	—
13. The policy limits of the athletic insurance are kept current and are adequate.	—	—	—	—	—
14. Athletic insurance coverage includes protection for non-students (general public) in the use of facilities.	—	—	—	—	—
15. All employees (coaches, etc.) are aware that they should have adequate insurance to cover them while transporting students in the course of their employment.	—	—	—	—	—
16. Each coach has personal liability insurance when coaching which is in excess of $500,000.	—	—	—	—	—

Total points scored _____

64 – (N/As x 4) = ____ Total possible points

Total points scored _____ / divided by total possible points_____ = school's %____

Facilities and Equipment Standards and Practices

	N/A	1	2	3	4
1. All equipment used in athletic activities is regularly and systematically inspected and complete repair on faulty equipment is done prior to any use.	—	—	—	—	—
2. There are clear, written policies for identifying and correcting potential hazards within the athletic environment.	—	—	—	—	—
3. The line of responsibility for inspection and repair of equipment is clearly defined so that a specific person or department is responsible for its duty of periodic inspection.	—	—	—	—	—
4. Accurate records are kept of all equipment and facility inspections. The records include the inspector's name, the date of the inspection, the condition of the equipment and facilities, and the recommendations for repair.	—	—	—	—	—
5. Facilities and equipment inspectors use a simple objective checklist of everything that needs to be inspected and the frequency with which inspection is needed.	—	—	—	—	—
6. Supervisors insure that inspections are done and that the recommended repairs are done properly and as soon as possible.	—	—	—	—	—
7. Coaches are requested to check equipment and facilities before each usage.	—	—	—	—	—
8. During equipment inspection, special attention is given ropes, ladders, lockers, and bleachers.	—	—	—	—	—
9. Hard walls, radiators, slick floors, glass windows, fire extinguishers, etc. are considered when evaluating the safety of the practice and playing areas.	—	—	—	—	—
10. Faculty and coaches are required to report unsafe facilities or equipment both verbally and in writing (retaining a copy).	—	—	—	—	—
11. The highest quality equipment is issued to all participants including varsity, junior varsity, and freshman level.	—	—	—	—	—
12. There are qualified personnel who know how to fit equipment and supervise the fitting of the equipment to ensure everyone has a proper fit.	—	—	—	—	—
13. All athletic equipment and facilities are within the guidelines of federal statutes, building codes, and executive orders.	—	—	—	—	—
14. If the school uses facilities other than its own, such as city or county parks and recreation facilities, a written agreement that indemnifies for injuries is drawn up indicating who is responsible for maintenance and repairs of equipment, facilities, and grounds.	—	—	—	—	—

	N/A	1	2	3	4
15. All catalogs and instructions furnished by the manufacturers of sports equipment for installing, fitting, and maintaining equipment are followed and kept for reference.	—	—	—	—	—
16. Appropriately designed and safe areas of play are provided and these areas are carefully and continuously maintained.	—	—	—	—	—
17. Athletic facilities and buildings are designed for the safety of spectators as well as the athletes.	—	—	—	—	—
18. Safety rules for use of athletic facilities are posted. The rules orient students, staff, and spectators to potential dangers in activities, facilities, and personal conduct. These rules are strictly enforced.	—	—	—	—	—
19. Safety rules include the regulation of vehicular traffic on or near all playing fields and other areas which athletes and spectators use.	—	—	—	—	—
20. All athletic apparatus are safely secured when not in use under supervision—either put away, locked, roped off, or covered with mats.	—	—	—	—	—
21. All passage facilities are safe and there is a safe system of pedestrian traffic within the athletic plant.	—	—	—	—	—
22. During assemblies and sport events athletic facility doors are locked from the inside according to Fire Ordinances.	—	—	—	—	—
23. A safe limit in the number of spectators has been determined for each area and the limit strictly followed.	—	—	—	—	—
24. Adequate fire extinguishers are available in every area and all staff members are trained in the methods of correct operation.	—	—	—	—	—
25. Potential risks are explained to athletes in such a way that they know, understand, and appreciate the potential risks involved in the use of equipment.	—	—	—	—	—
26. Athletic trainers and team physicians work with the coaches in selecting protective equipment.	—	—	—	—	—
27. Sufficient athletic equipment is purchased to ensure immediate replacement in case of damage or wear in hazardous activities.	—	—	—	—	—
28. Equipment is purchased on the basis of established criteria which ensures the selection of safe equipment.	—	—	—	—	—
29. There are established regulations for the use of school facilities by outside groups with regard to safety, accident prevention, and insurance coverage.	—	—	—	—	—
30. All sports equipment is inventoried at the conclusion of each athletic season, and replacement of defective equipment is made to ensure no unsafe equipment is issued at the start of the next season.	—	—	—	—	—
31. Bleachers and grandstands are inspected periodically by the manufacturer's engineers or other highly qualified personnel.	—	—	—	—	—

	N/A	1	2	3	4
32. Swimming pools and shower rooms are maintained in a hygienic and safe condition. Procedures to control fungal infections, rules of behavior for students and athletes, cleaning procedures, and control of temperature of shower water are included.	—	—	—	—	—
33. When, and if, serious injuries occur, items of evidence associated with the injury, such as pieces of equipment, are preserved.	—	—	—	—	—
34. Only reputable reconditioning equipment companies with high standards are used for reconditioning of equipment. For example, NOCSAE STAMP of approval should apply to reconditioned helmets.	—	—	—	—	—
35. Inspection of facilities and equipment is done with disabled athletes and spectators in mind in order to remove obstacles and provide them with adequate access and opportunity to participate.	—	—	—	—	—
36. The school has a written policy for crowd management which includes maintenance and inspection of bleachers, aisle space, and exit space, as well as location of fire extinguishers.	—	—	—	—	—
37. Athletic administrators anticipate potentially dangerous situations involving spectators and take preventative steps to reduce those risks.	—	—	—	—	—
38. Care is taken to ensure that movable bleachers cannot tip over.	—	—	—	—	—
39. Padding and other protective devices are used around playing areas to prevent injuries from sharp objects, poles, sprinkler, holes, etc.	—	—	—	—	—

Total points scored _____

156 – (N/As x 4) = _____ Total possible points

Total points scored _____ / divided by total possible points _____ = school's % _____

Supervision Standards and Practices

		N/A	1	2	3	4
1.	High risk activities are eliminated from the total program when qualified instructors and coaches are not available.	—	—	—	—	—
2.	All athletic contests involving physical contact are scheduled on the basis of equitable competition with regard to size, skill, and other controlling factors.	—	—	—	—	—
3.	The school has a "no hazing policy "that is strictly enforced.	—	—	—	—	—
4.	All coaches are under the direct supervision of an athletic directorwhose position holds a minimum qualification of an advanced professional degree in an area which includes study in coaching, competency areas such as first aid, care and prevention of athletic injuries, impact of sports competition, coaching techniques, anatomical and mechanical principles of sport, and training and conditioning.	—	—	—	—	—
5.	Activities are never placed in the control of non-qualified personnel for any reason.	—	—	—	—	—
6.	The selection of athletic personnel is done on the basis of the best qualified person and not "inbreeding" or hiring someone who is "on board" already.	—	—	—	—	—
7.	Each coaching position has a job description for selecting qualified personnel which includes a listing of safety procedures to be followed in the specific activities. Knowledge, skills, and understanding required of the job holder are also specified. Background checks are performed on applicants to ensure proper qualifications and to disqualify sex offenders.	—	—	—	—	—
8.	Rules and policies concerned with athletic safety have been established and are enforced. These policies are printed, posted, and/or distributed to students and faculty.	—	—	—	—	—
9.	Meetings are held to orient athletes to the safety and health requirements of athletic participation.	—	—	—	—	—
10.	Only referees who are competent and have passed both written and practical examinations are hired for officiating.	—	—	—	—	—
11.	There is a written policy of assigning an adequate number of supervisory personnel for groups engaged in athletic activities. The number of supervisors is determined by the nature and size of the group and the type of activity involved.	—	—	—	—	—
12.	There is a written policy that prohibits having unsupervised athletic practice sessions or leaving athletes unsupervised during practice sessions. This policy is strictly enforced.	—	—	—	—	—

	N/A	1	2	3	4
13. An attorney is consulted whenever there is un certainty regarding the legality of planned actions, such as contracts over $500, fund raising contests, and lotteries.	—	—	—	—	—
14. All coaches and/or administrators attend seminars and workshops that deal with tort liability and the prevention of injuries.	—	—	—	—	—
15. All coaches are administratively evaluated on how well they follow the school's safety and participation policies.	—	—	—	—	—
16. Records are kept of all safety and liability seminars which are attended by coaches and athletic administrators.	—	—	—	—	—
17. Administrators provide leadership in the development and implementation of sound policies, procedures, and safety regulation. This includes posting safety regulations in proper places; a standardized system of emergency care in the case of accidents; and a standard procedure of reporting accidents.	—	—	—	—	—
18. All coaches and other athletic personnel adhere to all the guidelines and procedures of the athletic department.	—	—	—	—	— —
19. There are administrative policies and guidelines stating how fans, cheerleaders, and announcers should behave during games and how they could be disciplined for unruly behavior.	—	—	—	—	—
20. There is an effort on the part of school officials to keep parents/guardians and the general public informed of the safety precautions that are undertaken to prevent accidents and to provide a safe environment.	—	—	—	—	—
21. The school's administration lends complete support and provides high priority to the school's safety program.	—	—	—	—	—
22. A safety audit is conducted periodically to check for possible safety and/or legal problems within the athletic program.	—	—	—	—	—
23. There is a written policy concerning use of equipment and hours during which fields can be used.	—	—	—	—	—
24. Records are kept concerning objective and fair evaluation of all of your personnel, including their background and training.	—	—	—	—	—
25. There are written policies and guidelines setting forth how practicesare to be conducted and who is responsible for them. These guidelines include use of volunteer workers, coaches, and teachers.	—	—	—	—	—
26. The school utilizes contracts extensively, including contracts concerning employees, team doctors, concessionaires, common carriers, insurance coverage, and game officials, as well as leases of your premises to outside groups and summer camps.	—	—	—	—	—

	N/A	1	2	3	4

27. Athletic personnel participate in and stay current with information reports from the injury-reporting systems and the equipment involved in injuries.

28. Coaches know and understand the rules of the association to which the school belongs.

29. Special supervision is provided for less qualified and less experienced coaches until they become more qualified.

30. School supervisors understand that if they assign unqualified personnel to conduct an activity, they may be held liable.

31. The following documents from parents are kept on file.

    A. "Agreement to Participate" consent forms signed by parents/guardians and students.

    B. Written permission from parents allowing their children to return from athletic trips with friends or relatives rather than returning on the school-provided carrier.

    C. Written permission from a physician allowing an athlete to return to practice and competition. Limits on the type and amount of activity are specified.

    D. Written permission from parents allowing a medical doctor to treat their child if injured in practice or a game.

32. The school conducts an annual analysis of accident data and trends in athletic injury prevention.

33. There are special emergency procedures for fire and other disaster emergencies. The coaching staff is aware of these procedures.

34. There is an established philosophy, which includes objectives and policies related to the school's sport safety program, and interpretation of this philosophy is presented to faculty, administrators, service personnel, students, and parents/guardians.

Total points scored _____

112 – (N/As x 4) = _____ Total possible points

Total points scored _____ / divided by total possible points _____ = school's % _____

Instruction Standards and Practices

	N/A	1	2	3	4
1. All coaches have either majored or minored in physical education, or they have completed a coaching minor, or have completed a systematic in-service program recommended by the state or an institution of higher education.	—	—	—	—	—
2. In-service programs are conducted to train athletic personnel in tort liability and first aid procedures.	—	—	—	—	—
3. Athletic coaches do not assign athletes activities that are beyond their ability and capacity. Size, skill level, age, maturity, and physical condition are taken into consideration.	—	—	—	—	—
4. Special care and training is provided athletes in gymnastics, tumbling, and other activities in which" dangerous equipment is used.	—	—	—	—	—
5. All coaches follow a written policy which requires them to teach sports skills starting with simple skills and gradually progressing to more sophisticated advanced skills.	—	—	—	—	—
6. All coaches involved with teaching gymnastics or wrestling are properly trained and qualified for specialized work.	—	—	—	—	—
7. The school uses "Agreements to Participate," rather than waiver forms, as means of assuring that parents/ guardians recognize the students' intent to participate in a sport and to inform them of the risks involved in participating in that sport.	—	—	—	—	—
8. Athletes and their parents are provided written and verbal warning of the possible dangers inherent to each sports activity. The warnings are clear and understandable. The written warning is signed by the athlete and parents and is kept on file. An audio recording is made of the verbal warning and the date noted.	—	—	—	—	—
9. Posters are placed around athletic facilities providing warnings of the risks involved in certain sports activities.	—	—	—	—	—
10. Players are well instructed prior to allowing them to perform in an athletic activity.	—	—	—	—	—
11. All coaching methods are analyzed by coaches and administrators for safety improvement and as a matter of public policy coaches are encouraged not to allow the use of tactics and techniques that increase hazards on the playing field.	—	—	—	—	—
12. Coaches stress safety in the performance of techniques taught to athletes.	—	—	—	—	—
13. Prospective players are given directions to follow and activities to perform for preseason conditioning.	—	—	—	—	—

	N/A	1	2	3	4
14. Drills or techniques that are disapproved by professional associations or respected leaders in the field are never used by coaches.	—	—	—	—	—
15. All of the coaches keep current on changes in equipment and skill techniques which will improve the safety and performance of the sports activity.	—	—	—	—	—
16. All of the coaches use a proper systematic and sequential coaching method of teaching and conditioning in order to prepare athletes for competition.	—	—	—	—	—
17. All of the coaches understand tort liabilities (negligence) as they relate to providing proper instruction and supervision.	—	—	—	—	—
18. All of the coaches are required or strongly encouraged to attend coaching clinics in order to stay current in the best coaching techniques.	—	—	—	—	—
19. Rules and regulations of games are strictly enforced in practice sessions as well as in games in order to reduce the risk of injury and keep players from developing bad habits.	—	—	—	—	—
20. School administrators do checks and periodic evaluations to ensure that coaches are instructing properly.	—	—	—	—	—

Total points scored _____

80 – (N/As x 4) = _____ Total possible points

Total points scored _____ / divided by total possible points_____ = school's %_____

Medical Standards and Practices

	N/A	1	2	3	4

1. All staff, volunteers, and visiting team coaches are provided with printed instructions on emergency care procedures. — — — — —

2. Coaches conduct a preseason conditioning program at least three weeks prior to the first contest and they encourage players to improve their physical condition between seasons. — — — — —

3. Local anesthetics are never used to enable an injured player to continue participation. — — — — —

4. There is a policy which prohibits the return of any seriously injured athlete to competition or practice without the permission of a certified athletic trainer or physician. — — — — —

5. Coaches are required to become knowledgeable with health and medical histories of the athletes under their care. — — — — —

6. Coaches are knowledgeable in the following areas and are able to apply this knowledge: — — — — —
   A. Routine first aid.
   B. Care of simple and common athletic trauma.
   C. Cardiopulmonary resuscitation.
   D. Water safety (swim coaches only).

7. Emergency care drills are scheduled and conducted during which all employees are provided the opportunity to practice specific emergency care procedures. — — — — —

8. All coaches obtain medical advice and approval for any medically related treatment beyond first aid. — — — — —

9. Accurate and up-to-date medical records are kept on each athlete. The information is used to provide appropriate medical treatment. — — — — —

10. Coaches and athletic trainers have a written policy on how to conduct first aid and emergency care. The policy specifies the limits to which they can go in treating athletic injuries. — — — — —

11. Procedures for handling emergencies include calling a nurse or doctor immediately and notifying parents. — — — — —

12. First responders to injuries (coaches, athletic trainers, etc.) use cellular phones or radio devices to expedite emergency communication. — — — — —

13. There is a well-equipped training room which is adequately supervised. — — — — —

14. Proper clearance is obtained when dispensing pharmaceuticals of any kind. — — — — —

15. Pharmaceuticals are kept under lock and key. — — — — —

	N/A	1	2	3	4
16. Comprehensive pre-participation medical exams by a qualified health care provider are required of student-athletes prior to participation.	—	—	—	—	—
17. There is a uniform procedure for reporting, recording, and investigating all accidents within the program.	—	—	—	—	—
18. There is a standard accident report form upon which all pertinent information may be recorded. The following are included in such a form:	—	—	—	—	—

A. Name, address, and telephone number of persons involved;

B. Date, time, and place of accident;

C. Sport activity involved;

D. Description of injury;

E. Brief on how the injury occurred;

F. Emergency procedures followed and final disposition of the injuries;

G. Names, addresses, telephone numbers, and, if possible; and signature of at least two witnesses.

	N/A	1	2	3	4
19. All accidents requiring medical attention are reported to the athletic director the following morning at the latest. Serious injuries are reported as soon as possible.	—	—	—	—	—
20. Head coaches or athletic trainers are responsible to fill out proper accident forms the following school day at the latest. These reports are kept on file for future reference.	—	—	—	—	—
21. Coaches or athletic trainers are required to make a follow-up call to parents on all injured players.	—	—	—	—	—
22. Each athletic team has a first aid kit available at all times. The kit contains adequate and proper first aid supplies.	—	—	—	—	—
23. A complete inventory of first aid and emergency medical supplies is assembled and maintained and these supplies are accessible.	—	—	—	—	—
24. There is a qualified person (doctor, athletic trainer, or paraprofessional) immediately available at all practices and contests who is designated to render emergency care to a seriously injured athlete.	—	—	—	—	—
25. There is planned access to a medical facility—including a plan for communication and transportation between the athletic site and medical facility—for prompt medical services when needed (away sites included).	—	—	—	—	—
26. Emergency medical transportation is available at all contact sport events.	—	—	—	—	—
27. Ongoing in-service programs are provided to the coaches of every sport on how to manage specific sport injuries.	—	—	—	—	—

	N/A	1	2	3	4
28. An athlete is not permitted, under penalty of dismissal from the squad, to insert himself/herself back into the contest after an injury.	—	—	—	—	—
29. Coaches or athletic trainers are required to withdraw obviously injured players from the contest.	—	—	—	—	—
30. Injured athletes are treated immediately.	—	—	—	—	—
31. Special procedures have been adopted for handling suspected spinal cord injuries.	—	—	—	—	—
32. Coaches and trainers are encouraged as a matter of public policy to err on the side of conservatism predicting the seriousness of an injury.	—	—	—	—	—
33. Recommendations by coaches concerning the gaining and losing of weight is done in a prudent manner.	—	—	—	—	—
34. There is a policy which recommends or requires updating first aid and emergency medical care credentials for all coaches.	—	—	—	—	—
35. Coaches are aware of the state's laws and their legal ramifications in case of injury to a player which results in a lawsuit.	—	—	—	—	—
36. The school has an athletic trainer who is certified by the National Athletic Trainer's Association.	—	—	—	—	—
37. There is a written agreement between team (athletic) physician and the school which identifies each party's responsibility in the event of alleged negligence.	—	—	—	—	—
38. Athletic trainers and other athletic personnel know and follow state laws governing the use of modalities, such as whirlpool and Ultrasound, and only qualified personnel are allowed to operate these therapeutic devices.	—	—	—	—	—

Total points scored _____

152 – (N/As x 4) = _____ Total possible points

Total points scored _____ / divided by total possible points_____ = school's %_____

Student Rights, Standards and, Practices

	N/A	1	2	3	4
1. Rules and practices are examined regularly to determine if they serve a justifiable public interest and not as ends in themselves.	—	—	—	—	—
2. All initial decisions and rulings which are appealed are provided full consideration, taking all factors of the individual's position into account.	—	—	—	—	—
3. Administrators and coaches understand the mandates of the federal laws regarding handicap and sex discrimination.	—	—	—	—	—
4. Periodic review is made of the current status of laws and judicial decisions concerning students' rights.	—	—	—	—	—
5. School officials voluntarily initiate programs that are in compliance with the law rather than await a judicial mandate.	—	—	—	—	—
6. Administrators and coaches permit athletes with disabilities to participate in sports according to Public law 94-142, Section 504 of the Rehabilitation Act, Individuals With Disabilities Education Act, and Americans with Disabilities Act.	—	—	—	—	—
7. The welfare of the individual is the basis of all decisions and is the paramount goal in the operation of the educational program.'	—	—	—	—	—
8. Adequate notice of charges is given to student athletes who have violated rules.	—	—	—	—	—
9. Student-athletes who may have violated rules are given adequate time to prepare answers to the charges and provide evidence in his or her behalf.	—	—	—	—	—
10. Student-athletes who may have violated rules are given a hearing to consider the evidence for or against them.	—	—	—	—	—
11. Student-athletes who may have violated rules are given fair and impartial decisions and the decisions put in writing.	—	—	—	—	—
12. Rules are published and announced in advance.	—	—	—	—	—
13. When rule violations occur, there is a prepared plan to deal with the problem.	—	—	—	—	—
14. Seminars and workshops are provided to faculty to improve legal knowledge and to keep them abreast of changes in the law involving student rights.	—	—	—	—	—
15. Due process is provided to student-athletes and students are made aware of the procedures available should they be accused of a rule violation.	—	—	—	—	—
16. A staff member is assigned to handle due process procedures for rule violations.	—	—	—	—	—
17. Rules are constructed so as to avoid rendering students ineligible due to circumstances beyond their personal control.	—	—	—	—	—

	N/A	1	2	3	4
18. Clear policies and practices concerning rules and regulations are published and students and coaches are aware of them.	—	—	—	—	—
19. All training rules, eligibility rules, and rules of conduct are reasonable and fair. They are specific and not vague or too broad and are rationally relatedto the school's interest, demonstrating function as a means to such ends preventing unfair competition, injury, or excessive pressure on young people, rather than an end in themselves.	—	—	—	—	—
20. Rules relative to conduct and eligibility are published, distributed, and thoroughly explained to athletic participants (student trainers, cheerleaders, etc.) prior to beginning the sport season.	—	—	—	—	—
21. Any written information concerning the student-athlete's character or ability is open and accessible to the athlete.	—	—	—	—	—

Total points scored _____

84 – (N/As x 4) = _____ Total possible points

Total points scored _____ / divided by total possible points_____ = school's %_____

Transportation Standards and Practices

	N/A	1	2	3	4

1. Transportation plans are canceled if school personnel are unable to be thoroughly convinced of the personal and prudent reliability of drivers, means of transportation and adequacy of insurance coverage. ___ ___ ___ ___ ___

2. The school has high standards required of all its drivers involved in athletic transportation. ___ ___ ___ ___ ___

3. When transportation is provided to an athletic event, parents, volunteers, and athletes are never used to transport participants. ___ ___ ___ ___ ___

4. Drivers used for transporting athletes are required to satisfactorily complete a systematic driver education program. ___ ___ ___ ___ ___

5. There are rules and regulations governing student-athlete conduct on transportation vehicles and drivers have the authority to enforce such rules. ___ ___ ___ ___ ___

6. There is a continuing training program for school bus drivers transporting student-athletes. ___ ___ ___ ___ ___

7. Age, experience, attitude, and emotional stability, as well as knowledge and skill, are used as criteria for selecting bus drivers. ___ ___ ___ ___ ___

8. The school's driver instruction program includes the following: ___ ___ ___ ___ ___

    A. Policies and procedures.

    B. Traffic accident problems.

    C. Human consideration in driving.

    D. Natural laws and their relationship to driving.

    E. A job description for the school bus driver.

    F. Responding to emergency driving situations and providing first aid to injured passengers.

    G. Proper care and maintenance of the school bus.

    H. Record keeping and required reporting.

9. Drivers are trained in traffic, including a variety of situations requiring the application of defensive driving techniques. ___ ___ ___ ___ ___

10. Athletic team members are required to go to contests as a team and return as a team (in the same vehicle, if possible). ___ ___ ___ ___ ___

11. There is a written policy forbidding overcrowding of cars and other vehicles. ___ ___ ___ ___ ___

12. If a number of vehicles are necessary for transporting athletes, the vehicles travel in a caravan and the car drivers are given complete instructions, which include speed, route, and meeting place. Whenever possible, the coach travels in the lead vehicle. ___ ___ ___ ___ ___

	N/A	1	2	3	4
13. The kind and amount of insurance is checked prior to the trip.	—	—	—	—	—
14. Coaches and other drivers understand whether or not they are adequately covered by insurance.	—	—	—	—	—
15. Vehicles are thoroughly checked before use.	—	—	—	—	—
16. School officials have adopted safe rules and policies for all travel of athletic teams.	—	—	—	—	—
17. School officials use commercial vehicles and competent adult drivers at all times.	—	—	—	—	—
18. Coaches are rarely, if ever, utilized as drivers to transport their own athletes to and from competitive sites.	—	—	—	—	—
19. Athletic personnel are aware of state laws pertaining to inspection requirements, proper licensure, age requirements, and other details, and adhere to them.	—	—	—	—	—
20. School owned motor vehicles or commercially approved carriers are used for transporting athletes to contests.	—	—	—	—	—
21. Athletic staff members understand the liabilities involved in allowing their athletes to drive their own vehicles to athletic contests.	—	—	—	—	—

Total points scored _____

84 – (N/As x 4) = _____ Total possible points

Total points scored _____ / divided by total possible points _____ = school's % _____

Profile of Safety and Legal Aspects
of a School Athletic Program

Directions:

1. Place the school's percentage score calculated from each section in the corresponding blank below.
2. Place an X or check mark in the appropriate column that represents the school's percentage.
3. Write the rating of your score in the rating column (Poor, Fair, Good).

			% of Possible Score & Numerical Score			
	Area/Section	School's % Score	Poor Below 74%	Fair 74-84%	Good 85-100%	Rating
1.	Insurance	_____	_____	_____	_____	_____
2.	Facilities & Equipment	_____	_____	_____	_____	_____
3.	Supervision	_____	_____	_____	_____	_____
4.	Instruction	_____	_____	_____	_____	_____
5.	Medical	_____	_____	_____	_____	_____
6.	Student Rights	_____	_____	_____	_____	_____
7.	Transportation	_____	_____	_____	_____	_____
8.	Total	_____	_____	_____	_____	_____

Interpretation of scores:

a. A score rating of Poor or Fair indicates need for concern. This area is highly vulnerable to safety and legal problems. It should be investigated thoroughly and corrective measures taken.

b. A score rating in the Good column indicates a sound area and should provide some sense of well-being; however, failure to comply with any of the standards listed could have serious consequences. A school should strive for complete compliance in all standards.

Footnote:

The above profile is only meant to be a guide or tool to identify safety and legal problems in the most vulnerable areas of concern. An exact rating of a school's vulnerability to a lawsuit or other legal problems is impossible to determine. No amount of precaution is going to prevent the possibility of a lawsuit; however, if the above standards and practices are diligently pursued the chances of a lawsuit are greatly decreased and the consequences, should one occur, diminished.

Chapter 26

Contracting with Suppliers, Staff and Participants

Charles Lynch, Jr.

Introduction

The sport manager must assume that "anything that can go wrong will go wrong," and provide accordingly. In order to protect against the unexpected, contracts are essential. Although faced with new transactions and factual patterns daily, many of the same protective devices will appear in all agreements. Each agreement must state clearly and concisely the basic terms of any matter agreed upon, and then provide a resolution for all anticipated or imaginable contingencies.

The sport manager must approach his job as the chief executive officer of a business. Sport has become big business and affairs must be conducted according to prudent business practices. This chapter is concerned with suppliers, staff and participants. It is not an exhaustive management treatise but merely a practical guide to alert readers to potential risks inherent in seemingly minor day-to-day transactions.

Importance of Contracts

The importance of reducing oral agreements or understandings to writing cannot be overemphasized. If a dispute arises, each party will have a different opinion about the details of an oral agreement. At a minimum, a letter to confirm an agreement with a space at the bottom for acknowledgement by the other party might well avoid any future misunderstandings. Of course, the letter should be well-written, to the point, and state in clear and concise terms the writer's understanding of the oral agreement.

Suppliers and Contracts

Realize that a business transaction is involved when dealing with outside suppliers. A supplier is any person or organization that contracts for supplies, services or events. Some of the primary areas of involvement with suppliers are merchandise and services, concessions, medical, agreements with other schools, joint facilities and leases.

A. Merchandise and Services

When ordering merchandise, know the terms of delivery and payment as contained on the order form or other agreement. When merchandise is delivered, make sure it is carefully examined for defects. Check the terms of payment to see if discounts for early payment are available. Also check to see if merchandise may be returned, and if there are any maximum time limits on returns. When contracting for services, check the references of the service provider to make sure that he is capable of adequately performing the agreed upon services. Get a list of references and check with the references. Be careful of persons who respond with "our standard contract." Normally, these form contracts are very unfavorable to the purchaser. Disputed matters will always be resolved against the purchaser thereby making careful review of these form agreements time well invested.

B. Concessions

How are concessions handled at events? Are they provided by the department or is a concessionaire used? If an outside concession organization provides the service, is there a written agreement with the firm? One should exist, and it should be carefully prepared with a detailed description of the duties and responsibilities of each party. For example, suppose a spectator at an event is injured by the explosion of a pressurized soft drink container at a concession stand. Who is liable? You may be, whether or not you had anything to do with the accident. If the concessionaire is liable, does he have adequate liability insurance? Your agreement with the concessionaire should provide that the concessionaire will indemnify you against all damages due to accidents which occur at or around the concession stands. However, if the concessionaire has no assets out of which to pay for damages, or if the concessionaire is inadequately insured, what good is such an agreement? The agreement should require the concessionaire to maintain some minimum liability insurance amount, and to provide you with a copy of the required insurance policy evidencing coverage and naming you as an additional insured under the policy.

C. Medical

Do you have a doctor present at all of your events? Are you required by law to have a doctor present at all of your events? If you do have a doctor available and present at all of your events, do you have an agreement with him or her? You should. The agreement should detail and describe the services to be provided by the doctor, the amount he or she is to be paid, and should include a schedule or list of the events requiring the doctor's presence.

If you do not have a doctor present at your events, should you? Perhaps you are reasonably close to medical treatment facilities, and you have ambulance service. If you have ambulance service, are the ambulance personnel trained in emergency medical services, and are they capable of handling athletic injuries, heart attack victims, and other similar traumatic injuries? Finally, do you have an agreement with your ambulance service? A short sample physician's agreement is included in Appendix 1 to Chapter 8.

D. Agreements with Other Schools

When you make up your athletic teams' schedules do you enter into a written agreement with each opponent, or do you merely confirm the dates and times by telephone? If your school, conference or association has a standard agreement which you complete by filling in the blanks, do you keep copies of the filled-in agreements for your files?

E. Joint Facilities

If you share ownership or use of a facility with another school, do you have a written agreement defining the rights and responsibilities of each owner or user? Does the agreement adequately protect you if an accident occurs while the other party is using the facility? A carefully drafted agreement defining the terms of use, supervision required during use and the specific responsibilities of each party could be very important in the event of an injury at the facility.

F. Leases

For each facility that you lease for your use, or that you lease to others, you should have a written lease agreement.

Contracts for Staff

At the end of each athletic season, our newspapers usually carry several articles about the firing of coaches. Frequently these articles disclose that the school or other employer must pay the coach's salary for the remaining years on his or her contract. Obviously, the coaches in these cases have written employment agreements with the schools providing for payment following termination by the employer. In the absence of a written employment agreement, the general law is that the term of employment is at the will of the employer, and may be terminated at any time without further liability for payment. For the protection of your school and your coaches, a written employment agreement should be prepared, and it should define the term, rate of pay, expectations and other matters agreed upon by the parties. The employment agreement may also include a listing of the fringe benefits provided for the coach. For most business executives these include insurance, both medical and life, retirement benefits, the use of an automobile, secretarial or other similar assistance and perhaps housing.

Common at the larger university level is the summer camp program, whereby the coach can operate a summer camp by leasing some or all of the school's athletic facilities. From the school's standpoint, the lease or other agreement with the coach should specifically eliminate the school's participation in the conduct of the summer camp. The coach should operate the camp entirely on his own, and the school should only act as a lessor of its facilities. It should not pay its personnel for working at the camp, and they should make separate employment arrangements with the coach. Again, the coach should be required to maintain adequate liability insurance coverage, naming the school as an insured, and provide the school with proof of the coverage prior to the effective date of the lease.

Contracts with Participants

A. Scholarships

The most common form of written agreement between the school and its athletes is the scholarship form. If there is no written scholarship agreement, one should be prepared. The scholarship agreement should outline the basic requirements that the athlete must maintain to keep his scholarship. If the scholarship is a one-year annually renewable agreement, this fact should be disclosed prominently to the athlete. If the athlete is to be adequately protected, the school should provide the athlete with some medical insurance program, either paid by the university, or paid at the option of the athlete or his family. Most medical insurance policies pay only a percentage of the actual medical bills, and by having only a regular family policy on an athlete, a parent may not have full medical insurance. Therefore, an additional policy, purchased by the athlete or his family, or provided by the university, may provide improved medical coverage for the athlete.

B. Injuries

If an athlete is injured due to lack of supervision or faulty equipment, does your school have adequate liability insurance? If so, does the insurance require you to make an annual report on the condition of your equipment and facilities? Who performs the inspection and certification to the insurance company? Do you have adequate amounts of insurance? Judgments are being handed down for millions of dollars. If your policy limits are the standard $100,000/300,000, then you may be inadequately insured in the event of an injury. Additional insurance is usually not as expensive as the base amount, and you may be able to purchase an "umbrella" policy providing coverage of a million dollars or more without significant additional expense.

C. Club Sports

If your school has a club sports program, does the school participate in or attempt to control the club sports? Are playing fields or other facilities for the club sports to use merely provided by the school or does the school control and administer club sports as part of the program? The more control and supervision one has, the greater the need for insurance and adequate supervision for these sports.

Do You Need an Attorney?

Consult with an attorney and choose an attorney based on his or her capabilities. The attorney must understand the needs of the sport manager and be experienced in dealing with matters which affect the sports program. Most laymen do not understand that all attorneys do not attempt to practice in all fields of law. In choosing an attorney, ask questions about his or her type of practice and areas of specialty. If the attorney's practice is devoted primarily to criminal law matters, it is doubtful that the attorney or sport manager would benefit by his serving as attorney for the program. Also, do not choose an attorney solely because he or she is a friend or neighbor or because he or she is a booster of the program. All of these are good qualities, but unless the attorney is capable and competent to handle the program's legal problems, the association will not be beneficial to either party. Invite the attorney to visit, show him around, and let him feel that he is a part of the program. Welcome his advice and opinions on all matters, even if it is occasionally contrary to what one desires. Do not be afraid to consult with the attorney because he will charge a fee. Selecting an attorney because he is the cheapest one in town may not be getting very good representation, since one gets about what one pays for. Have an understanding with the attorney about fees. He should discuss them frankly and fairly, including the billing system and expected terms of payment.

Do not try to be a lawyer. Do not assume that because a situation was handled in one way last year, that a similar situation will be handled exactly the same this year. If the law has changed, or if the circumstances are not exactly the same, then last year's solution may not work. Never simply retype an agreement which you have previously used and substitute names and dates. Often this procedure is employed in an attempt to save legal fees. Call your attorney, and discuss the situation in detail. Let the attorney decide on the appropriate course of action.

You should use the attorney in the planning stages of a proposed event or transaction, and you should avoid calling your attorney only after the "deal has been struck." Frequently, the attorney's advice at the planning or negotiation levels may lead to better results, and he can make suggestions which may be beneficial to both parties.

Summary/Conclusion

In order to reduce your legal risks, have a good understanding of the arrangements and affairs of all aspects of the sport program. Written agreements, however simple, are the only way that certainty can be achieved. Engage an attorney who is competent and who is experienced in handling contract matters and general business affairs. Consult with the attorney frequently, particularly during the planning stages of a transaction or an event. The attorney's advice can be invaluable and may save a great deal of time and money in the long run.

Chapter 27

The Law of Public Assembly Facilities

James F. Oshust

Introduction

Since the publication of this chapter in the first edition of this volume, a number of changes have occurred in the field of public facility management and particularly in the area of what has become more commonly referred to as patron rights. The dilemma facing management and their governing authorities or ownership remains. However, with the passage of several phases of societal conduct and the history of the past three decades, certain precepts remain.

There are few, if any, clearly defined court decisions related to public access to such facilities, or truly definitive criteria relative to maintaining the secure nature of events while protecting constitutional rights of all attendees. Yet with the required compliance with existing laws, codes and ordinances, there still exists the ever increasing need to provide sensitive and responsive customer service for any and all activities in which a facility or organizing group are engaged or plan. In certain cases, decisions regarding rights of access, the degree to which facility authorities, staff and associated law enforcement agencies may conduct searches and require rigid entry policies can be considered rather clear cut. In the main however, it normally comes down to the facility or event's management to develop specific policies and in the absence or pre-disposition by judicial review, to try to both observe individual rights and still assure the maintenance of the public good order.

Need for Legal Assistance

As originally espoused in the earlier volume, facility and event management were urged to acquire the assistance of legal counsel. After an incident or claim has been made it is proverbially locking the barn door after the horse has been stolen. Regrettably, too little legal review has been developed to give most attorneys' sufficient documentation to use as jurisprudence guidelines. It is the requirement of management to provide all proposed facility and/or event rules and conditions to review prior to issuance. And in doing so, to provide legal counsel reasoning behind such rules and regulations.

Stipulate what is desired in the implementation of such access policies. What are the major concerns regarding the attending public? What is the potential threat level to persons or property? What is the security precedent for any proposed measures? And most importantly, what is projected as the amount and type of personnel and accessories expected as the bulwark of any access plan. No legal counsel can definitively assess risk and potential litigable repercussion without a clear picture of what is planned, when and in that manner.

Only when the legal counsel has been given sufficient information on the particular type of operation and some of the nuances that distinguish it from other similar operations, can he or she best prepare defenses for potential reaction by those who claim offense, discrimination or excessive inconvenience. When provided this preparatory involvement, legal counsel can then become a part of the planning process. As sincere as their intent and as noble their calling in many past instances, dependence on local law enforcement agencies to develop such programs and approaches will more often than not, lead management more quickly into the quagmire of unnecessary litigation and public criticism.

The reader is cautioned that, like all aspects of society, the law itself changes. Oscar Pound wrote, "The law would be stable but not rigid." Too often we exist operationally by adhering to specific legal countenances. Yet, an esteemed justice of the High Court of India, stated in his book, *Elements of Law*, "…The value of law lies not in the happiness it creates but rather the suffering it prevents" (Ref. 1). Thus, be prepared for change within each jurisdiction. And not to forget, each session of the U.S. Supreme Court can and often does bring change in legal positions once considered inviolate but now altered to meet new circumstances.

To avoid as much confusion, conflict and possible criticism from media and public, be as prepared as one can be. Stay alert to reported public incidents and legal actions that directly impact your type of operation. As social mores and conduct of society in general shift ever so slightly in one direction or the other, so does the potential interpretation forthcoming from courts at all levels. To avoid such attention and ongoing dialogue with those associated with such matters is to face potential disaster. At best I can cast a shadow over the credibility of your operation and the facility or event's position in both the community and the industry.

Access and Availability of Facilities

This has been a major concern of management and local governments for years. Primary to its high visibility were three dramatic intrusions into the human fabric. In the United States it was the Vietnamese crisis of the late '60s and early '70s, and growing drug use fueled in the minds of many local authorities by the massive proliferation of the more strident pop music culture termed "hard rock." Overseas the numerous incidents of violence at major soccer competitions gave rise to the term "hooligans," tagged on English fans who seemed to bear a preponderance of the public scrutiny in these highly explosive situations. Coupled with the growth of rock music came a more aggressive style of performer and equal exuberance of their fans who ranged from early teens to mid twenties. Added to this sometimes volatile mixture was the Vietnam anti-war sentiment, again voiced by many of these music devotees. This was an integral part of this entire culture for almost ten years, waning in the late 1970s. As not to be at a loss for an ongoing connection with their fans, major music concerts often became forums for various causes involving the environment, endangered species and social and gender identification.

With the passage of much of the near hysterical entertainment scenes of the late 1960s to the late 1980s, a newer, more sophisticated era of concern arose for and adherence to citizen rights. In the world of facility and event operations, that always meant patron or customer rights. But to understand this current atmosphere, it is important to understand when and how public awareness became so acute.

When early pop music entrepreneur Alan Freed began developing local live concerts featuring black and white musical groups, he probably didn't realize what he had started. In the next few years pop music would become rock music. It was a short hop to what some referred to as hard rock, then heavy metal and eventually "rap music." Although each phase enjoyed startling success to be overtaken by the next musical genre. Yet it was with the advent of rock music and large arenas and coliseums that raised serious concerns with security at such events. Local governments, more often than not the primary operators of public assembly facilities in that period, saw an increasing danger in the mixture of loud and strident rock music with the rising use of drugs and alcohol by a number of concert attendees.

Two distinct issues became salient in community's efforts to control the use and accessibility of facilities, often supported by local tax funds. Oddly the dual concerns were far different than most at the time recognized. The first approach was the direct attempt to control access by rock music concert goers. This was accomplished mainly by use of local law enforcement agencies to enforce existing laws and local ordinances and codes regarding alcohol consumption, possession and transport. In addition, the prevalence of illegal drugs prompted many communities to create near fortress like atmospheres in trying to stem the rising tide of youthful possession and use of a variety of such items from marijuana to cocaine and a variety of multi-colored and equally dangerous substitutes.

Recognizing the futility of merely staffing facilities with an overload of police officers, undercover agents and private security personnel, the next step was to dictate standards of facility use. It then became a matrix for identifying and designating those events felt to be potentially harmful to the local public as a whole and the welfare of its citizens.

An excellent example of this attempt to diminish the problem before it might occur was clearly reflected in an incident in Green Bay, Wisconsin, early 1983. The then rather controversial rock performer "Ozzy Osbourne" was slated to appear in concert at that community's arena facility. Since a private facility management company operated the facility, local authorities felt that their exposure under prior restraint aspects of the First Amendment would be either vastly lessened or possibly non-existent. The management company's contract ostensibly gave them total control over the selection and booking of events. However, the management group stated they would accede to the local government's wish to preclude the appearance if the County would accept full liability.

Fortunately the county's legal counsel intervened declaring that any such arrangement, however seemingly protective on the exterior, did in fact conflict with existing law and applied constitutional freedoms. As it eventually occurred, the performer reportedly took ill and was unable to fulfill the concert commitment, thus avoiding what could have been another legal confrontation and media fodder.

In another instance, a facility was to be rented by a somewhat unusual event for its time, a "Gay Beauty Contest." Local church and civic groups protested violently; the event was cancelled due to lack of ticket sales and the inability of the promoter to provide the necessary deposit funding. Here, two separate types of events, potentially appearing at two different control situations, full governmental operation and private management, were faced with a similar dilemma.

In a 1993 high court decision concerning an accused obscene book sales operation (Ref. 2), one of the comments in the court's dissent was particularly relevant to the contended application of "community standards." "We have interpreted the First Amendment as providing greater protection from prior restraint than from subsequent punishments." In declaring this dicta, the high court continued to take a firm stand against pre-event or actionable restraint in the name of denying use, distribution or exercise of constitutionally protected free speech.

This bears directly on the basic premise, what right does a public assembly facility, however operated, have to restrict or, if desired, bar presentation of events or limit availability to an individual for a public program? An individual, high in the entertainment promotion sphere, quipped a few years ago, "you have no rights to stop such events—and your ability to do so by limiting access deteriorates from that point on." This has been tested time and time again. It more recently arises in the demand for sites to espouse a group's particular philosophy, however offensive their beliefs and commentary may be to normal community standards. Prime example, the highly volatile request of the then Nazi oriented, white supremacist organization to march through a Chicago suburb, whose population contained many members of the Jewish faith as well as numerous survivors of the Holocaust. More recent attempts by various elements of the Ku Klux Klan to hold rallies, march through downtown areas from southern states to major northern cities have created occasional concerns over potential violence.

In *Southeastern v. Conrad*, or the highly publicized "Hair" controversy, a Chattanooga, Tennessee theater sought to deny appearance dates for the then much debated Broadway musical that had in one scene a brief glimpse of nudity (Ref. 3). After a lengthy period of litigation and First Amendment claims and local standards argument, the court ruled the facility could not arbitrarily limit, regardless of any pre-determined criteria, access to what was, despite its critics, a legitimate theater production.

A variance to this non-exclusion aspect of the law can be the unique or pre-designated use of certain structures. For example, "Wholesome University" has constructed a rather large and well-equipped arena. It primary purpose, staging of the school's basketball competitions, gymnastics, wrestling matches, commencements and other events requiring substantial seating and accommodations. During the summer, however, when the student population is drastically reduced or during those periods when little other activity is planned, the student government desires to stage concert attractions. Kenny Rogers had been booked as well as Simon and Garfunkel, both very popular with that demographic group. But, the students also want more current acts; "The Blasters," the "Nobodies" and other groups from what is termed "heavy metal" to the more recent "rap" genre.

Along with the student population, the local community can easily support sell-out capacities for such events. And inasmuch as the local community has no similar facility and is not fiscally able to construct and support such a facility on its own, Wholesome University's new arena is the perfect answer. The University fathers decline to allow such events. But, other, perhaps less controversial or high profile events such as an ice show, or the circus or less aggressive music acts are to be permitted. And although the facility was not intended as a profit making structure, it suddenly comes into its own as a revenue producer when found that no competitive facility exists within miles of the community. Additionally, the University's fiscal situation calls for development of needed revenue, which such uses of the facility could provide. With the specter of increasing operational costs for the entire organization, what should the University do?

Simply put, can the school be selective in its choices of events? To forestall the "Blasters" or the "Nobodies," the University may be forced to curtail if not totally absent itself from booking other, less aggressive productions. What such a facility or the community and constituent group its serves, feel is "normal" or meets existing "community standards" or needs, may not, in the eyes of the court, be broad or general enough in its scope and criteria. Thus, unable to preclude the claim of First Amendment rights ostensibly being exercised by those requesting dates or usage of the facility. What are the specific purposes for the facility's operation? Are the constituent groups and uses clearly identified? Are the stated criteria and operating policies consistently applied to all applicants? These questions must be continually reviewed and updated to reflect changing conditions, both operationally and fiscally.

To the reverse of this situation is the designated use or structural style of the facility in question. Any use program must be consistent with the architectural and operational style of the facility itself. One does not book a rock act into a concert hall designed for the symphony, the ballet, musicales or stage productions—unless one desires an ongoing program of refurbishing, repair and replacement. This is true of exhibition halls and conference centers that may have the floor capacity and seating configurations to satisfy major meetings and exposition needs. If more contemporary events or major family entertainment spectaculars can reasonably be considered potentially injurious to the facility itself, its amenities and accoutrements, facility management has and the courts will sustain refusal for any problem bookings.

Before we leave this subject, the author would be remiss if he did not emphasize the importance of the lease agreement, its preparation and documentation. The subject alone can fill volumes but in the context of dealing with this question of access it is important to remember that there exist three "Ps" to any agreement: to Permit, to Provide and to Pay. If you are diligent in enumerating and detailing what is permitted in your facility, who provides what, when and how and equally importantly, who pays what for this permission and provision. Too often confusion as to the intent of an agreement, the preparation of the contract form, the documentation of conversations, correspondence and methods of resolving conflicts, can quickly lead from conviviality to the courtroom.

Your lease agreement, operating policies and regulations are your road maps. Drawn carelessly and without regard for inevitable change will soon prove fiscally and legally reprehensible.

Access to Records, Booking Schedules and Operational Details

When any facility "goes public" so do many of its records. Where once protection was provided certain privately owned and operated buildings, certain religious establishments offering space rental and college and school controlled facilities may lose that protection. Such is not the case in today's highly litigious atmosphere. It must be remembered that the courts hold adherence to the basic tenets of the First Amendment very sacrosanct. Any attempt to deny access to appropriate booking records, contract documents and accompanying correspondence can be considered by the courts as overt attempts to deny, by prior restraint, constitutionally mandated access. To merely stipulate that any set of conditions exists as a policy, understood by all applicants, is insufficient grounds for rejecting access claims without due process by both parties.

Privacy, once considered a dual right and inalienable in every facet of society, does not protect the facility owner/operator when its use may appear to deny appropriate redress for any litigant. Assure your records are consistent with developed and printed policies. Assure all access applicants have the opportunity, and can be required to provide adequate information regarding their event. History of event activity in other locations is a vital tool for determining potential problems. It cannot, in itself be a sole or even primary cause for rejection unless showing substantive reason for concern both to patron attendance and the facility operation and well being.

To paraphrase Clarence Darrow, noted attorney and one of the founding fathers of the ACLU, regarding the written word, "words are not as clear as the crystal. Rather they are covered by a membrane that changes in color and texture as viewed by the listener and interpreted by the reader." Unless you are prepared to defend your policy and operational criteria in a court of law, don't engage in hypothetical hyperbole or indistinct language. It merely places you in legal harms way. Document all such requests. Prepare your legal counsel in advance for various scenarios and how they may affect both constitutional elements and local laws and codes. Know your enemy before they learn that your word was written by a noted Chinese philosopher, general and poet centuries ago (Ref. 4).

Special Interest Access to Premises

The Courts have ruled during the past several decades that access to premises of any public assembly facility shall be granted under conditions which form a rather large umbrella of coverage. This coverage encompasses numerous types of assembly, protests, solicitation and public commentary. Our Founding Fathers envisioned the expression "freedom of speech" to counteract the excessive control over what a person could say that the other heard or the government and local authorities felt were demeaning, insulting, defamatory and seditious. Today that freedom covers a range of expression even the courts and legislators ever conceived of as late as the early 20th Century.

But this mandated latitude is not to say that anyone may enter upon the premises of any facility at any time to what they wish. However, in order to protect the guarantees of free speech, the courts have stated that access to the general populace cannot be "severely restricted or unnecessarily hindered." If, however, the facility is located well within the confines of a secluded campus area, situated well within a larger landmass that serves as parking or service areas, there are certain imposed limitations to unfettered access that can be implemented. Is there little daily traffic? Is the location quite isolated from mainstream pedestrian or vehicular traffic? Is there any purpose for entry other than to access the facility for attendance at an event? Yet, if a facility provides daily boxoffice services that are located within this defined enclosure, and the public must enter the conclave to access these services, the facility becomes far more apt to be come a potential forum for assembled protest. Let us examine the five principal areas of facility management concern in this matter.

1. Protest

Too often the arena, coliseum, theatre, convention facility becomes the target for a multitude of protests for the simple reason it is more often than not the most visible site for media exposure. Often, the protest might not even refer to the facility or one of its activities. Rather, is well known, fairly accessible both by the protesting group or individual and especially by print and broadcast media. If isolated from normal public view, non-event hours are minimal opportunity for such groups. However, it is at event times when the greatest opportunity arises.

It has become common to both recognize the dissenting group's constitutional rights and yet provide a modicum of insulation from ongoing patron traffic interruption. This is the use of pre-designated "protest areas." Provide clearly marked, fenced or otherwise barricaded areas where the protesters may express themselves, be seen by at least a portion of the incoming patron yet not impede traffic flow or cause undue stress on all concerned. Make sure profanity, defamatory or derogatory comments or signage is utilized or noisemakers that create undue harassment are part of the protest. If this occurs, the protesting group has then crossed the thin legal line between legitimate expression and public nuisance. This then becomes a law enforcement matter if such activity violates local code or ordinances.

It is important to remember the group or groups must be visible to at least a measurable portion of the incoming patron traffic. Their location need not be adjacent to the facility itself so long as their positioning does not eliminate the visibility. Facility management has a right to insist the group be responsible for litter, repair and restoration of the area they occupied were their actions to create such problems. Preclusion of banners must be dictated by profanity, offensive allegations of a racial, religious, gender or political nature. Many facilities prohibit any type of political protest or solicitation in or on the premises. This must be clearly stipulated and rigorously applied to all groups including incumbent political parties. If political rallies are allowed for one party they must be allowed for all.

Prohibition of employees wearing political candidate buttons or other type pins, political or special cause bumper stickers or window decorations create a separate delineation of rights. Clear definition of facility personnel rules must be part of any job applicant's information packet. There is very limited and definitive case law regarding such activities. This is particularly true of bumper stickers on employee cars parked in areas visible to daily or event pedestrian traffic.

2. Sale of Items

One of the primary rules prohibiting contact with the attending public for sale of items and/or merchandise not both connected with the event and approved by facility management, is a keystone to the controls normal to such operations. Most simply put, the facility allows certain merchandise to be sold on its premises, has full control of food and beverage sales in and on the premises and prohibits sale of any devices or items bearing the likeness of the facility or reference to the particular event in question.

This control should be very clearly enumerated in all contract documents. Furthermore, it must be clearly specified in any public information handouts and operational rules and policies of the facility. Most important is to have sufficient local government backing in the support of such controls. This is best achieved in the formulating of codes and ordinances that protect both the premises and contiguous properties where possible. Define the areas of concern. Provide graphic representations of the areas to be covered. Monitor and enforce on a continuing basis to assure precedent compliance in the event of later litigation.

3. Distribution of Written Materials

The distribution of handbills, leaflets and other such written materials can be restricted so long as the restrictions do not in themselves stop the supplier from coming on the premises and having what is considered by the court "a reasonable degree of access" to passing patrons. This must be coordinated with the protest area adaptations and positioning. The inevitable litter problem is one that has dogged facility operations for years. To require payment for "additional clean-up labor cost incurred by this added distribution" is limited at best. The primary source for such charges is the conference and trade show industry where such distribution is an integral part of the event activity. In this instance, facility management builds in such costs and requirements to the lease agreement.

As for the non-contract aspects, until substantive hardship and cost can be documented by the facility, such charges may not be permitted. In essence, one cannot charge another for such allowed freedom of expression.

4. Solicitation of Funds

The past few years have seen an almost universal prohibition of solicitation of funds on premises at any time. The question of fund solicitation is at best a potential quagmire of opposing views. Once inside the physical structure of the facility, management policies supercede the previously broad powers allowed by First Amendment interpretation of this activity. As for such activity on the premises, the portals and particularly the escarpment leading to the entry doors, there are three elements to be considered.

First, has such solicitation been permitted within the event contract? Secondly, is the solicitation part of normal allowances—has it happened before and been allowed without management or law enforcement intervention. Third, is the solicitation contrary to the nature of the event, interfering with normal pedestrian traffic and inhibiting attendees? Is this a concert or athletic event at which solicitation of funds is not a part of the attendees understanding of the event. Often activities are geared toward increasing both public awareness and possible funding such as "Aids Concert," "Farm Aid Concert," "Cancer Fund Gala," or "Symphony Fund Raisers."

Consistency of approach must be the rule. Religious gatherings often have fund raising, donations, "giving" as an integral part of their event. Defining conditions by which and types of events at which such solicitation can occur may be the best method for setting and implementing a consistent approach.

5. General Principles of First Amendment Rights

The law appears rather clear regarding First Amendment Rights granted an individual. This has stemmed from its very broad nature and fertile ground for equally varied and broad interpretation. Our forefathers did not designate place or time or attitude of the expression and use of the freedoms encompassed therein. It might be best to remember that any overt attempt to regulate excessively, to restrict by imposing hindrances, or to impede by ignoring requests, creates a basic foundation for any forthcoming litigation.

To declare oneself totally cloaked by First Amendment right is not a clear statement of mandated obligations on the part of facility management. It does provide the initial thrust of the claimant. As indistinct as the early thinking by our forefathers as to exactly what was intended and the latitude to be allowed, the following truths are both evident and paramount to any management action and/or consideration.

The First Amendment is all-inclusive as shown in the many decisions by all levels of the justice system. We have arrived at the beginning of another century, the advent of the millenium, thoroughly school in our individual and composite beliefs in those freedoms. Finally, without its simple dictates, our current jurisprudence system might have become a jumbled, conflicting series of interpretations and adjudication.

In the realm of "freedom of the press," no other part of the First Amendment has been so heralded as the protector of free speech and assurance of an informed citizenry. Although true that the media enjoy vast liberties with presenting viewpoints, facts and information as they see fit, there still exists some basic parameters as to conduct and content. In 1931, in *Near v. Minnesota*, although claiming specific rights as encompassed in the freedom of press language in the Constitution (Ref. 5), the court set a particular standard of conduct. Apparently the defendant had published what had been termed "malicious, scandalous and defamatory newspaper or other periodical" in the past. In this instance, the court enjoined the defendant from future such publications based on its history of past transgressions of that nature. Again, not prior restraint but rather subsequent punishment for again violating certain previously agreed standards or conditions.

There is little the facility manager can do to offset media comment or attacks on the facility or personalities therein. Unless crossing that very narrow divider between assumed fact, permitted commentary or pursuit of information, and what could be intentional defamation and purposeful incorrectly statements, little recourse is available. The best defense is a policy offense. By this I mean, have a defined policy on what kind of information is available, from what source and in what time span. Identify the facility spokesperson. Set criteria for information releases and review said policies on an ongoing basis. More effectively, try to estimate what activities, what events, what announcements have the greatest potential for media inquiry and reaction.

The "public figure" classification becomes muddled and unclear when dealing with high profile events such as major celebrities and events, serious accidents or incidents at or during an event. The facility manager needs to assume required leadership roles and must expect that he or she will become, at least upon occasion, a *de facto* public figure. When that happens, as one old sailing ship veteran once stated, "and just hold on to the mainmast, cause sure as you're there, another wave will be coming."

Search and Seizure

Possibly no Amendment, other than certain parts of the First Amendment, have raise more legal inquiries and conflict between the law enforcement community and the judicial system than the Fourth Amendment involving constitutionally permitted search and seizure. At the present time there still exists little if any definitive case law particularly dealing with patron rights at public assembly facilities. By this I mean, litigation and questions of law reaching the U.S. Supreme Court where specific adjudication of certain rights and permitted procedures have been articulated. A number of lesser court decisions have tended to favor those complaining about what has been termed excessive, inconsistent and unregulated search techniques, seizure processes and resulting criminal charges being levied.

In the *Wheaton/Wheeler* case in 1976, a facility in North Carolina was sued in a combined plaintiff action brought by the ACLU. The essence of the charges included an inconsistent search and seizure pattern depending on the nature of the event. In addition, the litigants contended that positioning of identifiable law enforcement officers either at the door or actually participating in the questioning of incoming patrons to a rock concert constituted intimidation. Ergo, the patron did not feel he or she had any options but to accede to a search of their bags or personal clothing. The other litigant, assigned by the ACLU to verify inconsistency of procedure, claimed that patrons to the symphony, a large family shows, etc., were not required to undergo such questioning and searches (Ref. 6). Thus the procedure was selective by patron and event and a resultant "profiling" of those law enforcement and facility management felt were most likely to or be suspect of carrying illegal substances or prohibited items.

The judge's decision was interesting inasmuch as he gave the plaintiffs relief in the use of police officers to perform the inspection procedure but otherwise adjudicated on the part of the local establishment. He ruled that notwithstanding the intimidating affect of the uniformed officer at the door, trained law enforcement representatives do have the ability to sense by smell the presence of marijuana and when seeing alcohol containers plainly in view can react appropriately. Due to the monetary considerations, the city declined to appeal the primary ruling and the matter merely became another instance of a lost opportunity wherein there was initial judicial finding but without resolution.

Definite entry policies have resulted from the numerous local litigation. Glass containers, bottles, alcohol, weapons of various sources, have all become part of the prohibited items list plainly posted at entry doors, on the back of tickets and often within specific concert ads. However, the carrying in of illegal drugs, easily hidden weapons, distracting noisemakers at certain events (whistles at athletic contests) will remain as fewer facilities wish the risk both the cost of litigation and the probably adverse rulings by the courts. If search and seizure procedures are either mandated by local authorities or desired by the facility, it is suggested the following criteria be considered:

1. All checks, allowable searches, close surveillance of incoming patrons, requests for inspection of baggage, parcels, purses, etc., must be done by civilian garbed staff rather than uniformed police officers or security staff whose clothing closely resembles that of a bonafide law enforcement officer.

2. The language of any and all prohibitions should be very plainly displayed at each entry portal. In today's diverse society, such signs should respect the dominant minority Hispanic population in the area. The language must clearly define the limitations and access requirements and methods of implementation, inspection, inquiries, and surveillance.

3. Conversations with patrons must be clear but courteous. Questions regarding suspicious items and implementation concerns of the patron will do far more to facilitate patron flow than the more heavy handed and often blunt demand to their required compliance. If the patron refuses, and your policies are consistent and within legal guidelines, the patron is then asked to leave. Is he or she granted a refund? That is in the discretion of facility management and considerations for resulting customer and public relations value.

4. The procedure must be taught to and not only reviewed by every management, operations and event staff member, legal counsel, governing authorities and local law enforcement. The application of the procedures must be continually monitored.

It is the obligation of facility management to do his or her best to maintain the public good order. This can only be accomplished through due diligence to the intent of the law, recognition of inherent rights and compliance with those procedures and guidelines proven acceptable when judicially scrutinized.

Crowd Control

The term "crowd control" is a misnomer. One does not control a crowd, one manages a crowd. When conditions escalate to the level where management has failed to maintain control activity at an acceptable level you then are faced with implementing effective containment procedures to minimize damage, personal injury and further escalation. The amount of security forces, whether "T-shirt" style, private security or uniformed law enforcement cannot be found on any standards chart. Rather it is principally a matter of management judgment gleaned from industry experience regarding like facilities and situations—and a certain degree of luck. All planning must integrate three areas; facility management and event staff, on-site security personnel and the event itself, i.e., performers, bands, actors.

Security, in a managed and event trained format, is vital to securing the facility, controlling and easing escalation of crowd actions and assistance in emergency medical situations. Trained paramedics are invaluable regardless of the type of event. Some law enforcement units have the radio communication facility and accessory emergency medical and fire protection services to provide instant response as situations dictate.

However, at no time should facility management and its ownership ever relinquish its right to reasonable levels of security staffing at certain events, including their positioning, training and duty assignments. If these authorities and responsibilities are ever subjugated to outside resources or reduced in command level status, the patron is ill served and the very fabric of effective facility management structure will be seriously undermined.

Required and Desired Accoutrements and Facilities

1. Disadvantaged Patrons

Here again the courts have been slow to take on what is one of the more sensitive aspects of facility management, the reasonable access by those who are physically disadvantaged. This has become a clarion call by those groups advocating total resolution of past inequities and facility designers and operators who face measurable costs in implementing the Americans with Disabilities laws. ADA has undergone some major changes since its institution over a decade ago. The majority of costs have been borne by older facilities that over the past few years were required to refit their facilities. This has resulted in loss of seats, huge construction costs and a degree of closedown of facilities to effect the changes.

To the facility manger looking at many empty seats in the specially equipped sections for the physically disadvantaged, the revenue loss and constant comment by other attending patrons as to the vacant and often highly desirable locations is ongoing. In recent years facilities have developed systems by which for major, sold-out events, time limits are placed on these special customers and if not utilized at the time of the event, are made available to other patrons. Fortunately, many groups serving the disadvantaged constituents have come to realize they too must cooperate with facility management. Not only in this ability to resell unused seating but also during the initial design stage, to assist architects and planners in assuring such access needs are met.

The need to assist the disadvantaged does not stop at the ramped entry. It includes practical door openers for those unable to handle the standard door hardware, telephone equipment and positioning for those with hearing problems, special electronically enhanced listening devices for concert halls and conference centers. The ADA is very clear. Those with such physical difficulties, but with the mental alertness to provide their own thought processes independent of other assistance, need parking facilities close by, ramp access for wheelchairs and those with walking difficulties and elimination of hindrances or barriers to using restrooms and concession areas. When asked how he became so attuned to such needs, a facility manager replied, "for one half day I navigated my facility in a wheelchair. The next day I used crutches for most of the day. And finally, during one concert I used ear plugs and found to some degree what the world of silence was really about."

2. Emergency Medical Care

Possibly one of the most neglected areas of patron care in the early days of facility development and operation was medical service. Once the province of a volunteer first aid person or possibly a hired nurse at major functions, this has grown to relatively full service medical facilities featuring defibrillators, transport equipment, gurneys, staffed by professional emergency medical care personnel. The primary reason for this level of medical preparedness is simple. Through advertising, public announcements, provision of customer amenities, entertainment, ease of parking and often close access to public transportation, facility management has in fact induced the patron to attend. In doing so, the facility has assumed, however indefinable, a measure of liability for these patrons. To minimize their access to immediate emergency medical care provided by experience, capable staff borders on negligence.

Prepare for each type of event by categorizing potential age groups attending, emotion potential, considering the nature and duration of the event. Review differing needs with responsible medical care specialists.

There may be fiscal pressure from government and/or ownership regarding the acquisition of more sophisticated medical paraphernalia including oxygen, stretchers, defibrillators and a good supply of splints, bandages and other needed treatment material. However, the lessening of eventual liability far outdistances any monetary considerations. Coordinate on-site facilities with the closest emergency medical center, preferably by phone or in today's computer age, by data line. Accident and/or incident reporting systems are required. Designate who files the report, where this information goes and the degree of confidentiality required. When the emergency has passed the cold reality of administrative need and potential legal positioning takes precedence, too often revealing certain vital information is lacking.

By an ongoing review of medical treatments applied, accident and incident reports, the facility manager can soon determine patterns, both as to possible trends and levels and extent of care required for future events. This information also serves as an excellent format for staff training, critiques of all event personnel and possible areas of liability yet recognized.

Granted, budget considerations, availability of personnel and access to emergency transport all impact on the final medical care level that can be maintained. Many communities require the presence of emergency transport in the form of ambulances and trained EMTs (Emergency Medical Technicians) or paramedic personnel. Other facilities provide more complete medical or "First Aid" rooms with limited bed space, some degree of mechanical and electronic vital sign measurement and/or resuscitation.

Whatever the facilities, whatever the level of service and personnel, it is incumbent on the facility manager to insist that those attending the event have the most reasonable opportunity to receive emergency medical care available. To have less is to fail ones professional responsibility.

Summary/Conclusions

There exists no simple answers or clear matrix in viewing the numerous legal and socio-political questions and situations that will arise regarding the operation of any public assembly facility. If you look for the all-encompassing formula to create the proper mix you'll not find one. If you feel any one or group of facility managers has developed the proper mix between professional management needs and the often-fickle nature of government, the media and the patron, your search will be fruitless. But, if you utilize any working concept, research all avenues of approach developed or encountered by your peers, you will then have accumulated sufficient material for your first attempt at conquering the impossible. From then on it is a sometimes tedious and tenuous task of ongoing review and reasonable experimentation with policies, procedures and approaches.

What you can utilize is a practiced discipline in dealing with every situation, every problem, and every opportunity. Accept the preeminence of law as that cohesive element that binds the fabric of society into one massive tapestry. Communicate your needs clearly. Be concise and above all, sincere in your intent and expression of need and determination. Understand that flexibility and mobility in the blade of the fencing foil adds a dimension of strength and a capacity for endurance. It has been written that civilization hinges on the habit of obedience to criminal law and to some degree civil law. Although respect for civil law is less constant and not as engrained, it is still no less important. Professional management that strives for the better in whatever is undertaken requires patience, skill and ethical stamina. Less than this precludes the success of any worthwhile venture.

References

1. Hugh L. Markby, Chief Justice, Indian High Court, *Elements of Law*, (1868).
2. *Alexander, Sr. v. United States* 509 U.S. 544 (1993)
3. *Southeastern Promotions Ltd. V. Conrad*, 420 U.S. 546 (1975)
4. *Sun Tzu, Elements of War.*
5. *Near v. Minnesota ex rel. Olson*, 283 U.S. 697 (1931)
6. *Wheaton/Wheeler v. City of Greensboro, et al.*, 435 F.Supp. 1134, 1138, (M.D.N.C.) 1977

Chapter 28

The Americans with Disabilities Act and Sport Facilities

Gil B. Fried

In a watershed event for millions of Americans, President Bush signed the Americans with Disabilities Act (ADA) into law on January 26, 1990. The new law promised millions of Americans the opportunity to receive equality in ways never before experienced by some or long forgotten by others. The ADA has been dubbed the Emancipation Proclamation and the Bill of Rights for individuals with disabilities (Schneid, 1992). Approximately 4S million individuals benefit from protections provided by the ADA (Schneld, 1992).

The Civil Rights Act of 1964 is considered a sweeping legislative enactment entitling women and minorities the equality they need to be gainfully employed. The ADA is even more sweeping because while it is unusual for someone to change sex, nationality, race or religion; it is not uncommon for a healthy individual to be suddenly stricken by heart disease, diabetes, arthritis, or a variety of other maladies. These unwanted maladies become the basis for potential discrimination or exclusion. One of the primary purposes of the ADA is to ensure that facilities and organizations that provide public accommodations are usable by all people. It requires that any recreation/sports provider must make "reasonable accommodations, for participants who have a disability.

Nowhere can the ADA's effect be seen more prominently than in facilities. Sports and recreational facilities are especially prominent in ADA coverage due to the publicity generated by such facilities and the number of individuals who attend events or engage in activities at such facilities. Sports facilities have become the target for organizations such as the Paralyzed Veterans of America who have engaged in a concerted effort on behalf of their 17,000 members to challenge new sports facilities which do not meet ADA requirements. The group filed claims against several arenas claiming that while spaces are available at each site for wheelchairs, most seats do not offer a clear view of the action when surrounding fans stand up. Regulations under the ADA require all wheelchair seats to be designed so that the wheelchair using patron is not isolated, has the choice of various seats and ticket prices, and in places where fans are expected to stand, facilities must provide a line of sight "comparable" to the view from seats provided to other spectators.

Specific ADA rules are being proposed for various sports facilities. The United States Architectural and Transportation Barriers Compliance Board has put forth proposed ADA recommendations for sports facilities. Recommendations were developed for sports facilities, places of amusement, play settings, golf, recreational and boating and fishing facilities, and outdoor development areas. The sports facility recommendations are set forth in over 200 pages describing the layout of baseball dugouts, entrance turnstiles, and other sports facility components (See Exhibit A). It is obvious that the ADA does not operate in a vacuum with reference to sports facilities.

Other laws work with the ADA to create a complete compendium of laws covering all sports facilities. The 1968 Architectural Barriers Act and the Rehabilitation Act of 1973 provide an extensive regulatory framework for sports facilities. State and local laws can also effect facility design, construction, and renovations. Building codes determine specific issues such as how many steps can be built without needing a handrail, the number of inches required per person, per seat, in bleacher seating (usually 17-20 inches allocated for each seat), and the number and size of exits based on the number of individuals expected to use each exit.

These laws are all coming into play in a variety of sports facilities ranging from stadia and arenas to schools and bowling alleys. The scope and applicability of ADA facility requirements are best understood when analyzed in light of the express purpose of the ADA.

Purpose of ADA

The underlying principles of the ADA entail the equal opportunity for individuals with disabilities to participate, and benefit from programs and facilities in the most integrated setting possible. The goal of the ADA is mainstreaming; allowing individuals with disabilities the opportunity to mainstream into American society. To help bring about mainstreaming, facilities and programs must integrate the individuals with disabilities to the maximum extent possible, provide separate programs when required to ensure equal opportunity, and must not exclude individuals with disabilities from regular programs (unless there is a significant injury risk).

ADA Requirements for Sports Facilities

Title III of the ADA covers places of public accommodations and commercial facilities. For a facility to be considered a place of public accommodation, the facility's operation has to effect interstate commerce. Public facilities which meet this test include, but are not limited to, any establishment serving food and drinks, entertainment facilities (movie theaters, concert halls, etc.), public gathering places (auditoriums, convention centers, stadiums, arenas, etc.), public transportation centers, places of recreation (parks, zoos, bowling alleys, etc.), places of education (private schools), and places of exercise or recreation (gymnasium, golf courses, etc.). The only exception from Title III coverage are private clubs and religious organizations.

Under the ADA, a place of public accommodation is required to remove all architectural barriers to access if such removal is' "readily achievable." When an architectural barrier cannot be removed, the facility must provide alternative services. However, any new construction or facility alteration must comply with all ADA accessibility standards. New construction is required to be accessible and usable unless it is structurally impracticable to accomplish.

EXHIBIT A

ASSSEMBLY SPACES

UNIT 5: Technical Information Modifications to Spaces

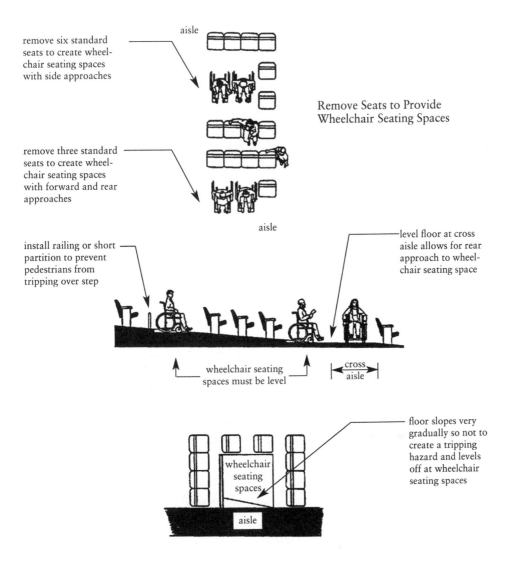

remove six standard seats to create wheel-chair seating spaces with side approaches

remove three standard seats to create wheel-chair seating spaces with forward and rear approaches

aisle

Remove Seats to Provide Wheelchair Seating Spaces

install railing or short partition to prevent pedestrians from tripping over step

level floor at cross aisle allows for rear approach to wheel-chair seating space

wheelchair seating spaces must be level

cross aisle

floor slopes very gradually so not to create a tripping hazard and levels off at wheelchair seating spaces

wheelchair seating spaces

aisle

Modify Floor to Create Access Route from Aisle to Seating Space

Commercial facilities are facilities not intended for residential use and whose operation affects interstate commerce. Examples of commercial facilities include factories, warehouses, and office buildings. Existing commercial facilities are not required to remove architectural barriers even if the removal is readily achievable.

Commercial facilities also do not need to provide alternative services as do places of public accommodation. Only newly constructed commercial facilities and alterations to existing commercial facilities need to meet ADA requirements.

The primary focus in analyzing sports facilities revolves around the public accommodation requirements. Public accommodations may not discriminate against individuals with disabilities. Disabled individuals cannot be denied full and equal enjoyment of the "goods, services, facilities, privileges, advantages or accommodations" offered by a covered facility. The ADA applies to covered facilities no matter whether they are owned by the private, non-profit, or government sectors.

Full and equal enjoyment covers more than just facilities. It also covers programs held within the facilities. The landmark case setting forth ADA requirements for sports programs under Title III is *Anderson v. Little League Baseball, Inc.* Little League Baseball adopted a policy in 1991 that prohibited wheelchair using coaches due to the potential collisions that could occur between a player and coach. Anderson, a wheelchair user who also was an on-field coach, contended that the policy change was instituted to prevent him from coaching during a 1991 season-end tournament. The local Little League office refused to enforce the rule and Anderson's team was eliminated early in the tournament. The issue arose again in 1992 when Anderson coached an all-star team.

The court questioned whether Anderson posed a risk to other participants. The court also examined whether Little League's claimed "direct threat" (to others) was based on generalizations or stereotypes about the effects of a particular disability. The court held that each coach had to be individually assessed. There was no evidence that Little League Baseball, Inc. undertook any type of inquiry to ascertain the nature, duration, and severity of risk, the probability that injury could actually occur or whether reasonable modifications of policies, practices, or procedures could reduce the risk. Thus, any rule developed by an organization (that utilizes places of public accommodation) must provide the opportunity to evaluate each program participant on his/her own merits. Any policy that results in an absolute ban on any handicapped individual(s) will always be struck down if there is at least one person who does not pose a "direct threat" or prove that he/she does not epitomize a generalization or stereotype.

The unfair and indiscriminate application of stereotypes has resulted in several successful suits against sports facilities. A California ski resort violated the ADA with its policy that prohibited persons in wheelchairs from riding cable cars to the resort's recreational facilities. The court concluded that the resort's policy responds not to an actual risk, but to "speculation, stereotypes, and generalizations." The resort was forced to modify its policies. A Philadelphia gym facing significant legal fees agreed to pay $35,000, adopt a non-discrimination policy and provide mandatory staff AIDS/HIV education to settle an ADA (Title III) lawsuit. The suit was brought by an AIDS victim who claimed the gym owner publicly humiliated him, threw him out, and told him never to return to the gym because he had AIDS.

What Disabilities Are Covered by ADA?

The ADA employment provision clarifies what constitutes a disability under the ADA. Individuals covered by the ADA include those with *significant physical or mental impairments, a record of an impairment,* and those *regarded as having an impairment.* A person with a record of disability is protected even though they might not currently experience any impairment. Thus a cancer patient in remission is still covered by the ADA. Furthermore, those regarded as having an impairment are protected even if they never had any impairment.

Not all physical or mental impairments constitute a disability. The impairment has to be *significant. To* help determine significance, the following factors are examined: the length of time the condition has existed, the number and types of life activities affected, the extent to which the disability limits opportunities, and whether the condition is medically diagnosable.

Common examples of protected disabilities include: paralysis, diabetes, arthritis, cancer, epilepsy, asthma, vision impairments, hearing impairments, speech impairments, learning disabilities, muscular dystrophy, heart disease, and manic depressive disorder. Conditions commonly regarded as impairments include dwarfism, albinism, cosmetic deformities, controlled diabetes, and visible burn injuries. The ADA specifically excludes homosexuals, bisexuals, transvestites, transsexuals, pyromaniacs, kleptomaniacs, and compulsive gamblers. Other conditions that are not covered by the ADA include: colds, broken bones, appendicitis, hair color, hair type, or left-handedness.

Disabled individuals are not the only ones protected by the ADA. The ADA prohibits discrimination against any individual or entity because they have a known relationship or association with a person(s) who is disabled. Thus, the roommate of a disabled participant cannot be excluded from attending an event at a facility. This does not mean that the roommate can get into a stadium free. If the roommate and the disabled patron both have tickets, they should be allowed to sit together. Furthermore, individuals who exercise their rights under the ADA or assist others in exercising their rights are protected from retaliation.

The above enumerated physical attributes and conditions present a complicated list of potentially disabled individuals. Unfortunately, most of the disabilities covered under the ADA are not readily visible. Thus, the notion that you can see when a disabled person uses your facility is a fallacy. Therefore, you have to prepare your facility for any and all potential users. The hallmark for proper preparation entails providing reasonable accommodation.

What Constitutes a Reasonable Accommodation?

Reasonable accommodation refers to correcting both architectural and program related barriers. An architectural barrier represents a building's physical element that impedes access for disabled individuals. Examples of architectural barriers include: steps and curbs rather than ramps, unpaved parking areas, conventional doors rather than automatic doors, office layouts that do not allow a wheelchair to move through an office, deep pile carpeting which is difficult for wheelchairs to traverse, or mirrors, paper towel dispensers and sinks that are positioned too high on a bathroom wall.

All covered facilities must reasonably modify their policies, practices and procedures to avoid discrimination. Modifications do not need to be undertaken if they would fundamentally alter the nature of the goods, services, facilities, privileges, advantages, or accommodations. A perfect example of this rule was seen at the inaugural Disney World Marathon. One disabled participant, a motorized wheelchair user, sued claiming the race organizers were not reasonably accommodating his needs. The race organizers replied that by having the disabled individual compete, the race would be fundamentally altered. The court agreed with the race organizers. The judge concluded that the race organizers were providing reasonable accommodation to disabled individuals through the running of a wheelchair-user division in the race. However, the disabled prospective participant who filed the claim was no ordinary wheelchair user. He used a motorized wheelchair. The court reasoned that the use of a motorized wheelchair would significantly alter the nature of the event. By allowing a motorized wheelchair, the court would have opened the door for a disabled person to claim the next year that they wished to participate while driving in a customized van. The court was unwilling to let the law go so far as to alter the very nature of the event.

There is no need to provide individual prescription devices that must be customized for individual use such as glasses, wheelchairs, or hearing aides. Neither is there a requirement to provide individualized assistance such as eating, dressing and toileting assistance. Thus, while it is fairly easy to determine what accommodations do not need to be provided, it is much more difficult to determine the appropriate level for achieving reasonable accommodation.

Do I Have to Prepare for Every and All Potential Handicaps?

Most facility operators when faced with possible access barriers often struggle with a prioritization process. Which repairs should be completed first? What repairs or changes can be implemented over time? In order to provide guidance, the Department of Justice has established priority suggestions for removing barriers. The primary concern and priority is the removal of any and all barriers that would prevent individuals with disabilities from entering the facility. The next priority is to provide access to areas where goods and services are made available to the general public. The third priority is to provide access to restrooms. The fourth priority entails removing all barriers to using the facility. Such repairs can include adding floor level indicators in elevators, lowering telephones and lowering paper towel dispensers in bathrooms. These repairs relate only to areas that are not exclusively used by employees as work areas.

Reasonable accommodation for ensuring equal communication can include a multitude of auxiliary communication aids such as: qualified interpreters, transcription services, audio recordings, speech synthesizers, telecommunication devices for the deaf (TDDs), telephone handset amplifiers, video text displays, written material (including large print), note takers, assistive listening devices, closed caption decoders or brailled materials. Besides purchasing needed equipment, any and all equipment must be kept in accessible locations and in working condition. Most auxiliary aids are relatively inexpensive, such as amplifiers for telephones. However, purchasing and maintaining a significant amount of auxiliary equipment can become costly for smaller businesses.

How Much Will It Cost Me?

Public accommodations are only required to remove barriers when such removal is "readily achievable" (ADA Section 302(b)(2)(A)(iv)). "Readily achievable" means that the repairs or modifications cal, be made without significant difficulty or expense (301(9)).

Several factors influence the costs associated with barrier removal. These factors include the nature and cost of needed remedial action, the financial strength of the facility or organization required to provide the accommodation, and the relationship of the facility in the overall financial picture of the parent company. Companies with significant capital will be held responsible for undertaking more repairs than a financially strapped business.

Cost is only one factor to be considered when attempting to make a facility barrier free. An alteration is defined as any physical change that affects facility usability. Such changes can include remodeling, renovations, rearranging walls, and other activities that affect a facility's use. Any alterations begun after January 26, 1992, must be useable by disabled individuals to the maximum extent feasible. An example of an unfeasible alteration can be demonstrated through analyzing a renovation project for a facility entrance. While performing renovations, the facility manager is told that the only way to increase the doorway size to accommodate a wheelchair would affect the building's structure. Thus, it would be technically unfeasible to widen the entrance. Only that portion of the accommodation plan can be avoided. All other ADA alteration requirements have to be followed.

Traditionally, landlords are responsible for facility repairs and modifications. Thus, landlords are typically responsible for financing required renovations or repairs. Lease agreements can provide the tenant with a right to modify a facility. If a lease agreement specifically allows a tenant to renovate a facility, it will be the tenants responsibility to pay for ADA required modifications. If a lease is silent concerning responsibility for required repairs, the Department of Justice could force both the landlord and tenant to pay.

While some accommodations might seem impossible for a company to afford, tax benefits can make such improvements attainable. Internal Revenue Service (IRS) Code, Section 190, specifies that up to $15,000 of allowable expenditures for ADA required compliance can be deducted rather than capitalized. All expenditures over $15,000 constitute capital expenditures. Furthermore, under IRS Code, Section 44, eligible small businesses with sales less than $1 million and less than 30 employees can receive a credit equal to 50 percent of the accommodation's cost for expenses that exceed $250, but do not exceed $10,250 in any tax year. This credit applies to expenditures that are both reasonable and necessary. These tax benefits are best discussed through an example.

Sam Jones is the owner of Health-T Fitness Facility. Jones employs 15 people and has sales of $400,000 per year. After hiring an ADA compliance consulting company, Jones discovered that he needed to modify the facility's front entrance so a wheelchair could enter through the front door. The company also concluded that a ramp had to be built to provide access between the aerobic area and a soon to be built tennis playing area. In year one, Jones spent $18,000 to modify the front entrance. Jones took a $15,000 tax deduction and capitalized the remaining $3,000 expense. In year two, Jones spent $12,000 on the required ramp. The amount by which $12,000 exceeds $250, but not $10,250 is $10,000. Fifty percent of $10,000 is $5,000. Thus Jones was eligible for a $5,000 tax credit on his next tax return.

What Will Happen If I Just Do Nothing?

The ADA is enforced through several means. Private citizens can file their own ADA claim in Federal court. Private claims are only entitled to injunctive relief and attorney fees. Thus, if a bowling alley does not provide any reasonable accommodation, a patron can sue to force the alley to build a ramp so a wheelchair user could reach the lanes, but not for monetary damages.

A private citizen can also file a claim with the attorney general. After receiving a complaint, the attorney general can then sue the facility owner and seek injunctive relief. The attorney general can also recover monetary damages and civil penalties.

Practical and Inexpensive ADA Solutions for Sports Facilities

The purpose of this chapter is not to scare facility administrators. However, it should be specifically noted that the Justice Department has clearly indicated that the days of ADA education are now over and the Department is now in a phase of ADA enforcement.

There are numerous ADA solutions that can be implemented at little or no cost. While facility renovation costs and repairs are hard to reduce, it is much easier to implement program-wide attitude changes which can significantly reduce the chance of incurring an ADA complaint and provide evidence that ADA compliance is being developed and fostered throughout the organizational staff.

For extensive repairs or renovations, facility operators can hire an ADA consulting firm to determine what repairs need to be made. Another option involves performing a complete facility review and program review to discover first-hand what potential problems exist. The first step necessary when undertaking your own ADA review is to designate one individual within your organization as the ADA expert. This "expert" will have to review literature in the field, become familiar with ADA regulations and specifications, and listen to the needs of employees and customers.

The second step involves the undertaking of a comprehensive facility audit. All facility components should be analyzed and evaluated for accessibility. A written evaluation should be prepared to track needed repairs, facility evaluation dates, repair dates, repair costs, priorities and similar concerns. Such documentation is critical when facing an ADA investigation.

A convenient approach to conducting a facility audits entails working from outside to inside a facility; following the same travel path a disabled person might use. The following represent specific concerns that should be examined. This is not an exhaustive list, rather a framework for further analysis.

Parking Area

- Does your facility have ample parking spaces for individuals with special parking needs?
- Are international symbols for the disabled used to identify parking spaces?

- Is there adequate spacing between a disabled individual's potential parking space and other spaces so a wheelchair could easily be moved around a car/van's side?
- Are there directional signs indicating the facilities entrance?

Sidewalks/Ramps

- Are sidewalks at least 68 inches wide to allow two wheelchairs to simultaneously move past one another on the sidewalk?
- Are ramps clearly set apart with colored paint and the international handicapped symbol?
- Can the ramp or curb be reached easily by someone parking in the handicapped parking space?
- Slope?

Entrance Ways

- Are entrance doors/paths unlocked and accessible?
- Is there a minimum of 60 x 60 inches of level space in front of the entrance door to allow maneuvering?
- Are doors easy to open? Push or pull doors need to be opened with less than 8.5 pounds of pressure. Sliding doors and interior doors require less than 5 pounds pressure. Fire doors require at least 15 pounds pressure.
- Are doormats at the most one-half inch high and in the proper place as not to obstruct access?
- Can doors be grasped with one hand without the need for a tight grip or wrist turning?
- Are automatic doors set to open only when someone is less than two feet away from the doors? (This could cause an individual in a wheelchair to be hit by the doors.)
- Are there accessible doors next to revolving doors?
- Is there any metal or wood plating on the very bottom 7½ inches of a glass door?
- Is the door threshold flush with the floor or entrance surface?
- Are interior floors covered with a non-slip surface?
- Is high-plush carpeting used in transit areas?

Stairs

- Are treads no less than 11 inches and covered with non-slip material?
- Are the stair's risers and do they run a uniform height?
- Are the stair's nosings abrupt and do they extend past the lip over 1 inches?
- Do the handrails extend at least 12 inches past the top and bottom stair?
- Is the handrail's height between 34 and 38 inches above the stair treads)
- Is the handrail grab bar less than 1½ inch in diameter and easy to grip?
- Are there tactile designations at the top and bottom of the stair run?

Elevators

- Is an elevator required for accessibility to all facility levels?
- Is an audible and visual signal provided to identify the elevator's travel direction?
- Are elevator call buttons located at most 42 inches above the ground without any obstructions such as ash trays?
- Are Braille or raised/indented floor level designation buttons within the elevator?
- Do the elevator doors open at least 32 inches and provide ample wheelchair accessibility within the elevator?
- Does the elevator stop flush or within ½ inch at each floor level?
- Is the elevator equipped with an automatic bumper or other safety closing mechanisms?
- Does the elevator have handrails mounted 34 to 36 inches above the elevator's floor?
- Is the control panel located no more than 48 inches above the elevator's floor?
- If an elevator's automatic doors are not functioning correctly is a maintenance plan in place to make immediate repairs?

Public Restrooms

- Is an accessible restroom available for each sex?
- Are restrooms and appropriate stalls clearly marked with international symbols?
- Are restrooms identified with Braille or raised/incised lettering on the door or by the door frame?
- Are mirrors and paper dispenser mounted within 40 inches from the floor?
- Is the toilet appropriately placed at the right height and distance from any hot plumbing fixtures?
- Is there an area of at least 30 x 48 inches provided in front of the toilet for a wheelchair to move around?
- How are faucets activated (levers, handles, or motion detectors)?
- Does the handicapped stall have a door that swings out and provides at least 32 inches of clearance?
- Are handrails appropriately placed in stall?
- Are toilet paper and seat covers within easy reach of a person on the toilet? Are flush controls mounted lower than 40 inches from the floor and easy to grasp?
- Is there unobstructed access to the bathroom?

Telephones

- Are the telephone dials and coin slots no more than 48 inches above the floor?
- Is the receiver cord at least 30 inches in length?
- Are phone directories usable at a wheelchair level?

- Is the handset equipped with an amplification mechanism?
- Are usage and payment instructions available in braille?

Water Fountains

- Is the fountain at least 27 inches high and 17-19 inches deep?
- Are there easy to control buttons, levers, or motion detectors?
- Is some signage available showing how to operate the fountain?
- Are drinking cups available for fountains that are too high?

The third step involves evaluating policies, procedures, and facility practices. All policies, procedures, or practices that may affect individuals with disabilities need to be addressed. These practices can be modified with little cost or effort. For example, a receptionist could be asked to answer all phones in a loud voice while clearly enunciating the company's name. Waiters could be instructed to ask each party being served how they can accommodate any special needs that any patron might have. The key to any such effort is co-opting all employees into the process with the view that they should not be afraid to ask how they can help or what they can do. For example, a sporting goods store's normal practice might be to require a driver's license when accepting a personal check. If someone does not have a license, the sales clerk should not automatically reject the check. The sales clerk should ask for other pieces of identification, or ask why the customer cannot produce a driver's license. Many individuals with disabilities do not have driver's licenses.

The fourth step involves acquiring and maintaining in readily usable fashion, any necessary auxiliary aids such as interpreters, taped text, Braille text, and assistive listening devises to name a few. There is no requirement that the most expensive method of accommodation needs to be pursued. Any method of accommodation or auxiliary aid needs to be effective for its intended purpose.

The fifth step involves following-up to make sure your plans are acted upon. In one case handled by the author, an individual with a disability defecated on herself in a restaurant even though the restaurant had accessible restrooms. The individual sued the restaurant for violating the ADA. While the restroom did indeed meet the ADA requirements, a food shipment had been received earlier in the day and the only place the employees thought about putting the boxes was in the hallway to the restrooms. While there was a wide enough path for a person to enter, there was no room for a wheelchair to fit through. Constant vigilance is required to insure that changing circumstances do not render a facility inaccessible.

Lastly, facility owners should always check with their accountant to determine if they receive a tax break.

Numerous solutions exist to solving ADA related compliance problems. Only technology and ingenuity limit the development of solutions that create accessibility. Assistive listening systems and devices present a perfect example of methods that can be used to provide accessibility.

Hear This

Under the ADA, integral components of an event or facility need to be accessible. Of special concern for sports facilities are sound-related issues. If sound, music, or other auditory components of a program constitute an integral component of an activity, then the facility needs to provide assistive listening devises. An example of an auditory component comprising an integral element of a sports activity is music for an aerobics class. Auditory related issues are also a key concern under the Architectural Barriers Act and Title V of the Rehabilitation Act of 1973 as the United States has over four million hearing-aid users and fifteen million others who have hearing losses that require some additional hearing assistance.

There are four different assistive listening services (ALS) that utilize input from existing public address (PA) systems to distribute sound. An FM system uses sound from a PA system fed into an FM transmitter to transmit sound to individual FM receivers. An FM system produces excellent sound quality, is highly reliable, allows the listener to choose their seating location, and installation and operating costs are also fairly low. A typical system costs about $1,500. However, the FM system transmits through walls affecting listeners in other rooms and access is restricted to those with FM receivers. Similar to the FM system is the AM system which can be received even with a small AM portable radio. However, AM systems often have poor sound quality and the sound may be especially poor in steel reinforced buildings. AM transmitters costs from $350 to $1,000.

Sound can also be distributed through an induction loop. This system involves a wire loop around a room that receives input from a PA system and retransmits the sound through a magnetic field within the loop. The receiver is equipped with an amplifier so the sound level can be controlled by the listener. Individuals with hearing-aids can use their aids without any additional devices. These systems are also easily installed, inexpensive and portable. Loop receivers cost about $75 each and a typical complete systems costs about $1,000. Their major disadvantage is that amplification only occurs when someone sits within the loop. Additionally sound quality is often uneven and fluorescent lights can interfere with sound transmission.

Infrared systems use invisible, harmless, infrared light beams to carry information from the transmitter to a special portable receiver worn by the listener. The system is easy to operate, not subject to electrical interference and provides the best system for transmitting confidential information. A typical infrared system costs about $2,000. The major drawback with an infrared system is that the listener has to be within the transmitter's sight line to receive the transmission.

Summary/Conclusion

The Department of Justice is past the stage of ADA education and is now aggressively pursuing ADA violators. Sports facility administrators have to develop a mind-set, and co-opt other employees into accepting the mind-set, of providing all potential facility and program users with reasonable assistance. The key to ADA compliance was recently highlighted in a youth baseball case in Hemet, California. The national governing body for the baseball league backed the youth league in not allowing an athlete to play in part, to prevent the player from "embarrassing himself." The choice of whether or not a person might be embarrassed is solely up to that person not others. Facility administrators and program coordinators cannot exclude anyone just because someone might be embarrassed. Participants should be provided the opportunity to determine if they, in fact, will be embarrassed. This is the mandate of reasonable accommodation.

References

Anderson v. Little League Baseball, Inc., 794 F. Supp. 342 (DC. Ariz 1992).

Assistive Listening Systems, United States Architectural and Transportation Barriers Compliance Board, 1991, Washington, DC.

BNA (1994). *Americans With Disability Act Manual Vol. 3*, 24 (December), 91.

—— (1995). *Americans With Disability Act Manual Vol. 4*, 3 (February 9), 18.

Schneid, Thomas D. (1992). *The Americans With Disabilities Act, A Practical Guide for Managers.* New York: Van Nostrand Reinhold.

Chapter 29

Safe Facilities: The Facility Risk Review

Todd Seidler

"Student-athlete Trips and Falls: $130,200 Awarded"
"Rough Field Causes Injury to Softball Player"
"Soccer Net Cross-bar Crushes Boy to Death"
"School Found Liable for Paralyzing Playground Injury"
"Overloaded Bleachers Collapse Killing One and Injuring Over 200"
"Pool Drain Cover Case Settled for $30.9 Million"
"High School Tennis Player Electrocuted"

These are real headlines of actual events. Thousands of people are injured each year as a result of participating in activities while using unsafe sport facilities and equipment. A claim of unsafe facilities is one of the most common claims made in lawsuits alleging negligence in sport and physical activity programs. Due in part to the expansion of programs, an increase in the number of participants, and the proliferation of personal injury lawsuits, safety has become one of the most important concerns for today's sport manager. The establishment of a good, effective, formal risk management program has become the expected standard of practice. A good risk management program will take all reasonable precautions to ensure the provision of safe programs and facilities for all participants, spectators, and staff.

Managers of physical education, recreation and sport programs have a number of legal duties they are expected to carry out. Among these legal expectations is the need to provide facilities and equipment that do not present an unreasonable risk of harm to the participants, staff and visitors to the facility. The responsibility of facility managers to provide safe facilities is often referred to as premises liability. According to Page (1988), premises liability comprises "one of the largest subcategories within the broad spectrum of tort law." This chapter will focus on one of the most effective methods of ensuring facility safety, performing a facility risk review.

It is important to note that throughout this chapter it is necessary to keep in mind that everyone who enters the facility has a right to expect that the facility will be reasonably safe. This includes participants, spectators, visitors as well as staff that work within the facility. Where safety is concerned, facility managers must not lapse into thinking that participant safety is more important than the others. A safe facility for all is essential and expected.

Legal Duties of the Sport Facility Manager

When determining the conduct expected of a facility manager, courts have ruled that they be held to a standard of a reasonably prudent and careful facility manager. More specifically, the facility manager must at least perform the following five duties in order to be considered reasonable:

1. Keep the premises in safe repair.
2. Inspect the premises to discover obvious and hidden hazards.
3. Remove the hazards or warn of their presence.
4. Anticipate foreseeable uses and activities by patrons and take reasonable precautions to protect them from foreseeable dangers.
5. Conduct operations on the premises with reasonable care for the safety of all.

If someone is injured in a facility and initiates a lawsuit claiming that the injury was caused by a situation that was dangerous and the facility manager should not have allowed to exist, the court will partially base it's findings of liability on the concept of foreseeability. Was it foreseeable that the situation in question was likely to cause an injury? If the court determines that a reasonably prudent facility manager would have recognized it as a potential danger and acted to reduce or eliminate the hazard, the chances of being found liable for the injury are greatly enhanced. However, if it is determined that a reasonably prudent facility manager probably would not have identified the situation as hazardous and likely to cause an injury, the likelihood of liability is greatly reduced. It is the legal duty of facility managers and program directors to address or treat all foreseeable risks in one way or another.

Critical to the determination of foreseeability is the concept of notice. There are two types of notice; actual and constructive. Actual notice occurs when a facility manager has direct information regarding a defect or hazard on the premises. This may come about by any number of means such as inspection, reporting of the hazard by a user, or from someone actually being injured. It is especially important to remedy a situation where actual notice occurs by way of a previous injury. It may be hard to justify not repairing a known hazard that later causes an injury but it can be especially difficult to justify not fixing a hazard that has already been responsible for a previous injury. If a person were injured by a given hazard, it then becomes highly foreseeable that someone else may also be injured by it.

The author recently observed a good example of foreseeability and actual notice which occurred in a high school weight room. The weight machines were old and had not been maintained properly. During a physical education class, a student was working on the lat pull station, an exercise where one grasps a steel bar overhead and pulls it down under the chin and then slowly allows it to return to the starting position. The steel cable connecting the bar to the weight stack was very frayed and had been for several months, as attested to by three coaches who supervised the weight room. During one set, the student was pulling the bar down toward his head when the cable snapped. The bar crashed into his head, knocking him over backward to the cement floor. The student was seriously injured but was expected to recover. Not only did at least three supervisors admit knowledge of the frayed cable and did nothing about it, but upon inspection several weeks later it was discovered that two other weight machines also had severely frayed cables and were still in use by physical education classes and athletic teams.

Situations like this with previous injuries are extremely foreseeable and must be repaired as soon as possible. The greater the foreseeability, the higher the likelihood of the court finding liability for negligence or even gross negligence. Once again, actual notice occurs when a facility has direct information regarding a defect or hazard on the premises.

Constructive notice, however, occurs when management should have known of a hazard and would have known if proper inspection procedures had been carried out. Facility managers are legally responsible to regularly inspect the premises to discover obvious and hidden hazards. Facility managers are held accountable for both actual and constructive notice.

Once a facility manager learns of a hazardous condition, the courts will allow a reasonable time in which to repair or compensate for it. This time period is determined by a jury and based on the severity and likelihood of possible injuries. For example, a loose railing on the end of the bleachers in a spectator facility would probably be expected to be repaired very soon after discovery, at least before the next event. Because of the probability and severity of the potential injuries, such a hazard should be corrected before the next time it is used. However, in a situation where the danger is less imminent and the seriousness of the potential injury is lower, a longer time will be allowed for repair. There is no set time allowed for the repair of hazards, it is whatever is reasonable. Whenever a hazard is recognized, the faster it is fixed, the better.

It is important to understand that whenever a recognized hazard cannot be immediately fixed or removed, it is necessary to warn patrons of the hazard and possibly rope it off until proper treatment can occur. An example would be if a basketball coach finds a puddle of water on the court just before practice. The ideal is to get a towel and soak it up. The hazard is eliminated. But if the puddle were caused by a leak in the roof, and it's still dripping, then it must be dealt with differently. In this case, it might be best to get a bucket to catch the drips and then surround it with orange cones. The leak should be reported to maintenance immediately. One more step is necessary whenever a hazard cannot be completely removed. Warn the players of the danger and instruct them to stay away. Depending on the location, it may also be prudent to station an assistant coach by the cones to stop anybody from coming near during practice.

It is the facility manager's responsibility to determine the best method for reducing the likelihood of injuries. The bottom line is, once actual or constructive notice is established, it is expected that appropriate steps will quickly be taken to remedy the situation.

The Basis for Hazards

Safety problems in facilities can usually be traced to one or a combination of two primary causes. These are:

1. Poor Facility Planning and Design
2. Poor Management

Poor design can typically be attributed to a failure of the planning and design team before the facility was constructed. It is not uncommon for a sport, physical education or recreation facility to be designed by an architect who has little or no experience in that type of building. For those without the proper background and understanding of the unique properties of sport and recreation facilities, many opportunities for mistakes exist which may lead to increased problems related to safety, operations and staffing. Design problems commonly seen in activity facilities include inadequate safety zones around courts and fields, planning pedestrian traffic flow through activity areas, lack of proper storage space, and the use of improper building materials, such as putting a slippery floor surface in the shower room. The author has also seen many facilities that have been built with major design flaws such as a gym that was constructed with no locker rooms, a varsity football field only 80 yards long, a competitive swimming pool that is only three feet deep under the starting blocks (which cannot be used in that depth), and a gym with stairs going down one flight that were placed less than four feet from the endline of the basketball court. It is essential that these facilities be planned and designed by professionals with activity-related knowledge and experience. Often the safety problems related to design are difficult, expensive, or impossible to fix once the facility has been built. On the other hand, just because a facility was constructed with a safety problem built in does not mean that there isn't anything that can be done about it. Good management can often alleviate or at least lessen safety problems that are the result of poor planning. For an in-depth discussion on designing safe facilities, see Planning Facilities for Safety and Risk Management (Seidler, 1999).

Safety problems attributed to poor management are also a source of great concern. It has been estimated that negligent maintenance is the single most common allegation of the cause of injuries in facility-related claims. Typical examples of poor management include water or dirt on floors, equipment left out or poorly maintained, limited access areas left open and inadequate supervision. Management practices that promote facility safety include performing a facility risk review, developing a safety checklist and applying it through periodic inspections, establishing a good preventive maintenance program, and educating staff about safety and risk management. A conscientious facility manager will inspect, identify, and properly treat hazards as they are discovered. Although there are innumerable different hazards possible in sport and recreation facilities, some are more common than others. Examples of commonly occurring hazards that result from poor planning and/or poor management are discussed later in the cahpter.

Facility Risk Review

One of the most effective means of promoting safe facilities is through the use of a facility risk review. This is a formal, step-by-step process for identifying and correcting hazards on an on-going basis. The facility risk review begins with the formation of a risk management team or committee. The size of the team is usually proportional to the size of the facility and the organization managing it. This committee may have as few as one person to as many as feasible. Typically, the larger and more complex a facility is, the larger the risk management committee will be. It may be feasible for one person to inspect a high school gym whereas it may take a team of six or eight to adequately inspect a large arena.

The facility risk review is broken down into three major parts:

1. Initial inspection
2. Risk Treatment
3. Periodic inspection

Initial Inspection

Once the facility risk management committee has been established, it is time to determine who will be part of the initial inspection team. This may include any or all members of the risk management committee but it may also prove to be advantageous to include others from different backgrounds. The director of maintenance will notice potential hazards which are different than those identified by the head of security or a teacher who holds classes in the facility. It may also be beneficial to include users of the facility on the inspection team such as an athlete, student, parent, or spectator. In order to do a thorough inspection, input must be gathered from all points of view. It can also be very beneficial to invite someone from outside the organization who is not familiar with the facility to come and inspect, thereby providing a fresh point of view. Often, someone who works in a facility every day becomes used to the way things are and may not notice a potential hazard simply because they have seen it too many times. It is surprising the seriousness of some hazards that have been overlooked until a "fresh set of eyes" finally spotted the problem. It can be very helpful for managers from two different facilities to trade off and each inspect the other's. In this early stage of the facility risk review, input from many different people is desirable.

Once the inspection team has been established, the primary task is to conduct the initial inspection. This begins by each member touring the facility trying to identify as many potential risks or hazards as possible. Any hazard that could possibly cause an injury, from minor incidents to major catastrophes, must be noted and written down. At this point, it is important to consider all situations as long as there is potential for injury to occur. The initial inspection should include all areas inside (gyms, locker rooms, storage areas, hallways, lobbies, pools, etc.) and outside (playfields, playgrounds, sidewalks, parking lots, fences, etc.) of the building as well as other areas that may be associated with it. Often, facility managers overlook the exterior areas of their facilities. It does little good to have a hazard-free gym if one of the patrons breaks an ankle by stepping in a pothole in the parking lot. Each inspector should independently tour the entire facility and make a list of potential hazards.

Taking notes, they should think about every possible activity that may take place in the facility and try to imagine how different circumstances might affect safety. For example, in a high school gym, each should try to imagine everything a student approaching the building for a physical education class might do. From entering the door, walking down the hallway to the locker room, changing clothes, participating in physical education class, showering and changing, and leaving the building for the next class. What potential hazards might students come in contact with? What different activities might they encounter throughout the school year? As these potential hazards are identified, they should be written down for further evaluation later. Then the next scenario should be evaluated. What about the gym during an athletic event when it is filled with spectators? It is likely that new and different hazards will be identified in the different scenarios.

Whenever possible, performing the inspections during actual events is most effective. Also, repeating inspections at different times may help to identify problems that are unique to a certain time of day or night. A college athletic department was performing a facility risk review and went out during the afternoon to inspect the track for potential hazards. At that time they thought they had identified all of the uses and hazards associated with the track. The inspection team later went back at ten o'clock at night and found that many people exercised at night and that there were no lights on or leading up to the track. Security lights were installed shortly thereafter thereby reducing the formerly unknown hazardous situation.

The individual lists are then compiled into one comprehensive list of potential hazards. This comprehensive list must then be prioritized into the order in which the hazards will be addressed. Hazards are usually prioritized by taking the following three factors onto consideration:

1. The likelihood of causing an injury—The more likely a hazard is to cause an injury, the higher it is placed on the priority list. A frayed cable on a weight machine may be more likely to cause an injury than a marginal safety zone around a softball field.
2. The severity of the potential injury—The greater the possibility of severe injuries or death, the higher it is placed on the priority list. A missing railing on top of the stadium may result in more severe injuries than a loose board in the gym floor.
3. The number of people potentially affected—Is it likely to involve one or two people, or fifty, or hundreds? The more people that are potentially affected, the higher it is placed on the priority list. Loose bolts in the bleacher supports may potentially cause more people to be injured than a pothole in the back of the parking lot.

Based on these three factors, the hazards are prioritized in order from the greatest hazard to the least. The sport manager must use his/her best professional judgment when making these decisions. The higher the priority assigned to a hazard, the greater the need to deal with that hazard quickly.

Risk Treatment

Once the potential risks in the facility have been identified and prioritized, it is time to start at the top of the list, or the most hazardous, and treat those risks so that they are eliminated or at least made as safe as possible. As each hazard is dealt with, the next one on the list can then be addressed. This does not mean that items with a lower priority on the list must wait until the ones before have been treated. If an item cannot be treated immediately, do not wait to go to the next hazard on the list and deal with it. Many situations can be quickly and easily treated and removed from the priority list while others may take some time. The decision on the best method for treating the risks will rely on the best professional judgment of the risk management committee. There are two primary ways to treat or deal with a facility hazard once it has been identified.

1.   *Eliminate it.*

Eliminating the hazard means to repair, remove or fix it so that it is no longer a hazard. If there is a hole in the middle of the soccer field, fill it in and inspect the rest of the field to determine if there are any other holes. Risk elimination is the ideal when treating risks. If it cannot be fixed or eliminated, then step two is necessary.

2.   *Reduce it and compensate for it.*

Some hazards, however, will not be so easy to fix. If it is determined that it is not feasible to repair or eliminate the hazard, it will be necessary to determine another way to compensate for it in order to reduce it as much as possible. This means to make it as safe as possible and then determine other methods of reducing the risk even further. This may include warning of the situation or changing the rules slightly to reduce the hazard as much as possible. An example is if the sideline of an indoor basketball court is only three feet from a concrete block wall. Although it is unrealistic to move the walls further away, there are almost always other ways to compensate and reduce the risk as much as possible. It may be wise to pad the walls or to get some floor tape and create a new sideline another three feet in from the wall, or both. Then participants should be warned of the hazard and of the use of the new sideline.

With some hazards it will be obvious how to best remedy the situation. If there is a wet spot on the gym floor, dry it immediately and determine it's source. If it was a one time accident, no more concern is necessary. If, however, it was caused by something that is likely to happen again, such as a leaky drinking fountain, it should be fixed as soon as possible. If it will take some time before the required repairs can be made, it may be necessary to warn patrons of the hazard and rope it off until it can be properly addressed. Warning of specific hazards is an excellent defense to claims of negligence in case of an injury. If participants are aware of the risks associated with a facility, it is then up to them to decide if they want to assume those risks and participate anyway.

Periodic Inspections

The next step is to develop a checklist with which to perform periodic facility inspections on a regular, on-going basis. This checklist should be developed for each facility and customized for that particular situation. All too often, facility managers will borrow a checklist from another facility, put their name and logo on it, and use it for their building. This is not an effective practice. Every facility and situation is different. Therefore, every checklist should be customized for each given situation. It can be very helpful to look at checklists from other facilities and borrow ideas from them, but make sure that each item is appropriate.

Creating an effective checklist is a balancing act between simplicity and complexity. It is important to keep the checklist relatively simple. If it is so long and complex that it becomes a major operation to perform, it probably won't be performed correctly, if at all. On the other hand, it is essential to make sure that all items of importance are included.

Next, an inspection schedule should be established. The frequency of inspections depends upon the type of facility and programs involved. In an activity facility it might be effective to establish a regular time table for inspection, such as on a bi-weekly basis. In a spectator facility, it may be more appropriate to perform an inspection immediately prior to each event. The risk review committee must determine what is appropriate for the individual situation.

In some organizations it may be suitable to develop two or even several checklists. It may be that a daily checklist should be developed to help perform a quick check of areas to identify factors that can easily change at short notice. This might include checking access doors, looking for water on the floor of an activity area, seeing that the stairs are clear of debris, or making sure there are no children in the weight room. Another, more detailed, in-depth checklist can then be used on a less frequent basis. This list could prompt the inspector to check for things such as loose bolts and frayed cables on the weight machines, or bent and broken rims on the basketball courts. Again, professional judgment will best determine the frequency and detail of the inspections.

Including the following items on a checklist is necessary for it to be as effective as possible.

> Name of the organization
> Inspector's name (printed)
> Date of inspection
> Location of inspection (if needed)
> Inspector's signature
> What problems were discovered
> If a problem is found, what action is recommended.

(See Figure 1 for a partial example of a checklist.)

It is very helpful to word the questions on the checklist so that they will be answered "No," only if a problem exists. This way someone can quickly scan a checklist and any point not checked in the "Yes" column will stand out. Otherwise, a person reading the checklist will have to read each question in order to determine if there is a problem or not. As an example, the following question can be rewritten:

> Holes in soccer fields　　　<u>yes</u>　　<u>no</u>
> Soccer fields free of holes　<u>yes</u>　　<u>no</u>

As a part of the checklist, it is recommended that an additional sheet be attached that prompts the inspector to report all items that require action. By including this one page action report when an inspection discovers problems that need to be addressed, it is less likely that any items will be overlooked. If the facility manager has to look at each item on every page of an inspection report in order to discover those that require action, there is more chance that some will be overlooked. Procedures must be established so that once a hazard has been identified, it will be treated as quickly as possible.

Establish Safety Rules

Another method of reducing the risks associated with facility hazards is to establish rules concerning safety. Safety rules must be considered carefully. It is im-

FIGURE 1

Edwards Recreation Center
Safety Inspection Checklist

Inspector's Name ___Kevin Finn_____Date ___6/17/00_____
Location of Inspection ___Main Gym_____
Inspector's Signature _____

Instructions for Inspector:

1. Inspect and complete all items.
2. Include comments on all "NO" responses.
3. Fill-out and report problems on completion of inspection.

# POTENTIAL HAZARD	YES	NO	COMMENTS
1. Floor clear of obstacles and debris	✔	—	
2. Floor clear of standing water	✔	—	
3. Floor swept, good traction	✔	—	
4. All standards, mats & goals properly stored	✔	—	
5. All other equipment properly stored	✔	—	
6. Gym rules clearly posted	✔	—	
7. Bleachers secure and in good repair	✔	—	
8. Warning sign on bleachers clearly visible	✔	—	
9. All lights undamaged and working	—	✔	Light over center court is out
10. Emergency procedures clearly posted	✔	—	
11. Emergency telephone accessible	✔	—	
12. Emergency phone numbers and directions to facility are posted by the phone	✔	—	
13. Rims unbroken, straight, & in good shape	✔	—	
14. Backboards unbroken—no loose bolts & in proper position	✔	—	
15. Wall pads in place	✔	—	
16. Access—Ingress and egress points opened or locked as appropriate	—	✔	N.E. outside door open
17. Supervisor present	✔	—	
18. No unsupervised children present	✔	—	
19. All of participants equipment properly stored in hallway	✔	—	
20. Other	—	—	

portant to make sure that all rules are appropriate and necessary. Once safety rules have been determined, they must be posted in plain sight and in locations that are appropriate to the given hazard. Some examples include "Do Not Drop Weights" in weight rooms, "No Diving" or "No Glass Containers" in pool areas, or "Protective Eyewear Required" in racquetball courts. Safety rules must be clear, obvious, and direct in order to be effective. It is not uncommon to see safety

FIGURE 2

Edwards Recreation Center
Inspection Checklist

Action Report

Item #	Problem	Recommendation
P 4	Drain in N.E. corner backed up	Report to maintenance immediately
P 7	Ladder in deep end loose	Report to maintenance immediately
P 13	Extension pole missing	Contact pool manager & replace it
MG 9	Light over center court is out	Notify Maintenance
MG 16	Side door unlocked	Have supervisor check regularly
WR 6	Frayed cable on bench machine	Replace cable immediately

_____Kevin Finn_____   ___6/17/00____
Inspectors Name   Date

_____
Inspectors Signature

rules typed on a sheet of paper and taped to the wall. This is not appropriate. If the rules truly exist for safety, it is important to post them where they will be easily seen and read.

Once safety rules have been established and posted, it is essential that they are strictly enforced. It is hard to justify making rules to protect patrons' safety and then allowing them to disobey the rules. Enforcement of safety rules is an important part of a risk management program. Once the rules have been established and clearly posted, the facility manager is entitled to assume that patrons will obey the rules.

Establish a Preventative Maintenance Program

A conscientious facility manager does not put off maintenance until something breaks or becomes a problem. Proper maintenance should take place before problems or failure occur. It is important to know, understand, and follow manufacturer's recommendations for maintaining and repairing equipment. Most equipment manufacturers will provide printed guidelines for preventive maintenance. These guidelines should be kept on file, followed, and documented upon completion. A system for developing and maintaining good written records of all preventive maintenance performed is essential (see Documentation). The lack of a good preventive maintenance program for the equipment is a common problem in weight training facilities. Most manufacturers of weight machines provide preventive maintenance schedules which outline cleaning, lubrication, testing, and replacement intervals for each. Many also provide specific procedures for repairing and replacing parts. It is important to follow these guidelines and procedures and then document it upon completion. If someone were to file suit after getting injured on a weight machine, it will be very important to show that the manufacturer's procedures were followed.

Staff Training

Another essential step in making a facility as safe as possible is to train staff members to become risk managers. They must understand the importance of risk management and know that safety is a top priority of the organization. Each staff person should be instructed on the kinds of hazards they are likely to encounter while performing his/her daily duties and to actively look for possible hazards. They must also be taught the process of reporting them and following up to ensure they are dealt with properly. This process allows for several sets of eyes to continually look for hazards instead of one person looking only during the periodic inspections. In order for the staff to truly help recognize hazards, it is important for the facility manager to follow up on their comments in a timely manner. If a staff person reports a few hazards and nothing ever gets done about them, they will probably quickly become discouraged and give up.

Documentation

An organized, thorough, consistent method of documenting facility safety efforts is an integral part of any risk management program. If litigation over an injury occurs, the court will want to see evidence of what the facility did to ensure the safety of the participants, spectators and staff. Keeping good records is essential if one has to demonstrate in court that safety inspections were done or what preventive maintenance was performed. The facility manager may have done a great job of inspection and maintenance but if there is no documentation to show it, why should the court take the manager's word for it? The old adage, "If it wasn't written down, it didn't happen" is a great one to apply to a risk management program. It is important to keep copies of all periodic inspection reports, accident reports, preventive maintenance programs, repair work orders, staff training, etc. It is necessary to document and save everything done that relates to safety.

If a hazardous situation is identified and cannot be immediately fixed, it should be reported to the party responsible for its repair, (i.e., maintenance, principal, owner, general manager, etc.) as soon as possible. It is important to notify that person in writing such as through a memo, letter or work order. Then a copy of each notice should be kept on file. If someone were to get injured because of the dangerous situation, the sport manager can show that he/she did everything within his/her power to fix it. This is an effective method of transferring responsibility to someone else.

If an injury does occur, the facility manager must be especially diligent in regards to documentation related to the incident. Thorough documentation as part of a good overall risk management program is one of the best defenses in court. How long should these records be saved? The statute of limitations, the length of time an injured individual has in which to initiate a lawsuit, varies from state to state. Usually it is between three and five years but can be as little as one year and even longer than five. Especially in the case of an injury to a minor, the time can be much longer. It is important for each facility manager to find out what the statute of limitations is in his/her state and maintain all records at least until it expires. Facility managers are expected to keep and be able to produce all records associated with an incident, even if it occurred several years ago.

It is also very helpful to develop a good system for organizing and cataloging all such documents. It is not a good idea to throw them into boxes and stick them in the basement somewhere. If it were necessary to find a checklist performed the fourth week of September, five years ago, how hard would it be?

Common Hazards

Although there are innumerable different hazards possible in sport and recreation facilities, some are more common than others. This section is a sample of some that more commonly occur than most.

Common Indoor Hazards

1. Improper storage of equipment
2. Inadequate safety zones around courts—Inadequate wall padding
3. Traffic patterns routed through activity areas
4. Improper building materials
5. Weight machines not properly maintained
6. High risk areas or equipment left unsupervised
7. Poor control of access
8. Improper maintenance of facilities and equipment
9. Non-safety glass in activity areas
10. Slick floors in wet areas

Common Outdoor Hazards

1. Playing surface abnormalities
2. Improper storage of equipment
3. Overlapping fields
4. Baseball team benches exposed to batted balls
5. Improper surface material on playground
6. Soccer goals not anchored or stored properly
7. Slippery pool decks
8. No warning track on baseball field

9. Unsafe bleachers
10. Improper fences for activity

Summary/Conclusion

Providing reasonably safe facilities is one of the primary legal duties expected of managers of sport, physical activity, and recreation programs. In order to do this, managers must truly believe that the safety of patrons, spectators, and staff is a top priority. A good facility risk management program can usually be achieved through effort and, for the most part, without great expense. Most hazards, once identified, take little time or money to repair, remove, or compensate for when facility managers use their imagination. The key is caring enough to recognize potential hazards and deal with them before they become a problem.

Suggested Reading

Appenzeller, H. (1993). "Equipment and Facilities," in H. Appenzeller, *Managing Sports and Risk Management Strategies*. Durham, NC: Carolina Academic Press.

Berg, R. (1994). "Unsafe," *Athletic Business 18*(4), 43-46.

Borkowski, R.P. (1997). "Checking out checklists," *Athletic Management*, IX (1), 18.

Coalition of Americans to Protect Sports (1998). *Sports Injury Risk Management & the Keys to Safety*. North Palm Beach, FL: CAPS.

Dougherty, N.J. (1993). *Principles of Safety in Physical Education and Sport*. Reston, VA: National Assn. for Sport and Physical Education.

Hart, J.E. and R.J. Ritson (1993). *Liability and Safety in Physical Education and Sport*. Reston, VA: National Assn. for Sport and Physical Education.

Hart, J. (1990). "Locker room liability," *Strategies, 3*(3), 33-34.

Hronek, B.R. (1997). *Legal Liability in Recreation and Sports*. Champaign, IL: Sagamore Publishing.

Kaiser, R.A. (1986). *Liability & Law in Recreation, Parks, & Sport*. Englewood Cliffs, NJ: Prentice-Hall.

Maloy, B.P. (1993). "Safe environment," Chapter 2.34 in D.J. Cotton and T.J. Wilde, *Sport Law for Sport Managers*. Dubuque, IA: Kendall/Hunt Publishing Co.

Maloy, B.P. (1993). "Legal obligations related to facilities," *Journal of Physical Education, Recreation, and Dance, 64*(2), 28-30, 68.

Page, J.A. (1988). *The law of premises liability*. Cincinnati, OH: Anderson Publishing Co.

Seidler, T.L. (1999). "Planning Facilities for Safety and Risk Management," *Guidelines for Club, Recreation, Sport, and Physical Activity Facility Design Development*. AAHPERD. Dubuque, IA: Kendall-Hunt.

Seidler, T. (1998). "Elements of a Facility Risk Review," Chapter 24, in H. Appenzeller, *Risk Management in Sport: Issues and Strategies*. Durham, NC: Carolina Academic Press.

van der Smissen, B. (1990). *Liability and Risk Management for Public and Private Enterprises*. Cincinnati, OH: Anderson Pub. Co.

Chapter 30

Overview of Player Contracts and Collective Bargaining Agreements for Professional Team Sports

Glenn M. Wong*

Introduction

The general manager and other executives of a professional team-sport franchise must deal with a number of different contracts while running their operation. These include player contracts, coach and manager contracts, front office employment contracts, facility lease contracts, radio and television contracts, minor league player contracts, winter league player contracts, waivers and releases of liability and others. The leagues and teams use standard contracts to deal with some of these areas, while in other areas the contracts are negotiated and drafted on an individual basis. The focus of this chapter is on the club-player contracts and collective bargaining agreements in professional team sport. The important documents for the general manager dealing in player contract negotiations are the standard player contract, the collective bargaining agreement, the league constitution, bylaws and rules. The first two impact most directly on the player contract negotiation area. The chapter is divided into three sections: (1) The standard player contract; (2) The collective bargaining agreement; and (3) Additional contract amendments. Other contracts that an executive of a professional sport team may deal with are discussed briefly under the heading, "Other Contracts." It should be emphasized that this chapter is designed to give the reader an overview of some of the different elements of professional sport player agreements. The chapter will mainly draw from documents of the National Hockey League (NHL), Major League Baseball (MLB), National Football League (NFL), and National Basketball Association (NBA). It is not intended as a comprehensive discussion of an extremely complex area.

---

* Author would like to acknowledge the research assistance of John B. Shukie, M.S. student, Class of 2000, University of Massachusetts, and also the students in "Professional Sports Law," who aided in gathering data for this chapter.

The Standard Player Contract

Each major professional league has its own standard-form player contract, that is generally included as part of a collective bargaining agreement. A brief discussion follows concerning some of the similarities and differences that are found in the standard player contracts. The following clauses are likely to be similar.

A. Termination Clause

This is the clause under which most players are cut, waived or released from the club. The most common reason for releasing, waiving or cutting a player is for lack of sufficient playing skill. In other words, the player who is competing with other players for a position on the team is deemed, in the sole opinion of the club, to have insufficient skill and ability. This clause often results in litigation, where, for example, the player feels that he has been terminated while injured. The player contends that he has not been terminated for lack of sufficient playing skill, but that he was injured and was not able to demonstrate his abilities.

B. Physical Condition

A player agrees to report in good physical condition and to keep himself in good physical condition during the season. This clause has been used in a few instances to terminate a player who was overweight or out of shape. For example, in the National Football League, a player may be fined $50 per day, per pound that they are overweight. This clause may also have been used to deal with players with drug or alcohol problems. However, most professional leagues have resorted to a specific drug policy to deal with such problems.

C. Renewal or Option Clause

Leagues may have a renewal or option clause in a standard player contract. The clauses vary from league to league, and in some situations, the renewal or option clause is mandatory. At one time, a renewal or option clause was found in all standard player contracts. However, player unions in many situations have made these clauses negotiable, and therefore they may be either included or excluded in the contract.

D. Filing

Player contracts in all professional team sports leagues are filed with the league office. A commissioner or president of a league has from 10 to 20 days, depending on the league, to disapprove the contract, if he or she deems the contract to be in violation of any league rule.

E. Compensation

This clause sets forth the salary that is paid to a player. Additional compensation is provided for in the collective bargaining agreement (discussed on p. 399 *infra*) and may be provided in additional contract clauses (discussed on p. 404

infra). Minimum compensation levels are set forth in the collective bargaining agreement.

F. Payment

The salary is generally paid during the regular playing season, NOT over the entire season. For example, an NFL player who earns $1,700,000 per year will be paid $100,000 per week for the 17 weeks of the regular season. The player is NOT paid during the off-season. During the pre-season, the collective bargaining agreement generally provides for compensation on a weekly basis. Post-season pay is additional compensation, apart from the salary provided for in the contract, and is usually provided to the participating players through a playoff pool (discussed on p. 403, *infra* O). Some leagues, generally those in formative stages, have attempted to pay the players over the entire year, rather than during the regular playing season. This assists the owner's cash flow situation. In at least one situation, however, this has adversely affected players that were not able to collect the balance of their contract which was payable after the end of the playing season due to a owner's financial problems.

G. Other Activities

A player agrees not to participate in outside activities that may involve a significant risk of injury. There have been a number of cases where a player has been injured in the off-season as a result of playing another sport. If the club knows the player is participating in an outside activity with a significant risk of injury, the club has the right to have the player stop participating. If the player is injured in such an activity, he may have breached his contract, and may not be entitled to future contract rights (such as guaranteed pay). The player may be able to protect himself by requesting permission from the club to participate in an outside activity. A club that is aware that a player has participated in a certain outside activity in the past, which the club deems is no longer in the club's and player's best benefits, may negotiate to include a clause in the contract specifically preventing the player from participating in that activity. For example, in the Standard Player Contract for MLB, the "Other Sports" clause states, "The Player and the Club recognize and agree that the Player's participation in certain other sports may impair or destroy his ability and skill as a baseball player. Accordingly, the Player agrees that he will not engage in professional boxing or wrestling; and that, except with the written consent of the Club, he will not engage in skiing, auto racing, motorcycle racing, sky diving, or in any game or exhibition of football, soccer, professional league basketball, ice hockey or other sport involving a substantial risk of personal injury."

H. Rules

A player agrees to abide by the club's training rules, as well as any of the club's in-season rules. The Standard Player Contract in the NHL, for example, leaves the specific rule-making to the team, but states that the player must follow the specific Club rules; "The Club may from time to time during the continuance of this contract establish reasonable rules governing the conduct and conditioning of the Player, and such reasonable rules shall form part of this contract as fully as if herein written. For violation of any such rules or for any conduct impairing the thorough and faithful discharge of the duties incumbent upon the Player, the Club may impose a reasonable fine upon the Player."

I. Assignment

A club is given the right to assign, sell, exchange or transfer a player to another club. In the NFL, NBA and MLB (Major League Baseball) players may have a no-trade clause in their contract. In the NHL, players may have a no-trade clause in their contract, but not until after their 32nd birthday.

J. Publicity

A player grants the club the authority to use his name and picture for publicity and promotional purposes. Players also give up the right to appear on radio and talk shows without the approval of the club. However, the club grants the player the right to use the name of the club to identify himself, truthfully, as a player of the club, past or present.

K. Grievance Procedure

This clause designates the procedure by which the club and a player may re-solve a dispute. The details of the grievance and arbitration clause are set forth in the collective bargaining agreement. The club and a player may have a dispute as to whether the club has properly terminated the player, whether the club has properly compensated the player, whether the club has provided the fringe bene-fits to the player as provided in his contract or in the collective bargaining agree-ment, whether the player has achieved the incentive performance bonus clauses in his contract, and many other issues. Depending upon the league, a grievance must be initiated by a player or club within 45-90 days of the occurrence. The griev-ance is filed by submitting a written notice to the league. For example, in the NFL, the Management Council has to issue a decision on the grievance within seven days of receiving it. If the player does not agree with the decision he has the right to appeal to a panel of 4 arbitrators whose appointment must be accepted in writing by the NFLPA (NFL Players Association) and the Management Council of the NFL. The arbitrator shall issue a final decision within thirty days of the sub-mission of briefs. Leagues may have an expedited process of grievance arbitration when they are dealing with volatile issues such as suspension and large fines. For example, in MLB, any player, upon receipt of a fine and/or suspension may appeal the decision directly to the league President or Commissioner's office within seven days, and is guaranteed a final and binding decision within 10 days.

L. Uniqueness Clause

The player represents that he has an extraordinary and unique skill and ability and that any breach of the contract will cause irreparable injury to the club. This clause is an extremely important one in professional sports today and throughout history. The uniqueness clause allows the first club to seek an injunction to stop a player from playing for a second club in another league, when the first club is able to prove a valid and binding contract. The uniqueness clause has been invoked against Napolean Lajoie, Rick Barry, Dick Barnett, Lou Hudson, Billy Sims, and many others. For instance, in the NFL, players who play in the CFL (Canadian Football League) cannot play in the NFL during the same year.

M. Collective Bargaining Agreement

All established professional team-sport leagues, with the exception of MLS (Major League Soccer), have a collective bargaining agreement.

The standard player contracts used in professional team sports have many similarities in the types of clauses contained in the contracts. However, there are some differences in the types of clauses and also in the content of the clauses. For example, in the standard player contract for the NBA there exists a specific clause dealing with 10-day contracts. This type of clause would not be relevant, and therefore does not appear, in the MLB standard player contract. A review of standard player contracts used in other professional leagues, such as Major League Soccer and the Women's National Basketball Association, reveal many of the same aforementioned clauses, although again there are differences in content.

While the standard player contract is important, what has become more important in this day of increased negotiating leverage and salaries for the players, is the collective bargaining agreement and the individually negotiated additional amendments to the standard player contract.

The Collective Bargaining Agreement

A collective bargaining agreement is an agreement by and between the management (the clubs, leagues, or representative council) and the union (as representative of the players). The collective bargaining agreement details the terms and conditions of employment. A professional team-sport collective bargaining agreement is different from most nonsport agreements in that the agreement sets forth the minimum terms and conditions of employment. This allows the player the ability to negotiate on an individual basis above and beyond the minimums set forth in the collective bargaining agreement and the standard player contract. This practice differs from the general practice in the labor sector, whereby the collective bargaining agreement sets forth the terms and conditions of employment and employees are not allowed to negotiate additional compensation and benefits on an individual basis. Therefore, employees in similar job positions, with similar backgrounds and/or experiences are paid the same wages or salaries. For example, all secondary school teachers within an administrative unit with a masters degree and five-years experience are paid the same salary. In professional team sport, not all quarterbacks, second basemen, guards and wings are paid equally.

As in standard player contracts, a comparison of collective bargaining agreements in professional team sports shows a number of similarities and differences. However, there are vast differences in the collective bargaining agreements, particularly in the content of the different articles. The current collective bargaining agreement of MLB contains 30 different articles, with numerous clauses, 22 attachments, and six exhibits. The entire document contains 174 pages. A detailed comparison of the collective bargaining agreements would be too lengthy of a process for this chapter; therefore, a brief discussion of the typical articles found in a professional team sports collective bargaining agreement follow. The focus herein is on those clauses which most directly impact on a player's individual contract negotiations. Collective bargaining agreements are much longer and more extensive than standard player contracts.

A. Free Agency

A free agent is defined as a veteran player who has fulfilled his contractual negotiations with his current club. Each major professional team-sport league differs in how its awards free agent status to a veteran player. In the NHL, there are five different groups of free agents, each category characterized by the number of accrued seasons the player has been in the league, and the age of the player at the time of the termination of his most recent contract. Free agents in the NHL are categorized as restricted or unrestricted. This classification deals with how a team will be compensated by the loss of their player team via free agency. The issue of compensation will be further discussed in the following paragraphs. A player in Major League Baseball must have six or more years of service in the league before he becomes eligible for free agency. A free agent in baseball, however, is free to negotiate with any team in the league, and teams are awarded compensation, in the form of draft picks (discussed below in C) for their loss of players to free agency. In the NFL, any player with three, but less than five, accrued seasons, is deemed a restricted free agent. The original team, however, is able to make use of their right of first refusal (discussed below in B). Similar to the NHL, his former team is awarded compensation, consisting of draft picks if he is signed by another team in the league. However, after five accrued seasons in the NFL a player becomes an unrestricted free agent, is free to negotiate with any other team in the other league, and his former team is not eligible for compensation from the team that signs the player.

B. Right of First Refusal

The right of first refusal is the right of the original club to match an offer obtained by a free agent from a new club. When a free agent is negotiating with another club, therefore, the original team has an opportunity to offer an equal salary, and therefore block the player from signing with the new team. If the original team decides to exercise this right it is obligated to sign the player. The NFL has the right of first refusal built into its standard player contract through the collective bargaining agreement.

C. Compensation

An original club is often granted the right to be compensated for the loss of a free agent. Football (NFL), baseball (MLB), and hockey (NHL) allow an original club to be compensated. Football's main area of compensation is with restricted free agents, and is based on the salary offered to the free agent by his new team. Generally, its is scaled so that the higher the salary offered, the higher the compensation received by the original team. The compensation formula for baseball is complicated and the compensation varies in accordance with where the free agent ranks statistically within his positional group. If the player ranks within the top 30% of his statistical category, he is deemed a Type "A" player and the original club is entitled to compensational draft choices. Type "B" and "C" players rank in the top 50% and 60%, respectively, within their statistical categories. Their original teams are entitled to less compensation from the latest team as a result of their loss to free agency. The system in the NHL is similar to baseball's. Each free agent is placed in a category from Group 1 to Group 5. Depending on whether the player is an unrestricted or restricted free agent, the former team may be entitled to draft pick compensation from the player's new team.

D. Supplementary Taxes

In recent years, professional sports team leagues have had to institute taxes to offset rising operational costs. These supplementary taxes may include a luxury tax or a payroll tax. Luxury and payroll taxes are taxes that are levied against teams that have a payroll above a certain set number. This is a way for a league to level the competitive playing field for smaller market teams, who may not be able to have a very high payroll.

E. Amateur Draft

This clause outlines the nature of the entry draft for a league: the number of rounds, a pay scale (if applicable), eligible players, and other issues involved with the entry draft are discussed in this section. For example, the collective bargaining agreement of the NBA sets forth that the draft shall consist of two rounds. It also describes how teams may conduct contract negotiations with rookies, and how underclassmen collegiate athletes, as well as foreign-born players, must apply for entrance into the draft.

F. Salary Caps

This clause sets a certain monetary figure that a team's total payroll cannot surpass when they are paying their players. Currently the NBA and the NFL are the two major professional sport-team leagues with a salary cap. The NBA has a soft cap, while the NFL employs a hard cap. A soft salary cap is one that has many exceptions, while a hard salary cap is one that has a set team salary cap that cannot be surpassed. Salary caps have been instituted by leagues to curb the heightened salary escalation in the past decade. In the NBA, the salary cap figure is decided by taking a percentage of the Basketball Related Income (BRI) of the league, which may include gate revenues, club seat revenues, licensing revenues, and many other sources of income, and dividing this amount equally among the NBA teams, and declaring that each team can not surpass this figure when paying their players. For the 1999–2000 season in the NBA, the amount available to each team for player salaries was $34 million. The NBA has many exceptions to its salary cap, including the resigning of your free agents not counting towards your cap number. The NFL salary cap is decided by calculating projected gross revenues for the league and dividing this number equally among teams in the league. In both leagues, the salary cap is an attempt to aid small-market teams who have more limited funds to spend on their players.

G. Grievance Arbitration

This article sets forth a dispute-resolving procedure for any disputes between a player and a club involving the standard player contract and the collective bargaining agreement. It is an alternative to the court system, which may be a lengthy and costly remedy. Disputes arising out of other agreements, such as the Constitution or bylaws may also be arbitrated, provided they pertain to the terms and conditions of a player's employment. This procedure is governed by a completely neutral arbitrator, who is agreed upon by both league management and the player's union. Each major professional league has a formal process for how a grievance must be filed, decided, and appealed. The decision of the arbitrator can not be appealed, except in very limited situations.

H. Injury Grievance Arbitration

The National Football League has a separate injury grievance arbitration clause, which allows a player to bring a complaint claiming that he was terminated by a club while injured. The collective bargaining agreements of other professional team-sport leagues do not contain this clause.

I. Salary Arbitration

This article allows a neutral arbitrator to resolve disputes between players and clubs relative to salary. The salary arbitration process is employed by the NHL and MLB, however, it is not a part of the NFL and NBA collective bargaining agreements. The arbitration process differs slightly between the NHL and MLB. In the NHL, the player and management present separate arguments to the arbitrator, stating the annual salary that they believe the player deserves. The arbitrator, after hearing the arguments, is able to choose *any salary* that he deems fit. However, in MLB, the arbitration procedure is different because the arbitrator is forced to choose *one* of the salaries that either the player or management proposes. In either case, the decision of the neutral arbitrator(s) is final and binding.

J. Minimum Salaries

The minimum annual salary that a club must pay a player is included in all collective bargaining agreements. In some sports, such as baseball, a minimum salary of $200,000 for the 2000 season applies to all players, regardless of their years of service in the league. However, in football, the minimum salary is determined by a sliding scale based on the number of years of service in the league. For example, in the 2000 season, a player with less than one season on an active team roster in the NFL must be paid at least $100,000 per year, while a player with two or more seasons on an active roster must be paid at least $150,000 per year. In the NBA, the minimum salary for the 1999–2000 season ranges from $301,875 for rookies to $1,000,000 for players with more than 10 years of service in the league.

K. Pre-Season Training Camps

The compensation for players during training camp and the earliest commencement dates for pre-season training camps are set forth in this article. For example, in 2000, NFL rookies are paid $700 per week for training camp, and a veteran is paid $900. For 1997 in MLB, the weekly allowance for spring training was $249.00, and the collective bargaining agreement allows for a cost of living adjustment to this number each year. In the NHL, a veteran (player with 52 or more games in the previous season), is paid $3000 for training camp. A non-veteran is paid $275 per pre-season game. Pay for pre-season camps is much less than the overall compensation for a player, which is only paid over regular season (discussed on p. 397, *infra*, F).

L. Travel

This article sets forth the travel benefits a club must provide for players on road trips. This may include some specific guidelines for management. For example, in the NFL, clubs are required to make their best efforts to make the following arrangements for their players while they are "on the road":

1. To have their baggage picked up by porters.
2. To have them stay in first class hotels.
3. To provide first-class transportation accommodations on all trips.

M. Moving Expenses

A player who has been traded, assigned or obtained on waivers is provided reasonable moving and travel expenses for himself and his family. Reasonable expenses may include, but are not limited to, board, first-class airfare and first-class hotel accommodations.

N. Meal Allowances

The players are given a per diem allowance when they are on the road. For example, in the NFL for 1999–2000 season, each player received $15 for breakfast, $21 for lunch, and $39 for dinner.

O. Playoff Money

This article provides for the money to be received by players who participate in the playoffs. In some collective bargaining agreements, such as baseball, a pool is established from gate receipts and players receive a percentage of the pool. For example, 36% of the playoff money goes to the winner of World Series, while the rest of the money is split up by the rest of the playoff participants, with the losers of the first round series' receiving the least compensation. In the National Football League, a player's share is predetermined and set forth in the collective bargaining agreement. For example, each qualifying player of the Super Bowl winner receives $63,630, while each loser receives $34,000.

P. Insurance

These articles provide for medical, life, disability insurance coverage and dental plans for players. For example, in the NHL, all players who play at least one NHL game are given a life insurance policy of $200,000 (U.S.).

Q. Pension Retirement Fund

A pension/retirement fund is established for the players and is usually funded by management. The players generally do not make direct contributions, such as deductions from salary. However, they may contribute indirectly, for example, by participating in an all-star game. In baseball, the proceeds of the all-star game are contributed to the pension fund. In hockey, the NHL Player's Association agreed to pay 25% of the cost increase in pension benefits. The Association would pay its share from its proceeds of all international hockey games. A former player becomes eligible for the pension plan after a certain waiting period, which is outlined in a separate league pension plan document.

R. Termination Pay

A player who has been terminated from a club may be provided with termination pay in a situation where the contract is not guaranteed. The amount of termination pay varies according to the league. In basketball, a player does not receive any termination pay if he is terminated prior to or on the 55th day of the club's season. If he is terminated on or after the 56th day, the player receives his full salary for the season. In baseball, if a player is terminated during the off-season or during spring training for lack of sufficient ability shall be paid the equivalent of 30 days of the contract. A player is given 60 days pay if he is terminated during the regular season.

There are many other clauses contained in a professional sport collective bargaining agreement which a general manager must deal with. The articles vary depending on the sport and league involved. However, some of the articles which have not been discussed include: off-season training camps, exhibition games, days off/scheduling, limitation on deferred compensation, pay and cable television, the college draft, union dues check off, agent regulation, waivers and loans of players to minor league clubs, international games, game tickets, endorsements, apprentice players, temporary injury contracts, prohibition of no-trade contracts and all-star games.

The collective bargaining agreement is an extremely important document for the general manager. The variation in collective bargaining agreements among the different leagues is great and much more pronounced than the standard player contracts. In addition to the collective bargaining agreement, a general manager must also be aware of any arbitration decisions which have interpreted the collective bargaining agreement.

Additional Contract Amendments

Amendments to the contract, which have been negotiated in addition to the standard player contract and the collective bargaining agreement, have been a problem area for professional team sport contract negotiators. The major problems are that some of the clauses are vague, ambiguous or unclear.

There is a tremendous variety in additional contract amendments, and the number of additional contract amendments varies from contract to contract and from sport to sport. One method in professional team sport is the use of standardized additional contract amendments. These standardized clauses are contained in the collective bargaining agreement in basketball and hockey, while the club's management council drafts standardized clauses in football. In basketball, for example, the standardized clauses, referred to as "allowable amendments," include amendments that provide for: (1) A player to be compensated if he is injured while playing or practicing for the club; (2) A player to be compensated despite failing, refusing or neglecting to maintain standards of good citizenship, good sportsmanship or obey the club's training rules; (3) A player to be compensated despite his lack of skill, and (4) A player to be compensated despite suffering a mental disability. In hockey, the collective bargaining agreement sets forth standardized clauses for certain amateur players, a player's option contract and a player's termination contract. In football, the club's management council has drafted a bonus clause standard form, which may be used by the clubs.

The free agent journeyman or marginal player is not as likely to have many additional contract provisions, and the additional provisions he may negotiate are often standardized. The superstar player (or the player in a good bargaining position) has, in many cases, the leverage and ability to add unique and non-standardized clauses to his contract. When the standardized forms are not available, the clauses are drafted by management or the player's representative.

There have been some contracts which reportedly have run hundreds of pages, but most add no more than a page or two to the standard player contract. Listed and discussed below are a number of typical clauses that are added as amendments to the contract. This discussion will only be a brief overview of possible additional amendments, as imagination and creativity have resulted in some atypical and extraordinary clauses being drafted. The more typical clauses are discussed first.

A. Performance Clauses and Award Clauses

Players may have clauses in their contract where they awarded extra compensation for reaching certain statistical levels. For example, a player in baseball may receive added compensation for reaching 500 plate appearances, or for playing in 140 games. Other examples of performance clauses are plays (football); interceptions (football); sacks (football); games (football and basketball); innings pitched (baseball); at bats (baseball); roster bonuses and percentage of the plays (football). Another type of incentive clause is an award clause. This rewards a player with added compensation if they receive a post-season award. For instance, a baseball player may receive bonus money if they are named the MVP of a playoff series, or are named the Gold Glove player at their position. Many professional athletes, in all different sports, have a large number of performance and/or award clauses in their contracts.

B. Compensation Guarantees

1. *Skill Guarantee.* A player will be paid his salary in the event that the club deems that he does not have sufficient playing skill.
2. *Injury Protection Guarantee.* A player will be paid his salary in the event that he is unable to play because of an injury. This clause may be drafted so that a player will be paid only if the injury is football-related or may also include a nonfootball-related injury.

3. *Full Guarantee.* A player is paid regardless of skill, injury, mental disability, death, strike or any other event. One additional consideration concerning guarantees is how the contract is guaranteed. Most contracts are guaranteed by the club, that is, the business which owns the club. If the business is a corporation, then none of the stockholders of the corporation are personally responsible for the debts of the club if the club declares bankruptcy. Therefore, some players, especially those that sign contracts with a new team or league, require some type of personal guarantee from the owner. This may take the form of a letter of credit or a personal services contract.

C. Additional Monetary Compensation

1. *Attendance Clauses.* A player is paid for every spectator over a certain number of spectators.
2. *Weight Clauses.* Either a bonus payment if a player makes weight or a fine if a player does not make weight.
3. *Loans.* A player is loaned money at a low interest rate or no interest at all.
4. *Real Estate Partnerships.* A player is given a share of a partnership for the tax advantages and the possibility of future appreciation of the property.
5. *Annuities.* A club purchases an annuity for a player which gives a player a stream of income in the future.
6. *Publicity Clauses.* A player is paid for public relations appearances on behalf of the club. These appearances are over and above the appearances required in the standard player contract. For example, a player may be compensated for his participation in an off-season promotional campaign.

D. Assignability Restrictions

1. *Full No-Trade Clause.* A player cannot be traded during the term of his contract.
2. *Partial No-Trade Clause.* Either a player cannot be traded for part of the term of his contract (i.e., he cannot be traded in the first year of his contract) or a player cannot be traded to certain teams.
3. *Buy-Out Provisions.* A club can buy the right to trade a player for an agreed upon amount.

E. Nonmonetary Compensation

1. *Lodging on Road Trips.* A club provides the player a single room on road trips. Some collective bargaining agreements specify that there are two players to a room.
2. *Lodging During the Regular Season.* A club provides the player a house or apartment during the regular season.

3. *Transportation for a Player.* A club provides an automobile during the season.
4. *Transportation for the Family.* A club provides round-trip airline tickets for the player's family to attend games.

F. Educational Clauses

Educational clauses provide for tuition reimbursement and a bonus to be paid upon graduation. They are most prevalent in baseball since baseball drafts college juniors. Major League Baseball has standardized language relating to education within the National Association rules. The clause may be modified or deleted by agreement of the parties. Under baseball's current plan, a player may resume his studies, with aid from the MLB Scholarship Fund, within two years after his last day of service. In other sports, educational clauses are negotiated on an individual basis.

G. Charitable Contributions

These vary tremendously and include the establishment of charitable foundations, scholarships, donations, and contributions. In some cases, the contribution is based on a player's performance. For example, a baseball player may contribute $1000 to a charitable organization for every home run that he hits.

H. Atypical/Extraordinary Additional Amendments

1. *Weight Clauses.* Although this clause was discussed above, many feel that it falls into the "extraordinary" category.
2. *Lodging.* Reportedly there was a basketball player who had a clause in his contract requiring that the team provide him with a single room and a waterbed on road trips. His room also had to be on a different floor from his teammates.
3. *Uniform Numbers.* The selection of a certain uniform number.
4. *Employment of Players.* Some players have negotiated employment clauses into their contracts, whereby the player will work for an owner's business after retiring from the game. Ted Turner, owner of the Atlanta Braves and a cable television conglomerate, has included this type of clause in some player contracts.
5. *Employment of Relatives.* Some contracts with players have included the hiring of a relative as an employee, usually as a scout, for the team.
6. *Free Agency.* Some players have negotiated clauses in their contracts which have changed the clause defining either free agency, right of first refusal or compensation from those in the collective bargaining agreement.
7. *Buy-Out Provisions.* If a club releases a player with time remaining on his contract, then it must pay a player a termination fee. However, the termination fee is usually less than the salary amount. For example, the last year of a player's contract calls for a salary of $1,000,000. If the club chooses to terminate the player, it must pay him $250,000. This clause is most prevalent in Major League Baseball.

Additional contract terms and amendments are a very integral component of contract negotiations. For example, with the introduction of salary caps in the NBA and the NFL, general managers have become more adept at using bonus clauses to uncover loopholes in the system. The nature of these additional contract amendments vary widely from sport to sport. Clauses that are prevalent in contracts in one sport, may not be applicable to another. However, no matter what the sport, it is imperative that these amendments are clear and well-written so there is no ambiguity in their interpretation.

Other Contracts

There are a number of other contracts a general manager might deal with. In some situations, a standard form contract is a starting point, while in other situations an individually negotiated and drafted contract may be the norm.

A general manager in baseball and hockey who deals with a minor league system must be familiar with minor league contracts and a working agreement with a minor league team. Professional Baseball is governed by the National Association Agreement. In addition, baseball is unique among professional team sports in that certain players play Winter League Baseball and a standard player contract is used for these players. In addition, the general manager must deal with employees, manager's, and coaches. A team executive must also deal with waivers and releases of liability with respect to facilities, concessionaires, spectators and players.

A league, as representative of the member clubs, also negotiates marketing, licensing and promotional contracts with the business sector. As a general rule, the clubs give up most of their licensing rights to the league. A team executive may be involved in negotiating contracts for the remaining marketing and licensing rights. A league is also responsible for negotiating television and radio contracts, and the contracts for umpires, referees and officials. The contracts for umpires, referees and officials are generally negotiated through collective bargaining and not on an individual basis. A separate entity, such as the Management Council in the NFL, sometimes apart from the league, represents the clubs for purposes of collective bargaining.

The final contract areas are stadium leases and television and radio contracts. Since each agreement is unique, these are generally negotiated on an individual basis, obviating the need for standard form contracts.

Summary/Conclusion

A mistake in the contract negotiation area can be a severe blow to a professional team sport organization. The resulting adverse publicity from a mistake can hurt a club by losing a player and also gate revenues. Sometimes a mistake is never known to the public, but has resulted in giving a player leverage to demand a trade. A club makes the trade, but may not receive full value for a player and the public wonders why the club made the trade.

Mistakes have occurred in the past. Many of these situations have resulted in arbitration cases. The contract interpretation cases involving Hall-of-Famers Carlton Fisk and Jim "Catfish" Hunter in baseball resulted in both players being declared free agents. Also, the case of Rudy Hackett in basketball resulted in an arbitrator's decision which found that the contract was "guaranteed" by the first team, and that the contract law principle of mitigation of damages did not apply. Therefore, Hackett was allowed to keep the salaries he received from two different teams for the same season.

There have also been a number of arbitration cases involving a player who was cut from a club for "lack of sufficient playing skill." In several of these cases, a player was successful in arguing that he was cut for reasons other than a "lack of sufficient playing skill." For example, basketball player Ken Charles contended that he was cut because of his high salary. The arbitrator agreed with Charles and awarded him the balance of his salary for the season in which he was improperly terminated.

The standard player contracts, collective bargaining agreements and additional contract amendments in other sports are important to a general manager for two reasons.

First, a general manager may be dealing with a player who has a contractual obligation with another league or another sport. The Cincinnati Reds in MLB are probably very familiar with the standard player contract and collective bargaining agreement of the National Football League, having employed Deion Sanders, of the Dallas Cowboys.

Second, the knowledge of other league's contracts and collective bargaining agreements may give a general manager a new idea or approach in contract negotiations. The allowable amendments and other standardized forms used in other leagues should be time and litigation tested. In addition, it would help the general manager to have background information on arbitration decisions and court decisions which have interpreted the contract and the collective bargaining agreement.

It is easy to see why lawyers are used in professional sports. A general manager may also be a lawyer, and while this combination may have some advantages, and is found on some professional sport clubs, it is not a necessity. It is also not easy to find an individual with a sport law background and the expertise with all the other areas, such as player personnel and business matters that a general manager must deal with. General Managers generally know and understand the standard player contract, collective bargaining agreement, constitution, bylaws and other legal documents. In some instances, a general manager may need legal assistance, such as in the drafting of an additional contract amendment, an interpretation of a legal decision in another sport (such as a drug case or eminent domain case). In such instances the general manager then uses the legal counsel for the club. A trend in professional sports is hiring in-house counsel or outside counsel to make sure that an expert is engaged in contract interpretation, drafting, and negotiations.

About the Authors

Herb Appenzeller, Ed.D, Co-Editor, is the Jefferson-Pilot Professor of Sport Management Emeritus and former athletics director at Guilford College. He is a member of four sport Halls of Fame — National Association of Collegiate Directors of Athletics, National Association of Intercollegiate Athletics, Chowan College and Guilford College. He is co-editor of *From The Gym To The Jury* newsletter and special consultant to the Center for Sports Law and Risk Management. Appenzeller is the author or editor of sixteen books, fourteen of which are on sports law and risk management. He is the recipient of numerous national awards for sport safety and is a pioneer in the field of sport law and sport management. He was appointed Executive in Residence and Director of Sport Management at Appalachian State University for 2000-2001.

John Billing, Professor of Exercise and Sport Science at the University of North Carolina at Chapel Hill and Director of the graduate program in Sport Administration. Billing has over 23 years of administrative experience in sport and physical education at three different collegiate institutions. His research and writings have been published in a wide variety of textbooks, scholarly journals and trade publications. As a consultant, he has designed and administered special projects with groups as diverse as the Connecticut Commission on Fire Prevention, Xerox Corporation and Nuclear Security Forces. His responsibilities included personnel, budget and facility issues. He teaches courses in sport organizations, finance and NCAA compliance.

William T. Brooks is one of the nation's most highly sought after speakers, trainers and writers in the area of time management and personal productivity. He annually conducts in excess of 150 seminars from coast to coast. An Honors scholar and All East football player at Gettysburg College, he holds a masters degree from Syracuse University. A former college football coach, university dean and professor, he now heads his own firm that specializes in seminars, workshops, consulting and professional speaking. William Brooks clients range from Fortune 500 firms to professional sport team, educational institutions, and every imaginable organization that is seeking to improve the performance of its most valuable asset — people.

Don Canham was the successful former athletic director at the University of Michigan. He served on numerous Big Ten Conference and NCAA committees, including the all-important television committee. He served as a consultant to many institutions. Canham is sought as a speaker throughout the nation with an emphasis on marketing, promotion and business practices. He participated in major marketing seminars. He was the key mover in the construction of new recreational sport facilities that gave Michigan one of the largest indoor complexes in the nation. Under Canham's leadership, the University of Michigan's athletic program was self-sufficient and never used state, federal or university funding for buildings or operations. He was recognized nationally for his ability to raise funds for the intercollegiate sport program.

Gil B. Fried, Esq. is an associate professor in the Management of Sport Industries Program in the Business School at the University of New Haven. He teaches and writes on various topics including sport law, finance, risk management, facility administration and human resource administration. Mr. Fried is an active attorney, expert witness and financial analyst with a specialization in issues affecting smaller sport facilities and on the buying, selling and/or financing of sport business. Mr. Fried is a prolific director and has written many articles, chapters in numerous books and several texts such as *Employment Law* and *Safe At First*.

Lynne Gaskin is a professor in the department of physical education and recreation at the State University of West Georgia. She is a former coach who has focused on teacher certification, coaching preparation, and the legal aspects of sport and physical education. She is actively involved in a variety of professional associations at the state, regional, and national levels. She is the recipient of numerous honors and awards, a noted researcher and writer. She received the Ethel Martus Lawther Award and the Research Excellence Award from UNCG, Honor Award from the N.C. Alliance for Health, Physical Education, Recreation and Dance, UNCG Golden Chain Honor Society and held numerous offices in Delta Kappa Gamma International Society for Women Educators. Gaskin is regarded as one of the outstanding writers and speakers in the area of sport and physical education law. She received her doctorate from the University of North Carolina at Greensboro.

Jerald Hawkins, Ed.D., ATC, FACSM, is professor and director of sports medicine education at Lander University. He was the 1999 recipient of the South Carolina Governor's Award as Professor of the Year. In 1998 he was named the Lander Foundation Distinguished Professor. In 1996 he was the outstanding college and university teacher for the South Carolina Association for Health, Physical Education Recreation and Dance. He is the author of over 22 articles, eight book chapters and the author of five texts in the field of fitness, administration and sport medicine. He has made over 100 presentations on the state, regional and national level. He served on the United States Olympic Committee Medical Staff and was the athletic trainer for the U.S. Junior Luge Team at Italy, Germany and Japan.

Patricia M. Henry is senior associate director of athletics at Harvard University. She was responsible for scheduling men and womens' sports at the University. She has also served on the United States Olympic Committee and was a member of the Womens' Olympic Rowing Committee.

Guy Lewis is a consultant for sports business studies. He completed a thirty year career in higher education prior to his retirement in January 2000. His academic tenure was devoted to developing, implementing and administering degree programs in sports business. He held appointments to Penn State University, the

University of Massachusetts (Amherst) and the University of South Carolina. He was the recipient of a Fulbright Scholarship and had an appointment to Bochum University in West Germany. He is a pioneer in the field of sport management.

Chester Lloyd is a specialist in the delivery of emergency medical care for mass gatherings and/or large facilities. For years he has been involved with the planning, training and patient care aspects of emergency medical services. His experience included work as a coordinator of emergency medical teams for large capacity stadia. He received his Master of Science degree at the University of Illinois, Urbana-Champaign where he researched emergency medical preparedness at mass gatherings. He is an independent consultant and provides advice on emergency response to entertainment and sport facilities in corporate or industrial settings, and at any facility or event which attracts large crowds.

Nancy L. Lough is an assistant professor in the sport administration graduate program at the University of New Mexico. Prior to assuming her present position, Dr. Lough served as an assistant professor at Iowa State University and Kent State University. Her 14 years of experience in the sport management field also include coaching and teaching in NCAA Division I and II programs in California and Texas in addition to public and private high schools in Colorado. Dr. Lough's research has focused primarily on corporate sponsorship and marketing of women's sport, as evidenced by numerous national presentations and publications.

Charles Lynch, Jr. is a partner in the law firm of Keziah, Gates and Samet. He is a graduate of the University of North Carolina and the law schools of the University of South Carolina and New York University. The major focus of his law practice is on the matters of corporate and tax law.

David Maraghy is the President/CEO of Sports Management International, LLC, in Richmond, Virginia. He has a B.A. from Williams College and J.D. From Wake Forest University. He was admitted to the North Carolina and Virginia Bar. He was a special consultant to the 1997 World Cup of Golf (Kiawah-Ocean course), the 1996 Sang Yong International Golf challenge and the 1995 Hyundai Motor Golf Classic in Korea, the AMG Signet Open, the Golf Championship of Virginia (1988-1997, Fantasy Golf, Senior Softball World Series, and the General Chairman for the 1986 Greater Greensboro Open. Maraghy is the author of "Defamation in Sports" in *Law and Sport: Contemporary Issues, Availability of the Duress Defense in Prison Escapes* and also a writer of articles for *On Tour* and *Meetings and Convention* magazines. He is also adjunct professor of sport administration at Virginia Commonwealth University.

Geoffrey Miller is athletic director at Goucher College with six conference titles and seven NCAA Championship bids. He was president of the United States Intercollegiate Lacrosse Association and served for six years on the NCAA Men's Lacrosse Association Committee. Miller teaches sport administration courses in the graduate program at Goucher. Before joining the Goucher staff, he was director of athletics at Washington College for seven years and an administrative assistant and associate director of athletics at Guilford College. His duties included coaching the lacrosse team and was named coach of the year in Division III NCAA. He managed the Ragan-Brown Field House, a cooperative effort between Guilford College and the Guilford College YMCA. He is a 1976 graduate of

Amherst College and participated for four years in football and lacrosse. He was a recipient of the NCAA postgraduate scholar award and earned his M.S. in sport management from the University of Massachusetts.

John Moore was the sports information director at Guilford College for three years. After graduation from Guilford College, he served as the Associate Sports Information Director at Duke University. At Duke his responsibilities included extensive involvement in promotion and advertising. He is president of Moore Productions (1990-2000) specializing in producing TV and radio shows.

David Dominic Morelli is head football equipment manager at the University of North Carolina at Chapel Hill where he has managed the equipment room operations for over 20 years. His duties include bidding, ordering, inventorying, issuing and organizing equipment. Morelli supervises a staff of 10 assistant equipment managers and has developed a computer program to assist in his operations. He has contributed to several publications dealing with equipment control. He is a leader in the field regarding players' equipment and assists in analyzing apparel and shoe contracts. He is a member of the Athletic Equipment Managers Association and the Advisory Board for the NIKE Company.

Bernard Mullin has 23 years of highly successful experience in the Sport Management and Sport Facility industry. He started his professional sport team career in 1986 and served five seasons as Senior Vice-President of Business for the Pittsburgh Pirates. In three years, the Pirates did a complete turnaround going from drawing only 700,000 fans and losing $10 million annually to an all time attendance mark with a $3 million operating profit. In November 1987, Sports Inc. called him the "Pirate of Profitability" for his outstanding accomplishments. In 1991, Mullin became Executive Vice President for the Colorado Rockies. Under his leadership the Rockies broke every major league baseball record for attendance and they still hold many records for merchandise and ticket sales. *Sport Illustrated* dubbed him the "Guru of Ticket Sales." He then ran both team operations and business affairs for the expansion Denver Grizzles of the International Hockey League. The Grizzles were highly successful in every area and in 1993, Mullin was given credit for the team's accomplishments. He was named Vice Chancellor of Athletics at the University of Denver and was one of the authors of the best selling text book *Sport Marketing*. He is currently a principal in the Aspie Group, a full line Sport and Marketing consulting firm with a long list of clients in professional sports. Mullin was named to the newly created position of the National Basketball Association senior vice president for team marketing and business operations.

James Oshust is Director of Broadcast Administration for the Salt Lake Olympic and Paralympic Games. Oshust has been involved in public assembly facility, major event and entertainment/sports production, and management since 1959. He has managed coliseums, arenas, theaters and convention exhibition facilities in South Dakota, New York, Tennessee and North Carolina. Oshust has been involved in 40 facility management, design and operations consulting projects domestically and internationally. He is a member of the Men's Olympic Basketball Committee, the Director of Venues, 1998 Goodwill Games and the Director, Broadcast Administration of the 2002 Winter Olympics, Salt Lake City, Utah. He was Senior Venue Manager of the 1996 Summer Olympics in Atlanta, Georgia. He is a member of the Board of Director of the International Association of Auditorium Managers.

Gary Rushing is associate professor and currently coordinator of Sport Management Studies in the Human Performance Department at Minnesota State University, Mankato, Minnesota. His research and teaching areas include a variety of Sport Management courses such as Legal Aspects of Sport and Physical Activity. He is published in several law reporters and coaching journals. He has over twenty years of experience in athletics as a coach and athletics administrator.

Frank Russo, Jr. is vice president of Sales and Client Services for Ogden Entertainment Services. His responsibilities included worldwide business development of private management contracts for arenas, civic and convention centers, stadiums, theaters, and other public services facilities. Russo has 22 years experience in the fields of municipal and facility management. He has been an active member for the International Association of Auditorium Managers (IAAM), serving in various capacities — sitting on the Board of Directors, Vice President and Membership Chairman of District I, and National Membership Consulting Board. Russo received his B.A. from St. Michael's College, Vermont and his M.A. in public administration from the University of Connecticut.

David Scott received his B.S. degree from Texas A & M University, his M.S. from Midwestern State University and doctorate from Northern Colorado University. He taught at Southern Illinois University and now teaches graduate courses at New Mexico University in sport administration. His research centers around organizational behavior and development in sport organizations with an emphasis on leadership and team building. He conducts workshops dealing with various aspects of training for coaches. He is currently a member of the North American Society for Sport Management and the American Alliance of Health, Physical Education, Recreation and Dance.

Todd Seidler is the coordinator of the graduate program in sport administration at the University of New Mexico, one of the few programs that offer both the master's and doctorate in sport administration. He received his B.A. from San Diego State University, his master's and doctorate from the University of New Mexico. He was the coordinator of the graduate sport administration program at Wayne State University for six years and the undergraduate sport management at Guilford College for two years. He is active as a consultant on facilities and risk management for sport programs. He is called upon to make presentations at professional meetings and publishes widely in the field of sport and recreation. He is on the Executive Council of the Sport Management Council, past chairman of the Council on Facilities and Equipment within the American Alliance for Health, Physical Education, Recreation and Dance, President-Elect for the Society for the Study of the Legal Aspects of Sport and Physical Activities and a member of the North American Society for Sport Management.

John Swofford is the Commissioner of the Atlantic Coast Conference. He is the former athletic director for the University of North Carolina at Chapel Hill where he managed one of the most successful and well balanced athletic programs in America. The basketball and football teams traditionally ranked among the Top 20 in the nation. The non-revenue sports were among the top programs in the nation. Swofford served on numerous NCAA committees and chaired the football television committee. He was a Morehead Scholar at UNC and a quarterback and defensive back on the football team. He is recognized as one of the top commissioners in the United States and the Atlantic Coast Conference has prospered under his capable leadership. In his fourth years as Commissioner of the ACC he has been named the Bowl Championship Series (BCS) Coordinator. The BCS is the six-conference confederation designed to determine the NCAA Division 1-A football champion.

Jeaneane Williams is a lifelong sports fan who began her career as the first female sports editor of her high school newspaper. She was director of public relations and publications at Guilford College, an editor and writer at the University of North Carolina at Chapel Hill and the University of Colorado. She directed advertising and promotion at McGraw-Hill Book Company and Garrett Press in New York. She has been a consultant for numerous non-profit organizations and social service agencies. She holds a B.A. from the University of North Carolina at Greensboro and has done additional work in marketing and advertising at the University of Colorado and New York University.

Glenn Wong joined the Sport Management Department at the University of Massachusetts in 1979. He served as Department Head from 1986 to 1998. He teaches courses in Sport Law and Labor Relations. He served as Interim Director of Athletics and Dean of the School of Physical Education in 1992-93 and was awarded the Chancellor's Medal after serving as Athletic Director. He also served as an adjunct professor in the Labor-Management Relations program. in 1999, he was selected for the University's Distinguished Faculty Lecture Series for which he received his second Chancellor's Medal. He authored *The Essentials of Amateur Sports, 2nd edition* and co-authored *Law and Business of the Sports Industries Volumes I and II* and *The Sports Lawyer's Guide to Legal Periodicals*. He also contributed chapters to *The Management of Sport: Its Foundation and Application, Successful Sport Management,* and *Law and Sport: Contemporary Issues* and co-authored chapters in *Cases in Sport Marketing* and *Principles and Practice of Sport Management*.

Index